MURDER IN
MEMPHIS

MURDER IN MEMPHIS

The FBI and the Assassination of Martin Luther King

MARK LANE AND DICK GREGORY

THUNDER'S MOUTH PRESS

Published by
Thunder's Mouth Press
54 Greene Street, Suite 4S
New York, NY 10013

Library of Congress Cataloging-in-Publication Data

Lane,Mark.
    Murder in Memphis / Mark Lane and Dick Gregory.
  —1st ed.
        p.   cm.
    Includes index.
    Originally published: Code name Zorro. Englewood Cliffs :
Prentice-Hall, c1977
    ISBN 1-56025-056-9 : $13.95
    1. King, Martin Luther, Jr., 1929-1968—Assassination:
2. Afro-Americans—Biography.   3. Civil rights workers—
United States—Biography.   4. Baptists—United States—
Clergy—Biography.
I. Gregory, Dick.   II. Lane, Mark. Code name Zorro.
III. Title.
E185.97.K5L34   1993
364.1'524'0976819—dc20   92-44534
                                                   CIP

Quotation from "Letter from Birmingham Jail," abridged from
pp. 77, 78, 83-84, 92, 100 of "Letter From Birmingham Jail"—
April 16, 1963—in *Why We Can't Wait* by Martin Luther King,
Jr., copyright © 1963 by Martin Luther King, Jr. By permission
of Harper & Row, Publishers, Inc.
"I Have a Dream," by Martin Luther King, Jr., copyright © 1963
by Martin Luther King, Jr., reprinted by permission of Joan Daves.
Quotation from "I've Been to the Mountaintop," by Martin Lu-
ther King, Jr., copyright © 1968 by the Estate of Martin Luther
King, Jr., reprinted by permission of Joan Daves.
Quotation from "The Drum Major Instinct," by Martin Luther
King, Jr., copyright © 1968 by Martin Luther King, Jr., Estate,
reprinted by permission of Joan Daves.
Eulogy of Dr. Martin Luther King, Jr., Atlanta, Georgia, April 9,
1968, by Benjamin E. Mays, reprinted by permission of Charles
Scribner's Sons from *Born to Rebel: An Autobiography*, by Ben-
jamin E. Mays, copyright © 1971 by Benjamin E. Mays.

Distributed by
Publishers Group West
4065 Hollis Street
Emeryville, CA 94608

(800) 788-3123

Contents

INTRODUCTION i

PART ONE / TWENTY-FIVE YEARS AGO

   1 ON THE DEATH OF GREAT MEN
      by Mark Lane 2
   2 TWENTY-FIVE YEARS AGO *by Dick Gregory* 5

PART TWO / MARTIN LUTHER KING AND HIS MISSION

   3 MARTIN AND CORETTA KING *by Dick Gregory* 12
   4 KING AND KENNEDY CALL *by Dick Gregory* 20
   5 BIRMINGHAM *by Dick Gregory* 26
   6 "PEARLS BEFORE SWINE" *by Mark Lane* 32
   7 BIRMINGHAM JAIL *by Dick Gregory* 42
   8 "I HAVE A DREAM" *by Dick Gregory* 45
   9 "A FAR DEEPER MALADY" *by Mark Lane* 50
  10 THE LAST CAMPAIGN *by Dick Gregory* 55

PART THREE / CODE NAME "ZORRO"

  11 HOOVER'S FBI *by Mark Lane* 60
  12 ONE MAN *by Mark Lane* 72
  13 THE OBSESSION *by Mark Lane* 77
  14 THE DESTROY KING SQUAD *by Mark Lane* 88

PART FOUR / PRELUDE TO MURDER

  15 MARCH 28, MEMPHIS *by Mark Lane* 98
  16 MARCH 29, MEMPHIS AND WASHINGTON
      by Mark Lane 105
  17 APRIL 3 and 4, MEMPHIS *by Dick Gregory* 112

PART FIVE / THE MURDER

  18 APRIL 4, MEMPHIS *by Mark Lane* 124
  19 APRIL 4, ATLANTA *by Mark Lane* 136
  20 DIRECTOR HOLLOMAN *by Mark Lane* 139
  21 APRIL 5, MEMPHIS *by Mark Lane* 145

PART SIX / THE STATE OF TENNESSEE VS. JAMES EARL RAY

22	THE CASE AGAINST RAY *by Mark Lane*	148
23	THE DEFENSE *by Mark Lane*	158
24	THE AFFIRMATIVE CASE *by Mark Lane*	171
25	THE PLEA *by Mark Lane*	188

PART SEVEN / KALEIDOSCOPE

26	"THEY/HE SLEW THE DREAMER" *by Mark Lane*	216
27	*THE MAKING OF AN ASSASSIN* *by Mark Lane*	230

PART EIGHT / FOR A DAY IN COURT

28	THE APPEAL *by Mark Lane*	254
29	THE BEGINNING *by Mark Lane*	259

POSTSCRIPT

APPENDIX

1	THE FUNERAL *by Dick Gregory*	288
2	SPEECH OF SENATOR ROBERT C. BYRD	295
3	PERCY FOREMAN LETTER	300
4	THE RIGHT TO KNOW *by Mark Lane*	301

INDEX

INDEX 305

INTRODUCTION

by Mark Lane

This work had its origin during 1977 when *Code Name "Zorro"* was published by Prentice Hall. Written less than a decade after the murder of Dr. King and before the United States Congress, through its House Select Committee on Assassinations (HSCA), had investigated the murders of President Kennedy and Dr. King, it was fashioned both to provide evidence about the death of Dr. King, including the role of the Federal Bureau of Investigation in that murder, and to encourage Congress to conduct a serious inquiry.

The inexorable passage of time and events has confirmed the essential allegations which comprise the work; it has, therefore, been modified only to make it current, both in reference to elapsed time and to provide additional corroborating evidence not available sixteen years ago.

Two historic events have taken place more recently regarding the circumstances surrounding the investigation into the assassination of Dr. King.

The essential eyewitness, apparently the only one, to an aspect of the murder, Grace Stephens, was released from the silence illegally imposed upon her by the State of Tennessee, and in her first moments of freedom offered evidence that James Earl Ray was innocent.

The other occurrence, really a continuation of events, was orchestrated by the secret police, the Central Intelligence Agency and the Federal Bureau of Investigation, in an effort to prevent the HSCA from probing too deeply into the affairs. Before long Richard A. Sprague, the brilliant and determined staff director and general counsel of the committee, was driven from that position by the skillful misuse of the news media (*see pages 266-269), visits to members of Congress by FBI and CIA officials, and through the intimidation of members of Congress. With Sprague gone the HSCA was moribund. With the appointment of his successor, G. Robert Blakey, the intelligence organizations had captured the committee.

GRACE STEPHENS

I met Grace Stephens one November morning during 1977. I had heard about her from Renfro Hays, the original defense investigator for Ray.

Hays, a massive and lumbering man cared to effect a Tennessee country boy countenance. The image is quickly dispelled as soon as the work begins. His blinking eyes and open face could not hide his uncanny ability to analyze the facts quickly, and the rugged determination that has constrained him to keep at it for almost a decade after the matter was concluded as far as the courts were concerned.

When we met he looked at me for a long, silent moment and then said, "I knew this day would come. I did not know it would be you. But I knew this day would come and this case would get on the track for the first time. And I'm ready. I've been ready for years."

Sammye Cook, a woman who lived in Memphis and was deeply concerned about justice, drove Renfro Hays and me seventy miles to a state mental institution in Bolivar, Tennessee, so that I might interview Grace Stephens. I brought with me a tape recorder and the hope that I might be the first person to record the words of the most important witness to the murder of Dr. King. The fact that more than nine and one-half years after the murder no one had recorded the words of the essential witness to the crime was evidence of more than neglect and carelessness.

As this work establishes, a statement secured by the police from Grace Stephens' husband, Charles, under the most questionable circumstances constituted the entire case against Ray as the murderer. Stephens alone alleged that he saw Ray flee from the bathroom just after the shot was fired. The prosecuting attorney conceded that Stephens was jailed as a "material witness" to preserve his testimony. The court ruled that he had been illegally incarcerated and ordered him freed.

Assistant Attorney General James Beasley told the jury: "At approximately 6:00 P.M., Mr. Stephens heard the shot coming apparently through the wall from the bathroom. He then got up and went through this room out into the corridor in time to see the left profile of the defendant as he turned down the passageway that leads to an opening into a stairwell going down to Main Street."

The one witness who might have challenged that assertion was Grace Stephens. Yet she was illegally placed in a mental institution by the Tennessee authorities soon after the assassination. When Hays sought to question her, she was transferred to another institution under a different name.

We found her on November 12 at the institution in Bolivar, where she was confined under the name Grace Waldon. She had met Hays briefly nine years previously. Hays approached her, offered her his hand, called her Grace, and asked if she remembered him. She answered, "Why, of course I do, Renfro. I haven't seen you in a long time." Hays introduced me, said I was investigating the King murder, and asked if she might be willing to talk with me. She said, "Yes, I'll tell you what I know about it, but, you know, it's the same thing I said before."

We sat together in an open waiting room that was comprised of nothing more than a few chairs placed where two wide corridors met at right angles. Sammye Cook sat to the right of Grace Stephens, and I sat in front of her and to her left. I asked if she minded if I used the tape recorder and she said, "I don't mind at all if it makes it easier for you."

Mrs. Stephens' appearance might not impress a jury at the outset. She was dressed in a rumpled, inexpensive, and shapeless garment. She had no teeth. Her hair was thinning and uncared for. She *looked* as if she had been confined to a Tennessee mental institution since April, 1968. Yet she was alert. Her eyes were alive. She spoke with clarity and humor. When I asked her about Charlie, she deprecated him in an almost kindly and philosophical manner. "Well, he never said much. He always was very quiet unless he had nothing to say." She told me that she had had a drinking problem herself. "Trouble was I never did stay away from those beer joints."

I spoke with her for a few minutes. She was calm, completely in control of her thinking processes, and quite certain about the events of April 4. Mrs. Stephens suffered only from being poor and from the neglect of an institution that did not provide adequate custodial care. If she had been properly dressed, equipped with dentures, and had her hair received a small fraction of the care that approximates the national average, she would have been indistinguishable from the millions of women her age who remain at home, work, or shop in the fashionable new malls that mark the landscape.

I asked her if she remembered April 4, 1968. She answered, "Yes. Sure. Very well."

Lane: What happened that day?

Stephens: I was lying in bed reading. Then my husband came in and said that he couldn't get into the bathroom. He had to go around to the other side to use the other bathroom. So he went off. I don't remember exactly how long he was gone. Then I heard this shot.

Lane: You heard a shot?

Stephens: Yes. I recognized it as a shot. My father was a great hunter. He taught us all about guns. In fact, two of my husbands collected guns.

Lane: After you heard the shot, what happened?

Stephens: In a few minutes the bathroom door opened. I could see that. My door was partially opened and I was propped up in bed, as I said, reading.

Lane: You could see out into the corridor?

Stephens: Yes, and the bathroom door was right next to us.

Lane: Did you see anyone come out of the bathroom?

Stephens: Yes. I saw this man come out. He had something in his hand, but I couldn't see what it was because he was carrying it next to the railing.

The railing she referred to was to the right of the man leaving the bathroom. It is near the bathroom and it tops the stairwell that provides a rear exit for the rooming house. It was that staircase that Charles Stephens had used in his search for an unoccupied bathroom. The room that the Stephenses occupied was across the corridor from the stairwell. Consequently, Mrs. Stephens did not have an unobstructed view of the object carried by the man, since his body came between her and the object. Mrs. Stephens described the physical layout of the building to me with absolute accuracy, remembering some details that I had forgotten. I had seen the interior of the building on several occasions earlier that year. Mrs. Stephens, who had spent a great deal more time there than I had, had not been there for more than nine years preceding out conversation.

She told me that the man carried the object "in his right hand, near the railing that goes on down the back stairs."

Lane: Since then have you seen pictures of James Earl Ray?

Stephens: I've seen pictures of James Earl Ray, but I never saw that man in person.

Lane: Was the man who you saw come out of the bathroom James Earl Ray?

Stephens: No it wasn't James Earl Ray I saw. It didn't look anything at all like him.

Lane: Did anyone from the police talk to you afterward?

Stephens: Yes. We had police, reporters, and more reporters. It was a mess.

Mrs. Stephens said that the police showed her a series of pictures to see if she could identify the man she had seen.

Stephens: There was a picture that looked like the man I had seen. I pointed it out [to the police], but they never did pay any attention.

She said that the picture she picked out was not a picture of James Earl Ray.

Later, after Ray became known as a suspect, she said the police "tried to get" her to say that she had seen Ray leave the bathroom. She consistently refused to make a false identification, she said.

Lane: You have seen pictures of James Earl Ray?

Stephens: Yes, since then.

Lane: Is there any doubt in your mind that the man you saw was not James Earl Ray?

Stephens: There's no doubt in my mind. That wasn't James Earl Ray. It was an entirely different man. He was older, had dark hair; he was a brunette.

Lane: Do you remember what he was wearing?

Stephens: A windbreaker. I called it a hunting coat then. And under the coat he had on a checkered shirt, a loud, checkered shirt. The coat was open.

Lane: Did your husband Charlie ever see that man?

Stephens: I don't think he did. He couldn't see without his glasses, anyway. He didn't have his glasses on; they were on the bed, in the room.

Mrs. Stephens explained that her husband left his glasses in the room for the short trip that he contemplated taking to the bathroom that was next door to their room.

When that bathroom was occupied, a fact he determined by "banging on the door," according to his wife, he went down the nearby stairs and then outside. "A few minutes" after the shot was fired, according to Mrs. Stephens, her husband returned to their room.

Lane: When he returned, did you tell him what you saw?

Stephens: Yes. I told him the man went down the hall, and he [Charles] went down to look down the stairs. He motioned me to come down there and look, but I was afraid that he might take a pot shot at me, and I wouldn't go.

Since some minutes had elapsed after the shot and before Charles Stephens returned to the room, it seems unlikely that Stephens could have been in a position to have seen the killer. Since he was apparently not wearing his glasses and evidently would have required them to make an accurate observation, it appears that his assertions were valueless. Yet Stephens is the only witness that the state has been able to discover to point the finger at James Earl Ray.

Just after Grace Stephens told me that she believed that her husband had not see the man who murdered Dr. King, a man in charge of the building at the institution and a woman employee of the institution approached me. The woman, who identified herself, only after my repeated request that she do so, as Daisy Cox, said, "You cannot talk to Grace." The man, David West, agreed. They were joined by another woman employee and then others. Daisy Cox ordered Grace Stephens to leave. Mrs. Stephens was taken away by attendants. West and Cox then told me that I would have to surrender the tape upon which I had recorded the interview. I told them that I represented James Earl Ray, that the recording was important evidence, and that I planned to keep it. They then told me that they were going to take the tape cassette from me. I said that since there was not the slightest chance of my surrendering the tape, it might be profitable for them to devote their energy to some other, and more realizable, task.

At that moment another employee arrived on the scene. She said, "You are not allowed to talk to Grace. No one is. At my switchboard I have a note from the administrator that says that she is not to receive any visitors or any telephone calls without them being cleared through the administrator." I asked for her name and she said, "I'm the switchboard operator, and that note is right at the switchboard." I asked for her name again and she said she was Georgia Young. I then asked her if the rule requiring clearance for telephone calls and visitors applied to any person at the institution other than Grace Stephens.

Daisy Cox answered for her. "We are not talking about the other patients—we're talking about Grace."

I asked Young if the note at her switchboard applied only to Grace Stephens. She said that it did.

As the employees of the State of Tennessee moved toward me, I walked around them and urged Sammye Cook and Renfro Hays to prepare to leave. Sammye and I exited quickly from the building while Renfro engaged the state employees in conversation, his bulk providing a barrier behind which Sammye and I were able to flee.

Armed with the taped interview I approached the Memphis office of the American Civil Liberties Union. The ACLU, after meetings and discussions, refused to assist Mrs. Stephens in her effort to be released from the illegal confinement. First the local officers stated that they did not have adequate funds, some $450, available to them to bring a writ of habeas corpus. I immediately donated $500 to the organization, earmarked for the Stephens action. Ultimately the ACLU decided it was "just not a good First Amendment case." They declined to act and never did return my donation.

I was far more successful when I turned to Rev. James Lawson, who had worked closely with Dr. King and who had recently moved to Los Angeles where he continues his good work and his ministry. Rev. Lawson and I organized a meeting of representatives of all of the religious faiths in Memphis who demanded the immediate release of Grace Stephens. Together with legal action which I brought and the airing of the Stephens tape on radio and television programs the movement to free Grace Stephens became irresistible. She was released from custody and was then free to tell the truth about what she had seen on April 4, 1968.

The statement of Grace Stephens might have been a significant factor had the HSCA conducted an honest inquiry. However, after Richard Sprague was replaced as staff director and general counsel by G. Robert Blakey, it became clear that a political solution, rather than one based upon fact, was the new order of business.

THE CONGRESSIONAL INQUIRY

Sprague had resisted the efforts of the CIA and the FBI determined who should be "cleared" among for his own staff of investigators and had steadfastly insisted upon using the power of subpoena to examine and secure all relevant intelligence files. Indeed, subpoenas issued by Sprague to the intelligence agencies either promised or threatened, depending upon one's perspective, to dismantle the secret police cover-up. Blakey instead became a willing extension of the intelligence organizations, firing former Sprague staff personnel the CIA and FBI were less than pleased with, and then in an almost unprecedented act of self emasculation, he yielded his only weapon, the power to subpoena essential documents.

So incurious was Blakey that he accepted only those documents which the CIA and FBI were eager to press upon him. The cowardly members of Congress agreed with Blakey that it might be counterproductive, even dangerous, to conduct a real inquiry. Walter Fauntroy, the delegate from Washington, D.C., to the House of Representatives, and the chairman of the sub-committee assigned to investigate the King assassination, told the authors of this book that while his investigation was underway the FBI had tapped the telephone in his office, his home and his church, and might kill him, *"as it had killed Dr. King,"* were he to conduct a serious investigation. The frightened chairman of the committee seemed certain of just two things: the FBI had assassinated Dr. King and he, Fauntroy, would never reveal the truth.

If there is a redeeming aspect to our political system it is that our elected officials fear, almost as much as full disclosure, the retribution that may be visited upon them by their informed constituents. For most members of Congress there is but one commandment: Thou Shall Get Thyself Re-elected.

A number of the members of the committee were African Americans who were given their assignments to assure the populace that the report could not be coerced. Would these men, we were to ask ourselves, falsify the record about the death of their leader? The answer was yes, at the very least if applied to Fauntroy. Those closest to the throne when John Kennedy was president, including Thomas "Tip" O'Neill, Nicholas Katzenbach, and a passel of other jesters and cronies also demonstrated that political loyalty is no more immortal than the man upon whom it is bestowed.

Thus, schizophrenia in its most virulent form, the strain which afflicts that portion of the mind in which conscience and courage repose, reached epidemic proportions among the members of the Congressional committee.

Unable to tell the truth after years of slavish devotion to the maxim that inconvenient facts must not be disclosed, and unwilling to appear mindless to their voters by denying that which all reasonable observers know—that there had been a conspiracy to assassinate both President Kennedy and Dr. King—they entered into a bizarre compromise. In their effort to please, or at least mollify, they instead revealed their own confusion and lack of intellect and commitment.

Thus *The Final Assassination Report*, as it was hopefully but inaccurately entitled when it was published in a commercial version by Bantam in 1979, with introductions by Tom Wicker and G. Robert Blakey, was a curious document.

Wicker did not like it; it caused him discomfort. He wrote, "I was dismayed in 1978 when the House Select Committee on Assassinations said in a preliminary report that John Kennedy was 'probably assassinated as a result of a conspiracy.'" (Wicker, Forward, *The Final Assassination Report*, Bantam, 1979, unnumbered page) Why was this objective journalist upset? He explained somewhat defensively that he had never tried to discourage investigation into Kennedy's death even though "virtually from the hour of Oswald's arrest, I had been among those who rejected the idea of conspriacy."

In the 1979 report, Wicker complained that he had even "endured a good deal of scorn from the most persistent theorists, a breed all too likely to believe that anyone who disagrees with them must be a conspirator himself."

Having cleared himself, Wicker never did offer evidence to support the monumental preconceptions he formed "virtually from the hour of Oswald's arrest," when no evidence was available to demonstrate Oswald's guilt, that Oswald fired the weapon and that he had acted alone.

Wicker was an important witness. He, among many others, saw the police officers charge up the grassy knoll toward the wooden fence from which the fatal shot had been fired. It was Wicker's first and probably only relevant observation that day. Why had he immediately shared it with his colleagues and then ignored it as soon as he heard that Oswald had been arrested? Perhaps it was not part of all the news fit to print.

Wicker's subsequent excuse that it was but a "minor detail" appears inadequate in view of the belief held by the vast majority of the American people, the overwhelming majority of the eyewitnesses and earwitnesses in Dealey Plaza that day, and the belief of virtually all serious students of the case that the events which had occurred at the area which the officers charged toward were of the utmost significance.

Wicker said he was less surprised, and no doubt less concerned, that the committee also found "a likelihood"* that a conspiracy was responsible for the death of Dr. King. (*same unnumbered page)

King, after all, had not been a president and the safety of the republic seemed less in danger from the revelation of some of the truth regarding the crime.

Wicker then skillfully assessed the befuddled and conflicting conclusions of the Blakey report. The document was, he revealed, at war with itself. Blakey had offered a laundry list of those he had apparently exonerated.

As Wicker's analysis disclosed, Blakey and his bemused and obedient group of Congresspeople accepted conspiracy as a premise, then rounded up all the usual suspects—and cleared them all.

Wicker wrote that "blows away virtually every conspiracy theory of any real consequence..." Wicker found this result "troubling" but also strangely "reassuring."

The established media and the craven members of Congress could accept the reality of a conspiracy for each assassination as long as it was understood that they did not know who was behind each murder, but were quite certain of who was not involved. For them, "small-timers" apparently were acceptable. For the rest of us, questions remain.

Blakey in his introduction places much of the responsibility upon me for having persuaded the American people that the assassination of President Kennedy was not the work of a lone gunman and also for having "espoused a theory of conspiracy in Dr. King's death." (*Blakey, Introduction, page unnumbered.)

He then admits, in a one sentence summation of his own report: "The final line in both assassinations is conspiracy." (*Ibid.)

He adds that although the report did not find conclusive evidence of a government "coverup" in either Kennedy's or King's death, there was substantial proof of a "failure to uncover" evidence which would indicate a conspiracy. "To put it bluntly, the official findings on the conspiracy question in both cases were wrong."

Blakey added, "Realizing that there would be an opportunity for others to fill in the details...we chose a cautious approach."

So cautious indeed that there have been no indictments, no trials, and no investigations since the publication of the Blakey report.

Blakey asserts with generosity founded only in bias and in the face of a body of evidence to the contrary that no agency of government was even involved in a "coverup." To understand the unshakeable preconceptions that he and his Committee brought to their task we need only examine the pathetic public record which they created. A rather dramatic example of the deliberate misconduct engaged in by Blakey and his associates surfaced during the testimony of James Earl Ray before the HSCA.

Ralph Abernathy, Hosea Williams, Dick Gregory, Andrew Young, Rev. James Lawson, Jesse Jackson, and other leaders of the African American community with whom I had worked over the years in a myriad of projects spoke with me about the death of Dr. King. Each expressed his own absolute lack of faith in the official version and each asserted his own belief that Hoover's FBI had murdered their friend and colleague. Each man also urged me to look into the matter. Coretta Scott King agreed.

Later when my inquiry began it took me to the Brushy Mountain State Penitentiary in Petros, Tennessee, where I met James Earl Ray. In time the evidence convinced me that there had been a conspiracy and that Ray had been, at the most, an unwitting participant. Ray asked me to represent him in his effort to secure a trial. I agreed to do so and when the HSCA called him to testify he asked me to appear as counsel.

It was a hot mid-August day in Washington, D.C., during 1978, when Ray and I sat together before the Congressional inquisitors and the bright television lights and exploding flash bulbs of the photographers. The event was carried live to millions of homes in the United States via radio and television. We had answered the inquiries and posed a few questions of our own which appeared to stun the uninformed committee members. Blakey's battalion, with its cherished commitment to prove Ray's guilt to the American people, was suffering defeat after defeat.

Following a luncheon recess the Committee reconvened, armed with "MLK Exhibit Numbered 92," Blakey's secret weapon. Rep. Samuel L. Devine of Ohio had been chosen by Fauntroy and Blakey to carry out the skulduggery. Rep. Richardson Preyer of North Carolina presided. Fauntroy, the chairman of the subcommittee on the King assassination, was a silent observer, no doubt afraid of a public confrontation with me for he had after all confessed his belief to me that the FBI was the culpable agency. Just before lunch, the committee had given me a copy of the document. Blakey and his staff had shrouded it in secrecy until then, although they had the document in their possession for approximately ten days. Surprise, stealth, and subterfuge were their allies; not just James Earl Ray but an open and full inquiry were their enemies.

The document which I had seen for the first time perhaps one hour earlier, at the same time it was provided to the news media, was the transcript of an interview with Alexander Anthony Eist, a veteran English police officer who had served as "a Detective Sergeant with a group of men stationed at Scotland Yard known as the Flying Squad." Eist stated that he "was under the command of a man called Butler, Thomas Butler, who was a *Chief-Detective Chief Superintendent.*"

The transcript was of an interview with Detective Sergeant Eist conducted by Edward Evans, Blakey's Chief Investigator, Charles Rogovin, special counsel to Blakey's committee, and Robin Lindley, another attorney reporting to Blakey.

Eist was described in the document as having served with the Metropolitan Police for twenty-eight years and having left "at the rank of Chief Inspector."

According to Eist he had been assigned a decade earlier, on June 8, 1968, to guard James Earl Ray at the Canon Row Police Station. He said that he talked with Ray over a period of several days and that he had gained Ray's confidence. In answer to impermissibly leading questions posed by Blakey's assistants, Eist said that Ray had admitted that he hated blacks, that he especially had hated Dr. King, that he had murdered Dr. King, that he expected to be paid more than a million dollars, that he had had no assistance in his escape from a Missouri prison, and that he had made a mistake in throwing the "gun" away which he had used to murder Dr. King since it had his fingerprints on it.

An example of the questions and answers follows:

Mr. Evans: During these conversations about the hatred of blacks, did he discuss with you his feelings about blacks relative to he would kill some black or he had a plan, or based on what he'd say did you get from that that he had a plan to kill some black?

Mr. Eist: Yes, very much so.

Every question was posed to secure an affirmative answer which would support the false case Blakey was attempting to construct.

Two questions were immediately apparent. Why had Blakey decided to send three of his most important aides to Cambridge, England, to conduct an "interview"? Why had they not instead taken a sworn statement from Eist or invited him to testify in person before the committee?

The unsworn answers given by Eist could have no legal import although they were designed to seem impressive to a waiting television audience. If Blakey and his staff of attorneys and investigators suspected or believed that Eist was not telling the truth the technique they decided to employ, securing remarks which were not given under oath, would spare *them* the potential embarrassment of prosecution for subordination of perjury. It also permitted Eist to make false statements with the knowledge that he could not be prosecuted for perjury. Blakey had issued a license to lie to Eist.

In addition it seemed more than odd that Eist, to whom Ray had allegedly made a full confession, would remain silent about the matter for ten years. Blakey's Chief Investigator had raised the question most gently:

Mr. Eist: Recently, about two months ago I think it was, there was a bit of publicity over here about certain things happening to do with Earl Ray and the shooting of Martin Luther King. There were inquires and things going on. And I have a lot of Americans coming here, and I was talking to an American couple who said this was probably important to the country's sake and I should do something about it and get in touch with the authorities, which I did, I phoned the FBI.

Mr. Evans: You phoned the FBI office in London?

Mr. Eist: Yeah.

Mr. Evans: And were you subsequently interviewed by two agents from the FBI?

Mr. Eist: I was, yes.

Mr. Evans: And did you relate to them basically the same story that you have now related to us?

Mr. Eist: Yes, the same.

Mr. Evans: Would you give me the name of the couple that you spoke to?

Mr. Eist: Well, I'd rather not, you know, because I only know them casually and they didn't, they don't come into this at all. They just in actual fact advised. I mean I never went into the conversation with them. I just said I had certain knowledge and this and that. And then they advised that I should contact the appropriate authorities.

Mr. Evans: And then you thought that you would contact the FBI?

Mr. Eist: That's right.

Mr. Evans: Are there any additional questions?

Mr. Rogovin: Have you had occasion to talk to your former department?

Mr. Eist: On this subject, no.

Mr. Rogovin: And you are in retired status of the Metropolitan?

Mr. Eist: Yes, yes. I'm on pension, yes.

Mr. Rogovin: I think we noted, but for the record, you retired as a Detective Chief Inspector?

Mr. Eist: Yes.

Mr. Evans: And that was a total of some thirty—

Mr. Eist: twenty, twenty-eight and a half years.

Mr. Evans: twenty-eight and a half years. Okay, is there anything additional that you would like to add that might be of some assistance to us?

Mr. Eist: Not really, except to say if you want my impression of Earl Ray, Earl Ray, and from what he told me. Gentlemen, for what it is worth, I haven't any doubt in my mind that he did that on his own. For whatever reason he did it on his, but he did it on his own. If it had been anything, or anybody behind him on that particular job that during the various and many conversations I had with him it would have come out.

Mr. Rogovin: Should it become of interest to the Committee of the House of Representatives in Washington, Mr. Eist, would you be willing, if requested, Mr. Eist, to do so to come to the United States at Government expense, of course, to testify at a public proceeding with regard to the knowledge you have of this matter?

Mr. Eist: Yes.

Mr. Rogovin: Thank you, sir.

Mr. Evans: Okay, thank you very much Mr. Eist for allowing us into you business location and taking the time to be interviewed by us.

Mr. Eist: It's fine.

And thus the interview was concluded. The Eist comments were entirely without corroboration although certainly one matter was susceptible to further inquiry—the name of the "American couple." Evans's acquiescence in Eist's demurer in that regard leads one to believe that he suspected or knew that the couple was apocryphal.

Eist said he was willing to testify, either in England or in the United States. I wondered what Blakey might have known that led him to offer, in place of legally acceptable testimony either through a deposition or a personal appearance, a legally valueless document explicitly entitled by Blakey "Interview with Alexander Anthony Eist."

While it was clear to me that much was legally amiss, it also seemed that Blakey's sudden and unprofessional sneak attack was calculated to prevail as a publicity stunt which might forever preclude the truth about the death of Dr. King from being revealed.

Moments before the HSCA commenced I was handed a note stating that an English barrister urgently wished for me to call him. I had never before absented myself from a hearing or proceeding upon such a nebulous, not to say, illusory, foundation. Desperation fueled my faint hope and after Devine had offered the interview in evidence and had begun to read the entire document into the record, I spoke:

Mr. Devine: This is captioned "Interview with Alexander Anthony Eist at the Greenman's Pub, Six-Mile Bottom, Cambridge, England, on August 4th, 1978.

Today's date is August 4th, 1978. We are at the Greenman's Pub, Six-Mile Bottom, Cambridge, England. We are about to commence with the interview of Alexander Anthony Eist. Mr. Eist, we will start off by identifying the persons in the room, starting with Mr. Eist. Mr. Eist will you identify yourself please?

Mr. Eist: Yes. My name is Alexander Anthony Eist. I am now a licensee of the Greenman Public House, Six-Mile Bottom, Cambridge, here. I served in the Metropolitan Police for twenty-eight years.

Mr. Lane: I am sorry to interrupt you. Since I read the document and there is some pressing other matter I might attend to, I wonder if I might be excused if all you are going to do is read that document and I will be back before you finish. Is that all right, Mr. Preyer?

Mr. Preyer: Is that all right, Mr. Ray?

Mr. Ray: Yes.

Mr. Preyer: That is agreeable with the Chair.

I rushed to a public telephone in the hallway of the House of Representatives office building in which the hearing was taking place. I called the number and waited while it rang many times with no response. I hung up, my fragile Pollyannish expectancy now gone. I tried once more, hoping that I had misdailed the first time

What I did not know then, but learned much later, was that the English barrister, then visiting his cousin in California, had called me earlier; his message had been held by Blakey's assistants until I appeared in the hearing room and only then given to me. The barrister had waited at the telephone for my call while watching the hearing on television. When he saw the proceeding continue with me at the witness table he was convinced that I would not call, and he and his cousin left for lunch. In the carport he heard the telephone ring—my initial call. He rushed back toward the house but was thwarted as I hung up. When he heard the telephone ring again he realized that the keys to the house were in his automobile and that he would not have time to fetch them. He broke into the house through an opening in the door used for the family's large dog. He ran to the telephone and arrived there just before I was about to leave. We talked. Then I returned to the hearing room as Devine began to question Ray about the Eist statement. Ray was responding:

Mr. Ray: Well, first, Mr. Devine, I think that is probably the most damaging statement that has been made against me. It quotes me as making an oral statement admitting guilt in a murder charge. I

think it refers to me as insane. So I would like to comment rather extensively on this statement and it is false, but did you say you wanted to ask me questions about specific allegations in the statement directed against me?

There are certain allegations in the statement referring to me. Did you want to question me about those allegations? Then after you did that I would appreciate if I could comment just briefly on some of—

Mr. Devine: Well, if you would care to comment in any way you wish, you go ahead, you have the freedom to do so.

I watched Blakey as he looked at me; he looked away suddenly as I stared at him. He seemed nervous and anxious, fidgeting in his chair, his hands flexing and unflexing.

Then I spoke:

Mr. Lane: I wonder if I could make a very brief comment because I agree with Mr. Ray, this is perhaps the most damaging statement that has ever made against Mr. Ray, and I am impressed with your statement, Mr. Devine, that you are going to investigate further.

I want to thank the indulgence of the Committee for giving me a few minutes to leave to talk with an English barrister who told me that Mr. Eist was dismissed from the Metropolitan Police force in London in disgrace under charges of theft and perjury which were lodged against him, that he was investigated by A-10 of the Internal Police Branch of the Corruption Department of Scotland Yard and they concluded he was guilty of corruption. The Crown or the prosecutor, one Henry Pownell, recently charged in open court that your witness, whose record you read to the American people, is "a corrupt police official, a disgrace to the English police force."

Mr. Preyer: (interupting) Mr. Lane.

Mr. Lane: (continuing) He has been placed on trial for accepting bribes and involvement in jewel robberies throughout London, including the Great Hatton Garden jewel robbery in the Hatton Garden Jewelry District in 1974. Further, it has been alleged in open court that Eist set up and established conspiracies on numerous occasions to commit jewel robberies throughout all of England. Mr. Eist has given evidence in court. It has been stated under oath by others that he invented oral confessions and committed perjury in relating them. If this information about Mr. Eist is true, which has just been given to me, if it was all public knowledge in England, in all of the newspapers as this lawyer told me, then I don't know why your investigators in London couldn't have found that out by reading any of the newspapers. If this is true, and if it was in the newspapers, this Committee has engaged in the most irresponsible conduct probably in the long history of Congress, and that is an awfully long history of irresponsible conduct.

Mr. Preyer: In a desire to be completely fair to you, the Chair has allowed you to bring out those matters which you would have been allowed to bring out, although more properly they would have come at the end of Mr. Ray's testimony, under our rule.
I will point out once again that Mr. Devine indicated this testimony is not being offered as evidence of the truth of those statements. The Committee does not make any statement as to the credibility of the witness and Mr. Ray was only being asked whether the statement was true and any comments he may—

Mr. Lane: If you knew of this man's background, it was a height of irresponsibility not to inform the American people about that background. Yet, if I did not receive a phone call from the English lawyer, the American people would not know of the deceit of this Committee. This is perhaps the most outrageous thing this Committee had done. It is outrageous, and the American people are watching this and are judging you more than they are judging anyone else here in the arena. Under these circumstances, I want to talk with my client. I am not sure it is possible to go on any further with the kind of deceit and deception of this Committee. I would like a recess to talk with my client to see how to proceed. I have never in twenty-eight years of practicing law ever seen anything as terrible, as outrageous—

Mr. Preyer: At this time, we will consider that.
    The Committee will stand in recess. Is five minutes sufficient for you? Ten minutes?

Mr. Lane: Half an hour

If one had placed a live hand grenade in front of Blakey and similar explosives at each of the television cameras in the room the Committee members could not have fled from their chief of counsel and the news media with greater alacrity.

After the recess, the Committee members straggled in, still shaken and confused. Preyer attempted to explain away the Committee's blatant misconduct. Weakly, he said:

I think that has been completely misconstrued. Mr. Ray was given this document over lunch. We wanted to give him the opportunity to comment on it. We will call this witness before the Committee so that his credibility can be assessed. He will have the chance to explain any statements that he may have made.

He added, "This committee does not vouch for the credibility of this statement, and we intend to call this witness to explain his statement at a later time."

I sought to respond.

Mr. Lane: May I have one—

Mr. Preyer: You are recognized, Mr. Lane, for one minute.

Mr. Lane: Thank you, Mr. Preyer. First of all, during the questioning, it was clear that this witness told your investigators that he did not mention this to anyone for ten years, evidently. Even when Mr. Ray was involved in an extradition hearing in London when the United States Government couldn't get any reliable evidence to extradite him, this man, this Chief Inspector had all this information, *his full confession*, and never mentioned it to anyone.

Now, years later when an American couple, who he was not required to name, he was not required by your investigators to supply, asked him about the case, he decided to come forward and issue this statement.

Devine, who had been so full of himself and questions for Ray before the recess, had become so disheartened, when invited to proceed, could only mumble, "I have have no further questions, Mr. Chairman."

Earlier in the day Fauntroy had been running about proclaiming to representatives of the news media that his questions of Ray would "nail him to the cross," an odd observation from a Christian minister. Now his moment was at hand.

Mr. Preyer: The Chair recognizes the Chairman of the Martin Luther King Subcommittee, Mr. Fauntroy.

Mr. Fauntroy: Mr. Chairman, as you know, we have three mandates in this Committee. One, to determine who killed Martin Luther King, Jr.; secondly, was he assisted in any way by anyone and, third, what was the performance of the investigative agencies of this government with respect to that assassination.

I have been preparing myself to interrogate Mr. Ray with respect to a number of some twenty-one conspiracy allegations and those conspiracy allegations will require a considerable time to cover, and I

am under great time pressure at this point to not only include at least three or four other witnesses that I think the Committee and the American people ought to hear today, but also to go through the complexities of several conspiracy allegations which we are mandated to explore.

For that reason, as reluctant as I am to give up the opportunity to question our witness with respect to these allegations at this time, I think it better wisdom that as a committee we continue the interrogation of Mr. Ray at a later time, at a time that would give me the time I need to raise the very serious questions which I have and enable us to get on to two or three very important witnesses that I insist, Mr. Chairman, that we as a committee cover today. I do very reluctantly give up that opportunity now, but I insist, again, that I have that opportunity to interrogate Mr. Ray on these matters.

The Committee members then began a dance in which each sought to distance himself further from Blakey's tactics. Each expressed, possibly feigned, surprise, that Ray and I had not been given the Eist interview transcript and other documents in advance.

Chairman Stokes: Will the gentleman yield?

Mr. Fauntroy: I will be very happy to yield to the distinguished Chairman.

Chairman Stokes: I would just like to say we were given that assurance from them that they had everything they needed.

Mr. Fithian [Rep. Floyd J. Fithian]: Will the gentleman yield?

Mr. Fauntroy: I will be happy to yield to the gentleman from Indiana.

Mr. Fithian: Mr. Chairman, I want to be sure, before you proceed, that the witness and his counsel do, indeed, have in their possession the 20,000 words and any other documents that we are going to proceed from, any documents of substance that we are to proceed from when we deal with the conspiracy question. Does Mr. Ray have in his possession now the 20,000 words which his counsel raised this morning?

Mr. Lane: No, we raised it yesterday. We do have this document. I think there may be less than 20,000 words, but I know you call it "the 20,000 word document." We have this document. We asked for it yesterday. We have it today. We don't have everything we may need.

For example, if you are going to try to add any more documents of this kind from England, this kind of trash, we would like to have

some advance notice. We don't know what you're planning, but so far as we're concerned, I believe that we are prepared to proceed now that we have this material and Mr. Ray has had an opportunity to read it. That is not to say that if you start asking Mr. Ray questions about secret reports that you have or new police officers whose memories have been refreshed a decade later materialize that we are not going to ask to look at that document or any document referring to it.

So far as we know, we are prepared now to answer all the questions.

Mr. McKinney [Rep. Stewart B. McKinney]: I would just like to say to the Chairman as ranking member of the Martin Luther King Subcommittee, as you know, I was prepared to go into somewhat extensive questioning this morning. I had read all of the testimony that Mr. Ray has given to the committee at Brushy Mountain, and my impression from the testimony was that the Committee had given the witness, as well as his attorney, everything that they desired. I found out that was not true as far as the counsel is concerned for the witness. So I, too, would like a chance again, but I want to make doubly sure that we have a definite statement from both the witness and counsel before they leave here today that, except for new material which we will give them, I am sure, well in advance, that they have absolutely everything they want at the present time so that we won't have this problem with delay and all the other problems we have had at these hearings.

Mr. Preyer: But I do want to assure you that the committee will make available to you, will take under advisement any requests that you have before we resume any hearings here.

Mr. Lane: One more point, if I could, about this and that is Mr. Ray believes that this is not the completed Huie material [William Bradford Huie . . . .]* and I have never seen this until today. Perhaps he can tell you what's missing.

Mr. Preyer: Well, we will go into that at the appropriate time. The matter before us right now is whether to recess or not.

---

*William Bradford Huie was the author of a book that asserted that Ray was the assassin of Dr. King. For a period of time Huie, posing as an objective journalist, recieved documents and cooperation from Ray's lawyer. Ray suspected that Huie was covertly working with the FBI. Later, it became clear that Huie did have a relationship with the FBI and had been fed false and derogatory information about Ray by the FBI.

This is the first week of a series of hearings in this matter. We will resume again in November. The Committee does have several other important witnesses to hear today. We have inconvenienced those witnesses long enough. It is the opinion of the Committee that we should recess the James Earl Ray portion of the hearings until a later date, probably in November. So at the time and in the meantime, we will make available to you and discuss with you whatever documents you might need, and we will make available today's transcript, of course, to you.

Mr. Lane: I take it that we can make a closing argument—

Mr. Fauntroy: Mr. Chairman.

Mr. Preyer: When we resume again, we will, of course, at the conclusion of the testimony make the time available to you for closing arguments and closing statements

Mr. Lane: Thank you.

To state that the day had not quite turned out the way Blakey and the congressmen had planned would be to engage in the kind of British understatement apparently foreign to Chief Inspector Eist.

The session ended with the members of Congress pledging to investigate Eist, permit Ray to return to answer the false charges and to give me the opportunity to summarize our case to the American people in closing arguments.

For months I had requested the relevant documents; Blakey and his staff had refused to make them available. Now the congressmen, eyes toward the televison cameras, were graciously inquiring if I had all the material I needed and wondering if they could assist me in any way.

Every promise made by the Committee was broken. Eist was forgotten, no additional documents were forthcoming and Ray was denied the opportunity to testify.

I never much admired the tactics utilized by Joseph McCarthy. Yet compared with Blakey, Stokes, Fauntroy, McKinney and the other activists of the House Select Committee of Assassinations, he was moderately fair. After all, he generally afforded to his victims the opportunty to respond.

These members of Congress demonstrated that they did not have the courage to speak truth to power. That executive power, represented formally during the past four years in the person of George Bush, the former Director of the Central Intelligence Agency, and informally long before that, has been modified by the election of Bill Clinton and Al Gore.

The desperate state of the economy and the mandate to attend to it will, in all likelihood, command the immediate attention of the new administration.

Yet somewhere on the agenda, in the section marked Justice, there remain other unresolved matters for our nation. The American people await a satisfactory response to the unsolved mysteries in the deaths of President John F. Kennedy and Dr. Martin Luther King, Jr. We all have an interest in a just resolution.

There is to this matter also a sense of urgency.

Now, twenty-five years later, an innocent man still remains in a Tennessee prison.

Mark Lane
Washington, D.C.
1993

PART
ONE

TWENTY-FIVE
YEARS AGO

Chapter One

ON THE DEATH
OF GREAT MEN
by Mark Lane

Twenty-five years ago Dr. Martin Luther King, Jr., the greatest civil rights protagonist in modern American history, was murdered in Memphis, Tennessee. Subsequently James Earl Ray was arrested and charged with the crime. Ray insisted that there had been a conspiracy and that after Dr. King's death he discovered that he had been an unwitting implement of the conspiracy.

No trial, or other public proceeding, has occurred since April 4, 1968, the day Dr. King was killed, which permits us to evaluate the evidence in the case. Ray entered what he has referred to, not without some supporting evidence, as an induced plea of guilty. A prearranged and rehearsed hearing was conducted without cross-examination or challenge by the defense. It raised more questions than it answered. Ray publicly contended, much to the embarrassment of his own lawyer, the Tennessee Attorney General, and the trial judge, that there had been a conspiracy to kill Dr. King. No one asked him what he meant or asked him to elaborate.

In this book, Ray's explanation of that provocative assertion will be explored. I have spent many hours with him at Brushy Mountain Penitentiary in Petros, Tennessee. I was the first person to visit him after his incarceration there in 1976, and I have met with him there on numerous occasions over the past quarter of a century. His view is presented here, as are the results of my investigation into his allegation. Ray is an intelligent and articulate man not without a sense of humor, some of it self-directed, some of it poured upon those who have assessed his role in the murder. I think that the reader will only be able to evaluate Ray's participation in the events of April 4, 1968, in Memphis after hearing Ray's account of the events and when that exposition is placed in its full context.

The troubling events surrounding the murder of Dr. King encompass much that is beyond the range of perception or knowledge of James Earl

2

Ray. A minor publishing industry developed after the murder. Much of the work it produced did little more than obfuscate the essential truth, through the promulgation of an army of irrelevant data and flawed reasoning.

With the exception of the incipient investigation of the murder by the Select Committee on Assassinations of the House of Representatives the only examination of the events in the nine years that have passed is a secret inquiry conducted primarily by a police agency that vowed to destroy Dr. King and a recent Department of Justice review of the work of that police agency. Such investigations can hardly be expected to win the confidence of the American people. It is, therefore, not surprising that just before this book was completed a national poll conducted by George Gallup disclosed that fewer than one out of five Americans believed the official version of the events—that James Earl Ray was the lone assassin of Dr. Martin Luther King, Jr.

That is why Dick Gregory and I decided that this book must be written now. So much new and profoundly disturbing evidence has come to light since 1968—some of it uncovered by Greg, some by me, some by other investigators—that the matter cries out for reconsideration by the most eminent of all juries, the American people.

Greg and I decided to divide the task of preparing the manuscript along purely practical lines. Greg knew King—was deeply involved in his work. I, on the other hand, had ready access to extensive documentation through the files of the Citizens Commission of Inquiry, which I now head. So it was decided that Greg should be primarily responsible for writing the first part of the book, the part dealing with Martin Luther King and events leading up to his murder, and that I should be primarily responsible for the later parts of the book, those dealing with the murder and its aftermath.

Through the work of Dick Gregory, Martin Luther King becomes alive again for the readers of this book. Greg stood with Dr. King in Birmingham and in a score of other cities throughout the Deep South, and in the Deep North of Chicago as well. Dr. King's assassination was a moment of history that traumatized this country, for in his life he was for a moment the conscience of mankind. Greg's work and Martin's words remind us again that not just a symbol died that day in Memphis. A man who could think, and inspire, and lead, and love, and be hurt was killed.

My task was different from Greg's. I have undertaken to tell the story of some particularly significant events that preceded the murder, to relate the evidence that we have uncovered about the murder, and to describe the efforts to suppress information that leads inexorably toward the prime suspects in the murder.

3

If the American people are not satisfied with the official rendition of the events, then they evidently spurn as well the quasi-official efforts by writers Ray refers to as "novelists." Who are these writers, and why might they have chosen to ignore some of the relevant evidence?

The death of great men often leaves behind a tumultuous wake that may inundate those who have stood too close to the event, or who may have inadvertently seen too much. In this case witnesses who lived in the rooming house from which the shot was presumably fired were unintentional witnesses to that moment of history. The rooming house was, if not what unkind fiction writers refer to as a flophouse, something akin to it. Those who were forced by events to live there were, for the most part, ill prepared to withstand societal pressures designed to alter their testimony, to forget their unmistakable observations, and to remain silent about official discrepancies. One of them, perhaps potentially the most important witness of all, remained for a decade after the event—in a Tennessee mental institution which she said was placed in as punishment for seeking to tell the truth.

In life as in drama, minor characters may be swept away by great events they do not understand and cannot even begin to comprehend. The real actors in the drama of Memphis, messengers who felt called upon to relate what they had seen, suffered grievously; some are suffering still. For those of us who were not witnesses that day, the suffering is of a different nature and of a different degree. We are, all of us, poorer for the death of Dr. King. We suffer still from the injury done to our right to know about events that have been contrived to shape our lives. If a major political and social leader may be murdered without a proper inquiry into the circumstances, our constitutional rights are in jeopardy. We have the power, I am convinced, to influence our own collective destiny. First, I believe, we must secure and understand the facts.

This book, we hope, will contribute to that body of knowledge essential to the mastering of the relevant evidence. Only when we know what things are may we hope to transform them into what they should be. Humans possess that unique ability. William Hazlitt perhaps said it best:

Man is the only animal that laughs and weeps; for he is the only animal that is struck by the difference between what things are and what they ought to be.

Chapter Two

TWENTY-FIVE YEARS AGO
by Dick Gregory

Martin Luther King and I fought together on the battlefield for human justice. This is where I learned to respect him as a leader, to admire him and love him for what he was doing for humanity. Martin had a tremendous influence on my life, on my commitment to nonviolence, and on my commitment to the struggle for human justice.

A convention of frozen food executives at the Playboy Club in Chicago started me on the road to fame in show business. My new status led to my first involvement in the civil rights movement of the 1960s.

I was a participant in most of the ''major'' civil rights demonstrations of the early sixties, including the March on Washington and the Selma-to-Montgomery March. During these marches, I was called an outside agitator so many times I went to check out my birth certificate to make sure I wasn't born in Iceland or someplace else. And the FBI used to infiltrate all of our marches, but we could always spot them by looking at their feet. Like whoever heard of walking fifty miles wearing patent leather shoes and white socks!

Under the leadership of Dr. King, I became totally committed to nonviolence, and I was convinced that nonviolence meant opposition to killing in any form. I felt the commandment, ''Thou Shalt Not Kill,'' applies to human beings not only in their dealings with each other —through war, lynching, assassination, murder, and the like—but in their practice of killing animals for food and sport. Animals and humans suffer and die alike. Violence causes the same pain, the same spilling of blood, the same stench of death, the same arrogant, cruel, and brutal taking of life.

I, along with millions of other blacks, was born into the world accepting certain negatives. I expected to be treated as less than a human being. Martin made the suffering and problems we blacks had undergone through so many years clamor for attention. He made it clear that we no longer had to accept a condition of servitude and second-class citizenship.

5

The moments I spent with Martin were many things. They were pleasant, stimulating, honest, and humorous. He enjoyed my jokes. Through him I was able to meet, associate with, and exchange ideas with many others who shared our concerns and convictions. My only regret is that my moments with him were not more relaxed. There was rarely an opportunity for lazy, reflective conversation. Either a demonstration beckoned, or I was rushing to entertain at some fund-raising event—or both.

I watched Martin as he grew large and vital on the American scene. And I watched and listened as a few powerful Americans attempted to make the world believe that what he was doing was wrong—that he was "picking on" America. They fought back by accusing Martin of being everything except what he really was—one of the most brilliant, dedicated, and admired spokesmen and leaders for the fight to gain humanity that this world has ever known. The FBI hated King with a passion. A clever criminal could have called the FBI and told them that King was organizing a march on one side of town, waited five minutes for all the agents to get there, and then have an open season robbing the banks on the other side of town.

I watched Martin as he dealt with issues concerning the plight of the poor and oppressed. I watched as he dealt with violence and injustice in America, and as he pointed out the country's lack of moral leadership. Then I saw him become the conscience of America.

Today, twenty-five years after his death, Martin Luther King, Jr., is still the conscience of America. I shall never forget how upset America was when he began his vigorous, adamant, and extremely vocal opposition to the Vietnam War. Through him I came to understand that a commitment to nonviolence is more than marching for a cause and singing "We Shall Overcome," or turning the other cheek when one was slapped by a Southern sheriff.

Clearly, those who feared for King's life and safety were not paranoid. His violent death in Memphis is proof. And the "white folk watchers" in the black community have been ever and acutely aware of what Mr. Charlie will and will not tolerate. When King left off antagonizing bigots and Klansmen and began attacking defense spending and pointing out the inconsistency between claiming to be a Christian country and committing unspeakable atrocities in Vietnam, they saw the gauge on the social Geiger counter go wild. Danger! Danger! Danger! was the only possible interpretation.

King, they felt, had crossed that invisible line separating black folks' business from white folks' business. The governmental policy makers, the industrial giants, the shakers and movers of American society do not use public accommodations. It was barely relevant to them whether or not blacks were served at Woolworth's counter, or where they sat on the bus. King was no longer a darky preacher leading the country in a rousing prayer meeting. He was attacking the power elite.

The twenty-five years that have lapsed since the assassination of Martin Luther King make it possible for one to look back realistically at Memphis, April 4, 1968. One can scrutinize the events that led to a motel balcony, to a sniper's shot, and culminated with a life and promise felled, a dream deferred.

It may be debatable that time heals wounds, but there is no doubt that it does place events in proper perspective, allowing one to study them without the drama and emotion of the moment, which must inevitably color them.

Momentous changes have occurred on the American scene. The Vietnam War is over. Richard Nixon was catapulted to the Presidency and then toppled by Watergate. Bobby Kennedy and J. Edgar Hoover, respectively King's staunchest ally and most bitter foe, are dead now, as is Lyndon Johnson who was tortured by the same war—if for different reasons.

Yes, it has been twenty-five years since that fateful day, April 4, 1968. Let us move back in time until we are there.

I was in the State of California, campaigning for the Presidency of the United States and lecturing at various colleges. Earlier in 1968 I had become a write-in candidate for the nation's highest office, with Mark Lane as my running mate.

At a little after 4 P.M. that day, California time, I was driving with a friend to Hartnell College where I was scheduled to deliver a lecture. Our conversation was interrupted by a radio bulletin. Martin Luther King had been shot in Memphis!

I began to remember Martin, clearly, vividly. I remembered his sweet innocence and his warm, gentle smile. I thought of the time when he and I had been riding on a plane and he expressed concern about my personal safety.

"Now Gregory," he said, "I want you to be careful. I'm just afraid they're gonna kill you."

I answered, "If they do, Doc, will you preach my funeral?" He said, "I sure will."

We continued our drive to Hartnell College in silence. Even now I can feel the numbness, still remember my disbelief.

Finally we arrived at the school. Standing up before an audience was the last thing I felt like doing that night. But, of course, I had to go out there and explain as best I could how I saw the situation. Many people were in the audience only because they wanted to know my thoughts and my opinions of the day's events. They knew Martin and I were friends and that I held him in great esteem.

At my lecture that night I realized for the first time that America was in trouble with her young white kids. I was surprised to see the effect King had on them. They had grown up hearing about him, seeing him on television, and being influenced by his national presence. No matter what J. Edgar Hoover, or their own mommas and daddies may have said about King, these young white kids knew he was not wrong and he was not bad. Martin was a living denial of all the racist myths perpetrated in the white community about black folks. Martin didn't lie, he didn't cut, he didn't steal, and he wasn't on welfare. These young white kids learned some truths about black folks from Martin Luther King, and he had a more profound impact on their minds and lives than anything they had heard around the family dinner table.

Martin Luther King had become a victim of violence while preaching nonviolence and it raised a crucial question. When I heard the conclusive word of his death at my hotel that night, the question became even more compelling.

Would the concept of nonviolence, already under brutal attack by many blacks and whites, die with King? Would black awareness and black progress be buried with him? Would the tremendous strides toward awakening the conscience of America to the plight of the poor and the oppressed be halted? Had Martin lived and died in vain? Was it possible that violence had conquered nonviolence?

For the first time since the news of King's being shot, I smiled, a reflective smile, sad and bittersweet, and I recalled the words of Gandhi.

My creed for nonviolence is an extremely active force. It has no room for cowardice or even weakness. When a man is fully ready to die he will not even desire to offer violence. History is replete with instances where, by dying with courage and compassion on their lips, men converted the hearts of their violent opponents.

King had faced his attackers; he did not beg, or scream, or whimper.

Martin Luther King, Jr., was laid to rest in the spirit which defined his days among us.

It was a poor folks' funeral, as sad as it was beautiful. I knew then there would never be another Martin Luther King, Jr., and further, that there did not need to be. A little bit of Dr. King resided in the heart and soul of every American. He had awakened it and brought it out into the open. He did what he had been placed on earth to do. There was no need for subsequent imitations of his life. America is a better place because Dr. King lived. History may prove him to have been his country's salvation.

Ironically, President Johnson was unable to attend Dr. King's funeral because he had to meet his generals and talk about Vietnam. Still I imagine the President spoke from the heart when he said, "We are shocked and saddened by the brutal slaying tonight of Dr. Martin Luther King. . . . I ask every citizen to reject the blind violence that has struck Dr. King, who lived by nonviolence."

I shall never forget the reaction of white America that night. The looks of horror, disbelief, embarrassment, and guilt. The haunting question was written on every face, "How will black folks react?" I saw it on California Governor Ronald Reagan's face on television. Black folks in California saw it too, and I really believe his tearful expression of personal shock and horror was largely responsible for keeping things cool in Watts.

The account of the assassination printed in *The New York Times* was typical of the press response throughout the country.

> The 39-year-old Negro leader's death was reported shortly after the shooting by Frank Holloman, director of the Memphis police and fire departments, after Dr. King had been taken to St. Joseph Hospital.
>
> "I and all the citizens of Memphis," Holloman said, "regret the murder of Dr. King and all resources at our and the state's command will be used to apprehend the person or persons responsible."
>
> The police broadcast an alarm for "a young white male," well dressed who was reported to have been seen running after the shooting. . . . Policemen poured into the area around the Lorraine Motel on Mulberry Street where Dr. King was shot. They carried shotguns and rifles and sealed off the entire block, refusing entry to newsmen and others.
>
> Dr. King had been in his second-floor room throughout the day until just about 6:00 P.M. central standard time (7 P.M. New York Time).
>
> Then he emerged in a silkish-looking black suit and white shirt. He paused, leaned over the green iron railing and started chatting with an associate, Jesse Jackson, who was standing just below him in a parking lot.
>
> Mr. Jackson introduced Dr. King to Ben Branch, a musician who was to play at a rally Dr. King was to address two hours

later. As Mr. Jackson and Mr. Branch told of Dr. King's last moments later, the aide asked Dr. King:

"Do you know Ben?"

"Yes, that's my man!" Dr. King glowed.

They said Dr. King then asked if Mr. Branch would play a spiritual, "Precious Lord, Take My Hand," at the meeting that night.

"I really want you to play that tonight," Dr. King said. The Rev. Ralph Abernathy, perhaps Dr. King's closest friend, was just about to come out of the room.

A loud noise burst out.

Dr. King toppled to the concrete passageway floor and blood began gushing from a wound.

Someone rushed up with a towel to stem the flow of blood. Rev. Samuel Kyles of Memphis placed a spread over the fallen head of the Southern Christian Leadership Conference. [Kyles was to have hosted a dinner for King and his associates that night before the rally.]

Mr. Abernathy hurried up with a larger towel. And then the aides waited, while policemen rushed up within minutes. In what seemed to be ten or fifteen minutes, an ambulance arrived.

"He had just bent over," Mr. Jackson went on bitterly, "I saw police coming from everywhere. They said, 'Where did it come from?' and I said, 'Behind you.' The police were coming from where the shot came."

Mr. Branch, who is from Chicago, said the shot had come from "the hill on the other side of the street." He added:

"When I looked up, the police and the sheriff's deputies were running all around. The bullet exploded in his face."

"We didn't need to call the police," Mr. Jackson declared, "they were here all over the place."

PART TWO

MARTIN LUTHER KING AND HIS MISSION

Chapter Three

MARTIN AND CORETTA KING
by Dick Gregory

Born: January 15, 1929, a boy child in the city of Atlanta. A black boy child. Of course the birth record in Atlanta was different. They had to put, Born: A boy child. A negro. Few people on this planet were aware that on January 15, 1929, a boy child would be born on this planet Earth to an environment and to a family that would touch the spirit of this boy child to the extent that another spirit would develop. A boy child was born on January 15, 1929. His name was Martin Luther King, Jr.

Martin Luther King reached the lives of each and every black person in America. He also affected the attitudes of nearly all white people living in America. He was loved and he was hated. His name and his face were known to just about every person living in the United States. He had been on the pages of every magazine and newspaper in the country. No other black person in America ever received as much attention in the media as Martin Luther King. The radio and television networks covered each and every demonstration led by King, and they followed the progress of the civil rights movement with dedication. Dr. King was a hero of the press. He was easily accessible to it and he always provided the dramatic impact that a hungry press was anxious for.

At the height of the civil rights movement, one could easily detect the optimism that had swept through black communities around the nation. Phrases such as "Black is Beautiful" and "Hey Brother" became a part of the new sense of black pride. Black people in America were changing. Fear began to disappear from the hearts of many older folks living in the South; for the first time in their lives, many black men and women were not afraid to stand up for their rights, to say to white people what they would no longer tolerate. The end to segregation was a reality because of Martin Luther King. This one man had more impact on the attitudes of black Americans than any other person in contemporary history.

This is not the place to try to give a full-scale biography of Martin Luther King, and still less, the history of the black civil rights movement.

I'd rather try to convey what the man and the movement meant to black people in America. But a few dates and facts may be helpful as background. King was ordained a Baptist minister in 1947. A graduate of Morehouse College, he continued his education also attending Boston University and The Crozer Theological Seminary in Boston, Massachusetts, gaining a Ph.D. in 1955. In 1957, he received a D.D. from the Chicago Theological Seminary. By that time he had already sprung to national prominence for the leading part he played in the black boycott of buses in Montgomery, Alabama, in 1956. This nonviolent protest against the bus lines' mistreatment of black passengers resulted in the jailing of more than ninety black protesters including King. The local court naturally found King guilty. He appealed the decision. Meanwhile, the bus lines, which were going broke, dropped the charges. It was a great victory, both for King and for the principle of nonviolence.

The next year, an impressed Congress passed the first civil rights legislation since 1875, and Martin Luther King founded the Southern Christian Leadership Conference (SCLC), the organization which was to be his main vehicle for promoting black civil rights in the years to come. Through the remaining years of the 1950s and the early 1960s, the SCLC, along with The Congress of Racial Equality (CORE) and the Student Non-Violent Coordinating Committee (SNCC), with the blessings of the older, more established organizations such as National Association for the Advancement of Colored People (NAACP) made the tactic of nonviolent protests as familiar to Americans as their morning breakfast cereal.

In April of 1963, this movement reached a kind of crescendo when Dr. King led an enormous protest march in Birmingham, Alabama. More than 2,500 black demonstrators were arrested. Three months later he led an even bigger march in Washington, D.C. In terms of mass demonstrations, probably the high point of the civil rights movement was that march. I'll deal with both these dramatic events in greater detail in later chapters. Within a year, the most extensive civil rights legislation in United States history, The Civil Rights Act of 1964, had been enacted into law. That same year, King was awarded the Nobel Peace Prize.

During the next four years, King continued his struggle for equality on many fronts, but by 1968 he had become convinced that still another mass demonstration was needed. This was to be The Poor People's March on Washington. He was deeply involved in plans for this event when, in the spring of 1968, he interrupted his work to go to Memphis, Tennessee, to lend his support to the striking sanitation workers there. On April 4, while standing on the balcony of his Memphis motel room, Dr. King was shot and killed. He had made the final sacrifice for the great cause to which he had devoted his life.

But then Martin Luther King had made many sacrifices during the period of time he spent organizing black people and leading demonstrations. He spent a lot of time away from his home in Atlanta, Georgia. His wife Coretta spent many nights alone with their four children. There was not much time for fun and recreation for a man who was putting his whole life into fighting for human rights. Every time Martin Luther King led a march, every time he felt the pain of a police nightstick against his body, and every hour he spent in jail helped black Americans wake up to the problems that existed and helped black America hold its head up high. It was a difficult time in Martin Luther King's life. There were many sleepless nights in strange hotels. There were thousands of strange phone calls and letters criticizing the civil rights movement. There were constant threats of death to Martin Luther King, members of his family, and many of his aides. Every day that Martin Luther King walked the streets, and every night when he lay down to rest, the reality of death was his shadow. But King learned to deal with the notion that death was a possibility, and he knew that fear would only make those around him afraid. King was not fearful of death; at least I can say that I never saw him show the strain and pressure that would normally burden a man faced with such grim prospects. It was his calmness and consistently positive attitude that made those around him feel comfortable. When word of possible danger was made known, Martin Luther King never panicked. He knew how to handle situations with whatever kind of tact was necessary. He was a master when it came to dealing with the pressures that were forever surrounding him. For these reasons, millions of people loved and respected Dr. King. Those who never got a chance to march in a demonstration or see King in person were with him in spirit. They knew him as their leader, and with the help of newspapers and television, Martin Luther King became the most well-known black person in America.

There were, of course, black Americans who felt that the black struggle might be more effective without King's nonviolent approach. Some of them tried to get King to change, but his beliefs were too strong for him to be swayed in any other direction. The efforts of these more radical civil rights advocates were short-lived. Allegiance to Martin Luther King was steadfast. Even through times when it seemed that nonviolence was ineffective, the people who believed in King's methods stood behind him. We used to get a kick out of hearing the Northern black guy who would say "I can't go down South because I'm too violent." Yet this cat was scared to talk back to his own white paper boy! It is ironic that

King's nonviolent movement brought on a violent reaction from much of white America. They were reacting to a type of attitude they didn't understand. America is accustomed to using violence as a tool to obtain whatever goal it is trying to reach, and for that reason it could not accept masses of black people acting peacefully in order to get their point across. Many whites felt Martin Luther King must have been planning something else. They just couldn't believe that this nonviolent approach was for real. Examples of the violence that stalked the nonviolent movement were spread throughout King's career. In January of 1956, less than two months after he became leader of the Montgomery, Alabama, bus boycott someone threw a bomb onto the porch of his home; no one was hurt. Two days before Christmas in 1956, blacks and whites rode integrated buses together for the first time. An unidentified gunman fired a shotgun blast into the front door of King's home; there were no injuries. On January 27, 1957, someone threw a bomb on King's porch; it did not explode. On September 3, 1958, King was arrested and charged with loitering while on his way to a Montgomery, Alabama, legal hearing involving his close friend and fellow civil rights advocate, Reverend Ralph D. Abernathy. On November 17, 1958, as Dr. King was signing copies of his new book *Stride Toward Freedom* in a Harlem bookstore, a black woman by the name of Mrs. Izola Ware Curry stabbed him in the chest with a steel letter opener, barely missing his heart. King was hospitalized for thirteen days in a Harlem hospital. On May 21, 1961, a mob of 1,000 angry whites upset over the Freedom Rides menaced Dr. King and 1,500 blacks holding a meeting at the First Baptist Church in Montgomery, Alabama. The National Guard escorted the blacks back to their homes. On September 28, 1962, during a Southern Christian Leadership Conference convention in Birmingham, a man who described himself as a member of the American Nazi Party hit Dr. King in the face twice, causing swelling and bruises. King did not press charges. The man was fined twenty-five dollars and sentenced to thirty days in jail. On June 30, 1963, people who were displeased by his nonviolent policies threw eggs at his car as King went to speak at a Harlem church. On June 18, 1964, Dr. King charged St. Augustine, Florida, police with brutality after they used cattle prods and beat people who tried to desegregate a motel. He asked President Lyndon B. Johnson to send in federal marshals. On January 18, 1965, as Dr. King registered at a previously all-white hotel in Selma, Alabama, a member of the National States Rights Party, punched and kicked him. The twenty-six year old assailant was sentenced to sixty days in jail and fined $100. On August 5, 1966, as Dr. King led marchers past angry white residents of Chicago's Southwest Side, he was struck in the head by a rock. He stumbled, but continued to march. Later a knife thrown at him missed and struck a white youth in the neck. On April 4, 1968, Martin Luther King was killed.

The violence that confronted King from the time he first led the civil rights movement up to the time of his death convinced many blacks to abandon their nonviolent beliefs. Though violence produced only temporary gains, many blacks felt it was the right direction to take. They felt they had been patient too long. It was the white police reaction and response to the rioting and violence that forced many blacks to reconsider King's methods, although they knew that King's way was not just for the benefit of those living, but was aimed at affecting unborn generations of black people.

One of the traits that made Martin Luther King popular as a leader and as a newsmaker was his dynamic speaking ability. He was a brilliant man with a widely diverse educational background and the soul of a country preacher. King reached millions with his echoing voice that made one feel a chill just listening to him. His choice of words was always perfect. He taught the world that it was both morally wrong and psychologically harmful to hate anyone. He believed that hate did more harm to the hater than it did to the hated. He urged people to try to solve the racial problems of the world through love and goodwill. He told parents to teach their children to fight injustice with an open heart and with an open mind. Martin Luther King believed that this was the only solution to the problems that plagued black America.

Despite his constant struggle to unite blacks and whites through nonviolence, and though he lost his life trying, some whites in America refused to give Martin Luther King his due respect. On the day of his funeral in Atlanta, many retail stores did business as usual, completely ignoring the fact that one of the greatest men that had ever lived had been shot to death. Most of white Atlanta was completely uninvolved in the sorrowful memorial that was taking place that day. Two major department stores did close, but many blacks felt it was not out of respect for King, but because they feared violence might break out if they stayed open. Governor Lester Maddox allowed all state employees to go home from work at two o'clock in the afternoon for what he called ''security reasons.'' Many city workers were not required to come in to work at all because their employers were trying to protect them from possible harm from angry blacks. But for blacks who had been around to see Dr. King fight for equality and for an end to segregation, it was a good feeling to see his mule-drawn coffin being pulled down the downtown streets, passing stores and restaurants that King himself had helped to integrate.

There are people who dedicate their lives to helping other people. We seem to take so much from them and give so little in return. We could always criticize Martin, but Martin never criticized the masses. He never complained that the crowds were not large enough, or that there weren't enough people supporting the cause in the black communities. But I guess that's part of being a leader; to lead a group of people who are so hungry for freedom and justice that all they see are the injustices and you. You weren't a man, you weren't a human being. You were something that wasn't supposed to get tired. You weren't supposed to get hungry, you weren't supposed to go to sleep, you weren't supposed to die. We need you; we need you here; we need you there. Hey Martin, come over here and help us. If you would just come they would listen to us. What about the other side? What about the family? Take a few minutes at home. Take the day off Martin, and rest. The family; no, we always forget about that. We talk about Mahatma Gandhi, but who was his wife? Who were his children? You were forced to give us so much. There was another side. There was a Coretta. There was a very warm side. There was Martin the father, Martin the husband. And it's like every other human being who meets another human being, and falls in love and gets married.

When Martin Luther King first met Coretta Scott they were both in Boston. It was 1951. She was twenty-four years old, fresh out of Antioch College and studying at the New England Conservatory of Music. King was working on his doctorate degree in theology at Boston University. After two years of dating, they were married. Coretta Scott had thought earlier, and had even said to her friends, that she and Martin would probably not think seriously of marriage. She was an accomplished concert singer and didn't think that being the wife of a minister would be her style. But, she soon changed her mind. They were married at her parents' home in Marion, Alabama. Their first child, Yolanda, was born two years later. Just two weeks after her birth, the Montgomery bus boycott began, and with it, the start of King's rapid rise to leadership and prominence. The couple's first son, Martin Luther King III, was born in 1958, followed by Dexter three years later, and Bernice in 1963. Coretta King spent a lot of time at home with the children during their preschool years. She spent her free time with local club work and singing with her church choir.

Coretta King was deeply involved in her husband's work. She taught their children about the civil rights movement and the importance of their father's involvement in it. She took her knowledge of the civil rights movement and expanded her own ideas. She was a member of the Women Strike for Peace movement where she, along with fifty other American women, went to the seventeen-nation disarmament conference in Geneva to encourage world peace. She even used her talents as a singer to benefit the movement. Not long after Martin Luther King was awarded the Nobel Peace Prize his wife said, "My life is either the church or the struggle for civil rights." Mrs. King did a series of cross-country freedom concerts which were solo singing engagements to raise money for the Southern Christian Leadership Conference. From 1965 until Martin Luther King's death, Coretta King barely saw a day pass without the threat of death surrounding her husband. She developed a philosophy that helped her live with the reality that he could be killed because of his commitment to the human struggle. She said, "If something does happen, it would be a great way to give oneself to a great cause."

Coretta King became involved in nearly every activity that her husband took part in; even after his death she continued to emphasize the need to carry on the movement. The Southern Christian Leadership Conference named her to its board of directors. Many felt that she would now emerge to carry on King's work. But those who knew Coretta King knew that she had always been out in front during all the demonstrations, during all the sit-ins, and throughout the entire movement. She was never just a behind-the-scenes companion. Coretta King was a strong, black woman who had long realized the necessity of her husband's work. She also knew the importance of her own association with it. She had stamina and patience. She was able to see ahead just as her husband did, to the time when injustice and segregation would be a thing of the past. It was this vision and the hope of a brighter tomorrow that allowed her to stand beside Martin Luther King in his fight for a better world.

Coretta King had suffered many periods of fear and grief long before her husband was killed. When King was stabbed she had flown to New York City to be with him. She always told the children what was going on, and she prepared herself for anything that could happen. She fully realized that danger was indeed a part of her husband's sacrifice.

Coretta King had become a well-known figure in the civil rights movement. Her name was a symbol of dignity, and her face mirrored the reflections of a woman dedicated to building her life around helping to solve the problems of the poor and the unfortunate. Coretta King's reputation as a hard worker with a genuine desire to keep the movement strong was evident as one read newspapers and listened to the news on television and radio. Reporters were beginning to mention her more and more, and many discovered that Coretta King provided a separate story, but one which would lead back to her husband—a story that would explain how important it was that she existed, how relevant she was to the entire civil rights struggle. Americans know who Martin Luther King's wife was because she made herself known through her involvement with him and with the movement. But it wasn't only this involvement that made her stand out. There were other wives of civil rights leaders who marched and demonstrated; even others who went to jail fighting for an end to segregation and racial inequality. I'm sure Coretta King helped to give these other wives strength and courage.

Chapter Four

KING AND KENNEDY CALL

by Dick Gregory

In May 1963 I received a call from Martin Luther King asking me to come to Birmingham. Then I received a call from President John F. Kennedy, asking me not to go.

I was at the height of my show business career and my involvement in the civil rights movement had grown to the point where I had become aware of a lot of things I was never aware of before. In the early days of the civil rights movement, I would get phone calls to come down South and perform. I had all the normal fears that one would have about going into the South. I had been told about the Ku Klux Klan, but the connection between the KKK, and the police, and the federal agencies had never been established. I think that was probably the most horrifying thing for me to find out—that it wasn't just the Klan.

Then I really started realizing the problems that black folks have in the South. I mean, that once the arm of the law grabs you, there is no way out. They could make you say things that you didn't want to say. They could say, "We can do this to your family; we can do this to your mother; we can get your wife fired from her job; or your father fired; or you're going to lose your home." It's amazing that the black folks had the strength and courage to stand up and push, because in America's wildest imagination, we could hardly believe that many of the things that were happening, actually happened. America could see the beatings and the jailings, but the political maneuvers behind the scenes were just as vicious and they fascinated me almost as much as they bothered me. It fascinated me when I went South, as informed as I always thought I was. It was almost as if I was not an American black, but was living on another planet, listening to someone say, "This is the way they treat them people."

Of course, it didn't just happen where it was obvious, as in Georgia,

Alabama, and Mississippi; it happened all over the country. Probably the one big difference between the black reaction in the North and the black reaction in the South was that black folks in the North weren't scared to walk down the street. This is the reason that the civil rights movement wasn't as effective up North—because we tried to use the same tactics that they were using in the South. The tactic in the South was to get a large crowd to walk down the street, because black people there were scared to walk down the street alone. This same tactic was followed in the North; we could have used ninety percent of our energy doing other things.

We were really trying to get that crowd to improve the news coverage. The one thing the press always asked us was, "How many people do you think you'll have for the demonstration?" For the evening news they had certain deadlines, and so they would come up and ask us to demonstrate early so it could be on the evening news. The press was managing our affairs, making things happen.

There was a certain type of closeness, in a hostile way, between black and white folks in the South. The whites had to dislike blacks for what was going on, but in the process of change, blacks became human. The movement started exposing our feelings, and making us human to the whites. When you are ill and your body goes numb, and then you start healing, you start tingling and the numbness gives way to real feeling again. I looked at the events, at black people showing their feelings, and saw a certain amount of beauty because years from now it would be different.

I knew the effect that those Southern street demonstrations were having on the young white kids. They would say, "Mommy, how come they let us treat them like that?" There was no more saying, "Oh, they're happy." There was no more Beulah singing in the kitchen. The old black man who worked around the house used to smile because his true feelings were hidden from white America. Now those feelings weren't hidden anymore.

There was an individual emerging who was becoming more than just a leader to black folks. Martin Luther King was more than just a leader in America—he was recognized worldwide. I started feeling the power and the effect of Martin by the way people talked of him. As much as certain people in the system tried to put him down, they always dealt with him with respect because of the way he carried himself. He was always the same.

I had such respect for everybody in the movement, I would never go to a demonstration until I was asked, and I would always call the leadership so they wouldn't think they were infringing on me because they looked at me as a celebrity. When I would go someplace, the cameras would go. I didn't want to go in without being officially invited. The first thing I would do, when I got into town, was brief myself, because the press would tend to walk away from the local leaders and start asking me questions. In the process of doing this, I became very familiar with situations. When I was picked up at the airport, they put it in my ear—what's happening, who's in jail, what the situation is.

King asked me to come to Birmingham, and I said, "Yes, Martin, I'll come." There had been strong rumors that the Birmingham problem was about to be resolved. President Kennedy and the city officials had worked out a deal, and there was speculation that King might be jumping the gun and ruining the deal. But I felt good because I was tired of white folks working out deals for black folks and I felt that King had to be in Birmingham and had to lead that movement. Whatever deal might have been worked out was no more.

We were to come in and solve this problem. The big problem in Birmingham was the police—Sheriff Bull Connor among others—and they became one of the main issues.

Arthur Hanes, the mayor of Birmingham, wasn't an issue to me because I didn't confront his side of the city. I confronted the Bull Connor street demonstration side—the hoses. The fire hoses had a tremendous effect on me because I had always loved firemen, and I used to follow firemen. I felt that the fire departments in America were making a mistake not to disassociate themselves from the white government. This eventually proved to be true, because in the North, when the firemen answered an alarm in the black community, bricks were thrown at them—at black and white firemen. The firemen couldn't be disassociated from the hosings down South. You kind of expected it from the police, but not from firemen. Firemen always seemed to have been good guys.

Firemen and fire hoses have become symbolic of black repression. This is the first time it ever hit us blacks; it had never happened before. This was the first time hoses were used against us. They had been used often in America's history, for crowd control, but now they were used against people who had thought firemen were heroes. The force of the hoses would sweep those kids around the corner.

The most horrible photograph that came out of Birmingham was that of the dog biting the black man in the rump, grabbing his pants. They tell me that he was one of the few blacks who didn't get bitten. It just made a beautiful picture. All the dog got was the pants, but that picture had a most significant effect on black folks and their relationship with dogs. The older black person always had to have a dog. *Someone* had to be below you. To watch dogs kiss folks on television really turned off black folk, because we had to keep that dog *a dog*. The dog had to eat the scraps, the dog could never be caught up on the couch and *the dog was the dog*.

Until Birmingham, the largest percentage of false alarms turned in, in major cities in America, were in black communities. This was before black folks started outnumbering white folks all through the cities, and living in distinct areas. There was something so beautiful, peaceful, and competent about the firemen's attitudes that you'd put in false alarms just to have them show up. After Birmingham, the false alarms decreased considerably in the black communities; it became something that you didn't want to see. The firemen and dogs are just examples of the tremendous emotional impact of the events in Birmingham.

When I got the call from Martin and he asked me if I would come down, I said, "Yes, Martin, I'll come." I was always scared when I had to go into the South—not the type of scared so that you wouldn't go, but the type of scared knowing that it can be your last time; you can be killed. The FBI, and the local police, and the state police were so vicious that anything could happen. My secret ambition, when I was a kid, was to be an FBI agent. I thought that was the epitome—higher than a fireman —and then the whole scene crumbled. I could see the FBI doing illegal things. No one had to tell me about it; I watched it happening.

When I went into Birmingham, what a funny feeling—only white police met me and asked me a bunch of questions when I got off the plane. The hostility from the press was unbelievable. Black folks had always accepted the white press as being factual. We were never in it so we could never document it if it wasn't factual. Until the civil rights movement, during which we started seeing our news being twisted and turned around, with hostile, vicious headlines, we had believed in the white press.

All over the world, Birmingham was making front pages—but in Birmingham, the stuff wasn't on the front page, it was on page three or four. The front page was just business as usual.

I had told Martin I would be there, and that a very interesting thing had happened. I had gotten a call from President Kennedy, but wasn't at home at the time. It was really interesting because Lil, my wife, said when I came home, "Where have you been!" She never snapped at me like that. I said, "Well, why?" She said, "Because President Kennedy has been trying to get you—he's called this house three or four times." I said, "I don't want to talk to him." Lil said, "He said he's going to wait up at the White House until you call him." I said, "But it's three o'clock in the morning, he's not going to wait up, no way, he's probably got a tie

23

line anywhere he is—you really think he's waiting up in the White House?'' She said, ''Yes, I talked to him personally and he told me it is very important that he talk to you.'' So I said, ''I don't want to talk to him anyway.'' I was getting ready to go to bed and she really had an attitude. She said, ''Well, you're not going to bed—you're not going to sleep.''

I really don't want to say I was drunk, because my life has changed so much, but I was. I'd been out drinking all day and Lil said, ''Well, you're not going to sleep until you call the President.''

Many years later, when Gerald Ford was in the White House, a call came from the White House; I wasn't home. About a week later a letter came from the White House saying they had called, that the President had wanted to ask Dick Gregory about something, and Lil said, ''Oh, God, I can't believe I forgot the White House, I meant to tell you the White House had called!'' I thought about the time Kennedy had called. I said to Lil, ''I would never have thought that there would be a day the White House would call and you would just forget about it.'' I guess that's growing up, or whatever you would call it.

I had to call President Kennedy, though, that night. The note said, ''Call Operator 18, Washington, D.C., the White House,'' and so I called Operator 18. I really was surprised, because when I said, ''Dick Gregory,'' Kennedy said, ''Oh, yes, Dick, I've been waiting for your call. I have a problem and I wonder if you'll help me with it?''

Martin had announced that I was going to Birmingham. President Kennedy said, ''Do me a favor and don't go down to Birmingham, because I feel that Dr. King is wrong. We reached a settlement there, and everything is going to be fine—your going there will create problems.'' So I said, ''I know Dr. King, and I know a lot of things are changing in the South that never started changing until Dr. King got involved. So I told Dr. King I'm coming down, and I'm going down, and I don't think he would have called me if he didn't need me and the last person who is going to put me in a trick is Dr. King.'' The President said that he wished that I wouldn't go. Then he said, ''Why don't you just wait for seven days? I'm sure the whole problem will be solved.'' I said, ''I told Dr. King that I'm going on Monday, and that's tomorrow—and I'm going.

''I want to go, you know. When I see what's happening to black folks on television, with the news, and the fire hoses, and whatever deal between white folks that's been made, the streets are where I need to be, and where I'm going.'' And Kennedy said, ''Well, I'm sorry you feel that way, Dick, but thanks for returning my call.'' Next day I got on a plane and flew to Birmingham with Jim Sanders, a brilliant comedy writer. All through the South, he was always with me. He was always arrested with me, but never got his name mentioned in the paper. When we got off the plane and met with King's people, I said that I really had to meet with Martin and tell him about the call I had from the President, because I thought it was serious and that there might be danger when we got to the 16th Street Baptist Church rallying point.

Chapter Five

BIRMINGHAM
by Dick Gregory

When we arrived at the church, I had a strange feeling, seeing the police surrounding the church. I think it went back to my childhood. My mother had told me about the lions eating the Christians and I thought that that period would never recur in history. I thought no one would ever violate the church. But then I saw the way the cops surrounded the church and realized how dangerous it could become to them if it were used as a water trough where people could gather to drink up the ideas of change. The church leaders said, "Until we rid ourselves of certain pressures, we will never find our true spiritual power." We can be happy belonging to an organized religion—it helps us put off the battle, it comforts us. But there's a universal God inside us and there are certain things that the inside of us will not tolerate, even if it means a confrontation to the extent of injury or death.

While I observed the activities in the church, my fear left me. I looked outside the church and what had been hate, and bigotry, and white evilness became fear. I was seeing the same expressions on their faces that I used to see on black folks' faces. They were afraid because officers of the law, knowing what a potential danger one person is, were now dealing with thousands, and, not knowing and not understanding non-violence, saw black folks losing their fear. The power was turning, and the police and their dogs were in trouble.

Those cops who "knew their niggers" suddenly realized that maybe they didn't know them. Cops used to say to black folk, "Get on down the street, boy," and now some black folks said, "Maybe I'm not going on down the street." The Southern cop was forced to do something that he had never done before; to deal with black folks that weren't scared, that couldn't be intimidated. Nobody seemed to mind getting bitten by a dog when there were three thousand people around to help.

A leadership was being developed that was above and beyond mere celebrity; Martin Luther King, the Southern Christian Leadership Conference (SCLC), and young people with new, different minds. Black kids listened to the news and gained a new awareness—their conscious mind was no longer locked into getting off the street when they saw white folks coming. Black folks got off the street not necessarily because all white folks wanted them to do that, but they didn't know which ones did and which ones didn't. I was looking out of the church at those cops, waiting to tell Dr. King about the call from the President, when someone said, "We've got a big march ready to leave, and we're trying to hold it, but the kids won't wait. The kids won't wait, and they're ready to go and take the streets downtown."

There were all groups and ages, but most of them were kids. I got arrested with one kid who was four years old. The whole town was under siege. This time, it was not business as usual in the whole town, white or black. Birmingham was the biggest thing happening in the world, on this planet Earth, and everybody was coming in from all over the world to cover it. Jim Sanders and I had to run out of the church to get in front of the group, and no sooner had we stepped off the sidewalk and walked across the street than we were arrested.

We were arrested for parading without a permit, but they didn't tell us at that time what the charge was. They just said, "You're under arrest," and they lined up the paddy wagons, and arrested close to 800 people at that particular affair.

There were so many blacks in the jail, this was the first time most of the niggers in Birmingham were eating good. There was a strong white reaction to the mass jailings; everybody was afraid. "What are we going to do with these blacks in jail? Do we feed them, and what about the whites there?" There was a big debate about whether we were going to get fed. The paper work of arresting so many was mountainous.

A white detective came over to me and said, "Dick Gregory, I'd like to talk to you. This is just a job for me but I really admire what you're doing and I know from what I see here that this whole thing is going to break. I'm one of the people who will be glad, but I have a job, and a wife, and a family, so I guess I'm part of it. I'm going to tell you about your rights, and I have some questions that I want to ask you, and you don't have to answer." I said, "I don't mind answering." "You don't have to. Do you understand your rights?" and he read them to me. "Do you choose to answer these questions?" I said "Yes." I sat down and it almost turned into a comedy. He thought I would be hostile with him after he had poured his whole soul out and that was a heck of a thing for a white cat to do.

He said, "What's your name?" I told him, "You know." "Where

do you live?" I told him. He said, "At what time did you get arrested?" I said, "I don't know." He approximated a time. He asked, "What street did you get arrested on?" I said, "I don't know." He stared at me. "What was the name of the church that you came from?" At that time I didn't know, having just gotten to town. I said I didn't know. The detective said, "Well, who were the people you were arrested with?"

I said, "Jim Sanders, who came to town with me." The detective asked, "Where's he from?" "Chicago," I answered. He asked, "Who were the local people?" I said, "I don't know 'em." He began to think I was pulling his leg—he *really* thought this and he really had an attitude because he said, "Now, wait a minute, I told you you didn't have to answer any questions, and you told me you wanted to." I said, "You really won't believe this, but I don't know anything. I just got off the plane and I haven't been in this town an hour and here I'm in jail now."

We were moved into the cell block, and rumors started that King had been killed and that there were bombings in town. None of this was happening at that time but these were things that people were bringing back to us. There were more rumors from people in jail, and we were worried about being hungry, and then they told us King was arrested. When you're in jail, you're totally out of the mainstream. You can't find out anything for yourself. The jail kept getting more and more crowded. That day I think two thousand people were arrested.

The youngest kid in jail was about four, sucking his thumb. I got to thinking about my kids at home, and I walked over to this little kid, and asked him his name, and he told me, and I asked him what he was in for, and he tried to say "Freedom" but he couldn't; all he could say was "Teedom." He just looked around at the rest of the people in the cells, and everybody ignored him; he stood there by himself, sucking his thumb. He was waiting for his mother to come and get him. I don't even know if his mother knew he was there.

The biggest crowds we had were young people. I was way back in the cell block, and there was a commotion up front. I told Jim Sanders, "I'm going up front to see what's going on."

Somebody was coming into the cell block, and the young kids wouldn't let them close the door. That's when I went up to the front of the cell block, and the jailer was yelling, "You close this door! We'll get this door closed!" He ran out, and I said to the youngsters, "You know we're really not in here to hassle around this door, so we better just close this door." The kids moved back, and I stood next to the door, with my hands around the bars, and forgot that I was in jail. I was at home with the kids and Lillian, and I had drifted out of that jail cell in my mind; meanwhile the jailer had just come back with help to get the cell door closed. I was the only person standing up there and he hit me across the knuckles. I had my hands around the bars, and when he hit me with that nightstick, I still didn't realize I was in jail. I opened up the cell door and leaped out on him and spit in his face and balled up my fists and knocked him down and—God, what did I do that for? They ran outside, and came back in with baseball bats, and cue sticks, and just about anything you could think of and I was fighting for my life. I'm sure the only reason I wasn't killed was that the hallway was too narrow and no one could draw back on me, and there were too many cops in there. There were about twenty-five, all shouting and beating me.

The door opened to a small hallway which led to a larger passageway. The kids started pouring out of the open cell door, and then the battle was really on. I was trying to stop the jailers, yelling, "Wait a minute, man!" and they didn't want to hear anything from me. We battled our way all the way into an office outside. Then there was screaming about a jail break, and somehow we ended up fighting back inside. I kept telling the kids to get back in the jail, and we pushed our way back in. I fell unconscious in the hallway and they just pulled me back into the cell.

The jailers were scared to come in. As long as we were back in the cell block, they were happy; they would settle for that. I went to the back of the cell and Jim Sanders said, "Damn, man, they just finished whopping somebody's ass up front," and I said, "That somebody's ass was whopped was mine!" We sat and talked the rest of the night in the cell, dozing on and off. When I woke, my arm was swollen; I had been severely battered. My hand, arm, neck and back were swollen and the kids were really concerned then because they saw how big my arm had gotten and knew the pain I was in.

The rumors started getting out about my beating, and people outside started hearing about it. That morning the federal agents came in from the Justice Department and asked me what had happened. I told them that I had been beaten up in the jail and then they decided to let me out. King had decided to come out. I didn't want to go to the doctor there and I didn't want to talk to the government. I did not want to talk to the agents but I knew I had to talk with someone because of the call from the White House. Then I decided to fly to Chicago and hold a press conference and tell what happened, and how I felt that the White House was not living up to its duty to show that this was not going to be tolerated any more.

At first, no federal troops came in; Kennedy's policy was strictly hands off. Finally, after many arrests, they knew our civil rights had been violated, and the federal government could get involved. I finally talked to the FBI in Chicago, went back to Birmingham, and stayed a week. There was so much going on; a lot of violence, and a lot of innocent people getting beaten up, and a lot of people losing their jobs.

I saw Martin Luther King at the Gaston Motel, which was bombed, but fortunately he had quietly left the day before. The Gaston Motel was his headquarters. I looked at the police around the motel and questioned the people around me to see if it was safe enough. There were so many bombings, and other violence, that I had a premonition. This was before the 16th Street Baptist Church got blown up, when the four little girls were killed.

Angela Davis went to that church as a little girl. Those were her friends that were killed. Nobody knows that side of the story; they just know Angela grown, but she's from Birmingham and that was her church and those were her friends that were killed.

I was invited to the home of A. D. King, Martin's brother, in Birmingham. His house was also bombed. I was considered a celebrity, and people invited me into their homes because they wanted to know what was going on in the world, how the movement was viewed outside of the South, and what other celebrities would be coming down to help. When I went to A. D.'s house for dinner, there were police sitting outside. Every black leader's home was surrounded by police.

Nothing could happen to A. D. unless the police were involved. They were watching the house. If SCLC headquarters were blown up, officers would be nearby. It was impossible for anyone to do anything without the police knowing about it. There were so many of them around.

The Gaston Motel was the nerve center, for a while, of the Birmingham movement. At the meetings were Fred Shuttlesworth, Ralph Abernathy, Hosea Williams, C. T. Vivian, of course Martin, and a great force, Jim Bevel. Many other people came in and out. I told King at the Gaston that I was worried about the police attitude around the motel. I thought that anytime that motel could go up in smoke, and wondered if there were enough security personnel. Martin said that he felt there was enough security. I didn't feel scared but I felt that the whole motel would go up in smoke and kill everybody in it.

I never understood why the federal government would tolerate the illegal actions of the local and state police. The intimidation of the black population could be seen. In most places, it was the white mob you had to worry about; in Birmingham, it was the police. What would happen to people who live in Birmingham after all this was over with, with that kind of hatred in the police department? What would happen to blacks who had to testify in various trials?

There was no doubt that the problem was going to be resolved. It was costing Birmingham too much money, and costing America too much prestige. Everything changed from that time in Birmingham, the turning point in the civil rights movement. The things that finally got all the black folks involved were things that shocked black folks—the fire hoses, the dogs, and children being beaten and jailed.

We knew that things would happen to the martyrs, to King and the leadership, but seeing dogs bite children, and fire hoses knocking down little kids—this was more than any normal person could take. It was a reaction against white America, against white, racist America. America had to deal with what would happen to her children. White Americans could easily hate an evil, militant black cat who was making demands on folks, and even some black folks didn't like that; but when it came to hurting children, Birmingham was the turning point in the movement.

Martin asked me to come to Birmingham and the President asked me not to go. The black folks in Birmingham were doing more than they should, and it was time for me to do what I could. So I said, "Yes, Martin, I'll come."

Chapter Six

"PEARLS BEFORE SWINE"

by Mark Lane

On May 10, 1963, it appeared that peace might come to the embattled city of Birmingham, Alabama. The two score bombings that had torn apart the city and set whites and blacks against each other passionately were, it was thought, a remembrance of a troubled and violent recent past. As homes, and churches, and meeting halls owned by blacks had been blown to pieces by dynamite, the anger of the black community began to focus upon the failure of the local and federal police authorities to determine who had planted a single bomb. Arthur Hanes, the Mayor of Birmingham and one of its leading segregationists, had been an FBI agent. Years later testimony revealed that the FBI itself had played a part in the campaign to elect him Mayor. When the bombings began, there was hope that Clarence Kelley, the newly-appointed Special-Agent-in-Charge of the FBI office in Birmingham, would act. However, during the years he occupied that position, not a single bomber was found, not a single case was solved. After Mr. Kelley moved to a new assignment, as Special-Agent-in-Charge of the FBI office in Memphis, Tennessee, his successor in Birmingham was no more effective.

Dr. King and his associates and the thousands who had witnessed for equality by marching in the streets of Birmingham, by kneeling-in in segregated churches, and by demonstrating at its city jail the previous month, had won a victory. The walls of apartheid had cracked and Birmingham, previously denounced by Dr. King as "the most thoroughly segregated big city in America," had at last agreed to change.

Dr. King greeted the new moment with a new approach. He said, "The city of Birmingham has reached an accord with its conscience. The acceptance of responsibility by local white and Negro leadership offers an example of a free people uniting to meet and solve their problems." He called upon the black community in Birmingham to "accept this achievement in the right spirit'' and to understand that it was not that they had won a narrow victory but rather that a victory had been won ''for democracy and the whole citizenry of Birmingham.'' Dr. King added, ''We must respond to every new development in civil rights with an understanding of those who have opposed us, and with an appreciation of the new adjustments that the new achievements pose for them.''

The same page of the *Birmingham News* that carried those conciliatory and healing words also reported that United States Senator Lister Hill urged President John F. Kennedy and Attorney General Robert F. Kennedy to use their ''influence and power'' to remove Dr. King, Dick Gregory, and other ''outside agitators'' from Birmingham, charging ''that these professional agitators have provoked and led demonstrations and lawlessness in open defiance of state and local laws and court orders.''

The *Birmingham News* that day also carried a headline announcing ''All But 119 of Arrested Children Free.'' The story reported that most of the 1,400 children arrested the previous week in demonstrations had been released on a $300 bond while some children remained in the county jail and others at ''emergency quarters at the State Fair Grounds.''

Another story on the same page said that ''a special report from the Jefferson County Grand Jury commended the Birmingham police department, and Sheriff Mel Bailey and his officers 'for the fine manner in which they have carried out their duties in the difficult situation which has existed here the last several days.' The commendation signed by the grand jury foreman stated 'We feel fortunate in having law enforcement officers of this caliber.' '' One column removed from the commendation release was the news story that an FBI investigation was underway into the beating of Dick Gregory in the Birmingham Jail. Clearly all was not well in the city but Dr. King, buoyed by the agreement, was hopeful that it signified change.

Reverend Wyatt Tee Walker, the executive director of the Southern Christian Leadership Conference, was concerned that the new agreement might further anger some segregationists and drive them to acts of violence. When several white men were observed, according to Reverend Walker, ''casing the Gaston Motel'' late that evening, he reported that activity to the police and asked for police protection. The Birmingham police officials agreed to ''keep a watch on the motel.''

Later that evening Roosevelt Tatum, a black resident of Birmingham, was in the vicinity of 12th Street and Avenue H. He reported that at approximately 11:30 P.M. he saw a police car slow down and then park on 12th Street directly in front of the residence of the Reverend A. D. King.

Tatum said that "a uniformed police officer . . . got out of the car, [and] walked behind the police car to Reverend King's house."

Tatum said that because he was curious about this late night visit by the local police to the home of Martin Luther King's brother, he remained in the shadows silently observing the events that were unfolding before him. The officer, according to Tatum, "walked to the front porch, at a moderate pace, stooped and placed a package at the right side of the steps of Reverend King's house," ran back to the car and entered it. Then "the driver of the police car tossed something out the window of the auto" and it landed, Tatum said, "approximately two or three feet from the sidewalk directly in front of the King residence." Almost immediately after the object landed there was an explosion that Tatum said knocked him to the ground. A second explosion took place. Tatum said he stood up, and as he approached the wreckage, saw a police car arrive "as if they were investigating." The two dynamite bombs had been effective. They demolished a corner of the home, and blew off almost half the roof and the living room wall.

At approximately the same time that dynamite tore apart the residence of A. D. King, the area in the Gaston Motel where his brother, Martin, had been staying was destroyed by another powerful dynamite blast. Two bombs exploded there, one through the registration office wall, directly below Room 30 where Dr. Martin Luther King, Jr., had been staying. Three women and a man were injured by this blast at the Gaston Motel. Dr. King had left the motel earlier to return to Atlanta.

According to some observers, Roosevelt Tatum entered into what was left of the King house and helped the children escape through the wreckage. Later Tatum told A. D. King what he had seen immediately before the explosions. A. D. King telephoned the FBI office in Birmingham and two agents reported to Reverend King's house to meet Tatum. They took him to the FBI office and immediately began to question him.

We may never know the presumed target of those Saturday night bombings in Birmingham since it is difficult to enter into the disturbed minds of the bombers and to know what their thinking process may have been. However, to many in the black community of Birmingham, it seemed apparent that attempts had been made to assassinate Dr. Martin Luther King, Jr.

The agreement for peace had been abrogated and for five hours hundreds of angry blacks filled the streets. It was Saturday night and the bars had been serving for hours a local homemade brew, called *Joe Louis* to describe its knockout potential. As the police moved into the streets they were targets of rocks and bricks. A white-owned taxicab was turned over and set on fire. The police reinforcements arrived with the dreaded police dogs. This time the anger and the resolve of the blacks was so high that the dogs, used to intimidate and assault the demonstrators during the previous weeks, merely provoked more anger and greater resolve. The police almost immediately withdrew the dogs. The response to the possible attempt upon the life of Dr. King was but a precursor on a local level of what was to come to the nation five years later on April 4, 1968. It made, therefore, the response to Dr. King's murder almost predictable. President Kennedy, alarmed by the bombings and by the reaction to them, issued a statement on Sunday in which he said that he was sending Assistant Attorney General Burke Marshall to Birmingham that evening to join with Assistant Deputy Attorney General Joseph Dolan and other Justice Department officials he had sent to Birmingham that morning. He said that he had also instructed Secretary of Defense Robert McNamara "to alert units of the armed forces trained in riot control and to dispatch selected units to military bases in the vicinity of Birmingham."

In addition, President Kennedy nationalized the Alabama National Guard. He explained these emergency actions by stating "I am deeply concerned about the events which occurred in Birmingham, Alabama, last night. The home of Reverend A. D. King was bombed and badly damaged. Shortly thereafter, the A.G. Gaston Motel was also bombed. These occurrences led to rioting, personal injury, property damage and various reports of violence and brutality." The response to the bombings by the President and his action in immediately sending high-level Department of Justice officials to the scene, together with the presence of a frightened but determined eyewitness to one of the bombings, gave the leaders of the movement the impression that, at long last, law and order might return to Birmingham.

Martin King returned with plans to lay nonviolent siege to the city. Together with Reverend Fred Shuttlesworth he prepared a bill of rights for Birmingham residents, including equal job opportunities in the large white-owned department stores, a realistic schedule for school desegregation, immediate lunch counter integration, and the appointment of a committee of blacks and whites to discuss the ongoing problems.

Two hundred and fifty blacks sought service at various lunch counters. Sheriff Bull Connor said he would "fill the jail full" and twenty demonstrators were arrested that day. The next day they were sentenced to six months in jail, the maximum provided by the trespassing statute. Other store owners declined to call the police and Bull Connor, powerless to make further arrests, said "We had to let them sit in. It's a disgrace." However, before the week was over more than seventy-five nonviolent demonstrators had been arrested. Some blacks and many white liberals urged Dr. King to leave town and initiate a thirty-day truce. But Martin King, his belief in the white legal structure more tenuous than ever before, pressed on. Easter was approaching and he urged blacks not to purchase new outfits, to boycott the downtown stores, and to attend church on Easter Sunday in blue jeans. He said that he would remain in Birmingham. ''The time is always wrong for some people,'' he said. ''The cup of endurance has run over.''

The importance of Roosevelt Tatum's statement was not lost upon the federal authorities in Washington. As the Klan rallied in Birmingham and as Dr. King proclaimed that the time would never be more right for a commitment to nonviolent action, Tatum was taken to the office of an Assistant Attorney General in Washington and questioned at length. He said that for three days beginning on Tuesday, May 14, he was interrogated by Justice Department employees and two men he could describe only as ''Washington lawyers.'' He also said that a member of Congress from New York was present during part of the questioning.

Upon his return Tatum was questioned by FBI agents in the Birmingham office and subjected to polygraph examination. He later reported upon what he considered to be the odd conduct of the agents who had administered the ''lie detector'' test. They had, he said, told him to answer each question negatively so that they could get a proper reading when he did not tell the truth. Because the questions he was asked did not pertain to the events that he observed on the evening of May 11, he said he was not suspicious at the time. He was told, he recalled later, to answer ''no'' to all questions about his ''family life'' and ''the names of his children.'' He said he did so, and when the polygraph examination was completed the agents required him to sign a statement admitting that he had made false statements. He said he was told that if he did not do so he would be prosecuted. He signed the statement.

Tatum had been employed at the Choctaw Pipe Company. His closest friend was his roommate and fellow worker at the pipe company, Morris Teasley. Teasley offered a form of corroboration for many of Tatum's observations. On May 12, Tatum told him that he had seen the police officers place and throw the dynamite at the King house. Teasley recalled that Tatum told him how he had been tricked into making false statements during the polygraph examination. One example Teasley recalled was that Tatum said that he was told by the agent, ''When we ask you if you have a child named 'Bronco' you say no.'' When Tatum was asked that question he told Teasley that he answered ''no'' and then the agent said that he could send him to jail for lying. Teasley observed, "They tricked him on that. But why? But why?"

On June 27, a federal grand jury was drawn in Birmingham for the United States District Court for the Northern District of Alabama. The drawing had been scheduled for July and the premature move was marked by another departure from custom. A deputy marshal is traditionally assigned to conduct that routine task. On this occasion the U.S. Marshal, Peyton Norville, selected the names of the jurors himself in the court of U.S. District Court Judge Clarence Allgood. Later in a conversation with Chief Deputy U.S. Marshal Daniel Moore, Norville said "Well, I have put my son-in-law on the grand jury." According to Moore, Norville explained to him that he had just "written in his name at the bottom of the list. I didn't select it. I just wrote it in."

In a subsequent investigation into a peripheral matter (an effort to remove Chief Deputy Moore for "speaking out too freely, particularly with regard to the illegal manipulation of the grand jury"), a Department of Justice report to the Administrative Assistant Attorney General confirmed the charge that "the then Marshal, Mr. Norville, knowing his son-in-law to be a qualified voter, wrote his name on a piece of paper and put it into the box."

Moore later said that he believed that the grand jury had been organized improperly for one reason. "It was," he told me, "to get Tatum. To indict him. He was a problem. They had to get him out of the way."

On July 26, 1963, Macon Weaver, the United States Attorney with jurisdiction in Birmingham wrote to the Department of Justice "requesting authority to prosecute one Roosevelt Tatum 'for making false statements to the FBI.' " Upon receipt of that request Assistant Attorney General Herbert J. Miller, Jr., responded for the Department of Justice. He wrote that the Department had concluded that "this is not an appropriate vehicle for prosecution" and advised against the prosecution of Roosevelt Tatum as recommended by the local federal authorities under Title 18, Section 1001.

The grand jury convened in Birmingham, nevertheless, and indicted Roosevelt Tatum. The minutes remain secret but an attorney, Orzell Billingsley, who represented Tatum was permitted to read them four years later and make contemporaneous notes. The notes reveal that among the witnesses to appear before the grand jury was James Edward Lay, a Civil Defense Captain, who said that "the Negro population of the City of Birmingham is under my supervision," and testified that "it is not the prevailing view by Negroes that the bombing was done by police officers.''

A police officer who drove a police car apparently testified that he was at the scene ''before the second explosion'' and that he did not normally patrol the area involved.

The first FBI agent to testify said that Tatum had told him of his observations on May 11, the night of the bombing. The same agent was later recalled to state that he talked with Tatum on July 3.

Another witness testified that he lived near A. D. King's house and that he did see a police car parked in front of that house. He said he saw only one officer in the car at that time.

Another local FBI agent testified about his ''investigation of Negroes'' and about ''their resentment.''

The FBI polygraph examiner, brought in from his assignment in Memphis, testified that he did ask a series of routine questions of Tatum ''about his family'' and ''other routine things'' and that he did talk with Tatum ''for about one hour before the examination was given.''

It appeared that substantial portions of Tatum's statement had received some corroboration even by hostile witnesses before a hostile grand jury. A police car was in the area, although not ordinarily assigned to patrol that area. It was parked in front of the King residence and when it was observed by one witness at that time there was only one occupant in it. Tatum was talked to at length before the polygraph examination was given and was asked routine questions about his family at the outset of the examination. Together with the direction from the Department of Justice not to prosecute, the improper selection of the grand jury, and the inflammatory and irrelevant information submitted to the grand jury, it seemed very unlikely that Tatum could be indicted.

On August 20 the home of Arthur Shores was bombed in Birmingham. Shores, a black lawyer, had represented two black students who had enrolled earlier that summer at the University of Alabama. Following that bombing U.S. Attorney Macon Weaver issued a public statement. The federal authorities in Birmingham had until that time been unable to solve a single bombing. Now Weaver felt that he had at last located a certifiable culprit. The *Birmingham News* carried a front-page story under the headlines ''False Charges Brought Attack on Police.'' The story reads:

U.S. Atty. Macon L. Weaver, in an unprecedented disclosure of Justice Department secrets, today said ''false charges'' that two policemen bombed a Negro minister's home in May resulted

directly in the violent aftermath of Tuesday night's bombing of Negro Attorney Arthur Shores' home.

After a fourteen-paragraph story which condemned Tatum, the U.S. Attorney referred at last to the bombing of the Shores home. He said "The FBI is working, as always, closely with the local police department to bring to the bar of justice the perpetrators of this crime against society."

The following day in a front-page story under the headline "Jury to Probe Negro's Lie" Judge Allgood said, according to the *Birmingham News,* "He will ask a federal grand jury to consider charges against a Negro who falsely alleged that Birmingham police bombed a Negro minister's home last May." If the newspaper report is accurate the good judge had evidently determined and publicly reported that Tatum had "falsely" implicated the police even before he was indicted.

The following week Roosevelt Tatum was indicted by the federal grand jury in Birmingham under Title 18, Section 1001, for making a false statement to the FBI. In the minds of the Birmingham black community, the connection between the local police, the U.S. Attorney's Office, the FBI, and the federal judiciary was never more clearly established. In the past there was the hope that the federal authorities might act as a restraining force against local police excesses but the indictment of Roosevelt Tatum shattered such hopes, particularly since it so closely followed President Kennedy's decision to send his Justice Department representatives to Birmingham. A presidential election was approaching; the black community, isolated and alone, had reason to feel alienated from the white system of justice.

Surely other witnesses would be afraid to come forward no matter what they saw. The government had indicted the one person who had come forward and said he was witness to a bombing. Upon reflection Orzell Billingsley said, "Why, no witness would dare open his mouth after they got Roosevelt for telling the truth. You'd have to be crazy to. They could do anything they wanted, bomb in broad daylight with a crowd watching and people would be too scared to say who did it. Man, to make a truthful statement to the FBI after that was like casting pearls before swine."

Approximately two weeks later the Sunday school at the 16th Street Baptist Church was blown up by dynamite. Four little black girls, Denise McNair, eleven years old, and Cynthia Wesley, Carol Robertson, and Addie Mae Collins, all fourteen years old, were killed.

President Kennedy sent Burke Marshall back to Birmingham and a special force of fifteen FBI agents was on the scene. The Justice Department said it would undertake the most vigorous manhunt since John Dillinger was captured.

Martin King delivered a moving epitaph. He said the four children "have something to say to each of us in their death, to every minister of the gospel who has remained silent behind the safe security of stained glass windows, to every politician who has fed his constituents with the stale bread of hatred and the spoiled meat of racism." He added, "We must be concerned not merely about who murdered them but about the system, the way of life, the philosophy which produced the murderers."

Roosevelt Tatum's case was to be tried in the continuing hysteria that was Birmingham before an all-white jury under the direction of Judge Allgood. His lawyer, Orzell Billingsley, had undertaken to handle the defense of some 3,000 persons who had been arrested in the previous weeks, a trial load so awesome that no lawyer could have adequately performed if he had been given ten years to do so.

He began by challenging the grand jury which returned the indictment against Tatum, charging quite accurately that blacks had been denied service on that panel. Billingsley was convinced then that Tatum was innocent, and now, in retrospect, he remains even more convinced that Tatum had told the truth and had been tricked. The record reveals that Tatum appeared in Judge Allgood's court on the morning of November 18, 1963. His lawyer was excused so that he could try another case that morning with the understanding that he would return to try the Tatum case at 2 o'clock that afternoon. Yet the afternoon session began with Billingsley entering the plea of guilty while Tatum stood silently by.

The lawyer was not present on the day of sentence and Roosevelt Tatum, standing alone, was sentenced by Judge Allgood to a penitentiary for one year and one day.

Years later the lawyer could not recall why Tatum, who insisted that he was innocent even on the day that the guilty plea was entered, pleaded guilty. He does recall the oppressive atmosphere, the hopelessness, and the isolation that marked those bitter days. He believes that the system coerced the plea.

It is impossible to determine with certainty whether or not Tatum was a reliable witness. Yet the federal and local police record remains intact. The chilling fact remains that the only person convicted in connection with a Birmingham bombing was a man who came forward as a witness, Roosevelt Tatum. If his plea was not freely entered into, but was a result of the hopelessness of the situation, then this attempt to murder Dr. King bears, in its legal conclusion, a remarkable similarity to the legal conclusion of the case against James Earl Ray, the man who allegedly did kill him.

Toward the end of 1964 Roosevelt Tatum was released from prison. He left Birmingham, where he could not find a job, to look for work in New York City. Before leaving his friends and his family he said that he had told the truth about the bombing of A. D. King's house. His friends say that he insisted that he would keep on telling the truth, whatever the cost.

He died in 1970, at the age of 46.

Chapter Seven

BIRMINGHAM JAIL
by Dick Gregory

Birmingham demonstrated how thoroughly American society was insulated against realizing what it had become. Birmingham forced America to face some terrible truths about itself. The world joined hands in outrage when television cameras recorded the grim pictures of children being clubbed and waterhosed, and dogs turned loose on nonviolent marchers. That's why the Lassie TV show got more hate mail from the ghetto than anyplace else.

At the same time, Birmingham was the wedge; it offered the opportunity for King and his followers to prove how powerful nonviolence was. And it made America recognize itself, the mightiest nation on earth, as a country whose practices were inconsistent with its creed. It exposed America as grossly hypocritical, woefully insensitive to the needs and plight of its minorities, its poor, and its old.

Countless numbers of us went to jail in Birmingham. I never did worry about staying in jail too long back in the 1960s because in those days I was earning more than a million dollars a year. So I knew the Internal Revenue was going to see to it that I didn't stay in jail too long. I remember the crowded jail cells and the inhumane treatment that was, for some of us, an introduction to Southern hospitality. Surprise lit the faces of the authorities when they realized how many we were and how unconditionally committed we were to going to jail and even dying, if necessary, to prove our utter dedication to the philosophy of nonviolence.

It was from such an inhospitable cell that King wrote his classic open letter to the clergy, entitled simply "Letter From Birmingham Jail." This letter was a response to eight white clergymen who wrote a public statement criticizing King for what they termed "unwise and untimely" demonstrations. In the reply, addressed to "My Dear Fellow Clergymen," King cleanly excised the meat, the nitty-gritty of the principles of Judaism, Christianity, and nonviolence, and proved them interchangeable.

42

Moving away from the American establishment as a target of criticism, King, here for the first time, dealt with the flaws and shortcomings of the church in America.

King said the church could do no more than reflect America, and that America, in turn, reflected the church. He saw the church as the moral barometer of the nation. He felt that religious institutions must be dedicated to humanity, equality, and justice; that this dedication was prerequisite to the development of a society in which all men and women could develop their highest potential.

I share with King the idea that America can be no worse than its churches. I would like to see American religious institutions become so clean and pure and just that the country could pattern after them, thus becoming all that it has ever claimed, striven, and hoped to be.

But we must let King's words of April 1963 speak for his position.

MY DEAR FELLOW CLERGYMEN:

. . . But more basically, I am in Birmingham because injustice is here. Just as the prophets of the eighth century B.C. left their villages and carried their "thus saith the Lord" far beyond the boundaries of their home towns, and just as the Apostle Paul left his village of Tarsus and carried the gospel of Jesus Christ to the far corners of the Greco-Roman world, so am I compelled to carry the gospel of freedom beyond my own home town. Like Paul, I must constantly respond to the Macedonian call for aid. . . .

. . . Perhaps it is easy for those who have never felt the stinging darts of segregation to say, "Wait." . . . But when you have seen vicious mobs lynch your mothers and fathers at will and drown your sisters and brothers at whim; when you have seen hate-filled policemen curse, kick, and even kill your black brothers and sisters; when you see the vast majority of your twenty million Negro brothers smothering in an airtight cage of poverty in the midst of an affluent society; when you suddenly find your tongue twisted and your speech stammering as you seek to explain to your six-year-old daughter why she can't go to the public amusement park that has just been advertised on television, and see tears welling up in her eyes when she is told that Funtown is closed to colored children, and see ominous clouds of inferiority beginning to form in her little mental sky, and see her beginning to distort her personality by developing an unconscious bitterness toward white people; when you have to concoct

43

an answer for a five-year-old son who is asking, "Daddy, why do white people treat colored people so mean?"; when your first name becomes "nigger," your middle name becomes "boy" (however old you are) and your last name becomes "John," and your wife and mother are never given the respected title "Mrs."; when you are harried by day and haunted by night by the fact that you are a Negro, living constantly at tiptoe stance, never quite knowing what to expect next, and are plagued with inner fears and outer resentments; when you are forever fighting a degenerating sense of "nobodiness"—then you will understand why we find it difficult to wait. There comes a time when the cup of endurance runs over, and men are no longer willing to be plunged into the abyss of despair. I hope, sirs, you can understand our legitimate and unavoidable impatience. . . .

. . . So the question is not whether we will be extremists, but what kind of extremists we will be. Will we be extremists for hate or for love? Will we be extremists for the preservation of injustice or for the extension of justice? In that dramatic scene on Calvary's hill three men were crucified. We must never forget that all three were crucified for the same crime—the crime of extremism. Two were extremists for immorality, and thus fell below their environment. The other, Jesus Christ, was an extremist for love, truth, and goodness, and thereby rose above his environment. Perhaps the South, the nation, and the world are in dire need of creative extremists.

. . . Let us all hope that the dark clouds of racial prejudice will soon pass away and the deep fog of misunderstanding will be lifted from our fear-drenched communities, and in some not too distant tomorrow the radiant stars of love and brotherhood will shine over our great nation with all their scintillating beauty.

Yours for the cause of peace and brotherhood,
MARTIN LUTHER KING, JR.

Chapter Eight

"I HAVE A DREAM"
by Dick Gregory

The March on Washington on August 28, 1963, was a drama of epic proportions. I will never forget it. It was wall-to-wall black folks and white folks, over a quarter of a million of us. I had never seen so many black folks and white folks together this side of a race riot. No event in human history was so feverishly anticipated, so fervently hoped for before it became reality. None has been so thoroughly analyzed, discussed and dissected when it was over. We made our point to the world—that the civil rights of black Americans must be respected.

It is not difficult to extract from the great panorama of the day the single most awesome, most inspiring, most moving aspect. What has come to be known as King's "I Have a Dream" speech was easily the gem that sparkled most brightly.

Those who were not present and have had to rely on published versions of the speech, however textually accurate, will never know the precise flavor. King's mood, the exhilaration he exuded are elements that cannot be reproduced on the printed page.

It seemed as if the very cells of his body were charged with new life and renewed spirit. As if the magic of the day, the nobility of the cause had been transformed into a potent elixir and absorbed into the very cells of his body, infusing him with optimism, courage, and joy. It was contagious. All of us there, black, white, young, old, rich, poor, Jew, Gentile, and Muslim caught King's spirit. Spontaneously, it was as if we all knew that after today we would never be the same, that whatever lay ahead: suffering, uncertainty, doubt, fear—even death—nothing would ever turn us around. We found a vigor, a lightness of heart, a gladness of soul that we had not brought with us, but which, miraculously, we were all privileged to take away.

Opponents of the March and its goals hoped for violence. We disappointed them. It was a picnic. I remember the March On Washington mainly because it was the only march I participated in that I wasn't

45

arrested in. As a matter of fact, the March On Washington set a record for an American city. It was the first time that a civil rights march was held that the police arrested more criminals that day than civil rights marchers. It was a day of jubilee.

I can see Martin now, walking to the podium, 'midst thunderous applause, waiting patiently until it was over, and then, with simplicity, honesty and human warmth saying:

Five score years ago, a great American, in whose symbolic shadow we stand today, signed the Emancipation Proclamation. This momentous decree came as a great beacon light of hope to millions of Negro slaves who had been seared in the flames of withering injustice. It came as a joyous daybreak to end the long night of their captivity.

But one hundred years later, the Negro still is not free; one hundred years later, the life of the Negro is still sadly crippled by the manacles of segregation and the chains of discrimination; one hundred years later, the Negro lives on a lonely island of poverty in the midst of a vast ocean of material prosperity; one hundred years later, the Negro is still languished in the corners of American society and finds himself in exile in his own land.

So we've come here today to dramatize a shameful condition. In a sense, we have come to our nation's capital to cash a check. When the architects of our republic wrote the magnificent words of the Constitution and the Declaration of Independence, they were signing a promissory note to which every American was to fall heir. This note was the promise that all men, yes, black men as well as white men, would be guaranteed the unalienable rights of life, liberty, and the pursuit of happiness.

It is obvious today that America has defaulted on this promissory note insofar as her citizens of color are concerned. Instead of honoring this sacred obligation, America has given the Negro people a bad check; a check which has come back marked "insufficient funds." We refuse to believe that there are insufficient funds in the great vaults of opportunity of this nation. And so we've come to cash this check, a check that will give us upon demand the riches of freedom and the security of justice.

We have also come to this hallowed spot to remind America of the fierce urgency of now. This is no time to engage in the luxury of cooling off or to take the tranquilizing drug of gradualism. Now is the time to make real the promises of democracy; now is the time to rise from the dark and desolate valley of segregation to

the sunlit path of racial justice; now is the time to lift our nation from the quicksands of racial injustice to the solid rock of brotherhood; now is the time to make justice a reality for all God's children. It would be fatal for the nation to overlook the urgency of the moment. This sweltering summer of the Negro's legitimate discontent will not pass until there is an invigorating autumn of freedom and equality.

Nineteen sixty-three is not an end, but a beginning. And those who hope that the Negro needed to blow off steam and will now be content, will have a rude awakening if the nation returns to business as usual. There will be neither rest nor tranquility in America until the Negro is granted his citizenship rights. The whirlwinds of the revolt will continue to shake the foundations of our nation until the bright day of justice emerges.

But there is something that I must say to my people, who stand on the warm threshold which leads into the palace of justice. In the process of gaining our rightful place, we must not be guilty of wrongful deeds. Let us not seek to satisfy our thirst for freedom by drinking from the cup of bitterness and hatred. We must forever conduct our struggle on the high plane of dignity and discipline. We must not allow our creative protest to generate into physical violence. Again and again we must rise to the majestic heights of meeting physical force with soul force; and the marvelous new militancy, which has engulfed the Negro community, must not lead us to a distrust of all white people. For many of our white brothers, as evidenced by their presence here today, have come to realize that their destiny is tied up with our destiny. And they have come to realize that their freedom is inextricably bound to our freedom. We cannot walk alone. And as we talk, we must make the pledge that we shall always march ahead. We cannot turn back.

There are those who are asking the devotees of civil rights, "When will you be satisfied?" We can never be satisfied as long as the Negro is the victim of the unspeakable horrors of police brutality; we can never be satisfied as long as our bodies, heavy with the fatigue of travel, cannot gain lodging in the motels of the highways and the hotels of the cities; we cannot be satisfied as long as the Negro's basic mobility is from a smaller ghetto to a larger one; we can never be satisfied as long as our children are stripped of their selfhood and robbed of their dignity by signs stating "For Whites Only"; we cannot be satisfied as long as the

Negro in Mississippi cannot vote and a Negro in New York believes he has nothing for which to vote. No! no, we are not satisfied, and we will not be satisfied until "justice rolls down like waters and righteousness like a mighty stream."

I am not unmindful that some of you have come here out of great trials and tribulations. Some of you have come fresh from narrow jail cells. Some of you have come from areas where your quest for freedom left you battered by the storms of persecution and staggered by the winds of police brutality. You have been the veterans of creative suffering. Continue to work with the faith that unearned suffering is redemptive. Go back to Mississippi. Go back to Alabama. Go back to South Carolina. Go back to Georgia. Go back to Louisiana. Go back to the slums and ghettos of our northern cities, knowing that somehow this situation can and will be changed. Let us not wallow in the valley of despair.

I say to you today, my friends, so even though we face the difficulties of today and tomorrow, I still have a dream. It is a dream deeply rooted in the American dream. I have a dream that one day this nation will rise up and live out the true meaning of its creed, "We hold these truths to be self evident, that all men are created equal." I have a dream that one day on the red hills of Georgia, sons of former slaves and the sons of former slave owners will be able to sit down together at the table of brotherhood. I have a dream that one day even the state of Mississippi, a state sweltering with the heat of injustice, sweltering with the heat of oppression, will be transformed into an oasis of freedom and justice. I have a dream that my four little children will one day live in a nation where they will not be judged by the color of their skin but by the content of their character.

I have a dream today!

I have a dream that one day down in Alabama — with its vicious racists, with its governor having his lips dripping with the words of interposition and nullification—one day right there in Alabama, little black boys and black girls will be able to join hands with little white boys and white girls as sisters and brothers.

I have a dream today!

I have a dream that one day "every valley shall be exalted and every hill and mountain shall be made low. The rough places will be made plain and the crooked places will be made straight, and the glory of the Lord shall be revealed, and all flesh shall see it together."

This is our hope. This is the faith that I go back to the South with. With this faith we shall be able to transform the jangling discords of our nation into a beautiful symphony of brotherhood. With this faith we will be able to work together, to pray together, to struggle together, to go to jail together, to stand up for freedom together, knowing that we will be free one day. And this will be the day. This will be the day when all of God's children will be able to sing with new meaning—"My country 'tis of thee, sweet land of liberty, of thee I sing. Land where my fathers died, land of the pilgrim's pride, from every mountainside, let freedom ring." And if America is to be a great nation, this must become true.

So let freedom ring from the prodigious hilltops of New Hampshire; let freedom ring from the mighty mountains of New York; let freedom ring from the heightening Alleghenies of Pennsylvania; let freedom ring from the snowcapped Rockies of Colorado; let freedom ring from the curvaceous slopes of California. But not only that. Let freedom ring from Stone Mountain of Georgia; let freedom ring from Lookout Mountain of Tennessee; let freedom ring from every hill and molehill of Mississippi. From every mountainside, let freedom ring.

And when this happens, and when we allow freedom to ring, when we let it ring from every village and every hamlet, from every state and every city, we will be able to speed up that day when all God's children, black men and white men, Jews and Gentiles, Protestants and Catholics, will be able to join hands and sing in the words of the old Negro spiritual: "Free at last. Free at last. Thank God Almighty, we are free at last."

Chapter Nine

"A FAR DEEPER MALADY"

by Mark Lane

Dr. King had become the most prestigious leader for liberation in recent American history. Future historians would in all probability consider this Southern black preacher, the son of a Southern black preacher, along with Abraham Lincoln. While others devised the "black is beautiful" slogan, a phrase which Dr. King admired little, in the ghettos of Montgomery and Birmingham and Selma and Jackson and Atlanta and Chicago, poor blacks looked toward Dr. King and said he was proof that they were not inferior. They said he had proved as well that they were not born to be victims; that by working together they had the power to control their own destiny, to shape their own lives.

In the spring of 1967, Dr. King risked all that he had achieved, his national reputation, a working relationship with the American news media, with black leaders and other national leaders, and the financial security of his Southern Christian Leadership Conference (SCLC). On that day he committed the SCLC to a formally sealed compact which unanimously condemned the war in Vietnam as "politically and morally unjust" and pledging to do "everything in our power" to end it.

A few days later, on April 4, 1967, Dr. King called upon all blacks and "all white people of good will" to boycott the war by becoming conscientious objectors to military service. He outlined a program designed to "begin the long and difficult process of extracting ourselves from this nightmarish conflict." He likened the use of new weapons against the farmers of Vietnam to the testing of "new tortures in the concentration camps of Europe" by the Nazis. Dr. King bitterly assailed American military policy from the standpoint of the Vietnamese peasants who

watch as we poison their water, as we kill a million acres of their crops.

They must weep as the bulldozers roar through their area

preparing to destroy the precious trees. They wander into the hospitals, with at least twenty casualties from American firepower for one Vietcong-inflicted injury.

So far, we may have killed a million of them—mostly children. They wander into the towns and see thousands of the children, homeless, without clothes, running in packs on the streets like animals. They see the children degraded by our soldiers as they beg for food. They see the children selling their sisters to our soldiers, soliciting for their mothers.

Dr. King added, "If America's soul becomes totally poisoned, part of the autopsy must read Vietnam."

One year later to the day, he was dead.

Dr. King's call for action to end the war was greeted with a chorus of public denunciation created by many of the nationally known leaders, including black opinion makers.

In an article published in *Reader's Digest,* a nationally known black communicator charged that Dr. King had created "doubt about the Negro's loyalty to his country." He had become "persona non grata to Lyndon Johnson," and he added that King's former friends in Congress will probably not be "moved by him the way they were in the past."

He then wrote that "talk of Communists influencing the actions and words of the young minister" had been revived. He added, "I report this not to endorse what King and many others will consider a 'guilt by association' smear, but because of the threat that these allegations represent to the civil rights movement." He wrote that since Dr. King had involved himself in "a conflict where the United States is in direct combat with Communism," he had imperiled chances for needed legislation to protect civil rights workers in the South and to ban housing discrimination.

The executive director of a national black organization agreed. He said that "urgent domestic programs of civil rights and the issue of the war in Vietnam should remain separate." The Jewish War Veterans (JWV) sharply attacked King. In reference to his comparison between German and American methods, the JWV charged, "It is utterly incredible that Dr. King's denunciation of our government should manifest itself in such an ugly parallel."

Another national black organization reported that its board of directors had voted unanimously against the proposal by Dr. King to "merge the civil rights and peace movements." The board called Dr. King's efforts "a serious tactical mistake" and added, "we are not a peace organization."

Senator Jacob Javits, a leading Republican liberal, said King's statement is "certainly bound to be resented by the country which is deeply involved in the war and which feels it can certainly do justice by the Negro at one and the same time."

Lyndon Johnson told a cabinet member, "That goddamn nigger preacher may drive me out of the White House." While Dr. King never evidenced such a desire, his call for peace, begun that day in early April and continued through the last year of his life, may have played an important part in President Johnson's decision not to seek reelection. It was the war and the growing opposition to it that led to Johnson's somewhat involuntary retirement.

What the President said with characteristic bluntness in private, the leading news media put more acceptably and more publicly.

Dr. King's last year on earth began in turmoil. He appeared to stand almost alone as a withering torrent of apparently orchestrated abuse engulfed him. He had expected that his public dissent from the war would create controversy. He had been advised that donations to the SCLC might sharply diminish and that public figures, major newspapers, and even some black leaders would express their displeasure. He was, nevertheless, unprepared for the depth of hostility he witnessed.

He was almost bewildered and thoroughly frustrated by the unthinking response to his call for an end to the war. He had reason to be frightened. For he appeared to stand almost alone, and to those who detested him, he appeared more helpless and vulnerable than ever before. Yet if he was frightened by the savage nature of the attacks, he never expressed that fear privately, and publicly his initial opposition to the war was honed through his almost prophetic reasoning into an analysis of the nature of American imperialism.

At that moment, and for the days that were left to him, his thoughtful bravery and his grace while under fire were never more apparent. Those who hid behind their shield of Congressional immunity, protected by a biased media and supported in their endeavors by the awesome power of the intelligence organizations, called into question *his* manhood and challenged *his* courage. Yet he was not blinded by panic. In private he wept as the reckless attacks against him increased. Yet through the tears of frustration, no doubt swollen by self-pity and righteous indignation, he saw the problem more clearly. He understood the goals of those who opposed him and took the full measure of their power.

And then he spoke. In 1967, a few months before he was murdered, he said:

The war in Vietnam is just a symptom of a far deeper malady within the American spirit. And if we ignore this sobering reality,

we will find ourselves organizing clergy and layman concerned committees for the next generation. They will be concerned with Guatemala and Peru; they will be concerned about Thailand and Cambodia; they will be concerned about Mozambique and South Africa. We will be marching for these and a dozen other names and attending rallies without end unless there is a significant and profound change in American life and politics.

Dr. King had been to the mountain top. And from the panoramic perception afforded by the lofty height, he set aside personal concerns for self and shared his view with those who could still hear him through the mounting din of false analysis.

He was a dangerous man. He had perceived some dangerous truths and he was so struck by the meaning of his discoveries that he incautiously, almost recklessly, spoke to us of what he had learned.

His words twenty-five years ago spoke to the developing efforts for national liberation in Southeast Asia, in Latin America, and in Africa. If we need not march off to rallies to protest American involvement there, then some small credit must be given to his words and his actions.

Newsweek reported in its news columns that Dr. King's opposition to the war was brought about because "he saw black students defecting to [Stokely] Carmichael and white liberals increasingly deserting civil rights causes for peace parades." *Newsweek* continued, "He considered his role as a Nobel peace laureate, a clergyman, even a prophet." Emmet John Hughes, writing in *Newsweek,* said, under a heading "A Curse of Confusion" and a sub-heading "False Image," King "achieves perhaps the greatest irony in his fancy that the civil rights movement can be strengthened by enlisting the moral passions exacted by Vietnam. . . . He propagates, even more remarkably, a confusion of moral and political values."

A nationally known black writer offered another motive for Dr. King's opposition to the war.

> **Some say it was a matter of ego—that he was convinced that since he was the most influential Negro in the United States, President Johnson would have to listen to him and alter U.S. policy in Vietnam.**

Perhaps Reverend Bernard Lee of Atlanta, Dr. King's close friend and aide, had better reason than most to understand why King had spoken out against the war. The Revered Lee recalled a day in the spring of 1967. "Martin and I were traveling to Jamaica. He was going to finish a book that he had been working on. Martin always carried a couple of really heavy suitcases. Never had any clothes in them, really. They were filled with books and magazines and various kinds of documents that he would study.''

The Reverend Lee said that before boarding the plane they stopped at a restaurant. Both ordered dinner. Dr. King had stopped off at a newsstand to pick up an armload of current magazines. The food arrived and both men began to eat. While he ate, Dr. King looked through the magazines. The Reverend Lee said, ''When he came to *Ramparts* magazine he stopped. He froze as he looked at the pictures from Vietnam. He saw a picture of a Vietnamese mother holding her dead baby, a baby killed by our military. Then Martin just pushed the plate of food away from him. I looked up and said, 'Doesn't it taste any good?' and he answered, 'Nothing will ever taste any good for me until I do everything I can to end that war.'

''That's when the decision was made. Martin had known about the war before then, of course, and had spoken out against it. But it was then that he decided to commit himself to oppose it. When we got back from Jamaica that is what he did.''

When he returned to the United States, Dr. King embarked upon a militant program designed to gain political and economic rights for blacks. He continued and increased the marching and organizing in Chicago, announced a twenty-city boycott campaign against companies with discriminatory hiring policies and began to mobilize white college students for work in political education campaigns.

Dr. King said that the war was morally wrong and itself a barrier to the realization of the dreams of black people. ''Many of the very programs we are talking about,'' he said, ''have been stifled because of that war in Vietnam. I am absolutely convinced that the frustrations are going to increase in the ghettos of our nation as long as the war continues.''

Dr. King pointed out that blacks were serving in Vietnam in disproportionate numbers. Twice as many blacks as whites died each day in Vietnam in relationship to their numbers in the whole population.

He answered those who insisted that he should work only in the civil rights movement with but two sentences. He said he opposed segregation, and that he would refuse to segregate his principles. He said the war was wrong, and that he would oppose it until it ended.

Chapter Ten

THE LAST CAMPAIGN
by Dick Gregory

Martin Luther King had become the true voice of America. When you read the United States Constitution, you hear all the beautiful things we teach in our grade schools, and our high schools, and colleges of what America should be all about. Martin brought those dead words alive. America needed a voice; America needed millions to speak out and yell; America needed to be heard the world over, and it was—through Martin's commitment. Through his suffering and unselfish attitude when it came to helping others, Martin earned the right to be that voice. Not just to be the spokesperson for black America, but he spoke for what the true, real, America should have been speaking about and sounding like. Because of that, every section of the country and the world that was having problems and was reaching out and crying for help was reaching for Martin. Come Martin, help us Martin, be with us Martin, lead with us. If you were here we could survive. Yes, we could survive. Oh God, if we could just get Martin here it would be all over. The white folks would listen to him. If we could get Martin here we could raise enough money. If we could get Martin here he would say it like it's supposed to be said. Martin Luther King developed into the real, true, honest voice of America. Because of him, every town, village, and city in America where there was suffering going on called on King for help. It wasn't just black folks who needed him. The Jews, the Gentiles, the Catholics, the Irish, the Baptists, the old and the young, men and women; they were all calling for Martin. Come and help us, talk to us, give us some encouragement. Tell us what we would not accept anyone else telling us. Tell us Martin, tell us rich, white, sophisticated folks what this America is all about. Because he was the voice for an entire nation, King was always in demand. As important as Memphis was, it came at a bad time.

The need for King to return to Memphis in April 1968 to help the striking garbage workers came at an inconvenient time. Martin Luther King was getting ready to do something that neither he nor any other civil rights leader had tried to do before. He was preparing for the Poor People's Campaign and March on Washington. Never before had masses of poor folks come together and talked about being poor and disadvantaged. This was different from all the other marches and demonstrations that Martin Luther King had led. Organizing a one-day march was simple. King had proven to America and the world that large numbers of black people could be organized for short periods of time. Many of the people participating in King's previous marches were not the poor and the hungry, but mainly middle-class people, celebrities, and working folks. This was going to be different. This time the force would come from a different group of people. The ones without jobs, people without enough food to feed their families, and the people whose faith in the American system had been shattered because of years of discrimination and injustice. The Poor People's March on Washington would go down in history as the biggest demonstration that the nation's capital had ever been confronted with—and it would be nonviolent. Imagine Dr. King coming into Washington, D. C., with thousands of poor people of all colors quietly asking America for a chance to be part of that respected segment of society reserved for the chosen few.

King knew that the Poor People's March would need a lot of careful planning. Everything had to be just right or it would not work. All things had to be considered. A lot of money would be needed, and King himself would be influential in raising funds. People might be reluctant to contribute to a cause that seemed as farfetched as thousands of poor folks marching into the nation's capital. King would have to convince both blacks and whites that it would work. And even if the money were raised, there were so many other problems that would have to be considered with so many people living in such close contact for an undetermined length of time. Husbands and wives would be together. Some pregnant women would come to Washington and give birth while they were there. Others might become pregnant, and there would be the problem of having the proper medical care available for them. There would be sickness, and problems of taking care of young children. Everyone would have to be fed properly, and while all these necessary things had to be taken into account, King still had the burden of watching out for government *agents provocateurs*. They might try to undo all the hard work and effort that had gone into the planning of this demonstration. King knew that he had a big job waiting ahead of him, and he was hoping everything would work out. He knew that if the Poor People's March was a success, black people and poor folks of all colors would be on their way to a better life.

The two things that upset the Establishment most about Martin Luther

King were the fact that he came out against the war in Vietnam and his plan for a Poor People's March in the nation's capital. King's plan to bring thousands of people into Washington, D.C., would broaden his base from civil rights to human rights. He would not only be concerned with equality under the law for blacks, but for all citizens who were not getting a chance to earn their fair share of what America had to offer. They would demand jobs and decent wages. This would be a new era in American history.

Many whites have always had a basic fear of black people, and that fear alone makes them resist anything that even appears as though it might have an effect on them. If Martin Luther King's bringing poor folks to the capital was going to jeopardize their jobs, or their life styles, then they didn't want the Poor People's March to take place. The government, too, was worried about masses of poor people pitching tents in Washington. What would this do to America's reputation in other countries? What would this do to our image as the richest nation in the world? What about those countries who were not aware of America's racial problems and problems of poverty and hunger? A Poor People's March on Washington would be an absolute embarrassment to the President of the United States and his entire Cabinet. It would be an embarrassment to all of America. The United States has always been able to hide its poor. People with no jobs, no homes, and no money have always been separated from the rest of American society. There are vagrancy laws that keep these people from being on the street. When they are caught mingling with the so-called decent people, they can be picked up and taken to jail for loitering.

White reaction to the planned Poor People's March was astonishing. A headline in *Reader's Digest* magazine a few days before King was killed read: "The United States may face a civil crisis this April when a Poor People's Army pitches camp in the nation's capital." The article stated that authorities must be prepared for the worst: a Washington paralyzed by a so-called Poor People's Army. At the White House, the Justice Department, the Pentagon, and the Metropolitan Police Headquarters, dozens of conferences were held to coordinate strategy. All of Washington knew, from the President on down, that if King's Poor People's March really took place, there was a possibility that nearly anything might happen. It could not be predicted, and the government with all its methods of tapping phones and sending out spies did not know how to prepare to handle this massive demonstration that was about to take place. The press was busy trying to find out each and every detail of the march. What would happen if the police told them to move? What if the government ordered an end to the demonstration? What if the police used force to physically remove the crowd? Was there a possibility of violence? And more than anything else, could this thing work without Martin Luther King?

It did work. Ralph Abernathy and other SCLC leaders led thousands into Washington, D.C. They lived in tents through the sweltering summer heat and through many days of hard rain. They were determined to make their voices heard, and they did it without chaos or violence. America had to listen.

PART THREE

CODE NAME "ZORRO"

Chapter Eleven

HOOVER'S FBI
by Mark Lane

The torrent of violence that greeted the nonviolent protesters in Birmingham dramatized again the problem that had beset the civil rights movement from the beginning: *Why was the law not being adequately enforced?* No one was naive enough to expect much help from local law-enforcement agencies in the Deep South, but what about the FBI, the federal agency sworn to uphold the Constitution and enforce the laws of the land on behalf of *all* the people? With its already broad criminal investigative authority, backed by a growing body of Supreme Court decisions and Congressional legislation on civil rights, surely the FBI had all the power necessary both to defend the legal rights of protesters and to arrest the lawbreakers who confronted them with acts of violence.

Why, then, was the law not being adequately enforced? FBI apologists, of course, said that the problem was too big, that the Bureau's manpower was inadequate to cope with widespread civil disorders. Yet the complex problems can hardly be understood solely in those terms. Who were the men who made up J. Edgar Hoover's FBI? What were their motives and how dedicated were they really to enforcing *all* the laws for *all* the people? Since Hoover's death the American public has already learned some of the dismaying answers to these questions. In three consecutive chapters, beginning here, we shall examine these questions again and try to determine what bearing their answers might have on the murder of Martin Luther King, Jr.

Although books have been written by FBI agents, and reports have been made by committees of the Congress detailing the aberrations, eccentricities, and illegal acts of J. Edgar Hoover's FBI, little has been done to effect a cure.

The reformation of the FBI cannot be achieved by the passing of Hoover. His fifty-year tenure was longer than the reign of most monarchs, and certainly longer than that of most dictators. Hoover was able to devise a classic carrot-and-stick employment bureaucracy, so that employees of the FBI became enmeshed in a system that left them little opportunity for free thinking. According to one former employee we talked to, "All the agents ever talked about was ball games and women. And their house. The house that they'd just bought. And their pay raise; mainly their pay raise. Talk about pay raise until you'd go crazy."

On November 27, 1976, I interviewed Arthur Murtagh at his home in Constable, New York. Before retiring, he had been a Special Agent of the FBI, for twenty years and nine months.

Murtagh, who later practiced law in Constable and taught at Clarkson College, had testified before the House Select Committee on Intelligence, chaired by Otis Pike, Democrat of New York, generally called the Pike Committee. Informing the Committee that he had "loyally served the Bureau for twenty years," and that he had been "assigned to the FBI's internal security intelligence squad in Atlanta for 10 years," he hoped he "could give this Committee insight into the Bureau's intelligence practices not from the theoretical viewpoint of a policymaker but from the practical viewpoint of a field agent."

Murtagh said, "it is possible for the structures of an organization such as the Bureau to be responsible for much wrongdoing without any measurable culpability on the part of individuals working in the lower levels of the organization." He gave one example:

I was at one time asked to obtain through my informants handwriting samples of a gentleman who is now a member of your body, the Honorable Andrew Young of Atlanta. I was also asked to obtain handwriting samples of several of his associates in Dr. Martin Luther King's Southern Christian Leadership Conference. I was an agent with a lot of experience at the time this request came to me from my superiors. I was aware that the matter in which the request was made was such that the information was to be used for one of the illegal purposes of the Bureau.

Murtagh also said that he was requested to order his informant in the SCLC to steal some stationery. The agent surmised that the plan was to effect a blackmail with forged love letters from "Andy Young to somebody's wife." Murtagh told his superior that "those fellows at SCLC will laugh at you." Although Hoover's interest in sexual blackmail is well-known, one wonders how seriously love letters on SCLC stationery would have been viewed.

Murtagh "flatly refused to comply" with the request, made after regular working hours, "orally in private." He turned to his supervisor, who was known among the agents as "Colonel Klink," and told him

". . . he could tell his counterpart at the Bureau who had called him on the WATS line seeking the information that I knew damn well it was going to be used in an unrecorded counterintelligence operation to destroy Mr. Young's chances of getting elected to the House of Representatives." The request came only a few days after Mr. Young had announced that he was seeking a seat in the House. Murtagh threatened to go to the Civil Service Commission or to somehow publicize it, so his supervisor backed down and said, "We will make some other arrangement." Assuming that the Bureau failed in this attempt on Mr. Young because his "supervisor had no other source at that time who could get the information for him," Murtagh also remarked that "no record of the above incident" would be found "in the Bureau files."

In an unsigned response to Mr. Murtagh's testimony, the FBI said: ". . . a review of the files disclosed no information to support Murtagh's allegation and that personnel, who would be knowledgeable of such a request of Murtagh, had no recollection of any such request. FBI headquarters files did not contain information which would substantiate Murtagh's allegation."

Murtagh added, in his testimony, that "if the same request had been made to most agents who had reached [my] level in the Bureau . . . they would have routinely complied with their supervisor's request, simply because they would have gone through a process which would have eliminated all those who saw anything wrong with the type of activity contemplated by their supervisor."

An agent with years of Bureau experience explained how this mind set was achieved. Because the Bureau was "exempt from Civil Service" regulations, it was free to set up its own criteria for the selection and training of personnel. Murtagh, in his testimony, confirmed that "Mr. Hoover was able over a period of nearly 50 years to bring in thousands of carefully selected agent-personnel who were as politically disposed to the right as he was and then through a personnel system, which offered no possibility at all for an agent to question Hoover's ethics or methods, to force thousands of those selected to leave the Bureau in utter disgust simply because they had no avenue through which they could air grievances involving unethical or illegal conduct."

The process of breaking down an agent's resistance to objectionable activities was, besides that of selection, one of occasional choices. Murtagh told me, "The average agent on a day-to-day basis might have to falsify a record for some purpose to keep the Bureau from some little scandal, but they'd go through 20 years and they might not have to, to any great extent. Except in the little administrative things. They'd have to lie about how many hours they'd worked. They broke 'em in on that kind of lying, and then when they got to the point where they had to lie for something big, their character—their self-respect—had been deteriorated. Agents said to one another, 'I have absolutely no respect for myself. I am a broken man.' Another was reported to have said, 'When I shave I close my eyes.' ''

An example of this debilitating dictatorship was the weight program of the Bureau. Arthur Murtagh suffered personally because, although he did not look or feel overweight, he did not accord with a chart provided to the Bureau by an insurance company.

Hoover was a very clever man—he was a clever dictator. He knew that if he could divide and conquer he'd be successful in controlling people. One of the things he used was the weight program. If we just talked about the weight program we'd laugh about it because it in itself was of no importance, but it accomplished the purpose of dividing the troops. Some people couldn't get their weight down to chart weights. The charts were such that it was an absolute impossibility for some of us to get to it. They were later done away with by the insurance company that had recommended them. And they weren't even used the way the company said they should be used.

The weight requirement obviously never applied to Hoover, or to John Moore, who was directly under him. Murtagh's supervisior asked him his weight every day—and Murtagh insisted on telling the truth. ''My supervisor would come and say, 'What do you weigh, Art? You're supposed to weigh 168.' I'd say I weighed 182 or 187. *And he put down 168.*''

Transfers to undesirable posts were used as punishment. This device was used so arbitrarily and capriciously that the lower echelons in the Bureau developed a defense against it. Murtagh's noncompliance with the weight charts was eventually discovered and he was ordered transferred. ''By the late fifties and sixties, the internal workings of the Bureau had broken down. If Hoover wanted to punish somebody, the manipulators under him would create a kind of cushion between him and us. They'd transfer us—but they'd give us the best damn transfer that we could get!'' Murtagh was transferred from Charlotte, North Carolina, to Atlanta, Georgia.

Hoover's methods of control of over 7,000 agents were worthy of

Machiavelli. He always cited national security and efficient law enforcement. In creating the Bureau, Hoover invented an institution that presented a polished, competent exterior to the public, an exterior hard-won by rigid rules of conduct and secrecy. Murtagh testified, "Secrecy served many useful purposes to the Bureau. It made it impossible for the public or Congress to know anything about what was going on internally. It gave the Bureau operation an aura of mystery and created a type of fear and respect for the Bureau which I personally feel is unhealthy in a society that strives to be both democratic and open."

The FBI's unsigned response to Murtagh's testimony was:

Annual appropriations [for the FBI] were based on Hoover's testimony before Congressional Committees which were at liberty to examine all areas of the Bureau's operations in conducting their inquiry for budget justification. As members of the Congress and representatives of the people, Committee members have always been in a position to know of the Bureau's internal as well as external operations and to make Congress and the general public aware of their observation *within their prescribed mandate and subject to the rules of confidence* [emphasis added].

Budgets of individual investigations never find their way into reports accessible to the public, however. Murtagh told me that a reluctant FBI was prompted, perhaps constrained, by the media to act after the murder of three civil rights workers in Mississippi. The investigation was designed to find the bodies he said. Murtagh was told by a supervisor that the Bureau spent $250,000 a day for over three months.

"We had about seventy agents on the case, and agents in the field, U-2 flights taking pictures, and about 150 backup agents in the state of Mississippi doing work that was directly related to recovering leads. It was a massive investigation." Ultimately the bodies were found when an informant was paid $10,000 for the location of each of the bodies.

Murtagh said that in a "normal criminal investigation, the Bureau should get high marks, in things like bank robbery, car thefts, kidnappings—there was some doctoring of statistics, but those things were played straight. But," added the same agent, "it was when they got into the intelligence area, an area with political overtones, that things began to break down. The Bureau's approach was so predominantly right that they might look at an ordinary citizen as a threat to the internal security of the United States. Anybody who wore a beard, in the mid-sixties—they'd take pictures of people in parades and pick the ones with beards—they were the dangerous ones."

An agent who had served in Detroit informed me that the "Two Squad," which was usually an intelligence squad, had conducted an investigation of Walter Reuther because of President Eisenhower's appointment of Reuther to an atomic energy conference in Europe. "The Bureau had to give him a clearance—the Bureau didn't call it that." The agent, in discussing the Reuther investigation with veteran "Two Squad" members, found that

> the famous Walter Reuther letters which were used against Reuther and published in the papers back in the thirties were actually written by a guy who is now a vice-president of General Motors. They were forgeries.
>
> When Reuther was trying to organize the CIO, back in the thirties, there were riots and several people were killed and a lot of people went to the hospital. During the riots Reuther made a trip to Russia, about 1932 or 33, and during the riots, these letters came out in local papers, and they were allegedly written by Walter Reuther, from Moscow, praising the Communist system.
>
> Reuther denied that he had written the letters—and there is information in the Bureau files to show that this General Motors guy had. I don't know whether the Bureau worked with this guy, using the FBI laboratories to create forgeries, or whether he wrote them independently and the Bureau found out about it. But at any rate, the Bureau never told anybody about this. They let Reuther bear the burden of the allegation. This extreme rightist approach is typical of Bureau history.

A Special Agent commented that when the FBI had to deal with other than "ordinary criminal behavior," it applied its own standards to formulate a judgment as to correct and moral politics. "Walter Reuther was a rabble-rousing labor leader by the Bureau's standards."

Two agents were assigned to investigate the applications of two young women who had applied for clerical positions with the Bureau in Atlanta. "They had worked in a rag-rendering plant in the mid-sixties. They had had a dispute and won it through the National Labor Relations Board. The investigation on their background went up to the Bureau, and Clyde Tolson wrote across it, 'What are we doing, fooling around with people who've been connected with labor unions? Close immediately.' They were denied jobs on the basis that they had something to do with labor unions—this was in the mid-sixties."

An agent who had been with the Bureau for many years remarked that, to J. Edgar Hoover, the Bureau was the "Seat of Government," and that the head office in Washington, D.C., was therefore referred to by agents as "SOG." Hoover regarded Presidents as transients passing through his administration. "Now to the average agent, after he'd been in fifteen or twenty years, there wasn't any government other than the Bureau. Kennedy couldn't have brought Hoover down, Johnson didn't bring 'im down, and Nixon didn't dare to bring him down—I don't think Nixon wanted to." He added, "Nobody dared cross him, he had built an impregnable dictatorship. It's still there today."

Because the primary mandate of the Bureau was to protect the Bureau's image, agents often were placed in humiliating situations to fulfill this mandate. An agent who had served in Atlanta recalled the plane crash at Orly Field in Paris, in which 130 prominent Atlanta citizens were killed.

The Bureau wanted to get a lot of good publicity out of that situation; they wanted to get in on the identification of the bodies and the French government didn't want to let them in. So we flew the identification crew from the Bureau over to France and then we had to go through Atlanta and collect pantyhose and shoes and bras and things like that and get the sizes from the various families.

Well, the families were all in mourning, and some of these mansion houses were under the control of lawyers, and we had to go through the lawyers in order to get permission to get in. Now this was pertinent information—you've got inheritance rights, was the person actually on the plane, or did they miss it—there was nothing wrong with collecting it.

But we kept having conferences—they had used all the agents in the office—and the conferences didn't concern solution of the case—they dealt with this guy who was the head of the identification unit, who wanted to get a promotion in the Bureau. He was an assistant director who wanted to be an associate director, and he needed this case to go to Hoover as a great publicity success. The only way it could be a great publicity success would be if the press and those involved in the investigation said it was.

So two days after the investigation was finished, we got a call from the Bureau, and this guy, back from France, called in all the Atlanta agents and said, "Gentlemen, I talked to [the assistant director], and he wants us to go back out to the families, and make under pretext some second contact or third contact with them, and subtly suggest to them that they write a letter to the FBI Director, thanking him for the FBI's part in solving this case."

They were still in mourning! And I walked out with some

agent, saying, "I'll be damned—I'm not going to cover those leads." I just didn't do it! And some of the other agents didn't do it. Most agents would do it, so that would be enough. Then they could satisfy the Bureau.

Now everyone knew what was going on. The telephone operator talked to me about how rotten it was that they'd ask us to do that sort of thing. Demoralization took place. That was a prelude to [the attempt at] bringing down Dr. King by taking stuff off the wiretap and feeding it to the press. It's all part of the same process. You would have to have a control system and restructure the organization so that the Orly crash incident wouldn't happen. So that a guy wouldn't dare do it!

Another agent reported that the FBI had its own kind of "dirty tricks" operation.

We had files—counterintelligence files where you had to periodically submit schemes for counterintelligence. I had a guy, working under me, to whom this intelligence file was assigned. He was thirty-nine years old—one of the wildest, drinkingest, women-running-around guys that I have ever known. He would come in the office half crocked nearly every morning.

The intelligence files came up for review every ninety days. So every ninety days he would say—and he used that awful language, he used to swear all the time—slam it down—"I'VE GOT TO WRITE ANOTHER SO-AND-SO!!" Then he'd come over to me a few minutes later and say, "Hey, give me some ideas." And I would get the steno, and out of the blue think of some kind of a scheme that would satisfy the Bureau. And we'd send it up as a proposal. Every ninety days you had to send something in telling them something dirty we were going to do, in order to accomplish the purpose of counterintelligence.

Any kind of scheme would do—it didn't make any difference. They were directed against the Klan as well as against blacks in civil rights, but mostly against blacks.

The Bureau had a penchant for forged letters, and for attacking people on the sex angle. Sex seemed to be—because they were all from the right wing, churchgoing moralists—they figured that's the way you blackmail somebody.

An agent remarked that this attitude was prevalent in areas other than the Bureau.

Nothing surprised me about Watergate—there were no surprises. Nor did it surprise my wife. She was privy enough to all that was going on in the Bureau. We watched the Watergate hearings and we said, "Why doesn't he ask this question? Why doesn't he ask that question?" And the reason they didn't ask the questions was evidenced by what Senator Baker said to McCord once.

He said to McCord, "What I'd like you to do now is go home"—it was Friday—"and think over the weekend what questions we should ask you." Baker could see that he didn't know enough about what was going on to know what kind of questions to ask. I wished to God I could talk to Baker.

They should have gotten some advice. But where could they go to be briefed? Anyone who filters up through the system, and particularly in the Bureau, and in the government generally, goes through this culturization process. By the time he gets to the top, it's very doubtful if his perceptions will be accurate—if he'll be able to see what's going on. He's up there because he wants promotions, he wants power, he's gone through the system, and he has compromised himself.

Murtagh told me a story to illustrate how far this "compromise" could extend.

We had jurisdiction in selective service matters, and a guy we'll call "Pedro" was arrested in Chicago and he didn't have a draft card with him. So the police turned him over to the FBI, and Chicago called Detroit, and they said, "Pedro says he's registered with Board 91 on Taylor Street in Detroit." So the supervisor made the phone call, and he made a mistake and didn't check the right board. There are four on Taylor Street and he checked three, not the one Pedro was registered at.

He told Chicago that the guy wasn't registered. Well, Pedro was of a minority, and this was before the *Miranda* warning, and Pedro was brought before a Federal District judge and asked if he was registered and he said, "Yes, I registered at Taylor Street," and some FBI agent testified, "No, he didn't," and they sent Pedro to jail for eighteen months.

The Bureau didn't find out about this until over two years after it happened. Pedro's number came up at Board 91, and they wanted to know where Pedro was, so they could induct him. They looked for him, and couldn't find him, so they turned the case over to the FBI—told them to find Pedro. They searched the indices and found that—Jesus, we put Pedro in jail for *not* being registered, now we're looking for him because he *was* registered. WE MADE A MISTAKE!

I was with a group of agents in the squad room when this one agent—a loudmouthed little guy whom no one liked—he certainly didn't measure up to my idea of what an agent is—came running into the room showing this to everyone. We all knew the supervisor had made a mistake. He had eight kids. He was going to get transferred.

Then there was a closed-door conference in the supervisor's office—something very unusual. Then this supervisor walks out, and walks into his supervisor's office. And then, nothing happens for another two years.

We hear no more about it until a guy—Charlie—was testifying—he was an accountant for the Bureau—testifying in Grand Rapids, in Federal District Court, and somebody said something derogatory or unfavorable to the Bureau or about the Bureau's investigation and Charlie didn't ask the prosecuting attorney for an opportunity to refute the testimony. It wasn't very important—at least he didn't think so. By the time he got back to the office he had been transferred, because this thing had hit the wire and had gotten to Hoover's office, and the Bureau had been criticized and this guy hadn't defended the Bureau. Hoover transferred him—by teletype. Charlie, normally very reflective, was absolutely beside himself, and he wasn't going to take the transfer.

He quit, took another job, there were lots of jobs at that time. The thing kept stewing at him all the time, "this goddamn Bureau is doing these things to people." We all knew about a lot of things—not as bad as Pedro's—but there were all kinds of coverups on a day-to-day basis. We spent more time covering things up, even in the fifties—a lot more time writing memos covering things up, creating the record—than investigating. It certainly was the more important part of the work.

Anyway, Charlie was bothered so much that he went to a priest, and out of the confessional told him this Pedro thing, and that the Bureau had covered it up. So the Catholic priest, as I got the story, went to Washington, and went to the Bureau. The Bureau, up to this time, knew nothing about Pedro. But the cat was out of the bag, and somebody else knew about Pedro. So the Bureau came to Detroit and the supervisor and his supervisor and the little guy who had found the truth were called into the boss's office. I know all the details of this because the little guy came to see me after he quit.

The boss said, "What's this story about Pedro?" My supervisor says, "Jeez, boss, I don't remember any case like that at all," and his supervisor says, "I don't remember any case like that," and the little guy says, "You lying sons of bitches, you told me to take that case and put all that information about the previous investigation in the details, and to put all the other stuff in the synopsis, and that the Bureau wouldn't catch it because they don't read the details, and that would cover it up." I saw the damn door close with the three of them in the room when it was being talked about!

The supervisor said to the little guy, "We never knew anything about that; you must have just slipped and not put it in the synopsis."

The boss ordered them to go down to the files to see if they could find it. So they started walking down into the files and the two guys were walking on either side of this little guy—his supervisor and his supervisor's supervisor. This little tiny guy, with bulging eyes and great big teeth, was telling them about the case, and they both turned to him and said, "Now, for Christ's sake, don't! We'll tell him we can't find it." Even at this late date they were still lying.

The little guy says, "What do you mean, we can't find it? The damn thing's down there! We talked about it!" The supervisor says, "We never talked about it!" They find the file and bring it back, and the two supervisors persist in stating that they know nothing about it at all.

So the little guy took out his credentials, and his badge and his gun, and threw them down in front of the boss, and said, "If I have to work with a bunch of lying bastards like this, guys, you can take this gun, and credentials, and badge, and do so-and-so with it!" And the boss says, "Well, don't get hot—you're entitled to have it checked out. Who do you know who can tell your side of the story?" The little guy said that he had told the guys in the squad room about it, and named five of us. I wasn't named, for some reason. All five named said they didn't know anything about it, they'd never heard of it. But we'd all discussed it, and we knew as much about that in the Detroit office as we did about the Kennedy killing.

So the little guy said to me later, "When I knew they were all going to lie, I figured—my brother-in-law has a sugar business in Charleston, and offered me a job with $500 more than I was getting in the Bureau, so I figured I was better off to get away from those lying bastards."

I offered to go to the office and write a memorandum and

bring it to the boss—this was back about '55 or '56—and blow the whistle on the whole goddamn thing. He said, "Nah, it wouldn't do any good. You can't fight that kind of system." He didn't want me to do it. He said, "I wouldn't take the job back from the Bureau even if they gave it to me." I said, "Okay, if you don't want to do it, we won't do anything about it."

Later, I walked into the office, and saw this one agent, one of the five named, alone there, and went up to him, and said, "Hi, how ya doing?" and he said, "Fine, how are you?" and I said, "Why in Christ's name did you and those other guys throw him to the wolves? He wasn't a nice guy, I didn't like him myself, but why would you lie, and let him get it?"

He said, "Well, the supervisor has eight kids. There's the moral basis. The supervisor couldn't afford the transfer and the little guy could."

And this takes us back to Watergate. Who outside of the Bureau would know the questions to ask? Even those inside the Bureau, asking questions, were not able to get the truth—if they wanted it.

They didn't ask the right questions because they're part of the system and they know which questions to ask, so that they can shape the story the way they want it to come out. That's the way it's done. That's the secret of the whole thing.

Chapter Twelve

ONE MAN
by Mark Lane

When he testified before Otis Pike's Select Committee on Intelligence, Arthur Murtagh wept as he told the Committee of his years of frustration and pain.

Although now retired and on a pension, Murtagh knows he could have retired at a higher grade with a larger pension if he had been more cooperative.

When Murtagh failed the weight program, he was transferred. He said,

They had methods worked out so that they could manipulate the transfers and they could kind of cushion the blow. What it amounted to was that the guys who were trying to enforce Hoover's rules had to deal with us because we had so much on them and the organization that they didn't dare fire us. They were afraid that we'd blow the whistle and the whole thing would blow up.

When I was transferred to Atlanta, I went in and told him "I got a royal rooking in Charlotte. My wife isn't going to move down here until spring, and I need to get on per diem where I can make extra money." He sent me off to Macon, Georgia, to stay for five months on nine dollars a day, which was a lot of money in those days. I got a room at the YMCA—the cheapest one I could get. And I stayed there; there was no work. I was an extra man on the totem pole—just somebody farmed out to cool off. You know, they figured I was madder than hell and if they left me there I'd cool down. They didn't dare fire anybody, because they might have to face the issues before a Civil Service board. They didn't want to be in a position where they'd have to answer for anything because they knew they were wrong in what they were doing. So I was in the YMCA in Macon, at seven dollars a week and

actually making money. There were five agents there. I'd go in, in the morning, and anything they didn't want to do, I'd do. But they didn't need me—I mean they could've gotten along without me. I stayed there five months and I read, I read everything that I could find about dictatorships. I read the life of Martin Luther, and his difficulties with the Pope. I was Catholic and I had gone to a Lutheran college in Pennsylvania. I just went to the library and got all that I could find of the dictators throughout history, from Genghis Khan down to Adolf Hitler. I read and read, about Catherine the Great, Frederick the Great, the Tudor Dynasties, and the French revolution. Authoritarian systems, and "Jesus," I said to myself, "Hoover read all this stuff. Or he knew about it." The Bureau was a medieval dictatorship. . . . This is the Justice Department of the United States. The Bureau is an integral part of the Justice Department, and yet it is autonomous—no controls, no influence over it, getting stronger and stronger, and the core, Mr. Hoover's people, zombies. There was never any thought of whether anything was right or wrong—if Hoover said it was right, it was right. He was becoming godlike to a lot of us, particularly the old timers.

I saw this as a very dangerous thing. I used to talk to my colleagues in Birmingham during the civil rights troubles, and say, "Look, there will be a Congressional investigation of the FBI and the whole house of cards will come down. This can't work in a democracy, the way he's trying to run it." And they would always say, "You're right, Art, but there's nothing we can do about it."

Everything in the Bureau was secondary to how one was going to survive as an agent. The work itself was secondary. The questions were always who was going to get clobbered; was somebody going to go to the press; were they going to blow the lid on the Bureau? We had to do our work, cover our leads. But the interests of the agents centered around—if the Bureau comes down, are my kids going to be able to hold their heads up at school?

In 1960 I made up my mind. I decided I'd stay in the Bureau and I'd get to retirement, but I wouldn't violate the law, and I wouldn't lie. That was a hard order to come by in the Bureau.

The other agents tolerated me—"Art's a nice guy, but he's crazy, you know, he won't roll with the punches, he calls the shots the way they are." I had one boss who told me, "Art, I have a lot of respect for your principles, but you have to decide"—this was in 1968—"whether to give up your principles or get out of the Bureau. There's no room in the Bureau for a man of principle."

These circumstances, through the years, got me to a point where, by the time I retired, I was just washed out. I wasn't healthy. I had an intestinal tumor that had probably been there as much as fifteen or twenty years, and it was never taken care of because I kept moving around all the time.

Because of the stand Murtagh took, he was never compelled to commit perjury.

I think it was a matter of policy. The Bureau thought nothing of lying to protect itself, the main tool by which Hoover controlled his seven thousand men. But it didn't work, and resulted in the ultimate downfall of the Bureau.

Why did I make that decision in 1960? Well, I have seven kids, and my education, even though I graduated from law school, is not such that I can go out and get a comparable job anywhere.

Here's another part of the Bureau structure: the public was told that the Bureau had lawyers and accountants, but they hired football players and bank tellers with B.A. degrees and night school attendees who worked in the Bureau as clerks and just barely got enough hours together to get a degree. The Bureau would then make an agent of them, and they'd jump from $7,500 a year to $18,000 in a matter of a few months; they had no hope of getting anything comparable to that on the outside, because they had no particular expertise that they could sell. Only 7 percent of the work force in the Bureau were lawyers and accountants.

Even though I was a part of that 7 percent, my family background made me Depression-oriented. I had a great lack of confidence in myself, in my ability to make it in life.

The Murtagh family had arrived from Ireland in 1841 and settled in the upper New York State area. The family had never been able to make money or get any real security. Murtagh was sickly as a child, and his development was very slow.

At fourteen years old, I only weighed seventy-two pounds. I had something wrong with my throat. Every winter I had tonsillitis three of four times. I'd sit in school and fall asleep. I was in the first grade for two years and the second grade for a year and a half.

When I got into the seventh grade my mother finally decided I was sick. This wasn't through ignorance; it was a lack of medical care and lack of money. We owed the doctor $86.00 through the Depression and I used to hear my mother and father talking about how they couldn't pay the doctor.

Finally I came home one Friday, while in the seventh grade, at noon. My mother counted around the table, and I wasn't there. One of the eight was gone. She came up, put her hand on my head and said, "My God, you've got a fever! It must be 106!" And then they called the doctor.

That was the first time I saw the doctor, that I could remember, in six or seven years. The doctor said he thought I had tuberculosis and would die. They took the tonsils out, and I bled for months.

Then I went back to school and in the seventh grade I put on weight and grew taller and began to be able to learn. I got to where I could read a little.

I couldn't read at all, before that; I couldn't even read the newspaper, and I was in the seventh grade. Once my aunt gave me a *Saturday Evening Post,* and it took me three days to read a four-page article about some American scientists that went to Russia.

Then I went to high school and had a sense of being intelligent. I did fairly well in high school. I was in the honor society and in areas where I didn't have to read—like math—I got straight A's. Then into college and the service, and out of the service into more college, and then law school. I finally got to be a very accurate reader, although very slow. But once I've read something, it's memorized.

All of my youthful problems affected me terribly; I was almost twenty-one when I finished high school. This can't be the sort of thing that builds confidence in a young man. By thirty I was a lawyer and admitted to the New York State Bar.

I went into the Bureau because I wasn't sure I could make it elsewhere. I also wanted to make some money—still Depression-oriented. I drive old cars—because I won't be in debt. I've never used credit of any kind. I've been frugal my whole life. All of this has something to do with my unwillingness to give up something that was sure financial security—the Bureau.

I knew what was wrong, and not to be corrected. Trying to correct it at the time, while I was in the Bureau, would have been hopeless and disastrous. So I waited.

When the Watergate break in first appeared in the news, Murtagh's first question to himself was "What part did the Bureau and Nixon have in it?"

Murtagh waited some more. "I had never criticized the Bureau publicly. But then the Senate Watergate hearings started and I watched them for about three days and I said this is it, the whole house of cards is coming down and I'm going to be there when it falls."

Murtagh wrote to *The New York Times* to offer what information he had, especially with regard to the illegal activities involved in the Martin Luther King investigation. A *Times* reporter went up to see Murtagh, who said, "that was the beginning of the world beating a pathway to my door. Two weeks don't pass before someone calls or comes to see me . . . sometimes there are two or three a week."

Murtagh's interest, as he consistently told all the media and the Pike Committee, was in a "complete restructuring" of the Bureau. "Without that, we'd just be treading water."

Murtagh wanted to be sure that the abuses of the enforcement and intelligence agencies were made public.

Unless the younger generation learns about this, they're going to forget, and think they can wash it all clean with Mr. Clean. We could put Jesus Christ at the top of the Bureau and he could not change it unless the structure is changed.

Those who have to carry out the dirty work, Murtagh said, are the ones who need an opportunity to speak out. "Who knows about wrong-doing in government? Is it the guys at the top, or is it the clerks and secretaries at the bottom? Who knew that there was a wiretap on King? Who typed some of the memos? Some of the stenos and clerks came to me at different times—they knew that the system was rotten."

Murtagh felt that a thorough reconstruction of the Bureau would achieve what the Bureau had promised its recruits:

A due process system would work—it would be fair and better than secrecy, and the resulting image would make them proud to have their kids go to school and say they were an FBI agent's child.

Chapter Thirteen

THE OBSESSION
by Mark Lane

The United States Senate, through its Select Committee to study Governmental Operations with respect to Intelligence Activities (popularly known as the Church Committee) concluded in its final report:

> **The Committee finds that covert action programs have been used to disrupt the lawful political activities of individual Americans and groups and to discredit them, using dangerous and degrading tactics which are abhorrent in a free and decent society. . . . The sustained use of such tactics by the FBI in an attempt to destroy Dr. Martin Luther King, Jr., violated the law and fundamental human decency.**

The Senate Committee which issued the report represented the disparate philosophies and politics found within the Senate. Among the members of the Select Committee were liberals such as its Chairman, Frank Church, Walter F. Mondale, moderates such as Howard Baker, and conservatives such as its Vice Chairman, John G. Tower, and Barry Goldwater.

The chilling language of the Committee report is underscored by the refusal of the FBI to make available to the Select Committee evidence regarding its most extreme programs to destroy Dr. King.

For example, the Committee learned that Hoover's pathological obsession with Dr. King was so grand that even after Dr. King was murdered the FBI continued its attempts to discredit him and his widow, Coretta King. During March 1969, the Congress was considering a resolution to declare Dr. King's birthday a national holiday. The Crime Records Division of the FBI recommended briefing members of the relevant Committee of Congress considering the resolution because "they were in a position to keep the bill from being reported out of Committee" if "they realize King was a scoundrel." Assistant FBI Director Cartha De Loach wrote, "This is a delicate matter—but can be handled very cautiously." Hoover wrote back, "I agree. It must be handled *very cautiously.*"

The following month the Atlanta Field Office submitted a recommendation for a counterintelligence program "in the event the Bureau is inclined to entertain counterintelligence action against Coretta Scott King and/or the continuous projection of the public image of Martin Luther King." Hoover evidently had determined that the time was not right for the suggested action against Mrs. King or Dr. King's memory. He therefore informed the Atlanta office that "the Bureau does not desire counterintelligence action against Coretta King of the nature you suggest at this time." The Select Committee was unable to secure any information about the nature of the proposed program because the FBI, which ostensibly it was investigating, decided not to share the evidence with the members of the Senate Committee. The Select Committee reported only "the nature of the proposed program has not been revealed to the Committee."

On November 18, 1975, Frederick A. O. Schwarz, Jr., chief counsel, and Curtis R. Smothers, minority counsel of the Church Committee, testified before the Committee regarding the results of their investigation. In questioning them, Senator Mondale summarized the evidence "and the tactics they [the FBI] used [against Dr. King] apparently had no end." He then made specific reference to the methods employed by Hoover and his associates against King. "They included wiretapping. They included microphonic surveillance of hotel rooms. They included informants. They included sponsoring of letters signed by phony names to relatives and friends and organizers. They involved even plans to replace him with someone else whom the FBI was to select as a national civil rights leader." The record reveals that, as Mondale continued, counsel confirmed the accuracy of his summary, on occasion offering additional information.

> **Senator Mondale: It also included an indirect attempt to persuade the Pope not to see him [King].**
>
> **Mr. Schwarz: And many other people.**
>
> **Senator Mondale: It directed him [an FBI employee] to persuade one of our major universities not to grant him [King] a doctorate degree.**
>
> **Mr. Schwarz: That is correct. I think there were two universities.**
>
> **Senator Mondale: It included an attempt to send him a letter prior to the time he received the Nobel Peace Prize, which Dr. Martin Luther King and close associates interpreted to mean a suggestion that King should attempt suicide.**

Mr. Schwarz: That's right. Included in that were materials which the Bureau had gathered illegally or improperly through tapes and bugs and so forth.

Mondale then responded to his partial accounting of the evidence: "I must conclude that apart from direct physical violence and apart from illegal incarceration, there is nothing in this case that distinguishes that particular action much from what the KGB does with dissenters in that country. I think it is a road map to the destruction of American democracy."

Hoover began to travel that road regarding Dr. King during February 1962. The Church Committee said that it could not determine if "Hoover's animosity toward Dr. King" influenced the FBI's decision to initiate a "COMINFIL" (Communist infiltration) investigation of him "without full access to the Bureau's files." Again, the FBI had decided not to share the evidence with the Senate Committee authorized to investigate it. In January 1962, the Southern Regional Council released a report which was critical of the failure of the FBI to take action during civil rights demonstrations in Albany, Georgia. The report was updated and issued in November 1962. Press reports about the document were forwarded to the FBI office in Washington, D.C. FBI regulations seemed to require that the specific allegations in the report be examined. The Bureau rules provided that allegations about FBI misconduct had to be investigated and that "every logical lead which will establish the true facts should be completely run out unless such action would embarrass the Bureau." The FBI's determination to secure, as the Bureau so oddly put it, "true facts" appeared to be tempered by a Catch-22 clause. How could an honest investigation of a valid charge of FBI misconduct not embarrass the Bureau? In this instance the conundrum was avoided as the FBI decided to conduct no investigation of the charges, to describe the report as "slanted and biased" even before the full report was received, and to begin an investigation of its author instead.

Soon after the report was issued, Dr. King was quoted in the press as having said that he agreed with the conclusions in the report and that the FBI had failed to adequately investigate civil rights violations in Albany. He said:

One of the great problems we face with the FBI in the South is that the agents are white Southerners who have been influenced by the mores of the community. To maintain their status, they have to be friendly with the local police and people who are promoting segregation.

Every time I saw FBI men in Albany, they were with the local police force.

The SAC of the Atlanta FBI office immediately notified headquarters about those remarks. The FBI concluded that Dr. King's comments "would appear to dovetail with information" the Bureau knew of "indicating that King's advisors are Communist Party (CP) members and that he is under the domination of the CP." To Hoover and his associates any criticism of the FBI was proof that a critic was a Communist. The Bureau officials decided to meet with Dr. King in order to "set him straight." After considerable thought was given as to who should contact King it was decided that he should be contacted by both Assistant FBI Director William Sullivan and Assistant FBI Director Cartha De Loach "in order that there be a witness and there can be no charge of provincialism inasmuch as Cartha De Loach comes from the South and Mr. Sullivan comes from the North." Two telephone calls were made to the busy and often hectic office of the SCLC in Atlanta. King was not in on either occasion and when he failed to return the calls De Loach wrote:

It would appear obvious that Rev. King does not desire to be told the true facts. He obviously used deceit, lies, and treachery as propaganda to further his own cause. . . . I see no further need to contacting Rev. King as he obviously does not desire to be given the truth. The fact that he is a vicious liar is amply demonstrated in the fact he constantly associates with and takes instructions from [a] . . . member of the Communist Party.

While the FBI officials were upset when Dr. King criticized them, they became enraged when he ignored them. William Sullivan was the head of the Domestic Intelligence Division during the harassment of Dr. King. He later testified that Hoover "was very upset about the criticism that King made publicly about our failure to protect the Negro in the South against violations of the Negro civil liberties" and that "I think behind it all was the racial bias, the dislike of Negroes, the dislike of the civil rights movement."

Hoover detested criticism, blacks, and movements for change. Dr. King epitomized all that threatened Hoover's tenuous hold on reality. The FBI's unholy war against Dr. King was on. Before it ended Dr. King would lie dead on a motel balcony in Memphis.

In May 1962, the FBI included Dr. King's name on "Section A of the Reserve Index" as a person to be rounded up and imprisoned in the event of a national emergency.

During October 1962, the FBI began an investigation of the Southern

Christian Leadership Conference (SCLC) and of its president, Dr. King. The FBI conducted the investigation under a provision in its manual captioned COMINFIL—an acronym for Communist Infiltration. That provision authorized investigations into "Legitimate Noncommunist Organizations that are Communist Infiltrated" in order to determine the extent of the alleged Communist influence. If the FBI excesses visited upon Dr. King and his associates were a road map to the destruction of democracy, the assumption that the government, through its federal police, had the right to examine, through methods legal or illegal, the constitutionally protected exercises of citizens constitutes the compass that pointed the way. Yet it was that basic assumption that Hoover shared with President John F. Kennedy, Attorney General Robert F. Kennedy, President Lyndon B. Johnson, and others in positions of influence including Burke Marshall, Nicholas Katzenbach, and Byron R. White. The wide-ranging investigations into the SCLC and of Dr. King were conducted with the knowledge of the Attorney General in 1962. The investigation which was largely carried out through the illegal use of electronic surveillance and through the use of informants was predicated upon the suspicion that one of Dr. King's advisers was a Communist. Fourteen years after the investigation began Burke Marshall, the Assistant Attorney General for Civil Rights from 1961–65, testified that he "never had any reason to doubt [the FBI's] allegation concerning" the adviser. He added that the charges against the adviser were "grave and serious."

After Hoover and Attorney General Robert F. Kennedy conferred, President Kennedy decided to send Marshall to meet with Dr. King and urge him to disassociate from his adviser. Marshall did meet with Dr. King and Andrew Young. When Young later testified before the Church Committee he said that Marshall said at the meeting that the FBI had informed the Justice Department that there was in fact Communist influence in the civil rights movement and had explicitly mentioned the adviser. When Young asked Marshall for proof that the adviser was a Communist he said that he had none, and that he "couldn't get anything out of the Bureau."

Proof was still lacking thirteen years later. The Church Committee concluded that it was shown no evidence that demonstrated that the adviser was a member of the Communist Party at any time during the entire FBI COMINFIL investigation. The failures of the Church Committee were numerous. It failed to secure what were likely the most relevant and illuminating FBI documents; it failed to publish many of the documents that it did receive with the exception of a few excerpts; it failed to publish the testimony of those who appeared before it. Yet perhaps its greatest failure was its reluctance to challenge the concept that the government has the right, indeed the obligation, to monitor the lawfully protected actions of the people.

Burke Marshall occupied a position in the Justice Department which imposed upon him the primary responsibility for the administration of equal justice to those struggling for equal rights. Dr. King and his associates felt that it was to Marshall that they must look for protection against those violently committed to segregation. They saw Marshall and the two Kennedys as a bulwark against the excesses of the local police and the Hoover regime. In the end it appeared that both the Kennedy and Johnson Administrations shared with Hoover the belief that the government had the duty to determine which private citizens could give lawful advice to other private citizens. Starting from that premise, which contemplates governmental intrusion into private sectors of life, all that remained to be determined were the methods to be utilized and the extent of the intrusions.

The most sensitive survivors of the Kennedy and Johnson Administrations shrink when they are informed of the details of the war that Hoover launched against Dr. King. Sensitive as they are and as appalled as they may be when they hear of the atrocities in the trenches, the singularly important fact that emerges from the investigation by the Church Committee is the inescapable conclusion that they, the technicians in the Kennedy and Johnson administrations, had declared war against Dr. King.

The Church Committee wrote:

The extent to which Government officials outside of the FBI must bear responsibility for the FBI's campaign to discredit Dr. King is not clear. Government officials outside of the FBI were not aware of most of the specific FBI actions to discredit Dr. King. Officials in the Justice Department and White House were aware, however, of the investigation, of Dr. King; that the FBI had written authorization from the Attorney General to wiretap Dr. King and the SCLC offices in New York and Washington; and that the FBI reports on Dr. King contained considerable information of a political and personal nature which was "irrelevant and spurious" to the stated reasons for the investigation. Those high executive branch officials were also aware that the FBI was disseminating vicious characterizations of Dr. King within the Government; that the FBI had tape recordings embarrassing to Dr. King which it had offered to play to a White House official and to reporters; and that the FBI had

offered to "leak" to reporters highly damaging accusations that some of Dr. King's advisers were communists. Although some of those officials did ask top FBI officials about these charges, they did not inquire further after receiving false denials. In light of what those officials did know about the FBI's conduct toward Dr. King, they were remiss in failing to take appropriate steps to curb the Bureau's behavior. To the extent that their neglect permitted the Bureau's activities to go on unchecked, those officials must share responsibility for what occurred.

Perhaps the ultimate irony is found in the evaluation of that period by the FBI. Testifying for the Bureau in an appearance before the Church Committee, the Deputy Associate Director, James Adams, said, "I see no statutory basis or no basis of justification for the activity. . .as far as the activities which you are asking about, the discrediting, I know of no basis for that and I will not attempt to justify it."

Yet at the time the unjustified and illegal programs were not challenged. FBI Assistant Director William C. Sullivan testified that he "never heard anyone raise the question of legality or constitutionality, never." Sullivan was in charge of the program.

He told the Church Committee:

No holds were barred. We have used [similar] techniques against Soviet agents. [The same methods were] brought home against any organization against which we were targeted. We did not differentiate. This is a rough, tough business.

He also said:

This is a common practice, rough, tough, dirty business. Whether or not we should be in it or not, that is for you folks to decide. We are in it. To repeat, it is a rough, tough, dirty business, and dangerous. It was dangerous at times—that is, dangerous to the persons who are being affected, not to the Bureau persons—when you are trying to disrupt someone's family life. It was dangerous at times, no holds were barred. We have used that technique against foreign espionage agents, and they have used it against us.

The FBI, employing almost every intelligence-gathering technique in its arsenal, collected information about Dr. King, his family, his activities, his plans and his associates.

During September 1963, the FBI conducted a survey of Dr. King's home and the New York office of the SCLC. On October 7, Hoover requested permission from Attorney General Robert Kennedy for a wiretap "on King at his current address or at any future address to which he may move" and "on the SCLC office at the current New York address or to any other address to which it may be moved." On October 10, Kennedy signed the request and on October 21 he also approved Hoover's request to wiretap the SCLC's Atlanta office. In making his application to Kennedy, Hoover did not allege that any criminal conduct might be uncovered. He cited only the "possible Communist influence in the racial situation." Predictably Hoover interpreted the Attorney General's permission to wiretap King "at any future address" broadly and therefore placed wiretaps on telephones in hotel and motel rooms where King stayed and on the telephones of friends with whom he stayed temporarily. Telephones in the homes and offices of Dr. King's advisers were also wiretapped. In addition to wiretapping, the FBI placed concealed microphones in Dr. King's motel and hotel rooms in an "attempt" to obtain information about the private activities of King and his advisers for use to "completely discredit" them.

Tape recordings made on these occasions were "improved" at the FBI electronics laboratory and then played for friendly reporters. This technique was employed in an effort to develop "friendly" news sources which would publish derogatory information about Dr. King and to discourage objective reporters from writing fair stories about him.

On a personal note I might add that similar techniques were utilized against me by the FBI as I looked into the assassinations. FBI agents have made similarly "improved" and fabricated material available to contacts in the news media, to members of Congress, and to the late President Lyndon B. Johnson.

The Church Committee, through the efforts of Senator Richard Schweiker, discovered through the questioning of James Adams that in 1966, just after *Rush to Judgment* was published, a request was made by the White House for "personal data information and dossiers," on seven Warren Commission critics. Adams admitted that the request was not a normal one, since it bypassed the Attorney General. Adams explained:

This is not a normal procedure. It is not the procedure followed today. There was a period of time where, at the President's directions, Mr. Hoover reported more directly to him in certain areas, and it was apparently a feeling that he did not want the Attorney General to know certain things.

Adams agreed, when specifically asked by Sen. Schweiker, that a dossier did include documents regarding the sexual activities of a critic.

Schweiker understood that the technique employed by the FBI against Dr. King and his associates was also used against Warren Commission critics. He said:

I think what concerns the committee is that whenever you get to the nitty-gritty of investigations—and it doesn't relate to the Warren Commission, I will leave that alone—we get back to something like a photograph or a tape recording or some letter referring to some kind of human weakness or failing that is really very irrelevant to the investigation, is sandwiched in here. It just seems to me that it was a tactic. This just happens to be the Warren Commission I singled out, but it was a tactic that was used rather frequently as a lever, or for reasons which I am trying to discover, as an instrument of investigative policy. Would you differ with that or dispute that? What rationale would you use? Do we use sexual activities as a standard criterion for investigations?

Schweiker added:

And my question is, how is that relevant to being a critic of the Warren Commission? What standard do we use when we just pass photographs of sexual activities to the White House? Is this a normal proceeding when a dossier is requested? Is this normally included, or did they specifically request photographs of this kind, or what light can you shed on this?

And the FBI's Deputy Associate Director replied:

I can't shed much. I know they requested information on him. I think there was other material concerning that individual of a security nature that was included. Why the information in that respect was submitted I am unable to answer. I do know at the time there was a lot of concern following the Warren Commission report. Had all the answers been explored? Was the Soviet Union involved? Was Cuba involved? And who were the critics who now are attacking this? But I have seen nothing which would explain the rationale for requesting the material.

When Schweiker asked, "What other purpose would a photograph of this nature have, other than to discredit critics?" Adams replied, "I can't answer that."

I have explored this rather personal area at some length because unhappily it does not belong to the past alone. Even as I worked on this book during the closing days of 1976, the documents referred to by

Senator Schweiker were being circulated among members of the Washington press corps, primarily to "friendly" FBI news sources and to various members of the Congress. The purpose—to discourage the Congress from responding to the call for a thorough inquiry into the murders of Dr. King and President Kennedy by attempting to discredit a man who issued that call.

Thus the techniques used by the FBI to discredit Dr. King during his life were being used to discredit those who wish to learn about his death.

A microphone concealed in a hotel where King stayed picked up sounds of a party at which he was present. According to the Department of Justice, the tape recording indicated sexual activity. The problem with the tape, it has been conceded, is that it did not really relate King to the sexual activity and one could barely hear King's voice. Hoover and his friend Clyde Tolson decided to send the tape to Coretta King in an effort to cause the family to break up. William Sullivan testified that the tape was intended to precipitate a separation between Dr. King and his wife in the belief that the separation would reduce his stature.

Hoover ordered the FBI laboratory to "improve" or doctor the tapes so that Dr. King's voice could be clearly heard in a context that would prove embarrassing. The tape was then sanitized, that is, all fingerprints were removed from it. It was placed in a package which was also sanitized and then mailed to the SCLC. Hoover ordered that the tape be mailed "from a Southern state." Accordingly, an FBI agent flew to Florida with the small package, mailed it and then flew home. Hoover evidently reasoned that King would be emotionally weakened from the confrontation with his wife and the impending separation. He therefore ordered that a letter be sent to Dr. King, a letter that Dr. King and his advisers interpreted to mean that he would be publicly exposed if he did not commit suicide within the next thirty-four days. The letter was dispatched thirty-four days before Dr. King was scheduled to receive the Nobel Prize.

Hoover's conceived plot was seriously flawed. It was white-oriented and bureaucratically programmed. It certainly did not contemplate the problems and strengths of the civil rights movement. Hoover, Tolson, and Sullivan, for all their intelligence-gathering devices and their techniques and equipment for surveillance, had not even begun to understand the pace and priorities of the movement. Hoover knew that a personal tape addressed to him would be on his desk and analyzed shortly after its arrival.

The arrival of a tape at the Atlanta office of the SCLC was not a signal event. Tapes came in all the time. The SCLC was collecting tape recordings of Dr. King's speeches. This one took its place near the bottom of a substantial pile of tapes, packages, and letters. Eventually the tape was listened to. Coretta King heard it as did Dr. King. He read the letter as well. The sanitizing had removed FBI fingerprints, the old typewriter that had been used could not be traced, and the postmark read Florida, not Washington, D.C. However, to Dr. King the origin was clear. This ultimate scurrilous action—including what he believed (and many others have since come to believe) was a clear suggestion that he kill himself —could have come, he reasoned, only from J. Edgar Hoover.

The following day Dr. King met with Ralph Abernathy and Andrew Young. He had the tape played for them. Sadly, King said that he then knew that he could never again trust the FBI to protect him.

Chapter Fourteen

THE DESTROY
KING SQUAD
by Mark Lane

who   *what*   *why*

J. Edgar Hoover's attitude toward civil rights activitists was evident
from the first. FBI Special Agent Arthur Murtagh had served in Georgia
in the early sixties. He told me that the ways the Bureau had chosen to deal
with this delicate and potentially dangerous matter were hardly satisfactory:

> **This was in Albany, Georgia, in the early sixties, during dem-**
> **onstrations. I observed, in court, Dr. King, and Asa Kelly, the**
> **mayor, and the Judge—a Federal District judge whom I had**
> **investigated for the job—the mayor, the judge and I were the**
> **only white people in the crowded courtroom. Constance Motley,**
> **now a District Judge in New York, represented Dr. King.**

King and the city of Albany were seeking cross-injunctions against
one another. FBI agents were dispatched from Atlanta to Albany to
investigate the demonstrations.

> **The personnel situation at Albany was unbelievable. We had a**
> **guy at the office nicknamed RN. . . . He was a Special Agent in**
> **Charge (SAC). RN was forty-five years old then. He had come up**
> **in the Bureau when it expanded from 600 to 6,000. He was not**
> **excessively bright.**
>
> **Nobody had any respect for RN. He got interested in women**
> **when he hit the big salary, just about the time we hit Albany,**
> **Georgia. . . . If this had gotten to the Bureau, it would have**
> **resulted in forty or fifty agents being transferred from Atlanta.**
>
> **His behavior could have been reported. But it wasn't—the**
> **personnel structure of the Bureau was so decayed that an agent**
> **could challenge a supervisor with, "You can't do it to me—the**
> **consequences are too severe!"**

RN was SAC of the task force that went down to Albany. Another character in this story is nicknamed SF, the local agent in charge, in the field, what we call a resident agent. There was another local agent also, but he didn't count for anything—this Albany agent was second in command to RN when he came down. There were five agents in Albany when this case went to court, and RN and SF were pitted against the other three agents. They hated each other vehemently. . . . Some of it was religious-oriented. They couldn't stand being in the same rooms together, the three and the two.

The two brought down to Albany forty agents, and set up an office in the Holiday Inn, collecting information on the King demonstrations.

SF called the shots. He was better equipped to be the Grand Cyclops of the Ku Klux Klan. When he met me at the office, he said, "You want to be careful here. I just talked to my wife, and I told her not to come downtown. Be sure to keep all the doors locked. We've got an explosive situation—just don't take any chances, whatever you do. You can't tell how long it'll be before this thing blows sky high!" I went out later to find out what he was talking about—one hundred bedraggled, beaten-down blacks, surrounded by about four hundred policemen, who were marching around the block once or twice a day in protest against not being able to use the library.

SF controlled the Bureau's response to these activities. The civil rights cases in the Bureau, including police brutality cases, went through the office with special handling. They were even on different colored paper—green.

An agent familiar with this procedure explained, "The Bureau handled civil rights cases by collecting information and turning it over to the Civil Rights Division of the Justice Department in a type of preliminary communication." Agents were not empowered to interview, in a police brutality case, the sheriff, the officer, or the victim until the Bureau responded to the preliminary communication and ordered the interview. The Bureau's response was always very specific, naming those to be interviewed, and ordering that the agent inform the interviewer that the investigation had been ordered by a particular Assistant Attorney General, head of the Criminal Justice Division of the Department of Justice.

"The reason we told them that was because Hoover didn't want to be connected with any civil rights investigations," Murtagh said.

This was the only time when we told anyone that the Justice Department was ordering us to conduct an investigation. In any other kind of case, the Bureau would be glad to take credit—shipping, interstate commerce—we'd let someone know we were saving their ship or their trucks.

Hoover wanted to minimize the responsibility of the Bureau for civil rights. His way of doing it was to have guys like SF in key positions throughout the states. He didn't have to pick them and put them there—the system caused them to gravitate there. His type was a racist who didn't want any part of civil rights, and wouldn't ask the right questions.

Arthur Murtagh added,

The whole thing was structured so that we weren't going to scratch the surface on the civil rights cases, unless we were forced into it as we were in Philadelphia. Bobby Kennedy had, at that time—it was unheard of—a bunch of bearded assistants, who would go out to interview the blacks who had sent in civil rights complaints, and they would ask them what had happened. They would get a different story from the one we were giving on the green sheets at the Bureau.

King got word of this, and three or four blacks told me, and other agents, this—they were terrified of SF. He was a good guy to sit down with and talk to—as long as you were white—but he instructed all the new men who came to Albany not to shake hands with any black people—he said, "We don't do that down here!"

The situation was getting quite active—the Klan was shooting into houses at night, and burning churches. SF was manipulating the civil rights investigation. Dr. King called a news conference and said that the FBI wasn't doing its job.

Well, I was there, and I know that the FBI wasn't doing its job—it didn't surprise me; and I don't suppose that it surprised the Bureau—but that was the beginning of the vendetta against King. From that time on, the concentration of effort against King was greater than any other single investigation that I saw take place at the Bureau and I saw a lot of them in twenty years. There was a crew of people who did almost nothing for a period of seven or eight years, except investigate King and try to destroy him.

Murtagh said that while the anti-King effort came mostly out of the Atlanta office, it also came out of the New York and Washington field offices, and "some other" offices had a part in it.

90

It was an organized vendetta. They were going to get King in one way or another.

At first, it was difficult for Murtagh and other agents to perceive the anti-King effort as a personal one: "I thought that it was just that the Bureau was anti-civil rights and that King represented the movement.

I knew enough about the phony Communist domination theory on King to know that it had no validity. In fact, the whole Communist scare, even through the fifties, fell flat on its face because it didn't have any substance. I don't mean that there weren't some Communists, but they never were in a position to do us internal harm of any significance, and most agents that knew what was going on would agree with that.

Murtagh saw a shift from efforts against Roy Wilkins, Whitney Young, James Farmer, Stokely Carmichael, H. "Rap" Brown, and Huey Newton, to an intense concentration on King. "The Bureau was even considering trying to substitute a leader that they could control. I saw many memoranda on this—they were going to try to take over the movement and direct it from the Bureau. But they couldn't get to first base," Murtagh said.

Murtagh worked with two men in the Atlanta office who were in charge of the wiretaps on Dr. King.

There was Al Santinella and Bob Nichols. I liked them both—and I could never agree, but we were gentlemanly and pleasant with one another. Al I had a lot of respect for. A quiet guy, with little to say—but I could tell from the little bit he did say, that he was anti-King in the early sixties, and by the time the whole thing was over, he felt that the Bureau [performance] was a travesty, that they shouldn't have taken King in. He told me, years later, that he didn't think the Bureau had any substantive grounds for the wiretap on King, and that he was satisfied that King wasn't involved in any Communist movement, which could have justified the wiretap. And I think that he never approved of the peddling of the information, to the media, from the wiretap, which in fact was a clear violation of the law. I think he would not have done it by himself.

The Bureau maintained a two-bedroom apartment in the Peach Street Towers in Atlanta, close to the office, where the wiretap surveillance on King was conducted. "In that apartment, one of the rooms had panels; the whole room was filled with wiretap equipment. They had a man there all the time, twenty-four hours a day, monitoring the equipment and recording things he thought were pertinent," Murtagh said.

**This was all about King. They wrote down every word that
transpired over the King telephone, and identified all of the
people involved. It was estimated one time that there were five or
six thousand people that the wiretap actually got information
on—people that called him. My own doctor was in that file.**

**My doctor, a white man, was active in the King movement.
He and his wife were both graduates of Harvard Medical School.
We were neighbors and good friends.**

**I found his name when going through the wiretap files one
time—all of it was longhand notes. There was a string of file
cabinets twenty or more feet long, starting with Day One in the
wiretap, and every single communication that took place. This
was a form—the number called from, the number of the person
who answered. Identity of the person; what was said. And so on.
The files were in a special room, the room I worked in for eleven
years.**

Murtagh's squad was not just criminal or intelligence, but a hash of
both. "We called it the security squad. We handled racial matters,
applicant investigations, even antitrust. Very bluntly—I hate to say
this—the more intelligent, better-educated would be apt to be on this
squad. If there was an investigation where one had to talk to bankers
—they would need someone who could handle that kind of work, someone smooth. The ex-ball player would go in the bank robbery squad."

Wiretaps, when conducted legally, are performed at the order of an
appropriate judge or official, after a showing of probable cause. The use
of information received from wiretaps as evidence is so restricted and
subject to challenge by a good defense attorney that it often seems hardly
worth it. Murtagh said that the justification for the wiretap on King was
based on an investigation that had been conducted before the wiretap was
begun.

You'd have to have a whole staff to investigate just that area.

**I think this happened. Bobby Kennedy was Attorney General
and he signed the order permitting the wiretap. There were
agents, oriented to the right, who investigated King in New York
and found a lawyer working with him. . . . [The lawyer] had
had a flirtation with the Communist Party back in the late forties.
He'd been to meetings and worked with the CP in New York, so
you would say that he was connected with it and at that time
probably subscribed to some of the CP concepts.**

Whether [the lawyer] changed his view is neither here nor there. I don't think he had that much influence over Dr. King—and the things that he encouraged, King had a perfect right legally to do, and had nothing to do with Communist domination or influence. To be a dangerous Communist, you'd have to steal government secrets and feed them to the Russians.

But if you encourage a bus boycott in Montgomery, is that Communist or not? It may cause riots and riots are associated with Communist activity. Discord in the community is an opportunity for the Communists to take over. That may be true, part of the Communist doctrine and tactics.

But labor unions demonstrate also, and there could be a riot—it depends on who pushes first, who shoots first.

I never saw anything to indicate that King was influenced to create riots. Whether what was in King's mind was also in [the lawyer's] mind when they decided to demonstrate, I don't know.

Remember in Birmingham, when the Catholic priests begged King not to demonstrate, that it would create chaos? I could see that it would create chaos. But I couldn't see any other way, how the situation in Birmingham would change without chaos. As long as demonstrations were prevented in Birmingham, the segregationists could not be broken. If the segregationists started to riot, then they were the "Communists," as far as I was concerned

I saw it that way, and so did a few agents. But most of the agents, in the early sixties, figured this to be Communist rabble-rousing.

The Bureau carefully refrained from instructing its agents on any of King's or the Southern Christian Leadership Conference's ideology. It preferred instead to place a convenient label on that behavior. King achieved a melding, peculiarly for the American people, of Christian principles and Gandhian demonstrations of nonviolent civil disobedience. He knew, through long years of study and prayer, exactly what his ideals were and their sources; and he used this blend to force the Constitution to come alive.

This thrilling revitalization and its origins were treated by the Bureau with the deepest ignorance. One agent assigned to listen to King's conversations commented, after listening to King and . . . [the lawyer] that King had "stood fast" against a suggestion by . . . [the lawyer] that

King rehire a SCLC aide he had fired for unsavory political connections. The agent was so impressed with King's obvious dominance that he taped the conversation and took it home, and played it for his agent friends.

"This guy was an ex-football player with no real politics," a friend of his said. "He said, 'I'd always thought that King was just a dumb nigger, couldn't write a speech, couldn't make up his own mind. But he stood fast on all counts!' " His friend added, "The ball player's racism was so pervasive that he couldn't conceive of an intellectual being black. He wouldn't listen to his speeches. He shut them off when King was on the radio."

Of course, agents had to attend King's speeches; his movements were covered at all times. "But they wouldn't listen to the speeches; they thought they'd been written by someone else," said Arthur Murtagh.

Lively debate ensued between those agents willing to discuss Dr. King. Murtagh said, "One of the agents and I had a sparring match about King's alleged flirtation with Communism and what it meant, and the agent felt, at first, that King was some kind of a devil. There was a code name for King—Zorro." Zorro, the Spanish word for *fox,* was a legendary masked figure in the Spanish Old West, popularized by a television program of the late fifties; a nobleman in disguise, he was a political Robin Hood.

"Zorro" was followed and spied upon constantly, and concerted efforts were made to humiliate King. Murtagh related how his own doctor had been involved:

> **The wiretap had been on for a long time. King had been awarded the Nobel Prize, and a banquet was planned for King, to be in Atlanta, to which world dignitaries would be invited, thousands of people. It would be a testimonial.**
>
> **Bill Sullivan, an Assistant Director of the Bureau, from Hoover's office, came into the Atlanta office and called a field conference for security. I never heard of a field conference for security. The Bureau always has the agents go back to the Bureau—even from the West Coast. They don't send Assistant Directors out to the field—they bring the troops in.**
>
> **So they were coming to Atlanta to have a field conference on security, and they had one. But none of the security agents met Sullivan. There was no meeting. There was no discussion.**
>
> **I walked into the squad room in the morning and the agent came out of the meeting room and said, "They're going to get Zorro now! Sullivan's in there and we're really going to get him!"**

Sullivan was in there with the supervisor we called Colonel Klink, which was the best characterization we could give him; when he came out, because he was so much a Colonel Klink, he couldn't resist telling me how he was hobnobbing with the big shots. "I'm going out with Sullivan," he said. "We're gonna fix King this time."

I went out, and went about my work, and came back in, and Klink was back, saying, "We really laid it on."

Klink told Murtagh that he hadn't gone in with Sullivan to see Ralph McGill, editor of the Atlanta *Constitution*, a highly respected newspaper, but that Sullivan had been "closeted with McGill for an hour and a half."

"I don't think you'll find McGill giving King any favorable treatment from now on," said Klink to Murtagh.

A week later, Murtagh went to see his doctor. The doctor said, "Art, I'm glad you came in. I wanted to ask you something."

The doctor had accompanied the Archbishop of Atlanta to the Vatican II conference in Rome because the Archbishop was very ill. He died soon after at the age of forty-nine.

The doctor told Murtagh, "I went in to see the Archbishop a few days ago, and he was in bed, and he asked me why two FBI men from Washington would come to see him, and try to dissuade him from making a speech—the main testimonial speech for Dr. King at the banquet."

The doctor said that he didn't know why, and the Archbishop said they told him that there was going to be an exposé of King that would embarrass the Church if they had anything to do with him. He had better withdraw his support of King.

"Also," Murtagh continued, "the chief rabbi of Atlanta called the Archbishop, and said that two men from the Bureau in Washington had come to see him."

The Archbishop responded, "I respect Dr. King's public position on race, and I think he is a great leader in that area, and I intend to go ahead with the speech."

Murtagh supposed that Sullivan and Colonel Klink told prominent citizens and the press that they had something devastating on King —something, perhaps, from the wiretap. "I think they were clever enough. Divulging the material would be a crime. They probably merely made implications."

Although Murtagh was assigned to the King investigation, he did not work on the wiretap. "I told Klink I wouldn't do it. I thought the damn thing was illegal. And I knew the bastards were using it illegally. One time King was in a house and they called the fire department on him.

Reported a fire in the house, to harass him. All child's play. They mailed him things—a tape to his wife."

The bugging of King was so constant that his hotel rooms were bugged in advance of his arrival, and an agent said, "He was even bugged in Sweden when he went to collect the Nobel Prize.

PART FOUR

PRELUDE TO MURDER

Chapter Fifteen

MARCH 28, MEMPHIS
by Mark Lane

[handwritten annotations: "when", "getting ready for this", "different rules put money into poor"]

In March 1968, Martin Luther King was stepping up his activities in preparation for the Poor People's March, which was to begin April 29. The plan was to amass a multiracial army of the poor to "stay-in" the nation's capital until "human dignity" concessions were wrenched from a government then pouring billions of dollars into the Vietnam War. King's daring plan was attacked strongly by black moderates, including Bayard Rustin and Roy Wilkins. It marked a shift from civil rights to economic issues. It was this same shift in politics that brought King, somewhat reluctantly, to Memphis. Although he had wanted to devote all of his time to building a successful Poor People's March, King's new politics would not allow him to ignore the call for help from a nascent union of mostly black sanitation workers in Memphis. The workers were on strike for union recognition, an end to racial discrimination on the job, and better wages and working conditions. The strikers had gained the united and militant support of the entire black community and a handful of white sympathizers.

King's help was requested by SCLC member Reverend James Lawson, the leader of the Memphis Strike Strategy Committee. A plan was formulated—King would send in aides James Bevel, James Orange, Tyrone Brooks, Andy Young, and Hosea Williams to prepare a massive march in Memphis which would draw national attention to the strike. King's aides recruited the help of an organized militant black group, the Invaders. This group had repeatedly brought hundreds of black students to earlier marches. The Invaders were helpful at times, provocative at others.

On the day of the March 28 demonstration, a crowd of 8,000 people, spanning many blocks, awaited Dr. King's arrival. Reverend Lawson noticed many marchers he had never seen at strike sessions or civil rights demonstrations directly at the front of the march.

Shortly after the march began, the first windows were broken. In some areas, looting began before the marchers entered the area. According to eyewitness reports, police just watched this looting and did nothing to stop it until the marchers came through.

Soon the police entered, viciously and indiscriminately attacking the demonstrators. Dr. King's party commandeered a passing car and was taken by a police escort to the Holiday Inn Rivermont Hotel.

At a press conference the next day, King vowed to return to show that his tactics of mass nonviolent action were still viable. The violence in Memphis gave black Establishment spokesmen more ammunition with which to attack King's Poor People's March. The day before King was killed, NAACP executive director Roy Wilkins scored King in a story in the Memphis *Press-Scimitar*, saying he doubted that the SCLC leader could keep the Washington march nonviolent. "If a maverick at the rear ranks of the march decides to throw a brick through a window, there's nothing Dr. King up front can do to stop it."

The official explanation of the Memphis march-turned-riot is that the violence and looting were probably triggered by the Invaders. But a black reporter for *Newsday*, Les Payne, turned up evidence which adds a new dimension to the matter.

In an article entitled, "FBI Tied to King's Return to Memphis," Payne reached his conclusion in three steps:

1) Several FBI informants and at least one Memphis police undercover agent were among the most active members of the Invaders.

2) According to some witnesses, the Invaders led the March 28 riots which attempted to discredit King.

3) According to Jesse Jackson and Andrew Young, "Dr. King would never have returned to Memphis if the violence had not happened."

This seemingly farfetched thesis must be considered seriously when viewed in the context of the FBI's campaign to destroy Dr. King and their COINTELPRO (Counterintelligence Program) tactics to provoke and disrupt black groups. One FBI memo admitted the use of agents provocateurs ". . . in harassing and impelling criminal activities. . . ." During the late sixties, FBI provocateurs in the black movement repeatedly urged and initiated violent acts. In the Memphis setting, turning a nonviolent march into a riot would have furthered the FBI's goal of discrediting King.

In his *Newsday* article, Payne wrote, "One of the informants [in the Invaders] reportedly planned a large portion of the group's violent confrontations." The undercover policeman was at the scene of the violence on the day of the riot. He was a very active and vocal member of the group. A former leader of the Invaders told Payne:

He had a 7.62 Russian automatic rifle and he was armed every time we were armed. He was always suggesting actions that we should take; I never saw him physically attack anyone. But he was one of the most provocative members of the Invaders.

The group was apparently so well penetrated that, according to Payne, "Police and FBI officials were regularly provided with detailed information about the group's plans, activities and meetings." A source went on to tell him, "They knew what went on at Invaders' meetings. It was as if they had a tape recorder there."

Detective Ed Redditt, a member of the Memphis Police Department in 1968, described another agent provocateur within the Invaders in a conversation with me.

He left the police department . . . and the word was that he went to Washington, D.C. Then a couple of years after the King slaying i ran face to face with him in downtown Memphis. He was wearing a disguise.

When Redditt stopped and confronted the man, the former infiltrator pretended to be someone else, but finally acknowledged his true identity. "He acted very mysterious, saying that he was now with the Central Intelligence Agency, and begged me not to blow his cover," Redditt told me.

The infiltration of the Invaders touched directly on Dr. King. According to Payne, the undercover agent who carried around the automatic rifle was also part of an Invaders security detail for King. This detail left the Lorraine Motel—for unexplained reasons—just thirty minutes before King was killed.

As the head of the strike strategy committee, Reverend James Lawson tried to work with the Invaders during and after the strike. It was not always easy.

Lawson spent most of a 2½ hour interview with Jeff Cohen, an able investigator residing in Los Angeles, discussing the now-defunct group. "From the beginning, I said publicly at mass meetings that I thought the Invaders were provocateurs."

Reverend Lawson invited an Invader representative to join the broad-based strategy committee. The committee had to deal with the survival needs of the strikers and their families, plus the boycott of downtown merchants, daily marches, and tactical issues. Lawson said, "The Invaders made it difficult for us to do the work that was on top of us. They wanted to rearrange the agenda to make room for their rhetoric. It seemed like they wanted to create havoc.'' He continued:

At a time when we were strong and dynamic, when the strike was freezing up the downtown area, when our boycott was 97 percent effective, according to *Business Week*, when the business community was putting pressure on the Mayor to settle, when our weaponry was obviously effective, why then would you want to change strategy? It would be another story if your weapons weren't working. Why would these guys come around at public meetings, yelling about burning down and killing honkies? They talked nonsense.

Lawson remembered that on March 28 he confronted a man described as a ''Beale Street crook,'' haranguing the crowd to remove the posters from the sticks and use them as spears.

Immediately after the riot, Reverend Lawson launched an investigation into who was behind the violence. After studying photographs and conducting interviews, he concluded that much of the violence was instigated by known Beale Street muggers and crooks. ''They may or may not have been paid provocateurs, but they are all not Invaders,'' he told Cohen.

Lawson takes the issue of FBI provocation of the Invaders and others very seriously. He still wonders about a threat he received in the mail.

A few days after Martin's death, I received a package in the mail that had my picture and a bullet taped to it. It read something like, "We've got one for you too, nigger-preacher." Although I showed it to no one but my wife, I soon got a call from [then Memphis Police Director] Holloman on some matter and he said, "I understand you got a package." That's when, for some reason, I was convinced it came from the Invaders and that the FBI was in on it. It's funny, I didn't suspect the Memphis police. Probably because Holloman worked for the FBI for so many years.

One of the leaders of the Invaders, John B. Smith, told Jeff Cohen that:

The marching contingent, not the leadership, could have been infiltrated. They were mostly eighteen- and nineteen-year-olds. It's very possible that the FBI hired people to throw rocks and bricks. It's also possible that a paid provocateur would have then proclaimed, "I'm an Invader." Remember too, if someone got up and spoke loudly at a meeting, that didn't mean that they were part of the leadership.

Smith disagreed with Payne's statement that the Invaders provided a four-man security force for Dr. King, but he offered an explanation:

We provided no security for King at the Lorraine. There was a heavy-set, brown-skinned, baldheaded guy named Barracuda, who, along with three or four others, played a security role. They were probably not from Memphis. At least I hadn't seen them before . . . or since. They wore cutoff Levi jackets and could easily have been mistaken for Invaders.

The confusion about the Levi-jacketed security detail parallels the situation in certain places where anyone who wore a black leather jacket was considered a member of the Black Panther Party.

While Smith contests some of Payne's specifics in his defense of the Invaders' leadership, he would be surprised if the FBI did not provoke violence to discredit King. "Knowing how they tried to destroy Dr. King, I'd be shocked if they did not have a hand in it. But the premise that the FBI had to go through the Invaders' leadership to hurt King is wrong."

In an account published by the black-oriented *Tri-State Defender,* Coby Smith, formerly a senior member and adviser to the Invaders and later an administrator at State Tech Institute, called the *Newsday* article "not completely accurate." Coby Smith claimed that he and other Invaders were aware of infiltrators in the organization long before King's death. He said that although the Invaders decided not to take part in the march, many people were donning Invader jackets because "they were very easy to make." His comments agree with John B. Smith's that there were people posing as Invaders who could have provoked the march to violence.

The FBI's role in Memphis just prior to the assassination is a huge and ominous question mark. Most Americans believe that the FBI investigates crimes. But revelations about the COINTELPRO operation indicate that the FBI has been committing them.

Dr. King's nonviolent movement in Memphis had been jeopardized by a series of events, culminating in the massive use of weapons, tear gas, clubs, and mace by the police under the direction of Frank Holloman, against the marching black population of Memphis. The fact that some of the violence was initiated, or at the least was said to have been initiated by some of the demonstrators, created a crisis for King's movement. He had little choice. It appeared that he was constrained to return to Memphis, to preach nonviolence yet again and to carry off a successful demonstration as witness to his deeply-held beliefs.

King was under fire from almost all of the traditional national black leaders for having called for an end to the war in Vietnam. The federal police had weakened his movement through numerous illegal efforts that enjoyed uneven success. FBI-infiltrated groups of young "militants" condemned him for his adherence to nonviolence in the face of continued and unabated violence directed against him and those who marched with him.

Liberal publications and friends who had formerly supported him had turned against him. Andrew Young, who had served in the Southern Christian Leadership Conference with King and former United States Ambassador to the United Nations, told the Church Committee:

It was a great burden to be attacked by people he respected, particularly when the attacks engendered by the FBI came from people like Ralph McGill. He sat down and cried at *The New York Times* editorial about his statement on Vietnam, but this just made him more determined. It was a great personal suffering, but since we don't really know all that they did, we have no way of knowing the ways that they affected us.

If a meaningful and nonviolent march to Washington on April 22, 1968, appeared to be crucial to Dr. King, it seemed on March 28 that a similar action in Memphis was required as a precursor.

On March 29 the local press in Memphis removed any doubt. On that day the Memphis *Commercial Clarion* stated,

Yesterday's march, ostensibly a protest on behalf of the city's striking sanitation workers, was generally considered to be a "dress rehearsal" by Dr. King for his planned march on Washington April 22.

The Domestic Intelligence Division of the FBI, in a memorandum circulated the previous day, stated:

A sanitation strike has been going on in Memphis for some time. Martin Luther King, Jr., today led a march composed of 5,000 to 6,000 people through the streets of Memphis. King was in an automobile preceding the marchers. As the march developed, acts of violence and vandalism broke out including the breaking of windows in stores and some looting.

This clearly demonstrates that acts of so-called nonviolence advocated by King cannot be controlled. The same thing could happen in his planned massive civil disobedience for Washington in April.

The memorandum was accompanied by an "action" directive which read:

ACTION

Attached is a blind memorandum pointing out the above, which if you approve, should be made available by Crime Records Division to cooperative news media sources.

The memorandum was initiated by Hoover and carried his approval in the form of the "O.K." written by him. On the memorandum the notation, "handled on 3/28/68," was evidence that the suggestion had been given to "cooperative news media sources."

The Memphis *Commercial Clarion* was the first news media to publish an article that resembled the memorandum written by FBI agents. The Memphis *Commercial Appeal* the next day picked up the "dress rehearsal" phrase and reported:

Dr. Martin Luther King, Jr., came to Memphis to star in what was billed as a "dress rehearsal" for his April 22 "Poor People's Crusade" on Washington. By his own nonviolent standards, the rehearsal was a flop.

The article then presented the other point that had been made by the FBI news writers. "The question being asked in Memphis, the nation and the world is whether—with the increasing militancy of the black youth—anyone can say with certainty that a nonviolent demonstration will stay that way."

That same day *The New York Times* published an editorial entitled "Mini-Riot in Memphis . . ." which made the same point:

The disorder in Memphis that left store windows on Beale Street smashed and one Negro youth dead exposes the danger in drawing large numbers of protesters into the streets for emotional demonstrations in this time of civic unrest. The Rev. Dr. Martin Luther King, who organized the Memphis march, is organizing a "Poor People's Campaign" for Washington, D. C., next month. None of the precautions he and his aides are taking to keep the capital demonstration peaceful can provide any dependable insurance against another eruption of the kind that rocked Memphis.

Chapter Sixteen

MARCH 29, MEMPHIS AND WASHINGTON
by Mark Lane

On March 29 the Domestic Intelligence Division of the FBI drafted another "news story" and recommended that that article should also be furnished to cooperative news sources. It read:

> **Martin Luther King, during the sanitation workers' strike in Memphis, Tennessee, has urged Negroes to boycott downtown white merchants to achieve Negro demands. On 3/29/68 King led a march for the sanitation workers. Like Judas leading lambs to slaughter [sic], King led the marchers to violence, and when the violence broke out, King disappeared.**
>
> **The fine Hotel Lorraine in Memphis is owned and patronized exclusively by Negroes, but King didn't go there for his hasty exit. Instead, King decided the plush Holiday Inn Motel, white owned, operated and almost exclusively patronized, was the place to "cool it." There will be no boycott of white merchants for King, only for his followers.**

The FBI agents even provided a headline for the story; "Do As I Say, Not As I Do." The news story was accompanied by an internal Bureau memorandum, bearing the caption of its Counterintelligence Program, which read as follows:

> **The purpose is to publicize hypocrisy on the part of Martin Luther King. Background: Martin Luther King has urged Negroes in Memphis, Tenn., to boycott white merchants in order to force compliance with Negro demands in the sanitation workers' strike in Memphis. On March 28, 1968, King disappeared. There is a first-class Negro hotel in Memphis, the Hotel Lorraine, but**

King chose to hide out at the white owned-and-operated Holiday Inn Motel.

Recommendation: The above facts have been included in the attached blind memorandum, and it is recommended it be furnished to a cooperative news media source by the Crimes Records Division for items showing King is a hypocrite. This will be done on a highly confidential basis.

That document bore Hoover's approval as well. He wrote on it "O.K., H" which indicated his approval of the plan.

When the Church Committee examined the document it reported that the notation "handled" appeared on the document, but that the date next to the word "handled" was illegible on the copy of the document furnished to the Senate Committee by the FBI and that "we have not yet seen the original document."

Since the FBI maintained that the date of handling was April 3, 1968, the FBI was also able to maintain that its program was not put into effect in this instance. Dr. King arrived in Memphis on April 3. Yet the blurred date, the refusal of the FBI to furnish a clear copy or the original document, and the history of FBI officials in hastily putting programs against Dr. King into action immediately after they were approved by Hoover for fear of Hoover's wrath if they failed to do so, raises serious questions. The Church Committee, however, did not confront those questions.

Instead of closely questioning the FBI agent who wrote "handled" on the memorandum, in an effort to determine how he had acquitted himself of his responsibility to furnish the article to a "cooperative news media source" on "a highly confidential basis" before he wrote the note signifying that he had done so, the Church Committee asked the FBI to investigate. The Committee then reported, "The FBI questioned the agent who wrote 'handled' on the memorandum and informed the Committee that he did not recall the memorandum, and did not know whether 'handled' indicated that he had disseminated the article or simply cleared the memorandum through the Crime Records Division of the FBI." Since in intelligence jargon "handled" means that the job has been done, the doubt suggested by the FBI investigation as to what "handled" meant in this instance hardly seems justified. It also appears rather unlikely that an FBI agent who may have played an important part in moving Dr. King from the relative safety of the imposing and isolated Rivermont Holiday Inn to a very vulnerable location at which he was, in fact, killed the next day would "not recall" the incident or his own actions relevant to it.

106

Perhaps the best evidence presently available regarding the action taken by the FBI in reference to the promulgation of its own news article can be gleaned by an examination of the news media reports. For, in this instance, the proof of the plotting is in the reading.

The day after the agent noted that the matter had been "handled," the Memphis newspapers began referring to Dr. King's "posh" room at the Rivermont Holiday Inn. In an article the Memphis *Commercial Appeal* even disclosed the exact cost of the room, referring to it as "Dr. King's $29-a-day room at the Holiday Inn Rivermont."

The Memphis police reporters in contact with Frank Holloman began to speak of King's betrayal as evidenced by his "posh" accommodations at the Rivermont. The political reporters in contact with the Mayor made similar observations. According to Kay Pittman Black, a reporter for the Memphis *Press-Scimitar*, "there was even resentment in the Invader group about him staying at this fancy hotel." Ms. Black had covered all aspects of the sanitation strike and the visits to the city that Dr. King had made. The Church Committee offered the conclusion that "Dr. King always stayed at the Lorraine when he visited Memphis; with the exception of his prior visit." That conclusion, however, was not based upon an investigation by the Committee, but upon its acceptance of the assertion of the FBI and of one other person. Clearly, a cursory examination of hotel registration records might have revealed the facts.

When Ms. Black was told that it was alleged that Dr. King had always stayed at the Lorraine in the past, she said, "No. He did not. I covered his every visit to this city—even before the strike. He stayed at the Claridge, the big hotel downtown, right across from City Hall. The SCLC and Dr. King had almost an entire floor there. They had never stayed at the Lorraine. Not that I know of. In fact when I was told, I guess it was on April 3, that he was to be at the Lorraine, I was at the AME building. I spent a great deal of time there and it was my specific duty to keep up with Dr. King, to know when he was to arrive, to know where he was staying."

Ms. Black said that the coordinator of the sanitation workers' strike told her that King "would not be at the Rivermont—that he would be staying at the Lorraine as a commitment to patronize small black-owned businesses, as opposed to staying at a white-owned hotel." Ms. Black added, "I know it was the first time that I ever heard of Dr. King being at the Lorraine Motel because at that time I didn't even know where that hotel was. I knew, I guess, that it was generally in the black area, but I didn't actually know where it was located. I went over there in the morning and I sat in the coffee shop and talked to Andy Young and Jim

Bevel and Jesse Jackson. And that was the first time I saw the Lorraine Motel and I followed Dr. King closely whenever he was in Memphis.''

The FBI memoranda had accomplished their tasks. Dr. King had returned to Memphis to lead a nonviolent march for the sanitation workers and to salvage his national movement and his projected Poor People's Crusade. He was compelled to do so, at least partially due to the FBI memorandum of March 28 and the wide circulation given to that memorandum, at first in Memphis, and then throughout the country.

Senator Robert C. Byrd led the efforts in Congress to condemn Dr. King and said that he should be enjoined from carrying out the planned demonstration in Washington. He referred to Dr. King as a ''self-seeking rabble-rouser'' and predicted that King, if not stopped, would be responsible for ''violence, destruction, looting and bloodshed'' in Washington.

Approximately seven years later the origin of Senator Byrd's vehement attack upon Dr. King became evident as the Church Committee secured access to various FBI memoranda. On January 19, 1968, Cartha De Loach, then a high-ranking FBI official, reported to Hoover's personal friend and FBI colleague, Clyde Tolson, that he had met with Senator Byrd. According to the De Loach memorandum, Byrd had expressed concern over Dr. King's plan for demonstrations in Washington and said that it was time that ''King met his Waterloo.'' De Loach's memorandum states that Byrd asked if the FBI would prepare a speech about Dr. King which he could deliver on the floor of the Senate.

The speech, which was delivered on March 29, 1968, by Senator Byrd, then leader of the Democratic Party in the Senate, was vehement. Although Dr. King was the victim of the violence, Byrd said:

> **Yesterday, Mr. President, the nation was given a preview of what may be in store for this city by the outrageous and despicable riot that Martin Luther King helped to bring about in Memphis, Tennessee.**

He continued:

> **In Memphis, people were injured, stores were looted, property was destroyed, terror reigned in the streets, people were beaten by hoodlums, at least one Negro youth is known to have been killed, and massive rioting erupted during a march which was led by this man. It was a shameful and totally uncalled for outburst of lawlessness undoubtedly encouraged to some considerable degree, at least, by his words and actions, and his presence. There is no reason for us to believe that the same destructive rioting and violence cannot, or that it will not, happen here if King attempts his so-called Poor People's March, for what he**

plans in Washington appears to be something on a far greater scale than what he had indicated he planned to do in Memphis.

Almost all who admired Dr. King as well as those who despised him or were indifferent to his work agreed that he was a man of great personal courage. From his upholstered chair in what its members are pleased to refer to as the most exclusive club in the world, Byrd attacked Dr. King's commitment and questioned his courage.

When the predictable rioting erupted in Tennessee, Martin Luther King fled the scene. He took to his heels and disappeared, leaving it to others to cope with the destructive forces he had helped to unleash.

Returning to his theme of Dr. King's ''flight'' from danger again and again, Byrd said:

King intends to create a black hole of despair with people packed together with pigs and chickens in a "shanty town" lacking sanitation. Surely he must know that to change hearts it is not necessary to turn stomachs. It can be assumed that, however, if yesterday's flight by King from the disorder he had helped to generate was any indication of what he might do here, the "Messiah" himself will not share the squalor he plans and that instead he will be conducting a lay-in at a posh Washington hotel to dramatize some imaginary discrimination there.

Had the speech been prepared on Hoover's private stationery, the clues regarding its conception would have been little more apparent. The word ''Messiah'' figured prominently in FBI jargon regarding Dr. King. A high-level FBI memorandum suggested that the FBI create its own black ''messiah'' to replace Dr. King. The allegation that Dr. King would conduct a ''lay-in'' at a Washington hotel might be construed as a reference to the then still secret war against Dr. King waged through FBI sexpionage tactics.

The reference to the ''posh Washington hotel'' may have been a device calculated by the FBI to embarrass Dr. King and drive him from the Holiday Inn Rivermont Hotel into the more modest Lorraine. If so, the United States Senate was employed, along with the local newspapers in Memphis, in an effort to move Dr. King to the location at which he was ultimately murdered. Byrd charged that ''King lovingly breaks the law like a boa constrictor.'' He continued,

Apparently the hoodlums in Memphis yesterday followed King's advice to break laws with which they did not agree. This has been a cardinal principle of his philosophy—a philosophy

that leads naturally to the escalation of nonviolence into civil disobedience—which is only a euphemism for lawbreaking and criminality and which escalates next into civil unrest, civil disorder, and insurrection.

Mr. President, I have previously urged, in discussing this matter with the Justice Department, that the Federal Government seek a court order to enjoin Martin Luther King and his pulpitless parsons from carrying out their planned poor people's campaign in the Nation's Capital. In the light of yesterday's bloody chapter of violence which erupted with the visit of Martin Luther King to Memphis, I again urge that the Federal Government take steps to prevent King from carrying out his planned harassment of Washington, D. C. An ounce of prevention is worth a pound of cure. It is time for our Federal Government —which in recent years has shown itself to be virtually spineless when it comes to standing up against the lawbreakers, the hoodlums, and the Marxist demonstrators—at least to let the Nation know, in no uncertain terms, that it will not allow this Nobel Peace Prize winner to create another Memphis in the city which serves as the seat of the Government of the United States.

Byrd was joined by other Senators and Representatives who, no doubt, without understanding that they were doing so, followed closely the script that the FBI had prepared just the day before. Among those who focused upon the Memphis riot to demand executive action to bar the demonstration were senators Strom Thurmond, John Stennis, and various members of the House. Among those who "saw the possibility of violence" in Washington and who opposed Dr. King's march were Senator Edward W. Brooke, described by the media as "the nation's highest Negro office holder," and Senator Howard Baker, who said that "the March on Washington is like striking a match to look in your gas tank and see if you're out of gas."

Senator Strom Thurmond echoed Byrd's remarks and then revealed that he too may have been privy to an FBI briefing or two.

. . . I call upon President Johnson to make public the information about King which is available to him. This information is openly talked about in Washington. References to it have appeared in the newspapers. I challenge the administration to let all the citizens of this country know what kind of a man King really is, and what his true purpose is.

The campaign of vilification of Dr. King raged on unabated in the Senate, far from the slums of Memphis where children of sanitation

110

workers suffered from malnutrition, were ill clothed, and attended sub-standard schools.

Senator Stennis had a word of advice for those and other "colored" people:

I want to give a word of advice and counsel to the colored people and to any others who may be inclined to come to Washington from Mississippi. It is to stay out of the march. Nothing good for them or from anyone else can come from it. They run the risk that harm can come from it. They run the risk that harm can come to any individual or any group. I mean by that the possibility of personal injury and violence in the course of any demonstrations that may get out of hand.

Dr. King returned to Memphis. The riot required that he return to confront yet again the twin evils of economic and racial discrimination.

The FBI had prevailed. Dr. King was to return not just to Memphis but to the Lorraine Motel.

Chapter Seventeen

APRIL 3 AND 4, MEMPHIS

by Dick Gregory

Reading Martin Luther King's final message to America and reflecting on his last day of life was a profoundly emotional experience for me. As I re-read it and listened to it so many times on tape, the feeling recurs, that King betrayed in his comments a premonition of the vicious experience creeping up on him. The tone and content of the message suggests that he believed his life might end soon.

I try to reconstruct in my own mind how he may have been feeling that night in Mason Temple in Memphis. Was he sad, weary, but determined to fight on to the end? Was he lonely, misunderstood but still unwavering in his convictions? I wonder what went through his mind as he stood there, knowing the stark hatred many aimed at him and his cause. And I wonder if his thoughts were with his family; those I had met, his brother, A. D., his mother, Alberta, his father, Daddy King, his children, and Coretta; and those I didn't know.

And I listen again to the touching segment of his speech in which he drew an analogy between his reasons for being in Memphis and the Bible parable of the Good Samaritan.

King related how he and Coretta were in Jerusalem where they rented a car to Jericho, taking the same road traveled by the Good Samaritan and the victim of highway robbery that he befriended. As they drove along the ancient road King said he saw the application of the parable to contemporary American life.

I was struck by King's keen perception of the lesson of the parable. The question, he said, must be what will happen to my brother if I don't stop to help him—not what will happen to me, what will I lose, if I do help him. He posed the question to his audience, told them that his position was not what might he lose if he joined the sanitation workers in their dispute, but rather what terrible consequences might result if he failed to help them.

112

If Martin could return and sit down with me, there are a million things I'd want to say to him. But, if the time were very short and I had to choose one topic, it would be this:

Martin, I want you to know how grateful I am that you stopped. That you encountered a sick, mortally wounded society as you traveled the road of life and you refused to ignore it; that you offered a helping hand. Thank you for stopping in Memphis, Birmingham, in Selma and St. Augustine, in Cleveland, Ohio, and Chicago. You stopped, you interrupted your life to speak out against the War in Vietnam.

I would go on,

Thank you, Martin, for ensuring that we need never ask the tragic question that too often follows neglect of duty: "Would this have happened if. . ." Because of you, we don't have to go to the back of Birmingham's buses, we don't have to say "If Martin had stopped here, the buses and the schools and the stores and the restaurants would be desegregated now," because you came and they are. We don't have to say "If Martin Luther King had stopped to help with voter registration there would be more black voters in the country," because you did stop and there are.

Because of you, Martin, I can give thanks that I, as an American and human being, will never have to pose that question. Because you stopped, a thousand potential tragedies were eliminated before they could be set in motion. I'm glad I don't have to say, "If only King had been there, this might not have happened," because you were there, and it didn't happen.

I reflect on your final message and know it is one from which unborn generations will derive meaning and inspiration. How I wish I could have been in the audience that last night of your life. I wish I could have been there to listen as you delivered your talk, to watch as you touched your face with your finger in a characteristic gesture, as you moved your shoulders to make sure your coat hung properly. I'm sorry I missed your smile as your eyes swept the crowded auditorium, as you recognized so many of the folks and welcomed the ones who listened to you for the first time.

I wish I had been there to hear the following brilliant farewell message, although none of your listeners knew it was goodbye.

Dr. Martin Luther King's final words to America were spoken at Mason Temple, Memphis, Tennessee, on April 3, 1968. The next day he was murdered, but his vision for a humane world order will never die. Excerpts from his address follow.

I'VE BEEN TO THE MOUNTAINTOP

. . . if I were standing at the beginning of time, with the possibility of a general and panoramic view of the whole human history up to now, and the Almighty said to me, "Martin Luther King, which age would you like to live in?"—I would take my mental flight by Egypt through, or rather across the Red Sea, through the wilderness on toward the promised land. And in spite of its magnificence, I wouldn't stop there. I would move on by Greece, and take my mind to Mount Olympus. And I would see Plato, Aristotle, Socrates, Euripides and Aristophanes assembled around the Parthenon as they discussed the great and eternal issues of reality.

But I wouldn't stop there. I would go on, even to the great heyday of the Roman Empire. And I would see developments around there, through various emperors and leaders. But I wouldn't stop there. I would even come up to the day of the Renaissance, and get a quick picture of all that the Renaissance did for the cultural and aesthetic life of man. But I wouldn't stop there. I would even go by the way that the man for whom I'm named had his habitat. And I would watch Martin Luther as he tacked his 95 theses on the door at the church in Wittenberg.

But I wouldn't stop there. I would come on up even to 1863, and watch a vacillating President by the name of Abraham Lincoln finally come to the conclusion that he had to sign the Emancipation Proclamation. But I wouldn't stop there. I would even come up to the early thirties, and see a man grappling with the problems of the bankruptcy of his nation. And come with an eloquent cry that we have nothing to fear but fear itself.

But I wouldn't stop there. Strangely enough, I would turn to the Almighty and say, "If you allow me to live just a few years in the second half of the Twentieth Century, I will be happy." Now that's a strange statement to make, because the world is all messed up. The nation is sick. Trouble is in the land. Confusion all around. That's a strange statement. But I know, somehow, that only when it is dark enough, can you see the stars. And I see God working in this period of the Twentieth Century in a way that men, in some strange way, are responding—something is happening in our world. The masses of people are rising up . . . whether they are in Johannesburg, South Africa; Nairobi, Kenya; Accra, Ghana; New York City; Atlanta, Georgia;

Jackson, Mississippi; or Memphis, Tennessee—the cry is always the same—"We want to be free."

And another reason that I'm happy to live in this period is . . . we're going to have to grapple with the problems that men have been trying to grapple with through history, but the demands didn't force them to do it. Survival demands that we grapple with them. Men, for years now, have been talking about war and peace. But now, no longer can they just talk about it. It is no longer a choice between violence and nonviolence in this world, it's nonviolence or nonexistence.

That is where we are today . . . Now, I'm just happy that God has allowed me to live in this period, to see what is unfolding. And I'm happy that he's allowed me to be in Memphis. . . .

Now we've got to go on to Memphis just like that. I call upon you to be with us Monday. Now about injunctions: We have an injunction and we're going into court tomorrow morning to fight this illegal, unconstitutional injunction. All we say to America is, "Be true to what you said on paper." If I lived in China or even Russia, or any totalitarian country, maybe I could understand the denial of certain basic First Amendment privileges, because they hadn't committed themselves to that over there. But somewhere I read of the freedom of assembly. Somewhere I read of the freedom of speech. Somewhere I read of the freedom of the press. Somewhere I read that the greatness of America is the right to protest for right. . . . This is what we have to do.

. . . Always anchor our external direct action with the power of economic withdrawal. Now we are poor people, individually, we are poor when you compare us with white society in America. We are poor . . . collectively, that means all of us together, collectively we are richer than all the nations in the world. . . . Did you ever think about that? . . . That's power right there, if we know how to pool it.

We don't have to argue with anybody. . . . We don't need any bricks and bottles, we don't need any molotov cocktails, we just need to go around to these stores, and to these massive industries in our country, and say, "God sent us by here, to say to you that you're not treating his children right. And we've come by here to ask you to make the first item on your agenda—fair treatment, where God's children are concerned. Now, if you are not prepared to do that, we do have an agenda that we must follow. And our agenda calls for withdrawing economic support from you.''

. . . up to now, only the garbage men have been feeling pain, now we must kind of redistribute the pain. . . .

I remember when Mrs. King and I were first in Jerusalem. We rent a car and drove from Jerusalem down to Jericho. And as soon as we got on that road, I said to my wife, "I can see why Jesus used this as a setting for His parable." It's a winding, meandering road. It's really conducive for ambushing. You start out in Jerusalem, which is about 1200 miles, or rather 1200 feet above sea level. And by the time you get down to Jericho, 15 or 20 minutes later, you're about 2200 feet below sea level. That's a dangerous road. In the days of Jesus it came to be known as the 'Bloody Pass.' And you know, it's possible that the priest and the Levite looked over that man on the ground and wondered if the robbers were still around. Or it's possible that they felt that the man on the ground was merely faking. And he was acting like he had been robbed and hurt in order to seize them over there, lure them there for quick and easy seizure. And so the first question that the Levite asked was, "If I stop to help this man, what will happen to me?" But then the good Samaritan came by. And he reversed the question: "If I do not stop to help this man, what will happen to him?"

That's the question before you tonight. Not, "If I stop to help the sanitation workers, what will happen to all of the hours that I usually spend in my office every day and every week as a pastor?" The question is not, "If I stop to help this man in need, what will happen to me?" "If I do not stop to help the sanitation workers, what will happen to them?" That's the question. . . .

It really doesn't matter what happens now. I left Atlanta this morning, and as we got started on the plane, there were six of us, the pilot said over the public address system, "We are sorry for the delay, but we have Dr. Martin Luther King on the plane and to be sure that all of the bags were checked, and to be sure that nothing would be wrong with the plane, we had to check out everything carefully and we've had the plane protected and guarded all night."

And then I got into Memphis and some began to say the threats, or talk about the threats that were out. What would happen to me from some of our sick white brothers?

Well, I don't know what will happen now. We've got some

difficult days ahead. But it doesn't matter with me now. Because I've been to the mountaintop. And I don't mind. Like anybody, I would like to live a long life. Longevity has its place. But I'm not concerned about that now. I just want to do God's will. And He's allowed me to go up to the mountain. And I've looked over. And I've seen the promised land. I may not get there with you. But I want you to know tonight, that we, as a people will get to the promised land. And I'm happy, tonight. I'm not worried about anything. I'm not fearing any man. Mine eyes have seen the glory of the coming of the Lord.

April 4, 1968

Morning comes too quickly to suit the two tired men who sleep in the motel room. The night before both had participated in a long, emotion-charged rally. One was the main speaker and the other a kind of advance man.

One of them opens his eyes and realizes that the light coming through the window near the edge not covered by the heavy drapes is a sign of morning. It is indeed time to get up, and this, like many mornings, is one where both men would have liked to have been able to rest a while longer.

Ralph Abernathy sits up in his bed, and there is a creaking sound as he swings his feet over the edge of the bed to the floor. He sits there for a long moment and then succumbs to the inevitable. Stretching and yawning at the same time, he rises.

Then he glances in the bed next to his and sees that his friend is still sound asleep. He would like so much not to have to wake him, but there's a lot of work that has to be done, and they could not sleep late.

"Michael," he says in a kind, quiet voice. "Michael, come on now, it's time to get up." The response is prompt, though the voice is still heavy with sleep.

"Yes, David," he replies without making any motions to get out of bed.

"It's time to get up now. . . . You know we can't win this nonviolent revolution in bed. It's time to rise and shine. The early bird gets the worm."

Michael is fully awake now, and though he really isn't ready to get up, he is alert and jovial.

"Aw, David," he teases, "you're still a farmer. I'm never gonna get that Alabama soil out of you!"

They tease back and forth, lightly and easily, in a familiar pattern. It is a typical beginning to an ordinary day. I talked with Ralph Abernathy at

117

great length about his private relationship to Dr. King. I wanted to know more than the story of two men who were professional colleagues and who shared a philosophy that is unique in our violence-prone society—the philosophy of nonviolence.

Among other things, I learned that King called Abernathy by his middle name, David; and that Ralph privately addressed King by his real name, which was Michael. (King was christened Michael Luther but when he was six years old his father changed both their names to Martin Luther.) It interests me that King's original given name was Michael. This name, historically, is as eminent as that of Martin Luther. Michael, the archangel, according to the Bible, will be a leader in the war between God and Satan. It seems to me that King fulfilled the name of Michael more than that of Martin Luther. The legal act of changing his name to Martin did not alter the destiny of Michael. For it was certainly King's perception that he was engaged in a battle between good and evil.

Ralph Abernathy's reflections to me about King added another dimension to the man many have viewed as a saint, savior, and humanitarian. Because of Ralph's love for King, he was able to reveal a type of personal warmth when he recalled important times that he had spent with him. The events that took place on April 4, 1968, prior to the moment when King was shot, were typical of the daily routine of these two men.

After getting up that morning, they each showered and shaved as they had to get ready for an important meeting where they would discuss the forthcoming Poor People's March on Washington. Getting organized was never a problem. Though Ralph was always the first to get up, he was frequently the last to get dressed because while King would be dressing, he would request Ralph to make phone calls and take notes for him. It was Ralph's job to make sure everything was done right and on time. There was no man in whom King had greater confidence.

They held the meeting right at the motel. They were meeting with the leaders of a local militant group called the Invaders. A march held the week earlier had been disrupted by persons claiming to be Invaders who had infiltrated the ranks of the peaceful marchers and begun rioting when the group reached downtown Memphis. Police had intervened and the march had to be called off. Andy Young reported that the Invaders were asking the SCLC to pay them $50,000 and give them five automobiles. Abernathy recalls vividly King's response.

"This movement will exclude any person or group who uses violence as a tactic, as a strategy, or as a way of life." King, says Abernathy, was adamant that SCLC would not pay blackmail to any person or group for any reason.

King and Abernathy had not eaten breakfast that morning before the meeting. Normally, their first meal was around noontime. They were both hungry after leaving the meeting and they decided to have lunch in their room. Each ordered fried catfish and salad. When the waitress brought their meal to the room, Abernathy was annoyed that she had not gotten the order right. She had all the fish on one plate, along with two bowls of salad. Abernathy was about to send her back to get the order straight when King told him not to worry about it. Abernathy recalls King saying to him, "Leave her alone, David, it doesn't matter. You and me can eat from the same plate."

The two men spent the afternoon with other SCLC members, making plans, mapping strategy. Reverend Samuel Kyles, a Memphis minister who was in charge of the garbage workers' boycott, was one of those who came. King's brother, A.D., had come from Lexington to particpate in the boycott and rally. Abernathy remembers King teasing Jesse Jackson. "Look, Jesse, you can't take that whole band out to Sam's house tonight." SCLC had been invited to Reverend Kyles' home for dinner before the scheduled rally. "Sam's wife can't feed the whole bunch. And you be sure to dress up a little tonight, OK, Jesse? No blue jeans, all right?"

Abernathy was the next in line for the teasing that was going on. One of the ministers accused him of taking almost as long to introduce King at the rally the night before as it took King to give the main address.

King had spoken the night of April 3rd, and that address came to be known as the now famous "Mountaintop Speech." It had been cold and dreary in Memphis; there were even tornado warnings. King did not think that people would turn out to hear him because of the bad weather, so he requested Abernathy to go to the Mason Temple and speak in his place. "You go ahead and speak for me tonight," he told Ralph. "I'll stay here and relax." Abernathy asked Jesse Jackson to go with him that night, and when they arrived at the church they were amazed at the large number of television cameras and reporters who were waiting outside in the cold and the rain. Abernathy was surprised that such a large number of press people were there. He looked inside and saw that about three hundred people were inside the enormous church that could seat three thousand. It was at that point that he decided that King, not himself, should be there to speak. He quickly went to a telephone and called the motel. King was hesitant at first, but realizing that all these people had come out despite the severe weather warnings, he told Ralph he would be there. The church was very near the motel, and it was not long before King arrived.

After Abernathy's introduction, King came onstage. His opening words that night were, "I want everybody here to know that Ralph David Abernathy is the closest and dearest friend I have in the world!" He went on to give his historic address, but in Ralph Abernathy's gallery of memories, King's public acknowledgment of the devotion he felt for his chief lieutenant were the words that shone most brightly that night.

Abernathy was often described as King's "behind the scenes man," or "his assistant." It was only when I talked with Ralph and learned of their many private conversations that I realized how very much Ralph Abernathy meant to Martin Luther King.

"David," King would say, "I want you to know how much I appreciate your loyalty. I get all the attention from the press, but you're just as important to the movement as I am. I couldn't do my work if you were not here with me. Life is very arbitrary in choosing who will be idolized, who will be the leader. People often forget that a leader is no stronger than his foundation, the often invisible people who give him support. I'll never forget that, David. The newspapermen, the cameramen, some of our own SCLC colleagues may forget it, but I want you to know that I *never, never* will forget it." Abernathy recalls that during King's words to him, he felt that King was looking for a way to repay Ralph for all the work he had done. But Ralph said he always replied this way: "I don't want anything more, Michael, I just want to be here working with you. I'm pleased and satisfied about what I can do for you." Envy and jealousy were never present in the relationship between Ralph David Abernathy and Martin Luther King, Jr.

It is still April 4th, and King's mother, Alberta King, was elated at the fact that her two sons, Martin and A. D., were together this day, chatting and sharing precious memories. King had gone to his brother's room at the motel while Ralph rested in Room 306. Around two-thirty that afternoon, King rang Ralph in the room and told him how happy he was that his brother had come, and that they had just both spoken with their mother over the telephone. King always shared these kinds of personal joys with his friend Ralph.

Around five o'clock King and Abernathy prepared to leave the Lorraine Motel for the dinner which was planned at Samuel Kyles' home. Abernathy, at King's direction, had phoned Mrs. Kyles and had been reassured that it was indeed a soul food feast that awaited the hungry SCLC corps. They were all hungry, and Kyles' wife, who they had all heard was a terrific cook, had prepared a dinner that included roast beef, collard greens, chitterlings, black-eyed peas, cornbread, and fried chicken. Kyles' wife also told Abernathy that the dinner would be at six o'clock, not at five o'clock as he had told them.

Confronted with this discrepancy, Kyles admits a little sheepishly that he wanted to make sure they got there on time. Everyone, after all, was aware of "Colored Peoples' Time," meaning that blacks were notoriously late. Kyles said he simply wanted to insure that they would not be late for the special meal.

Now the two men are in Room 306 alone. Both have changed clothes and are freshening up. Both King and Abernathy splash on some Aramis after-shave lotion. Abernathy told me that he remembered saying something about the lotion being a real necessity because King had just used a depilatory shave powder that fouled the air in the room. He said that the two of them often joked about the smell left by King's shaving solution.

King goes out to the balcony leading from the room. Jesse Jackson is on the ground below. They talk about the music to be played tonight. King turns to Jackson's companion, Ben Branch, an organist from Chicago. "Be sure and play my favorite song tonight, okay?" Branch assures King that he will play the familiar tune "Precious Lord, Take My Hand."

Abernathy, meanwhile, continues to rub Aramis into his cheeks. He hears a noise, reminiscent of a firecracker popping. He looks to the balcony and sees King's knees collapse. "All I could see was his feet," said Abernathy as he recalled that fateful night. Abernathy immediately ran toward King and saw the blood as he lifted the head of his friend and looked into his eyes. Ralph believes that King did see and hear him that night. He recalls saying to King, "Michael, its going to he all right, don't you worry now because everything's going to be all right. I'll get help, don't worry. . . ."

All the rest has been recorded a thousand times. One thing sticks in Abernathy's mind though. It is Andy Young's voice saying, "It's over, it's over. . . ." Ralph told me that he kept telling Andy, "No, it's not over, it's not over."

It was Ralph Abernathy who stayed with King's body the rest of the night. It was Abernathy who stayed in the operating room though doctors and nurses had told him that he would have to leave. The world was shocked and the press was looking for Ralph Abernathy to talk to about what had happened. But Ralph Abernathy never left the side of his friend's body that night. It was he who was called to the morgue to identify the body. "I remember something that hurt me more than anything else that night. . . . I remember going to that morgue and seeing my good friend with a brown paper tag hooked to his toe. I'll never forget that sight."

PART
FIVE

THE
MURDER

Chapter Eighteen

APRIL 4, MEMPHIS
by Mark Lane

Directly across the street from the Lorraine Motel was a large rectangular building which served Memphis as Fire Station Two. From the rear of the building, which was built on an embankment, one was afforded a fine view of the Lorraine and, because it was raised high above the street, an almost eye-level view of the motel's second floor balcony. For some days the police had utilized Fire Station Two as a command post. It was ideal because it was so near the motel, had an unobstructed view of the scene in the motel court and of most of the rooms which faced the fire station, and because it provided cover for the police. During the previous week, on March 28, a march from Clayborn Temple, led by Dr. King, was interrupted by window breaking. The police then moved into the demonstrators. Police attack dogs were replaced by the first mass use of mace in the nation against peaceful demonstrators. The police charged the marchers, using night sticks and tear gas, and firing weapons. A sixteen-year-old boy, Larry Payne, was shot and killed. Two hundred and eighty people were arrested and at least sixty were injured by police violence. The state legislature mandated a nightly curfew at 7 o'clock and 4,000 members of the National Guard moved into Memphis.

The feeling in the black community against the city officials, who would not consider the minimal demands of the sanitation workers, and the police, who were at best unsympathetic to their fellow city employees, most of whom were black, was exacerbated by the brutal attack upon the demonstrators. The Invaders, a militant black youth group, demanded that the police be removed from the scene. Reverend Samuel Kyles asked the police to assign Ed Redditt, a black Memphis detective, to provide security for Dr. King. Redditt was assigned and set up the police command post at the fire station because of its proximity to the Lorraine and because it provided security from the Invaders and others who wanted no police, black or white, on the scene.

A very interested observer in the police surveillance of the Lorraine Motel and Dr. King and his associates was Floyd Newsum, an intelligent, articulate supporter of his fellow city employees. Floyd Newsum, a black fireman for the city of Memphis, was stationed at Fire Station Two. Newsum had marched with the sanitation workers. He had walked with and listed to Dr. King. He had been for many years an activist in the struggle for equal rights in Memphis. When I spoke to him he had just celebrated his forty-fourth birthday. His daughter lived at home; one son, who had a masters degree in art, teached art at the University of Houston while his other son was completing work for his doctorate at the University of Michigan.

On April 3, 1968, Newsum saw Detective Redditt at the fire station. That evening Newsum went to the Mason Temple to hear Dr. King, who had just returned to Memphis. Newsum saw Redditt at the rally that evening as well. Then Dr. King spoke. Newsum was deeply moved by King's words and those words still haunted him as he returned to his home that Wednesday night. He entered his home at approximately 10:30 that evening and "I found a message to call into the Fire Department; to call my lieutenant, Lt. Smith." He called Smith who ordered him not to report to Station Two the next morning but insisted he report to Station Thirty-one "on detail." A detail is a temporary transfer that is traditionally arranged so that a fire company with a surplus of men, or at least more personnel than are required for the task, can temporarily assign one or more employees to an understaffed company. Newsum told me, "I worked on a truck company. Our company simply could not operate with less than five men. On April 3rd our company was a company consisting of five men. When they detailed me out of Two they made that equipment inoperable, unless they sent someone in to replace me." Smith told Newsum that he did not know why he had been detailed to Thirty-one but that Newsum definitely had been ordered to report there in the morning and that he was not to report to Two.

On the morning of April 4th, Newsum reported to Thirty-one. He was assigned to a pumper company, a company that required four people to operate the equipment. He was the fifth man in the unit. He learned later that day that Thirty-one was sufficiently overstaffed to detail a man elsewhere. "During the entire period that I was at Thirty-one a man was detailed to another station."

He told me that on April 4th, "I asked the question over and over as to why I had been detailed. It just did not make any sense from a fire department personnel management viewpoint." Later, when Newsum learned of Dr. King's murder he cried. And in the agony of that moment, he said, "The fact that I had been detailed out so suspiciously became more important to me."

"Of course," he said, "the police knew who I was and that I supported the sanitation workers and Dr. King." Newsum explained how he knew that the Memphis police were tracking him.

I was definitely under police observation before April 4th. All during the movement I carried a little transistor radio that picked up police and fire calls. Just about everyone in the movement knew that I had that little radio with me all of the time which means, of course, that people outside the movement had access to that fact as well. One day we were conducting a sit-in at the council chambers. When I walked into City Hall a police officer transmitted over the police radio channel the fact that I was there. The voice on the other end asked if the officer was sure that it was me and he answered that he was reasonably sure. The officer was then instructed to make a picture of me. Then the officer reported, "He's got his radio and he might be listening to us."

An independent examination of Newsum's file confirmed the charge that he had been placed under police surveillance before April 4th.

Two weeks later Newsum decided to seek a leave of absence from the Fire Department or, in the alternative, to resign. He was deeply troubled about his transfer and the murder of Dr. King and wondered if the two events were somehow related. He asked to see the Chief of the Fire Department, but Deputy Chief Gerald Barnett made it clear to him that he would not be able to see the Chief. Newsum then submitted his letter of resignation to Barnett, who left the room and then returned a moment later. Barnett then told Newsum that he could see Chief Hamilton. Hamilton asked him why he was resigning. Newsum said, "I sensed that he was happy, very happy, that I was leaving the department." Newsum told me, "After I came out of the Chief's office I saw Barnett and I said, 'I asked you before and you never did answer me, you never did give me any kind of reason. Now that this is settled, now that I have resigned and my resignation has been accepted by the Chief, now will you tell me why I was moved on April 4th?' Barnett said, 'All I can tell you is that you were moved at the request of the police.' "

When Abby Mann interviewed Barnett in 1976 he was at first vague about Newsum's allegation, didn't recall that conversation with Newsum eight years earlier, and added, "Without going up there [to Fire Department headquarters] and briefing myself on the personnel records I might

126

tell you a story. I might be mistaken. Why don't you call up and talk to Chief Williams about that. He's sitting up there with the records.'' When Mann asked the question again Barnett said, ''He's got me mixed up with some other Chief.'' I asked Chief Williams if the personnel records supported Newsum's charge about being transferred and he replied, ''Our records show that Mr. Newsum was detailed, I mean detailed from one place to another. And our records show that he was on April 4, 1968, he was detailed to what we say is Fire Station 31. But it doesn't give a reason.''

I asked if the records revealed that there were only two black firemen at Fire Station Two and that both had been detailed out to other stations on April 4th. ''Well, yes,'' said Chief Williams, ''And they both were detailed to another station. The other one was named Wallace.'' I asked if he had any idea why the temporary transfers had taken place. ''We try to keep the fire department balanced by details. To even up the personnel to take care of the shortage at a fire station.'' I then asked whether Thirty-one, to which Newsum had been transferred, had been short. He answered, ''Well, like I say, a number of them were short that day. No, Thirty-one was not short. It wasn't below maximum strength.'' As for Wallace, ''He was detailed to number Thirty-three, which is at the airport.'' Was Thirty-three short that day? ''No, I don't think it was.''

Well, was there a shortage of personnel at Two immediately after the two black firemen were detailed out on April 4 to other stations which were not short? ''Yes, there was. In fact one man had to be detailed in, they were so short.'' When was this other man detailed in? ''April 4, the day that Mr. Newsum was detailed out.''

I told Chief Williams that Newsum had told me that Barnett had informed him that his transfer was the result of a police department request. Williams responded, ''We had a fire and police director by the name of Holloman in 1968, at the time that King was killed. If Newsum was detailed out because of a police request it would have to come from Mr. Holloman, the director at that time. He was over the fire and police departments.''

I spoke to Robert Walker, then the director of the Fire Department, told him what I had learned about the temporary transfers of Newsum and Wallace on April 4, 1968, and asked if he had any explanation for the odd events. ''I think the records will reflect that those men were temporarily assigned to other stations and I think the reason might have been that there was a lot of tension, with the black-white issue there. And I think there had been a few occasions where they were harassed. I think it was this kind of tension that existed at the moment.'' I asked if the transfer was for the purpose of protecting Newsum and Wallace. "Yes, Right. In other words it was to relieve them of the tension that was being built up in the neighborhood." I told Walker that Newsum had been told that the police department had requested the transfer.

It's kind of bad that Mr. Holloman was the fire and police director at that time. Now we have separate directors, one over fire and one over police. It could have been that an agreement was worked out. I don't know what his thoughts were at that time. But it could have been that they were using Two as a stakeout by the police and possibly the FBI. I have been told that there were FBI people at the firehouse. You could call the FBI to check that out. I'm sure they keep the records. I know they were using it as a lookout post because the Lorraine Motel is near, in the vicinity of it.

During my next meeting with Newsum I told him that Walker had told me, in essence, that both he and Wallace had been detailed out due to the racial tension and to protect them. Newsum laughed and said,

I don't believe that was the reason. I never had been threatened. I never was harassed. In fact I felt quite comfortable at Station Two. I felt a lot more comfortable there than where I was sent to. Two is in a black community and I was transferred from there into a totally white community where I was the only black in the company. I was then with a group of men I didn't know. That was a crucial time, a very difficult time, and I was very uncomfortable there. In fact, I was so upset about that new assignment and so uncomfortable there that I called the Chief on April 4th and asked how long I had to remain there and asked to be returned to Two. There just is no way that they could have thought that they were doing me a favor, protecting me or making me more comfortable by transferring me. I am sure that I was not moved because of considerations of my safety.

Members of the fire companies stationed at Fire Station Two often sat outside the station during pleasant weather. They would sit or stand around on a small patch near the rear of the firehouse, overlooking the Lorraine, or on a bench near the front of the station on South Main Street. If Newsom had been at the rear of the station on April 4th he might have seen Dr. King when he was shot. He might have responded by running toward the front of the station and looking to his right. If so, he probably would have seen the killer emerge from the rooming house door just a few yards down the street.

If Newsum had been sitting on a bench in front of the station, had he looked down South Main, he probably would have seen the murderer emerge from the rooming house.

Newsum was an activist. One cannot predict what his response might have been, but it certainly is possible that he might have interfered with the flight of the murderer from the scene, or at least have observed the man and perhaps his vehicle and reported that information to the police.

However, for reasons not yet adequately explained by the Memphis police and fire authorities, Newsum was not there. At Thirty-one all Newsum could do upon learning of Dr. King's death was to cry.

While Newsum was the only committed activist at Fire Station Two on April 3, he was not the only black fireman stationed there; N. E. Wallace was also assigned to Two at the time. On April 3 his company officer, R. T. Johnson, told him not to report to Station Two on April 4 for he too had been detailed out. Wallace asked Johnson why he was being transferred and Johnson told him, "Well, we hear that you have been threatened. You know, we don't want anything to happen to you."

Wallace told me that to his knowledge he had never been threatened while at Two and that he was certainly not afraid that anything would happen to him if he remained there. "That was a black community; there was another black in our station house and I felt comfortable there. I don't believe that I was threatened."

He said that approximately two and a half months after King was killed he was reassigned to Station Two and that he was never threatened or harmed after he returned.

I asked Wallace if he ever believed that the real reason that he had been transferred was because he had been threatened. "I've got my doubts. I always did have. I never believed I was being transferred for my own good." Prior to April 4th Wallace was in a position to observe the various strangers who appeared in and about Two. "I saw the two black detectives, Redditt and the other one. And there were also white men there in street clothes. People said they were FBI but you can't tell from just looking."

On April 4th there were no black firemen in Fire Station Two, since the only two blacks had been assigned elsewhere.

Detective Ed Redditt was at Two, however, and he was in charge of stationary security for King. His radio provided him immediate access to the mobile units in the vicinity. Assigned to assist him was a Memphis police officer, W. B. Richmond.

Redditt said, "The day of King's assassination I was at the firehouse. I could identify everybody who came and went. I knew the SCLC personnel, I knew Dr. King, I knew the cars, I knew the license plate numbers."

I asked if he had always provided security when King came to town. "Right," he answered, "So I knew who to look for. I knew the local Klansmen by sight. I knew the Invaders, the ministers, the militant groups, everyone involved in the leadership of the sanitation strike." I asked Redditt what his plan was in case of an attempt on Dr. King. "My thing was this. If something occurred in my sight Richmond would remain there, at the rear of the Firehouse, overlooking the motel. I would run to the front. I run a little bit faster, and I would try to cut off anybody in front. Richmond could radio a perimeter of security, a moving task force." I asked Redditt what the stationary security consisted of. "Just me and Richmond, that was the total security."

I asked Redditt how many police officers had provided stationary security for King in the past. "Normally we had ten, but this time it was reduced to two."

Redditt was at the airport when King arrived. He remembers one woman, no doubt still reacting to the police violence at the March 28th march, who said, "We don't want no security. We don't need no police." Redditt approached a black minister and said that he had come to provide security and the minister responded, "We don't need any security." Redditt said, "I could feel the anxiety and the bitterness because of the police macing and beating. I could understand this feeling, the reason that they didn't want any police around. But I said, 'Well I'm going to get him to the Lorraine' and I got in front of the car in which Dr. King was traveling and we proceeded on down to the Lorraine and when we got there, I saw him up the steps." A police inspector was at the Lorraine and he asked Redditt what the black leaders had said. Redditt informed the inspector that the situation was very touchy and that some people in King's party did not want the police around. As they were talking, Redditt recalls that someone walked up to them and said, "We don't want no police around him. Get the hell out of there." The inspector took out his radio and called back to headquarters; "Okay, pull out," came the response from headquarters. Redditt was surprised. "I couldn't understand what the police were doing. It always is the function of the police to provide protection for people who are threatened even if some of the people around them don't want it. That's the way it always was. But with Holloman there it was different all of a sudden. I told the inspector," Redditt later said, "I need to have some type of security for King. We can't just walk away after all the threats and violence." According to Redditt, the inspector asked, "Well, what do you want to do?" and Redditt replied, "Well, there at the firehouse at least we can see if it's open; if it looks out adequately on the motel. At least we can go there and establish stationary security. We won't even be seen." The inspector replied "OK, do what you want to do."

Redditt established a command post at the firehouse. The normal complement of ten men had been reduced to two until approximately four o'clock on the afternoon of April 4th.

According to Redditt, "About an hour and a half, no more than two hours before Dr. King's assassination, Lt. Arkin, who was in intelligence, came down to the station. He said, 'Ed, they want to see you at headquarters.'" Redditt was reluctant to leave his post, to abandon the entire security operation to Richmond. Redditt had difficulty leaving since his plan to cut off a potential escape from the scene, should there be an attempt on King's life, was predicated upon a functioning team of at least two men. Arkin told Redditt that Holloman himself had ordered him to report to him at headquarters. "So what could I do? I got into the car with Arkin, leaving Richmond all alone, and we proceeded to headquarters." Upon arriving at police headquarters Redditt was taken into the conference room.

"It was like a meeting of the Joint Chiefs of Staff. In this room, just before Dr. King was murdered, were the heads and the seconds in command of I guess every law enforcement operation in this area you could think of. I had never seen anything like it before. The Sheriff, the Highway Patrol, Army Intelligence, the National Guard. You name it. It was in the room."

Redditt recalled that, "I walked right in and Holloman addressed me at once. He said, 'Ed, there's a contract out on you.' I said, 'What do you mean?' I couldn't understand why I was there at this top-level meeting and why I was being told about a contract on me in front of that whole group. The whole thing didn't make any sense."

Redditt said that Holloman then introduced him to a man in the room dressed in civilian clothes. Redditt remembers very clearly that Holloman, indicating a man at the conference table said, "Ed, this gentleman is from the United States Secret Service in Washington, D.C. He has secured information from the Highway Patrol in Mississippi that a group in Mississippi has a contract out to kill you. This group has let the contract out to a hit man from St. Louis to get you. That hit man may be here in Memphis now. He, [indicating the Secret Service man again] has just flown down from Washington to give me this information."

131

The events and assertions were moving too quickly for Redditt to calmly evaluate them. A top-level police mini-convention to which he had been summoned to be informed that the United States Secret Service had sent its representative by plane from Washington to warn of a three-state conspiracy to kill him, a relatively unknown local detective, was difficult to assess and impossible for him to believe.

Later he told me that he could not believe that the United States Secret Service, which is primarily obligated to provide protection for Presidents, Vice Presidents, members of their families, and candidates for the two highest elective offices, had taken a real interest in him. Upon reflection he also found it somewhat troubling to consider that if the Secret Service in Washington really did have information that someone was stalking the streets of Memphis presumably armed with a gun and motivated by a contract to kill him that the agent in Washington would pick up the telephone and ask his secretary to book passage for him on the next convenient flight to Memphis, rather than report the threat by telephone at once to the responsible persons in Memphis. In fact, nothing about the story rang true. On reflection, and without the perspective afforded by the inexorable passing of time and events, in that room crowded with the police elite, all Redditt knew was that something was terribly wrong.

Holloman continued, "So, Ed, in order to protect you, I have personally made reservations for you and your family at the Rivermont Holiday Inn. You and your family are to move in there right now for your safety."

Redditt told me, "My first thought was that Dr. King was going to be leaving the Lorraine shortly and that I should be there. Then I thought about my mother-in-law who was really quite ill. I knew that if she heard this rumor that I had been threatened and if she had to move, it might be very bad for her. Anyway I knew that Richmond couldn't handle it alone there at the station house and besides I was the one that knew the people, the cars, the license numbers and I was the one that could spot trouble." Redditt responded to Holloman. "Sir, I'm not going. You can't stop a contract. If there is one on me I'll just stay on the streets and try to be cautious. But I won't involve my family. My family will stay at home. I'll stay on the streets. If they're going to get me let them get me on the streets while I'm nowhere near my family."

Holloman answered sharply, "Redditt you are going to the Rivermont with your family. That's an order and there is nothing to discuss."

Redditt made one more effort. He told Holloman that his mother-in-law was too sick to be moved and too sick to be left alone. Holloman thought for a moment and said "All right. You just go home and stay there.'' Redditt asked if he could finish his assignment at the Lorraine first. Holloman said, ''You are going home. You are going home now. That's an order.''

Redditt drove home with Memphis police officers. When they drove up in front of Redditt's house, the Memphis police informed him that they were going to stay in his house with him. At that point it became clear to Redditt that their assignment quite obviously was to watch him, not guard the house.

I thought they might sit outside in unmarked cars, maintaining radio contact with each other and with me, and in that way provide some protection. But their orders apparently were to stay in the house with me. That way they could watch me but they couldn't protect me. If someone threw a bomb in a window those two officers would just have been two more casualties. Then I really knew something was wrong. I sat in the car and thought about Dr. King. I had been with him so much, everytime he came to Memphis, I had heard him speak so often that I was practically one of his disciples. I thought about him at the Lorraine without adequate protection. I didn't want to leave the car, to go into the house, because I thought that the presence of the other officers was going to upset my mother-in-law. So we sat in the car for a few minutes and then the radio announced that Dr. King had been shot.

Redditt ran into the house as soon as he heard the news.

I thought that it would be too much of a shock for my mother-in-law. Anyway the excitement of having the police there watching me didn't help. And we thought she didn't have a radio. We were trying to keep the news from her. But she did have a small transistor radio and she heard that he had been killed. The next night she screamed out ''Dr. King, Dr. King, Dr. King. God, take me instead of Dr. King.'' And she died. She died of grief.

I asked Redditt when he returned to work and how the contract story was finally disposed of. ''It was Thursday, April 4, that they ordered me to go home. I called Thursday to see if I could participate in the homicide investigation. I called Friday. I called Saturday. When I called Sunday, the basic investigation was over and they ordered me to go back to work. The contract? Nothing else has ever been said about the contract on my life.''

When Redditt was removed from the scene, only W. B. Richmond, then a Memphis patrolman, was left on the scene. My interview with him was less than satisfactory. I began by introducing myself and then saying, "I've been told that you were the one police officer who was a witness to the murder of Dr. King." He responded, "I'd like to know who gave you my phone number." I told him that I had found it in the telephone book following his name. Then he said, "I have nothing to talk to anybody about the King killing because I don't know anything about it." He denied that he was at or near the Lorraine Motel on April 4; he denied he had been in a stake-out with or without Ed Redditt; and he denied that he had been near the fire station that day. When I asked him what observations he had on April 4, he said, "I had none." When I asked him how far from the Lorraine Motel he was when Dr. King was shot he said that he was "at police headquarters" and added, "I didn't hear the shot."

It was clear to me that Richmond had not told the truth to me. He told me that he had been "talked to by the Department of Justice" during the first part of July 1976. "They're the only people I'm supposed to talk to about it. I don't know anything about the man's killing." He told me that he had told the Department of Justice "the same things that I told you." Weeks later when I returned to Memphis I spoke with Richmond again. This time he told me that he had been at the firehouse and that he was there when King was killed. He said he had talked to his supervisors who said that he should give me that information. He said that was all he remembered about the murder.

Later two investigators for the Citizens Commission of Inquiry interviewed two firemen who were present when King was shot. One of them, Charles E. Stone, said, "And Lt. Redditt, I believe that was his name, was gone and the other boy was here. Only one was here at the time of the shooting."

The other fireman, William B. King, said,

Well, it was around six o'clock when it happened. We had a warning test and at six o'clock the alarm goes off. So I know it was right at six o'clock when he was shot. He had come out to the banister. He was standing there talking to his chauffeur who was on the ground. The chauffeur was on the ground and all of a sudden he kind of looked up, at least it looked like he looked up and there was this noise and he fell. And there were several people crying at the motel and this one guy come out, just fell down and started crying and crying. There was a lot of emotion at that time. We heard a lot of policemen shouting and hollering over there because the door was shut and I forget the exact words that was said but there was a lot of emotion. And I

think we all ran to see who was shot. And then this policeman, Richmond, he got on the phone and made a call. Well, in no time he left.

Since Richmond had a radio, which could have provided immediate access to the police mobile units in the area as well as to headquarters, it is difficult to understand why he did not use it. It becomes even more puzzling in light of the plan that Redditt had promulgated and shared with Richmond. That plan called for Redditt to cover South Main Street and for Richmond to use the radio to alert the mobile units. One must concede that Richmond could not have done both. The mystery lies in trying to determine why he attempted neither.

If the elaborate charade, which included the removal of Redditt and the detailing of Newsum and Wallace, was designed to strip away the security just before Dr. King was killed, in order to facilitate the escape of the sniper, it was an ultimately successful plan. The murderer fled, unobserved and unimpeded.

Chapter Nineteen

APRIL 4, ATLANTA
by Mark Lane

Arthur Murtagh, the veteran FBI agent, said,

> The day that King was shot, I was at the office, leaving for the day, with an FBI agent who was at the supervisory level. He was a young man, twenty-nine to thirty-two years old, handsome, nice dresser—reasonably intelligent and the women were crazy about him in the office. He was friendly with me.
>
> We heard the announcement, that King had been shot, as we were preparing to leave. This agent jumped for joy, literally leaped in the air, yelling, "They got Zorro! They got the son of a bitch! I hope he dies!"
>
> As we punched our salmon-colored cards out, the agent explained to me how King was nothing but a "goddamn Communist" troublemaker anyway. Then we heard that King had died. Again, he was elated. He just went crazy with joy.
>
> I said, "For Christ's sake, they killed a great leader," and as we walked to the parking lot, we had a discussion. The agent told me how King had been ruining the United States; that he was dividing our people; that he was Communist-dominated; and that "if the lazy goddamned niggers had worked, instead of demonstrating, they could make it just like anybody else in this country—for example, the Italians and the Irish!"

Following the murder of Dr. King a number of American cities were set on fire. The Attorney General was able to view part of the conflagration in Washington, D.C. A federal decision was made to investigate the crime. Murtagh said that the Department of Justice called upon the FBI to investigate. Hoover sent the request to the SAC in Atlanta. The SAC there turned it over to the intelligence unit—the Destroy King Squad. The very people who had illegally harassed him when he was alive, including the agent who celebrated when he died, were really in charge of the investigation. Memphis had the early lead material. The Bureau in Washington directed the early stages of the investigation. But it was directed out of Atlanta by the Destroy King Squad after a day or two.

Teletype leads would come in, and the case supervisor would assign the leads to various agents. "Now the assigning of leads would make a lot of difference," said Murtagh. "Up until civil rights were pushed hard in the sixties, I was never assigned to civil rights work at all. Only when they got to the point where they had to get some answers would they assign anybody like me. They had been assigning old-time Southern agents to handle civil rights cases."

How did the fact that those assigned to investigate King's death had been members of the get-King Squad affect that effort? "I think they might not have gotten the right answer on a lot of these things simply because there was no will to get the right answer," said Murtagh. "They didn't want to ask the right questions. The feeling against King, in the Bureau, was so strong," said Murtagh, that if the Bureau had had advance information of an assassination plot against King,

> **and no one else knew about it—they would sit on it. And let King get killed.**
>
> **The Bureau wanted to get the investigation wrapped up and get out of it. I think there was sentiment in the Bureau, also—an extreme sentiment, at all costs, to keep the blacks from making any inroads.**
>
> **I would not depend on an investigation, by the people I knew, to be very accurate. Statements came out from the Bureau, within twenty-four hours of each killing, that there was no conspiracy involved in the deaths of President Kennedy, Dr. King, and Bobby Kennedy.**
>
> **I talked about conspiracy in Atlanta regarding King, and thought about it in the Kennedy case. I was told that we weren't to think about conspiracy. Our jurisdiction was very flimsy anyway, since King wasn't a government official. What were we doing investigating it?**
>
> **I feel it was a political decision. I don't think the crime was ever investigated. In fact, I'm convinced it was never investigated. It wasn't investigated like the Mississippi killings, it wasn't investigated like the Hoffa disappearance. It wasn't even investigated as well as King was, when he was alive. I think eventually, if everybody keeps pushing, eventually some way, sometime, the whole thing will break open—you'll probably find a conspiracy.**

Maybe it's a movement. You've got to be able to think in terms of the fiendish minds of people in counterintelligence. If we're right, the King killing was some kind of a counterintelligence scheme, cooked up by somebody and it could be anybody. It could be anyone who could manipulate things in such a way to get them to happen. I think it can be done, and I think it was done.

There are too many questions about Oswald and Ray. How did they get all the way across the country? And where the hell did the money come from? How did they have their identities covered? No guy like Ray can do that sort of thing on his own. It just didn't happen that way.

Chapter Twenty

DIRECTOR HOLLOMAN
by Mark Lane

On July 27, 1976 my associate Abby Mann and I interviewed Frank Holloman in his Memphis office. Holloman was then the director of Future Memphis, Inc., a corporation established by one hundred leading businesses in Memphis to "cut off trouble before it begins" and to create a better image for Memphis. He was at first reluctant to talk about the King assassination. "The reason I resigned as director of fire and police," he told us, "was so that I would not have to answer questions about that case." Yet, Abby was persuasive and with a minimum shifting of emphasis regarding his credits and a somewhat more substantial but temporary shift of his perspective, he convinced Holloman that he was a sympathetic listener, and perhaps an advocate of Holloman's cause as well. For example, Abby did not spend a great deal of time explaining that he had written the American film classic *Judgement at Nuremberg* or that he had been a close friend of Dr. King. Instead, he pointed to the fact that he created *Kojak*, a fact which often has caused Abby to wince but caused, in this setting, a warm and welcoming smile across Holloman's face. Abby's most impressive moment came when he referred to the chairman of the Church Committee as "somewhat of an extremist," followed quickly by his observation that "it is easy to criticize the FBI but where would we be without it." As I pondered that proposition for a moment, I saw Holloman melt and heard him ask Abby, "Well, what can I tell you that will help you?"

Abby explained that he was writing an objective screenplay for NBC-TV on the life of Dr. King and that while the program would not dwell on his death, quite naturally it would refer to it. He introduced me as his assistant in the project and said that I had done some research on the subject and would like to ask him a few questions. Holloman stared at me for a moment or two and we were both aware, I believe, that I had not offered my own police-oriented credentials.

Abby began to ask Holloman about the March 28th demonstration and Holloman responded:

There was a large number of people involved; a large number of school students. From early morning until the time of the actual step-off of the march we were receiving numerous reports of students moving from their school areas to the area where the march was to start. When the march started Dr. King stepped out. He was in the lead. And behind him violence did break out. They began to break windows. We felt we had no alternative at that point except to stop the march. We ordered the march stopped and ordered dispersal of the crowd. The crowd at that point in the rear was completely out of hand and we did have to use tear gas in order to disperse the crowd. I do recall the break out, then the fight, then the riot situation developed all over town.

Abby asked, "There was a boy killed later, wasn't there?" Holloman replied, "Yes . . . he was dying in the south, as I recall it was in the south part of the city in which there was a connection with looting as I recall. It was controversial as to whether or not there was a justifiable killing. We thought it was a justifiable defense of a policeman's life because the policeman thought his life was in danger."

I asked Holloman what his assessment of the situation was just before Dr. King came to Memphis. "What were the feelings and what were the police problems in terms of potential racial conflicts?" Holloman said that "From the time of the first riots until he returned, the feelings in the community were naturally very high. He came back for the purpose of making a successful march. We felt that there was a danger to Dr. King by information that we received that there would possibly be more violence and possibly violence toward him. And so we felt so strongly about it that we went to the federal court in order to seek an injunction against the march which was scheduled whenever it was, I've forgotten." I asked, "What was the information you received about violence which would happen against King?" Holloman answered, "It was an accumulation of intelligence information we had received. I will not be more specific on that." I asked Holloman what security was afforded to Dr. King by the police in the light of the potential violence against him. He answered, "The security we provided for him was a peripheral security because his people refused personal on-the-scene security." Holloman then pointed to my tape recorder and said, "Turn this off a minute." Holloman's warm tone had cooled a bit. By dramatically altering the course of the discussion to more general and less troublesome areas such as his police

140

background, his "absolutely down the middle neutral position" regarding the strike and other trying events, Abby and I were able to secure his permission to turn on the tape recorder again.

Soon after the recording device was reactivated, I told Holloman that Ed Redditt had told me that he had always been in charge of security every time King came to Memphis. I asked Holloman if Redditt had been correct. Holloman stared at me and, in a harsh and almost angry manner that is quite noticeable when the tape is played, asked me, "Did you talk to Ed Redditt himself?" I said that I had and then again asked if Redditt had always been in charge of providing police security for King and if he had been in charge on April 4th. Holloman replied, "He could have been. I don't recall though." I then told Holloman what Redditt had told me about the exchange that took place between them in the conference room just before the murder of Dr. King. Holloman said, "I arranged for him to go to a hotel." I asked Holloman if there had been a threat to kill Redditt and he answered:

> Yes, yes. I got a report on the line for it and immediately pulled. See, I had been in court due to actual time I was in court until five o'clock. I think it was four, in federal court, and I came back in the office. I was then advised. I didn't know about this until I got back to my office. Shortly after I got back to the office I was then advised that a threat had been made against Redditt's life. I immediately ordered Redditt to my office. I cannot tell you frankly where the report came from. I don't know the source. I can't say. Some people say it was the Secret Service. Some say it was somebody else. I frankly do not know. As far as I recall it came from a substantial source that convinced me that it was true. So I immediately called him into my office, told him what the report was and then told him that his life was invaluable as far as I was concerned and that I would take every effort to protect him. And I made arrangements to have him placed in a motel in Memphis under an assumed name together with his entire family which he did not want to do because Ed Redditt is a brave man. But I told him there was no choice, that his life was in danger and I was going to do what I could to protect it. Ah, this was after five o'clock. At 6:01 as I recall I was still in my office by myself handling some work cleaning out my desk before I went home when the report came that Dr. King had been killed.

I asked, "When Redditt left your office was it your understanding that he would then be going home or to the motel but not to the Lorraine Motel?" Holloman said, "Right." I inquired, "Well, was he at that point in charge of security at the Lorraine for the police department? I don't mean the peripheral TAC [Tactical] squad which had its own operation but I mean the on-the-scene.'' Holloman said, ''At that point I cannot say whether he was or not. If he says he was I have no reason to question that as to whether or not he was in charge. He was not in charge of the operation. Let's put it that way.''

I reported that Redditt said that there was only one other person with him, a fellow officer. I asked Holloman if Redditt was replaced by anyone else. He answered ''Was he what?'' ''Replaced at the scene by anyone else at the Lorraine Motel?'' I asked again. Frank Holloman responded, ''I do not recall because at that point in time I was I had handled this particular thing. I was sitting there trying to do some work on my desk when 6:01, which was less than an hour, this happened, so I don't know. I was never in that direct contact. I had been in court all day and it happened; as far as a replacement, frankly I do not know.'' I asked Holloman if it was unusual for him to be notified that there was a contract out on a police officer. He answered, ''There was never any contract. I mean there was no contract. It isn't that dramatic in the modern day organized crime. I just was advised that a certain organization was going to kill him.'' I asked, ''Organization? Do you remember which it was?'' Holloman answered, ''Yes, but I'm not going to reveal it. It was an organization. Not locally. Not local; not a local organization.''

I wondered if Holloman had ever considered what might appear to some to be obvious; that the death threat about Redditt was developed for the purpose of stripping away King's security. Holloman answered firmly, not to say repetitively, ''Absolutely not. No way. No possible way. No way.''

In fact, the death threat, real or contrived, was responsible for Redditt's removal and that removal was useful, perhaps critical, to the murderer in his escape from the scene. I asked Holloman why the only two black firemen at Fire Station Two had been removed from that assignment on the very day of the murder. He said, ''I never heard about that. No. And I would say there's absolutely no connection with any of it. So for whatever reason he may have been transferred, he was not there in the first place with the King operation.'' When I informed Holloman of Newsum's information regarding his transfer, he answered ''I don't think it would be true. I knew what was happening as far as the police department was concerned. And I knew of no orders, no instructions of any kind. And I don't believe that it would have gone through except through me. And it did not.''

I again asked Holloman if he recalled the original source of the threat to Redditt's life. He said:

No. I don't recall. And so you're going into something that I haven't thought about before. I just cannot recall. I guess the events—of the shock of the next hour. That's really completely in my memory, as far as that part was concerned. And I don't recall. I do know it came from a reputable source. I would say an agency. Whether it was the Secret Service, I frankly cannot tell you right now. I couldn't testify to that fact.

I asked, "If it was the FBI you probably would have remembered it?" Holloman answered:

Not necessarily. No, not necessarily. No it could have been the FBI, it could have been the Secret Service—it's just right there it's a blank. I don't recall. The source was so positive, and so reliable, that I immediately took action. In spite of what was going on at that time, I believed it. And that's the reason I took the action that I did.

Almost immediately after Holloman gave that answer he picked up the microphone and tossed it towards me, saying, "All right, put that thing off for good now."

There is much that is troubling about Holloman's explanation of the events. Why was he reluctant to release the name of the organization that conspired to kill Redditt? Holloman had said that he felt that Dr. King was in danger and that he believed that there might be violence directed against him. Why then was the police detail reduced to two men on April 4, 1968? He then reduced the detail to one man. Under the circumstances why did he not replace Redditt if he truly believed that Redditt had to be removed? Why did he take no action to apprehend those responsible for conspiring to kill one of his police officers, a crime, from the viewpoint of law enforcement officials, more serious than any other? How could he fail to remember the agency or bureau that flew a representative into Memphis to warn him about the threat to Redditt?

Redditt was certain when he talked to me that Holloman identified the agent on April 4th as a representative of the Secret Service. Yet, Redditt later conducted an independent inquiry and discovered, not at all to his surprise, that the Secret Service had dispatched no one to Memphis that day and that the officials there had never even heard of the threat to Redditt's life. If Holloman could remember his source, his allegation could be verified or proven to be untrue. His loss of memory, due, he asserts, to the "shock" of learning of the death of Dr. King, is both convenient and speaks of a sensitive man deeply committed to the law.

If one secures the threshhold impression that Holloman's failure to take adequate precautions was due to his lack of experience or that his memory was erased due to the personal grief that he experienced when a man he respected was murdered, an examination of his background may alter that concept.

Holloman had been with the FBI for a quarter of a century. He was the Special Agent in Charge (SAC) of the FBI office in Atlanta, where Dr. King lived and where his church and family were; he had been SAC at the FBI office in Jackson, Mississippi; he had been the SAC at the Memphis office, as well, when many of the problems which led to the strike were developing. During eight of Holloman's years with the Bureau, he worked in the FBI headquarters in Washington, D.C.

Holloman said of that period, "I was the Inspector in Hoover's office. You might say the Inspector-in-Charge of his office."

When Abby asked him about the charges made by the Church Committee about the numerous illegal and immoral actions of the Hoover FBI, many of which emanated from that office when Holloman was the Inspector-in-Charge, Holloman said, "I have nothing to apologize for that we ever did when I was there. What we did we had to do and it was proper to do it. J. Edgar Hoover was a friend of mine and I saw nothing that he did that was wrong."

It is in view of Hoover's pathological hatred of Dr. King, an obsession which led him to commit numerous crimes in order to destroy him, and which apparently did not trouble Holloman, that one must evaluate Holloman's claim of amnesiac shock occasioned by Dr. King's death.

Chapter Twenty-One

APRIL 5, MEMPHIS
by Mark Lane

Wayne Chastain, a lawyer in Memphis, was a reporter for the Memphis *Press Scimitar*, one of the two major daily newspapers at the time of the assassination of Dr. King.

After the police concluded that the shot had been fired from the bathroom window in the rooming house, Chastain came across an unpublished photograph in the newspaper's files. Taken by an Associated Press photographer from the bathroom window, it showed the Lorraine Motel balcony as the sniper would have seen it if the shot had been fired from there.

Chastain noted that the view was obscured by branches from trees growing on the embankment between the rooming house and the motel.

Later that day he discussed that oddity in the case with Kay Black, another reporter for the Memphis *Press Scimitar*. Chastain told me that although the picture was puzzling he paid little attention to it, "because at that time I believed the shot had come from that window. I believed that the police were right about that."

Chastain has continued to maintain a growing file on the case and has talked with many witnesses since. "Now I no longer believe the shot came from there. Now I think that picture and those trees take an added significance," he told me.

Later Kay Black received a telephone call from William B. Ingram, the former mayor of Memphis. Ingram had called to inform Black that the city was cutting down the trees on the embankment between the rooming house and the motel. She later told me, "Now, I hadn't been in the rooming house looking through that bathroom window but I do recall Wayne Chastain having said that he didn't see how someone could shoot through the trees to the motel. He said that he was puzzled how a clear shot could have been fired because he didn't see how you could see through the branches."

I asked Ms. Black if she could describe the trees.

I was over there all the time after Dr. King and his regiment arrived because I was covering the black community during the strike. I would go over there and have coffee with people if anything was happening. And it was spring and the normal thing was to be in the parking lot, the motel court. Right above the lot, on this embankment there was sort of an overgrown place. And of course I noticed it. There were a good sized amount of trees there—and they made a screen, more or less between the motel and the rooming house. They were between ten and twelve feet tall. Oak trees, and perhaps willows.

I asked Ms. Black if, in her judgment, the trees would have interfered with a shot from the bathroom window to the motel balcony. "Well, it occurred to me that they might, and on reflection I think they might have. That is why Mayor Ingram called, I think. They provided very substantial screening. And they were possibly important evidence and they were being cut down just as the investigation began."

Ms. Black determined that the city of Memphis had arranged for the trees to be cut down and had ordered the city sanitation department to remove them. She said that Ingram had called her in the morning. She reported the information to her desk and that afternoon she visited the murder scene. "And those trees were down. The screen was gone. There was just no way any longer to know if that shot could have been possible."

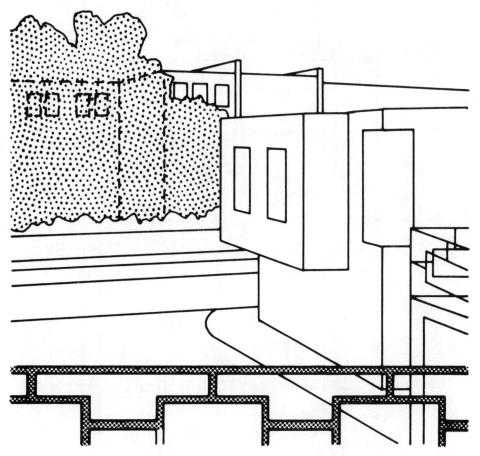

Drawing By Adam Schneider

The view from the balcony in front of Room 306 at the Lorraine Motel. The building to the left rear is 422½ South Main Street. The rear of the building which faces the motel is completely blocked by bushes and trees and cannot be seen from the Lorraine Motel. Yet it is that building that provides the entrance to the rooming house. One may pass through 422½ South Main and then enter the building which does overlook the Lorraine Motel.

The entrance to the rooming house at 422½ South Main provides internal access to the building to its left. It was alleged by the prosecution that Ray entered 422½, from which the Lorraine Motel could not be seen, walked through it to the next building, and secured a view of the Lorraine Motel balcony from the bathroom to the rear of that building. How Ray could have known of the internal connection between the two buildings and that the building housing Jim's Grill was part of the rooming house has not been explained.

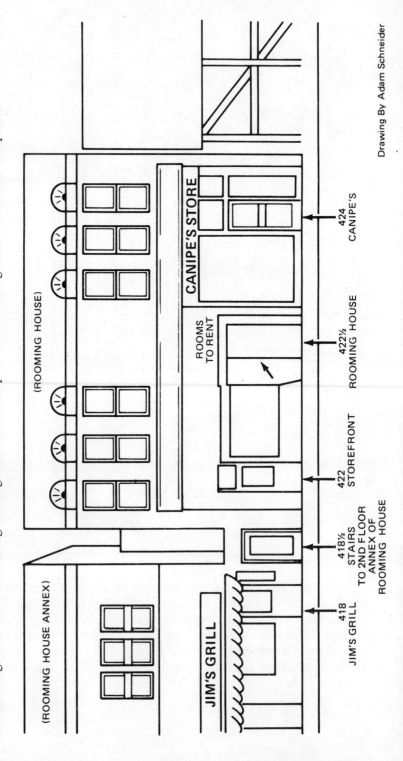

Drawing By Adam Schneider

Martin Luther King, Jr., in an unidentified jail cell.   © 1993 Flip Schulke/Schulke Archives

King delivers his legendary "I Have a Dream" speech at the 1963 March on Washington.

King shakes hands with the chairman of the Nobel committee, after King
received the Noble Peace Prize.   © 1993 AP/Wide World Photos

King, along with Coretta Scott King, Dr. Ralph Bunche, and Rev. Ralph Abernathy, leads the last leg of the Selma-to-Montgomery civil rights march in 1965.

© 1993 UPI/Bettmann

LBJ greets MLK at the bill-signing ceremony for the Civil Rights Act of 1965.

Left, MLK after being arrested for "loitering" in Montgomery.

© 1993 AP/Wide World Photos

Right, MLK and Rev. Ralph Abernathy in jail after leading a sit-in in St. Augustine, FL.   © 1993 UPI/Bettmann

King meets with Andrew Young . . .
© 1993 Ted Fahn/Globe Photos

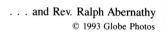

. . . and Rev. Ralph Abernathy
© 1993 Globe Photos

MLK during a drive to register new black voters in rural Alabama.   © Bob Adelman/Magnum Photos

Co-author Dick Gregory in St. Louis.   © 1993 UPI/Bettmann

PART SIX

THE STATE OF TENNESSEE VS. JAMES EARL RAY

Chapter Twenty-Two

THE CASE AGAINST RAY
by Mark Lane

On March 10, 1969, in Division III of the Criminal Court of Shelby County, Tennessee, James Earl Ray entered a prearranged plea of guilty in the murder of Dr. King. Judge W. Preston Battle accepted the plea after Ray's attorney, Percy Foreman, had worked out the arrangements with Memphis Attorney General Phil Canale, the prosecuting attorney.

Canale explained to the jurors:

> **It is incumbent upon the State in a plea of guilty to murder in the first degree to put on certain proof for your consideration.**
>
> **We have to put on proof of what we lawyers call the proof of the corpus delicti which is the body of the crime. We will also put on several lay witnesses or police officers to fill you in on certain important aspects of this case, and then we will introduce certain physical evidence through these witnesses, and Mr. Beasley, or Mr. Dwyer will question these witnesses, and Mr. Beasley will give you an agreed stipulation of facts that the State has gotten up which contains what the State would prove by witnesses if this went to trial, and you will have the benefit of all that information through this stipulation of fact which has been agreed to by the State and by the Defendant as to what the State would prove if this matter went to trial.**

Before the morning had ended and the jurors excused for lunch, the case against James Earl Ray for the murder of Dr. King had been spelled out in detail.

Several witnesses were called and questioned by Robert Dwyer, an Assistant Attorney General. Foreman did not object to any question put to any witness, even when the question was leading and improper. Foreman did not cross-examine any witness.

The first witness called was Reverend Samuel Kyles. He said he had known Dr. King for more than ten years. He had been with him in Room 306 of the Lorraine Motel for approximately forty-five minutes. "I had gone to pick Dr. Martin Luther King, Jr., up to go home, go to my house at 2215 South Parkway East for a soul food dinner." Dwyer asked, "Was Dr. King alive and in good health and in good spirits at that time and at that location?" Kyles answered affirmatively.

Dwyer asked Kyles what took place at 6:00 P.M.

Fairly close to 6:00 P.M. we were going to leave for dinner. Dr. Abernathy was also in the room. Dr. King came out. I was still in the room. He came out on the balcony and was greeting some of the people who were in the courtyard, and he came back in the room, I believe to get his coat, and the both of us came out together, and we stood at this point on the balcony for about three minutes greeting some people who also were going to dinner with us. And we stood together there about three or four minutes, and I turned to my right to walk away and said I was going and get my car and take some of the people who were going to dinner.

I got approximately 5 or 6 steps away from him and I heard what I now know to be a shot, and I looked over the railing. I thought it was a car backfiring, or something, and when I realized what had happened, I turned back to my left and saw Dr. King lying in a position thusly with a tremendous wound in his right side. He was laying in this position with the wound here [indicating].

Kyles said that when the shot was fired he looked in the general direction of the rooming house. "Yes, I looked over there because there were bushes and things."

Kyles was asked to describe the wound that had been inflicted upon Dr. King.

It tore this much of his face away that I could see, and I also noticed that the shot had cut his necktie, just cut right off at that point.

I remember that because he had been trying to find out—he thought somebody was playing a trick in the room—he couldn't find his necktie and he finally did find it, and we had had some conversation about his shirt and his necktie.

Kyles was asked if he had attended the funeral of Dr. King and he replied that he had.

Through the testimony of the first witness the state had established that Dr. King was shot at approximately 6:00 P.M. on April 4, 1968, and that he subsequently died.

Chauncey Eskridge, a Chicago lawyer who had represented Dr. King, testified next. He said that he had been "standing in the courtway looking up at door 306" at about 6:00 o'clock in the evening when Dr. King came out of his room. He said that soon "the sound came from my right ear and said 'Zing!' " He agreed with Kyles that the sound came from the general direction of the rooming house and that when he looked there he did not see anybody moving. Eskridge said that he had gone to the hospital with Dr. King and later attended his funeral.

Eskridge's testimony broke no new ground and was corroborative of Kyles' statement.

The state called no other eyewitnesses to the murder of Dr. King.

The next witness was Dr. Jerry Thomas Francisco, the Medical Examiner for Shelby County. He testified about the autopsy that was performed on Dr. King's body.

The examination revealed a gunshot wound to the right side of the face, passing through the body into the neck, through the spinal cord at the base of the neck, with the bullet lodging beneath the skin near the shoulder blade on the left.

Q. Cause of death was what, Dr. Francisco?

A. A gunshot wound to the cervical and thoracic spinal cord.

Q. In your medical opinion, how soon did death occur from that wound?

A. Shortly after death, shortly after injury.

Q. Did you recover anything from the body, Dr. Francisco?

A. Yes.

Q. I am going to show you an object and ask you if you can identify those, Dr. Francisco.

A. Yes.

Q. And what is that, please, sir?

A. This is the bullet that was removed from the body at the time of the autopsy.

Q. What, if anything, did you do with that bullet, Dr. Francisco, that you recovered?

A. This bullet was identified by number and delivered to a representative of the police department.

Francisco said that the bullet had angled downward from right to left passing through the chin, the base of the neck, and the spinal cord into the back. Francisco offered the opinion that the angle of the bullet through the body was consistent with a shot having been fired from the rooming house.

Francisco did not state that he knew where Dr. King had been standing, which direction he had been facing, or if he had been leaning over when he was shot, thereby considerably reducing the value of his opinion as to the origin of the shot.

Inspector N. E. Zachary of the Memphis Police Department testified that he had been the inspector in charge of the Homicide Bureau on April 4, 1968. He was at police headquarters when Dr. King was shot and when he heard that news on a radio broadcast he immediately went to the Lorraine Motel and began assigning men to the investigation. He then went to Main Street, he said, and stopped in front of the Canipe Amusement Company.

I found a package rolled up in a bedspread which consisted of a blue briefcase and a Browning pasteboard box containing a rifle.
At that particular time I put a guard on it with instructions to let no one touch it or move it until we could take photographs of it.

He said that the package had been wrapped in a bedspread when he found it. Zachary identified various articles that had been in the package including a box, a rifle that had been in the box, a pair of binoculars, a case for the binoculars, a pair of undershorts, a shaving kit, two cans of Schlitz beer, a hair brush, a transistor radio, a pair of pliers, a hammer, a paper bag, a copy of the *Commercial Appeal,* a Memphis newspaper, and some cartridges. He testified that he gave the evidence "to the FBI sometime around 10:00 P.M. that night" by delivering the material to "Mr. Jensen of the Memphis FBI." Zachary answered affirmatively when asked, "The purpose of turning these objects that you have identified here over to the FBI was to be sent to Washington for its examination, Inspector Zachary?"

Robert Jensen testified that on April 4, 1968, he was the Special Agent in Charge (SAC) of the Memphis Division of the FBI. He said that at about 6:05 P.M. he was told that Dr. King had been shot. He testified, "I called my Washington headquarters to advise them of the information which I had received, and then subsequently dispatched men to assist in the investigation." He said that he assigned agents to the investigation "probably around 6:30." The twenty-five minute hiatus, unexplained by the testimony or by subsequent official Bureau statements, leads to the conclusion that there was no federal effort to close off the area to prevent the murderer's escape. Since the city of Memphis borders on the states of Arkansas and Mississippi, both just minutes away, no local police blockade was likely to prove effective.

Jensen said that at 10:00 o'clock that evening he was in the offices of the Memphis Police Department. At that time, he said, "certain evidence was turned over to me." Dwyer inquired about the evidence.

Q. I am going to ask you, Mr. Jensen, to look at—there is a green spread here, here is some pliers and a hammer, here is a rifle, here is some shaving articles, binoculars, beer cans, newspaper, tee shirt, shorts, there is a transistor radio over there [indicating].

I will ask you if those objects were turned over to you by Inspector Zachary of the Memphis Police Department?

A. Yes, they were.

Q. And the purpose of that was what, sir?

A. In order that I could send them to our laboratory for examination.

Q. And did you do that, Mr. Jensen?

A. Yes, I did.

Q. And can you tell us briefly how that was done, sir?

A. Yes. The evidence was taken over to my office, was personally wrapped under my supervision, and when all the material was wrapped, I dispatched an agent to Washington to physically carry the material to the laboratory."

Jensen said that FBI agents discovered that a man named Eric S. Galt had registered at the Rebel Motel, although he did not say and was not asked for the date of that registration. He said that Galt had been driving a white Mustang. He testified that the FBI had discovered that the rifle had been sold by the Aeromarine Supply Company in Birmingham. Jensen said that the Mustang was discovered on April 11th. He said that the pliers and hammer may have been purchased from a hardware store in Los Angeles and that the tee shirt and shorts had been laundered in Los Angeles as well.

He then said that the FBI investigation culminated in the arrest of James Earl Ray. At that point Dwyer excused Jensen and said, "That is all the proof the State cares to offer at this time, if the Court pleases, except some stipulations by Mr. Beasley."

Through the testimony of witnesses the state had offered evidence that Dr. King had been shot on April 4, 1968, that he subsequently had died, that the shot had come from the direction of a clump of bushes and the rear of a rooming house, and that a package had been discovered near the entrance to the front of the rooming house. In addition, a witness had testified regarding the presence in Memphis of Eric S. Galt and his vehicle.

After a brief recess, the jurors were returned to the courtroom to listen to a lengthy narration by Assistant Attorney General James Beasley. He began, "May it please the Court, Gentlemen of the Jury, I propose at this time to narrate to you gentlemen a stipulation of the facts and evidence that the State would prove in addition to the testimony that you heretofore heard in the trial of this cause." Beasley contended that the state could prove that Ray had rented a room in the rooming house.

The State would show in the course of its proof, Gentlemen of the Jury, through Mrs. Bessie Brewer, who was employed as manager of this rooming house, that on the afternoon of April the 4th, between 3:00 and 3:30 P.M. in the afternoon, the Defendant appeared here at Mrs. Brewer's office or apartment that was used as an office in this rooming house. Under the name John Willard he requested a room for a week.

He added, "He was taken to room 5-B which is located in this section [indicating]. The Defendant did rent this room for a week from Mrs. Brewer." Beasley said that the state could prove that Ray had purchased Bushnell binoculars from Ralph Carpenter at the York Arms Company located one mile north of the rooming house.

A witness, Elizabeth Copeland, could testify, Beasley said, that between 4:30 and 4:45 P.M. a white Mustang parked near and to the south of the Canipe Amusement Company and was still there at 5:20 P.M. when she left the area.

Beasley said,

At approximately 6:00 P.M., Mr. Stephens heard the shot coming apparently through this wall from the bathroom. He then got up, went through this room out into the corridor in time to see the left profile of the Defendant as he turned down this passageway which leads to an opening with a stairwell going down to Main Street.

According to Beasley, Guy Warren Canipe and two customers were in the Canipe establishment and "saw the back of a white man going away from that area in a general direction on down Main Street, observing momentarily thereafter a white Mustang pull from the curb, head north on Main Street with one occupant.''

The package found in front of Canipe's, Beasley said, was wrapped in the green bedspread, previously identified, and contained the rifle, the binoculars and the other items in evidence. Beasley said that a crime scene search of the bathroom in the rooming house by officers of the Memphis Police Department "found marks in the bottom of the tub consistent with shoe or scuff marks" and that

> **The sill of this window in the bathroom was observed by Inspector Zachary to have what appeared to be a fresh indentation in it. This sill was ordered removed, was cut away, was subsequently sent to the FBI for comparison, and the proof would show through expert testimony that the markings on this sill were consistent with the machine markings as reflected on the barrel of the 30.06 rifle which has heretofore been introduced to you gentlemen.**

Beasley said the state could prove that Ray had purchased the 30.06 rifle that had been found in the package outside Canipe's Store and that he had used the pseudonym Harvey Lowmeyer when he bought the rifle in Birmingham.

The evidence would prove, said the prosecutor, that Ray had purchased the white Mustang for $1,995 on August 30, 1967, then using the name Eric S. Galt. At that point Beasley said that the evidence would prove that Ray entered Mexico on October 7 and remained there until the middle of November 1967. He said the State's proof would locate Ray in Los Angeles, New Orleans, and Birmingham in the intervening weeks. The State knew when Ray drove from Los Angeles to New Orleans and who accompanied him. The State knew that Ray was a customer of the Home Service Laundry Company located at 5280 Hollywood Boulevard and was prepared to offer Mrs. Mary Lucy Panella to testify that Ray brought his laundry in quite regularly between December 1967 and early March 1968. She was able, Beasley said, to identify her laundry marks on the undergarments found in the package.

Beasley continued,

> **Mr. Avidson, Rodney Avidson, who operated the dance studio at Long Beach, California, would testify with reference to knowing the Defendant as Eric S. Galt during the period from December the 5th until February the 12th while Mr. Galt was taking dancing lessons at his place of business.**
>
> **Through the testimony of Mr. Thomas Reeves Lau, the State**

would show that the Defendant, under the name of Eric S. Galt, enrolled in the International School of Bartending there in Los Angeles, and he attended this school from January the 19th until March the 2nd, when he graduated. We were able to obtain a photograph in color reflecting the graduation picture from Mr. Lau, which you will see does show the Defendant along with Mr. Lau, who was standing, as you gentlemen view the picture, to the Defendant's left and is holding the diploma in front of him with the name, Eric S. Galt.

Ray drove from Los Angeles to New Orleans and then spent the night of March 22, 1968, at the Flamingo Motel in Selma, Alabama, Beasley said.

The prosecutor continued:

We would show through Mr. Jimmy Garner, who operates a rooming house in Atlanta, Georgia, that he rented a room to the Defendant under the name Eric S. Galt on March the 24th, 1968; that he collected a week's rent and subsequently on March the 31st, collected a second week's rent from the Defendant as Eric S. Galt; that at the time of collecting the rent on March the 31st, that the Defendant did write his name out as Eric S. Galt on an envelope, and this envelope was subsequently turned in in the course of this investigation.

That on the morning of April the 5th, Mr. Garner went into the room that had been rented to the Defendant as Eric Galt, and for purposes of changing the linen, at that time he found a note in substance saying, "I have to go to Birmingham. I will be back later to pick up my, within about a week, to pick up my television set and my other articles"; that on April the 14th of 1968, some ten days after the murder in Memphis, Mr. Garner did give permission to the members of the Atlanta FBI office to make a search of the premises there at his rooming house which had the room which had subsequently been rented to the Defendant.

Mrs. Annie Peters would be called by the State to testify with reference to the operation of the Piedmont Laundry, which is located around the corner from Jimmy Garner's rooming house; that on April the 1st, the Defendant, as Eric Galt, left certain laundry and cleaning there; that on the morning of April the 5th, 1968, at around mid-morning, he returned and picked up this laundry and dry cleaning.

At that point those jurors who were observant realized that the prosecutor had taken them beyond the date of the murder. For the next twenty minutes Beasley spoke of the recovery of the white Mustang and of Ray's trip to Toronto, to London, to Portugal and his return to London where he was arrested by Detective Sgt. Phillip F. Birch of New Scotland Yard.

Toward the conclusion of his indictment of Ray the Assistant Attorney General offered the testimony of the FBI experts. He began with an assessment of the relevant fingerprints.

Mr. George J. Bonebrake, who has been working with fingerprints since 1941, would testify that at 5:15 A.M., April 5th, 1968, he received the following items as has been heretofore testified to; that is, the rifle, the items that, from the bag, that were delivered to him by the representative from the Memphis FBI office, with reference to this material from the front, recovered from the front of Canipe's Amusement place here, that he found a print of sufficient clarity, fingerprint of sufficient clarity on the rifle itself; he found another print of sufficient clarity for identification on the scope, the Redfield scope mounted on the rifle; he found a print on the after-shave bottle, which is in the little packet that was obtained or purchased from the Rexall Drug Store in Whitehaven, Tennessee, which was part of the items that we have heretofore mentioned to you. He found a print on the binoculars. He found a print on one of the Schlitz beer cans. He found a print on the front page of the April 4th issue of the Memphis _Commercial Appeal_. That on April the 17th he received this map of Mexico which was, the State would have shown, was obtained from the room, Jimmy Garner's rooming house in Atlanta; that he found prints of sufficient clarity on that map for identification purposes; that he started an extensive investigation through fugitive files consisting of some 53,000 fingerprint cards, and on April the 19th he identified all the above-mentioned prints that I have mentioned to you from these items as being identical with the records bearing the name and photograph of James Earl Ray.

An alert juror might have noticed that the State did not allege that Ray had left behind a fingerprint in the room that he had allegedly rented in the rooming house or in the bathroom from which the State alleged the shot had been fired.

Beasley then moved to what might have been the most difficult evidence for Ray to contend with. If the ballistics established that the bullet taken from Dr. King's body was fired from a rifle that had been purchased by Ray, the case against him would begin to take shape. Beasley now spoke slowly and loudly, his voice emphasizing the importance of his words.

Mr. Robert A. Frazier, the chief, firearms identification unit at the FBI, with 27 years' experience, would testify as to examination and firing of this rifle, 30.06, that has been heretofore introduced.

He examined the cartridges, the hull from the chamber of this rifle, the slug removed from the body of Dr. Martin Luther King, Jr., and would testify as to his conclusions as follows:

The death slug was identical in all physical characteristics with the five loaded 30.06 Springfield cartridges found in the bag in front of Canipe's. The cartridge case had in fact been fired in this 30.06 rifle. That the death slug removed from the body contained land and groove impressions and direction of twist consistent with those that were in the barrel of this rifle.

This, to the jurors straining for the damning and conclusive evidence, to the reporters seeking, quite literally, the smoking gun, was the climax of the undefended case against James Earl Ray. His rifle had killed Dr. King.

Beasley then appeared to establish as fact that allegation yet again. He added that Frazier had

also made microscopic comparison between the fresh dent in the sill of the window at the bathroom, 422½ South Main, and concluded that the microscopic evidence in this dent was consistent in all ways with the same microscopic marks as appear on the barrel of this rifle, 30.06 rifle.

The veteran lawyers in the courtroom smiled to themselves in much the same manner as professional magicians do when they observe an audience puzzled by a simple but well performed trick.

Moments later Beasley turned from the jury to Judge Battle and said, "If the Court pleases, that covers our stipulation."

This then was the case against James Earl Ray, fully and thoroughly presented by his prosecutors, uninterrupted by his counsel, and unrestrained by the rules of evidence.

Chapter Twenty-Three

THE DEFENSE
by Mark Lane

There is the truth. And there is the legal truth. It is not unusual for both truths to coincide. Yet the law, in its majesty, recognizes that this will not always be the case. The theoretical responsibility borne by the prosecution is to prove the guilt of the defendant, not by a fair preponderance of the evidence, but beyond a reasonable doubt. Therefore, continuing in a theoretical vein, a juror who was inclined to believe that the defendant was guilty—who had arrived at what was the truth for him but who was not convinced of the defendant's guilt beyond a reasonable doubt, would be obligated to vote for an acquittal.

For most Americans the technical problems confronting the prosecuting authorities in Memphis are of less concern than an examination of the facts which may lead to the truth. Yet those two areas of concern merge, entangle with one another, and make a clear understanding of the circumstances of the crime difficult to comprehend. It is because Ray pleaded guilty that the record of the crime is so barren. Had Ray been tried, certainly had he testified at the trial, the record would have been studded with, if not all or almost all of the relevant facts, a fair history of the events which had been tested in the crucible of cross-examination.

The search for the truth in this matter must, I believe, commence with an exploration of the anatomy of the guilty plea: its origin, its development, and the manner of its execution. In order to evaluate that bargained plea in the appropriate context it is necessary to assess the legal and technical validity of the case against Ray. For if he did kill Dr. King but the state was unable to prove that he did, then Ray is innocent under our understanding of the law. More important perhaps is the certain knowledge of the defendant and his attorney of this peculiar and marvelous dichotomy in our system of justice. In this chapter we will evaluate the viability of the case against Ray. If we conclude that the state could not have proved Ray's guilt beyond a reasonable doubt we will be constrained to examine his charge that his plea was improperly coerced.

Shortly after his arrest in England, Ray wrote to Arthur Hanes, Sr., the former mayor of Birmingham, and F. Lee Bailey of Boston, requesting that they each consider representing him. Bailey declined and Hanes accepted. Bailey explained that his friendship with Dr. King created a conflict of interest which barred him from representing Ray. Hanes had successfully represented defendants in the highly-publicized murder of Viola Liuzzo, a civil rights worker who had been slain in the South. Apparently Ray had been aware of that defense and of Hanes' skill and his empathy with Southern jurors. He wrote to Hanes from London:

Dear Mr. Hanes,

I am writing this letter from London, England. I am being held here on a charge of passport fraud, also I think for Tenn. in the Martin King Case. I will probably be returned to the U.S. about June 17, and would like to know if you would consider appearing in my behalf? So far [three days] I have only been permitted to talk to police and also have not seen any papers except a headline today. By accident, stating I had given an interview to a Mr. Vinson, which is false. Most of the things that have been written in the papers about me I can only describe as silly. Naturally I would want you to investigate this nonsense before committing yourself. For these reasons and others which I won't go into I think it is important that I have an attorney upon arrival in Tenn. or I will be convicted of whatever charge they file on me before I arrive there. An English attorney came to see me today and said he would also write to you. I don't know your address is why I am sending this letter to the bar asso. The reason I wrote you is I read once where you handled a case similar to what I think may be filed on me also whatever the papers might say. I don't intend to give any interviews until I have consulted with an attorney. In the event you can not practice in Memphis would you contact an attorney their who would?

Sincerely

R. G. Sneyd

P.S. Among the many names they have me booked under this one so if you should correspond use this one, address on envelope.

William Bradford Huie, an Alabama writer, almost immediately contacted Hanes and suggested that he would pay Ray a substantial sum for the exclusive rights to his story. Huie pointed out to Hanes that the sum could be used to pay lawyers' fees. Hanes left for England having decided both to represent Ray and to attempt to arrange a tri-party contract among himself, Ray, and Huie. Such a contract was agreed upon by the parties.

Hanes and his son, Arthur Hanes, Jr., diligently pursued leads, many of which were being developed by a private investigator, Renfro Hays.

I spent days at the Hanes law offices in Birmingham sorting through the voluminous investigative reports, trial briefs and working papers that the lawyers had prepared. They were kind enough to allow me to photocopy all those documents I considered to be relevant and I subsequently spent weeks studying that material. I also made available copies of that material to the Select Committee on Assassinations of the House of Representatives, with the permission of the Hanes law firm.

Interviews with the two lawyers and a thorough examination of their trial preparation work led me to conclude that they were ready for the trial. I began to defend against criminal prosecutions forty-two years ago. In the course of hundreds of trials, including prosecutions for murder, manslaughter, conspiracy to overthrow the government, conspiracy to blow up the Statue of Liberty, the Washington Monument, and the Liberty Bell, and conspiracy to seize federal property at Wounded Knee, South Dakota, I have come to understand and cope with our system of justice and to respect the vagaries of the jury system. I understand as well, I believe, the special problems imparted to the defense in an unpopular case, especially when the difficulties are compounded by extensive and prejudicial pretrial publicity. After taking into account the unusual problems posed for this defense by extralegal considerations, I believe that the essential case against Ray was so flawed that it would have been difficult for the jury to have returned a verdict of guilty. Had the case been tried the state would have undertaken the responsibility of proving beyond a reasonable doubt that James Earl Ray fired a rifle from a bathroom window of a rooming house and that the bullet from that rifle struck and killed Dr. Martin Luther King, Jr. This, I believe, the state could not do, partially due to the paucity of evidence linking Ray to the crime and partially due to the affirmative defense that had been established by the investigation conducted on his behalf.

Experienced trial lawyers know that there are no easy cases in which victory for either side is assured in advance of trial. In cases involving capital punishment, as in this one, the awful possibility of the ultimate penalty tends to diminish feelings of ebullience that defense counsel might otherwise experience following multiple assessments of the evidence. Yet in spite of the highly prejudicial publicity surrounding the charges against the defendant, and in spite of the awesome potential should the defendant be convicted, Arthur Hanes, Sr., and his son and their client shared a quiet optimism and a cautious confidence. That confidence was threatened primarily by the defense lawyers' everpresent fear that the state might be holding some decisive evidence in reserve. In this case such fears were groundless. All the authorities knew and much of what they suspected had been offered to the media and commented on repeatedly.

The case against Ray, all that could be proven and in addition all that the state said could be proven—although on occasion it lacked the evidence to follow through on that boast—was presented by the authorities on March 10, 1969, and fully reflected in the previous chapter.

Witnesses who testified offered evidence that Dr. King had been killed on April 4, 1968, on the balcony of the Lorraine Motel from a shot fired from the general direction of a clump of trees and bushes at the rear of a rooming house beyond the vegetation.

A pathologist established that a bullet was taken from Dr. King's body and he offered a vague and, as we have seen, poorly based opinion as to the possible origin of the bullet. A police inspector told of a package found on South Main Street, two blocks from Dr. King's location at the Lorraine Motel balcony, and he described its contents. The FBI SAC in Memphis said that the package had been received by the Bureau later that day.

At that point the Memphis prosecutor abandoned the usual method of presenting important evidence through the testimony of witnesses and offered instead his own unsworn and sometimes unsupported allegations about what the evidence would show. This technique is regularly and properly utilized by prosecuting attorneys for the purpose of offering an opening statement but in the ordinary course of events such a statement is not construed as evidence and is followed by witnesses whose testimony is considered as evidence. Thus the jurors may test the allegations of the accuser against the testimony of the witnesses. In addition, of course, in an ordinary trial the witness is subjected to cross-examination, a device which often proves useful in arriving at the facts. In Memphis there was no cross-examination and for the most part the evidence was not offered through the testimony of witnesses.

To the uninitiated jurors and the reporters the nice distinctions and precise language of the law no doubt proved misleading. The prosecutor alleged that the FBI firearms expert with 27 years of experience "would testify" that "the death slug [the bullet taken from Dr. King's body] was identical in all physical characteristics" with the cartridges found in the package in front of Canipe's. All that Frazier, the Bureau expert, had said was that both the bullet that killed King and the cartridges in the package were a common variety of 30.06 ammunition. That is not very dissimilar from a fingerprint expert testifying that the killer had ten fingers on two hands, five on each, and that the subject was similarly equipped. Then the prosecutor added that Frazier "would testify" that "the death slug removed from the body contained land and groove impressions and direction of twist consistent with those that were in the barrel of this [Ray's] rifle." To those without trial experience in assault and homicide cases, that allegation appeared conclusive or at least terribly damaging to Ray's claim that he had not killed Dr. King. Yet a knowledgeable defense lawyer would have welcomed that report and might have been tempted to call Frazier as a defense witness if the prosecution failed to call him as theirs.

As a bullet moves through a rifle barrel it spirals. Microscopic indentations which comprise the rifling inside the barrel cause that effect and remove particles from the jacket of the bullet. If the bullet is not substantially demolished a comparison with another bullet test-fired from the same weapon may yield conclusive results. The language of the government's firearms experts is standard, and their recitation is pro forma. In case after case the experts recite the conclusions that "my examination of this bullet proved beyond doubt that this bullet was fired from this weapon to the exclusion of all other weapons in the world." Any statement short of that one is considered to be valueless to the prosecution. In this case a substantial portion of the bullet remained intact. An expert who saw it but was not allowed to examine it under a microscope said that the bullet was sufficiently undamaged to permit a positive finding regarding the weapon from which it was fired. The failure of the state to prove that the "death slug" was fired from what was alleged to be Ray's rifle reflected very poorly upon the case against Ray.

The prosecutor sought to overcome this essential weakness in the case by stretching Frazier's identification of the mark on the bathroom window sill. Beasley said that Frazier would testify that the dent on the window sill "was consistent in all ways" with the marks on what was alleged to be Ray's rifle. No doubt, had Frazier been subjected to cross-examination he would have conceded that what he meant was that any metal object similar to the rifle barrel in question could have caused the dent. His refusal to inform the state that "Ray's" rifle did cause the dent meant that the state could neither prove that the rifle fired the bullet that killed Dr. King nor that it had been in the rooming house from where the shot was allegedly fired. Beasley's indications to the contrary may have been useful to obfuscate the record and mislead the jurors and the press in 1969, but upon sober reflection and in the context of the evidence now available his comments appear to have been a somewhat desperate prosecutorial effort to give the impression that there was a substantial case when in fact there was not.

If the state could not prove that the rifle fired the shot or that it had even been in the bathroom or elsewhere in the rooming house, the evidence that seemed to establish Ray's ownership of the rifle was rendered almost worthless. I believe that the state could have proven that Ray purchased the rifle from the Aeromarine Supply Company in Birmingham. Further, Ray told me that he had done so. Yet even if that weapon was judged to be the murder weapon by competent experts, proof of Ray's guilt would depend upon additional factors. Proof of ownership of a weapon employed in a murder case does not establish the owner as a criminal. In this case the state could not even establish any links between the defendant, James Earl Ray, and the bullet which killed Dr. King.

The state claimed that it could prove that Ray had been in the rooming house before the murder, during the murder, and immediately after the murder. For those assertions Beasley relied upon statements which he said were made by eyewitnesses. It is interesting to note that as the mythology of the case against Ray developed it became conventional wisdom to allege that Ray left fingerprints and palm prints around the rooming house. William Bradford Huie, whose book, *He Slew the Dreamer*, is discussed in Chapter 26 told Ray that his prints were found in Room 5 and in the bathroom. This inclined Ray to believe that his defense would be more difficult than he had conceived. In his book Huie wrote:

> **Part of the time between 4:30 and 6:01 P.M. Ray watched for Dr. King leaning out of the window of Room 5. Evidence of this comes from fingerprints and from the fact that, after the murder, a chair and table in Room 5 were found to have been moved to the window.**

Huie added that "a print of the heel of his [Ray's] palm was found on the bathroom wall." Huie informed Percy Foreman, Ray's lawyer, of his discovery and later Foreman declared in an article he wrote in *Look* magazine in April 1969 that Ray had left behind both fingerprints and palm prints and that he, Foreman, knew why. Foreman wrote, "he wanted to escape, but he didn't want to lose credit. As further precaution against such dreaded loss, he left his fingerprints in the side room that he had rented, and his palm print in the bathroom from which he fired the shot."

Huie, Foreman, and the many representatives of the news media who relied upon them for the facts, were wrong. The prosecution did not charge that Ray's fingerprints or palm prints had been found in the rooming house. At the outset, the Memphis police alleged that the shot had been fired from the bathroom window and that the killer had left scuff marks in the bathtub and a palm print on the wall over the tub. Captain Dewell Ray of the Internal Security Division of the Memphis Police Department and Sergeant Jim Papia discovered the palm print soon after the shot had been fired. Later, under the direction of Inspector Zachary, the chief of homicide, the palm print was dusted and examined. Fingerprints in Room 5 were also dusted and examined. Subsequently the state concluded that neither the fingerprints in Room 5 nor the palm print in the bathroom were left behind by Ray. On March 10 the prosecution made an apparent and deliberate effort to avoid the question. While Beasley considerably stretched, not to say entirely deformed, the statements of eyewitnesses in order to prove that Ray had been in the rooming house, he abandoned any effort to link either the fingerprints in Room 5 or the palm prints in the bathroom to Ray. Yet if the scuff marks in the tub and the palm print on the wall were evidence left behind by the killer, as the police had previously charged, it might be useful to discover whose hand matched the print. If the police did make such a determination they declined to reveal it.

With Ray's attorney and his biographer going far beyond the prosecutor and the evidence in their zeal to prove his guilt while the facts indicated that the case against Ray was largely conjectural, his hopes for an adequate defense diminished.

As we have seen, Beasley relied to a considerable extent upon Mrs. Bessie Brewer, the manager of the rooming house, to establish Ray's presence in the rooming house before the shot was fired and he relied upon her entirely for his assertion that Ray, using the name John Willard, requested a room for a week. Beasley said that the state would prove, through Mrs. Brewer, that Ray had entered the rooming house "between 3:00 and 3:10 P.M. in the afternoon" and that "the defendant appeared here at Mrs. Brewer's office or apartment." Yet Mrs. Brewer never made such a statement. Mrs. Brewer consistently refused to identify Ray as the man she rented the room to and as the man who used the name John Willard. She refused to make any such statement, written or verbal, in spite of the pressure upon her to do so. As Beasley, the Assistant Attorney

General, made those declarations to the jury and to the press, Phil Canale, the Attorney General, sat at the prosecution table.

Years later, Pamela Spack and Leona Zanetti, two researchers for the Citizens Commission of Inquiry, interviewed Canale. Canale admitted then that Mrs. Brewer had never identified Ray. He said, "Mrs. Brewer did not positively identify Ray as being the Willard who had checked in there. She said she said she never looked him full in the face or anything like that. That was her testimony."

The state alleged that only one other witness could place Ray in the rooming house. According to Beasley, Charles Q. Stephens, a resident of the rooming house, heard the shot and went "out into the corridor in time to see the left profile of the defendant as he turned down this passageway." But Stephens did not make a positive identification of Ray. He only said the man looked "very much like" an FBI picture of Ray. That modest assertion was challenged by other statements, including earlier statements made by Stephens himself.

Approximately one week after Dr. King was killed I visited Stephens in the room which he shared with Grace Stephens, his wife. At that time he told me that he had seen the man who fled from the bathroom just after the shot was fired. He said that the man was "very small, quite short and certainly not heavy." He also told me that he had been the primary source for the artist's portrait of the presumed killer which was at that time being circulated by law enforcement authorities. Ray is five feet, ten inches tall and in no manner resembles the artist's drawing. At that time I was unable to ask Stephens directly if the man who fled after the shot was fired was James Earl Ray, since Ray was not a police suspect then, and his name was not known. After Ray was apprehended I sought to question Stephens again but by then Stephens had been placed in jail by the Memphis authorities and held as a material witness. Canale explained why Stephens had been held: "He had a reputation for being an alcoholic and he frequented places that we thought if somebody had it in their mind to harm him they could." Although Pamela Spack and Leona Zanetti pressed Canale for an explanation, he could think of no other. He added only, "So we talked to him and his lawyer about putting him in protective custody, which he agreed to; then later on he got tired of sitting over at the jail and requested that he be released and he was." Canale added that "We were worried to some extent about his personal safety and we considered he was a material witness in the case although I think we could have presented the case adequately without him."

However, Canale did not tell the court in 1969 that Stephens was an alcoholic who should be imprisoned for his own protection. He filed an affidavit with Judge Battle in which he swore that he was concerned that Stephens "might leave the state and not testify." Based upon that affidavit Stephens was held involuntarily in prison under a $10,000 bond. The record reveals that Stephens did ask to be released on numerous occasions but that Canale refused. Stephens finally secured counsel and brought a writ of habeas corpus before a judge other than Battle. Judge William W. O'Hearn ruled that the incarceration of Stephens was "illegal" and ordered him to be freed at once. In contesting that ruling Beasley argued that the prosecution has no other witnesses who can "testify to the same material facts."

For two weeks before Stephens had been placed in jail police officers had been assigned to be with him all day and night. As soon as he was released the officers began to accompany him again around the clock. Canale later admitted that no one had ever threatened Stephens in any way. In retrospect it appears that the Memphis authorities were less concerned about protecting their witness from harm than they were about protecting him from interviews, particularly with the team of defense lawyers and their investigator.

Stephens was a disabled veteran with a severe drinking problem. Apparently he was drunk when the shot that killed Dr. King was fired. His wife told me in the week following the assassination that "Charlie didn't see anything. He couldn't have. He was on the bed trying to sleep one off." That statement received independent corroboration from James M. McCraw. The month before the plea of guilty was entered by Ray two investigators questioned McCraw. They prepared a rather odd document entitled "Statement of James M. McCraw" in which McCraw began speaking in the first person and then was referred to in the third person. The document, in its entirety, reads as follows:

> On April 4, 1968, I was driving for Yellow Cab Co. and was dispatched to 422½ So. Main St. to pick up a fare. When I arrived at this address, I double parked as there were cars and trucks parked at the curb. I observed a Cadillac auto, owned by Mr. Jowers, owner of Jim's grill on So. Main, 526-9910. I also observed two white Mustangs parked at the curb and several delivery trucks. All of this traffic was parked on the East side of So. Main St. facing North. A woman who ran the rooming house directed Mr. McCraw to a certain room, stating that the occupant of that room directed that a cab be called. The door of the room was open and McCraw went in the room and found Charles Stephens lying on the bed fully clothed, he was in a very

drunken condition. Stephens was well-known to McCraw, as he had picked him up many times before. Mr. McCraw refused to transport Stephens as a fare because of his drunken condition. McCraw stated that Stephens could not get off the bed. Mr. McCraw left the rooming house, got back into his cab, made a U-turn went South on South Main St. When Mr. McCraw got to the corner of So. Main and Calhoun Sts. the dispatcher said that Mr. M. L. King had been shot and for all cabs to stay out of the So. Main area. Mr. McCraw, after he got back into his cab, received a call to Frankie and Johnny's Boat Store on the Mississippi River at the Bridge. Mr. McCraw estimates that he was in the rooming house about three minutes and that from the time he left the rooming house until the time the dispatcher called about King being shot was about two minutes.

McCraw has driven Stephens to many liquor stores through the city at many different times. Stephens drank all kinds of whiskey or beer. Mr. McCraw could not tell whether Stephens drank more on the first and fifteenth of the month as he [Stephens] was a heavy drinker at all times.

McCraw's statement, ignored by Beasley when he ostensibly presented the facts in the case to the jury, provides strong support for Grace Stephen's earlier comment to me. The gravamen of the declaration made by the taxi driver is that Stephens, the only man who the state said could identify Ray as the fleeing gunman, was drunk on his bed two to five minutes before Dr. King was killed. The statement, of course, also raised the question of not one but two white Mustangs in front of the rooming house entrance.

Lloyd Jowers, the proprietor of Jim's Grill, located on the street level floor of the rooming house, was interviewed by Memphis police authorities on February 6, 1969, at four o'clock in the afternoon. Almost a year had passed since the murder and the state and defense were making last-minute preparations for the trial. Jowers, who was to be a prosecution witness, told two local investigators, according to their written statement, that "Charlie Stephens was drunk on April 4, 1969, in the afternoon." The report added that Jowers "remembers because Stephens and his landlady were having trouble about Stephens' rent."

Thus further corroboration for Mrs. Stephens' statement was available to the police and prosecution.

At this point the state's case against Ray crumbled. There was no reliable evidence that placed Ray in the rooming house at any time. No reliable witness would testify to his presence there before the shot was fired. The only witness who on occasion identified Ray as the man who fled through the corridor, and who had previously described a different man in size and facial characteristics, was evidently too drunk to observe the culprit and could not have seen him from his position on the bed, in any event. No fingerprints or palm prints placed Ray in the rooming house and indeed those that were located seemed to point in another direction which evidently was not explored by the police. No evidence demonstrated that Ray's rifle had fired the bullet which struck Dr. King and there, too, the evidence appeared to point in another direction which arrarently the police also failed to examine.

Although neither Beasley nor Canale mentioned her, Grace Stephens was an important witness. She was sober on the afternoon of April 4, 1968, and she was in her room at the rooming house. She heard the shot. She said, "At about six o'clock I heard a shot. I cannot tell where the shot came from. I know it echoed in the arcade beneath my window."

She said, "Right after the shot a man left the bathroom and went down the hall and down the steps to Main Street. I saw the man as he passed the door of my room. My guess of this man's age was in his fifties. This man was not quite as tall as I am. He was small-boned built. He had on an Army-colored hunting jacket unfastened and dark pants." She said that the man also wore a "plaid sport shirt." The man, Mrs. Stephens said, had "salt and pepper colored hair." She added, "He had something long in his right hand but I cannot swear what it was." She said that she heard "screaming at the motel" and that later reporters came to their room. Police officers did not visit her room for four hours. When they did arrive, she said, she accompanied them to Police Headquarters where she gave a statement to Inspector Zachary.

At last the Memphis authorities apparently had uncovered a reliable witness. Yet when Ray was arrested her statement was inconvenient. Ray was taller than average and Mrs. Stephens had described a man approximately five feet, five inches tall. Ray was well-built and muscular and she described a small-boned man. Ray was in his thirties and she described a man twenty years older.

While Charles Stephens was illegally held in jail by Memphis authorities, Grace Stephens was illegally taken from her home by other Memphis authorities and placed in a mental institution. Tennessee law requires that a commitment proceeding be initiated by a relative, guardian, licensed physician, or the director of a health and welfare institution. The proceeding against Mrs. Stephens was initiated by an assistant administrator at a hospital in Memphis. While the law required that the subject be notified in writing by mail of the proposed commitment hearing, that was not done in this case. Notice was not given to relatives as required by law. After Mrs. Stephens was illegally placed in the mental institution, the Memphis prosecutors removed her records from the hospital, according to her lawyer, C. M. Murphy.

Murphy also charged that his client had no history of mental illness and that she was able to care for herself. He said that the Memphis prosecuting attorneys committed her to safeguard their case against Ray. While one of the two prosecutors denied the allegation, he said that he did not know who really was behind the effort to commit her. Murphy said,

The reason she was placed in the psychiatric hospital was because her testimony would have been unfavorable to the position taken by the Shelby County attorney general [Memphis prosecutor] and his staff.

She was not mentally ill at the time and has at no time since been mentally ill. She charges further that although she was a material witness and that she informed the Memphis police . . . as to the details of her knowledge, such information was deliberately concealed . . . and she was unlawfully shuttled off to the psychiatric department of the city of Memphis' hospitals.

In 1970, two years after Mrs. Stephens was committed, Murphy brought an action for her release. A reporter for the *Washington Post* who attended the hearing said that Mrs. Stephens, "was heavily sedated" and that she "stared blankly." He reported as well that "attorneys say that ordinarily she is bright, articulate, and reads a great deal and that she completed three years of college."

Murphy was struck by the evident deterioration of his client. He said that a doctor at the mental institution had said in January 1969, two months before the Ray case came to trial, that her condition did not warrant commitment and that she should be released. Despite the evaluation by the institution's psychiatrist that her condition would "decline and deteriorate" if she was not released at the time of the evaluation in 1969, she was not released and she remained at the institution, almost a decade after her incarceration.

Charles Stephens originally offered evidence which cast doubt upon the state's case against Ray. He was incarcerated and was released after he recanted. Mrs. Stephens has not recanted. When she was visited at the institution where she is confined she was asked if she remembers what she saw on April 4, 1968. She answered with a sad smile, ''Oh yes. I remember what I saw and who I saw run away. That's why I'm here, you know.''

The tragedy of April 4, 1968, apparently did not end that day.

Chapter Twenty-Four

THE AFFIRMATIVE CASE

by Mark Lane

The defendant in a criminal case need not offer any evidence. He need not testify. The jurors may not draw any conclusion from his failure to testify. The defendant is not obligated to offer an alibi or an affirmative defense. He need not present the testimony of a single witness. The defendant may rest secure that if the state fails to prove his guilt beyond a reasonable doubt the jury will acquit him.

It is generally advisable for defendants and their attorneys to remind the jury of these components that comprise the presumption of innocence and then to place no reliance upon such shibboleths for in all probability the jurors will not.

While the state was unable to prove that Ray was in the rooming house, that he had fired a weapon, or even that the weapon which he had purchased fired the shot which killed Dr. King, curious jurors might be interested in trying to comprehend his strange behavior.

Ray had purchased the rifle in Birmingham under an assumed name. He had purchased binoculars shortly before Dr. King was killed and both the rifle and the binoculars and other articles were tossed to the sidewalk near the entrance to the rooming house within minutes of the firing of a rifle. Ray had registered at the Rebel Motel the previous night using a pseudonym. And while Ray had traveled by automobile from Los Angeles to New Orleans and from Canada to Mexico, he appeared to have no legal and visible means of support.

Had there been a trial the defense might have faced a dilemma. If the charge against Ray had not been dismissed by the trial judge after the presentation of the prosecution's case, the defense would have been constrained to determine whether Ray should testify. Very likely Battle, given his disposition to convict, would not have granted a defense motion based upon the failure of the state to present a *prima facie* case. While such a motion perhaps merited a serious hearing it seems doubtful, in a case of this magnitude, that it might be considered by the court. Through

171

the cross-examination of the prosecution witnesses the defense in all probability would have established in the minds of the jurors that the overblown promises made by Beasley could not be sustained by evidence. A well-planned defense seeks to answer the questions that remain for the jurors when a prosecution case dissolves. Although it is not necessary for jurors to have a reasonable alternative theory of the crime presented to them in order to acquit, indeed it is contrary to law even to suggest that the defense has such a burden, it is generally helpful for the defense to suggest that the crime may have been committed in another way. Similarly while the defendant need not explain where he was when the crime was committed—it theoretically being sufficient for the finding of innocence that the state be unable to prove that he was an activist at the scene of the crime at the appropriate moment—if the defendant can make a showing as to his actual whereabouts without jeopardizing his legal defense it is often useful to do so.

After talking with the relevant witnesses and after reading interview reports and official records comprising the entire defense and prosecution cases, I am convinced that the state was not prepared to prove that Ray was in the rooming house on April 4, 1968. I am equally convinced that he was there shortly before Dr. King was killed. Ray, himself, told me that he had been in the rooming house earlier in the day and that he had in fact registered that day. He told me

I signed the name John Willard in the registration book. I was really amazed when the prosecutor never mentioned that at the mini-trial. They said that the registration book was lost.

It is difficult to imagine how the registration book, an important, almost an essential document in the case against Ray, could have disappeared. The police were at the rooming house within minutes after the shot was fired and questioned the occupants of the house shortly thereafter. They were seeking information about who had occupied the various rooms that day. The registration book was an obvious prime target of their search. Ray's handwritten registration was the only evidence that the state could use to prove his presence there. Yet, the prosecuting authorities made no reference to that document and relied upon poor Mr. Stephens instead.

I asked Ray if he could understand the disappearance of the book. He said, "I don't know for sure but I can guess that maybe there is something else in that book, perhaps someone else who registered, that they don't want anyone to know about. It would have to be something important for them to give up the only evidence that could prove I was in that rooming house."

Ray's narrative of the events that led to the murder of Dr. King involve him in the commission of a number of crimes. If he admitted in court that he had committed those crimes he might have been prosecuted and the cumulative penalties that could be invoked against him for those crimes, when added to the penalty for the crime of escaping from jail and then added to the time that he owed the State of Missouri at the time of his escape, might have kept him in jail for the rest of his life. Yet Ray was anxious to testify at his trial in order to deny that he shot King or even knew that King would be shot. His first attorneys, who were confident that Ray would be acquitted, were reluctant to place him on the stand.

Ray did testify in an action that he subsequently brought against Foreman, Huie, and Hanes, Sr. On that occasion he testified that he had not fired the shot that killed Dr. King. Ray was willing to accept the risk that he might be required to spend a substantial portion of his life in jail for the opportunity to explain how he was used, without his knowledge, by those who murdered Dr. King. It is in this light that one must examine the statements by Huie and Foreman that Ray wanted to be caught so that he could proclaim that he murdered King. Both said that Ray's glory was in letting the whole world know of his guilt. Yet, as we have seen, Ray has insisted that he was innocent, denied that he shot King, and proclaimed himself to be an inglorious and unwitting dupe of others.

Ray's explanation to me of his movements through the United States from Canada to Mexico, his purchase of a rifle in Birmingham, and ultimately his presence in Memphis on April 4th in the vicinity of the murder scene is either basically true, or the intricate and comprehensive work product of a brilliant mind. For the narrative explains in a cohesive fashion all of Ray's otherwise inexplicable actions. Ray's relationship with a man he refers to only as Raoul becomes the Rosetta Stone of the defendant's odyssey.

According to Ray he fled to Canada after escaping from the Missouri penitentiary in Jefferson City. While in Montreal, he said, he "let the word get around" in the Neptune Tavern, a bar that welcomed seamen, that he had been in trouble in the United States and that he was seeking identification papers and money. Ray made it plain that he had been involved in criminal activities and was willing to undertake similar low-risk activities if his needs could be met. According to Ray a man he subsequently referred to as Raoul approached him and indicated that he could provide adequate documents and sufficient funds if Ray helped him to accomplish various projects. After a series of meetings Ray said the two men reached an agreement.

In furtherance of that agreement Ray began to surreptitiously deliver articles across the border from Canada to the United States and from the United States to Mexico. Ray was not told, and he states that he did not ask, about the contents of the packages. He, of course, presumed that he was smuggling contraband from one country to another.

Ray said that for one episode Raoul paid him $3,000 in cash. According to Ray, Raoul suggested that he go to Alabama from Montreal. "I didn't want to go back to the United States," Ray said to me. "Raoul told me he operated out of New Orleans and that he wanted me to help him in that area. He said I should go to a place near New Orleans and he suggested Mobile." According to Ray he chose Birmingham over Mobile because "I'm allergic to salt air." He added, "When you're living underground a bigger city is safer than a smaller one and Birmingham is bigger than Mobile." Raoul told Ray to buy a car in Birmingham.

In September 1968, Ray wrote, "I suppose I became involved in the plot to kill King when I took those packages into the United States from Canada. I would think it had all been decided before the car was bought in Birmingham, as no one would have given me $3,000 in Birmingham just to haul narcotics across the border. But nobody told me about any planned murder of King or anyone else." Subsequently Raoul arranged for Ray to drive his white Mustang into Mexico after Raoul had exchanged the spare tire in the Mustang for another one. After Ray had cleared Mexican customs Ray's tire was returned by Raoul who removed the one that Ray had driven across the border. "I never thought I was smuggling a spare tire," Ray told me later. "Obviously something was in the tire."

Ray said to me that Raoul gave him $2,000 in cash for that episode. "It was all in twenty-dollar bills. And he said he would have $12,000 more for me to go into a business within another country and he would also have a passport for me." Ray told me that Raoul said "he would probably need me in about two or three or four months. This was in October 1967. He said I should call him at his New Orleans telephone number once in a while. I told him that I would be in Los Angeles and he said that he would write to me there."

Ray said that approximately four months before Dr. King was killed he returned to New Orleans to meet Raoul in a tavern on Canal Street on the border of the French Quarter. At that time Raoul told Ray that he would have a job for him to do in about three months and that it was to be Ray's last assignment. "He told me that when that job was done he was going to give me $12,000 and all the documents that I would need to travel wherever I wanted to outside of the States. He wouldn't tell me what the job was, told me not to ask about it, and gave me $500 in cash," Ray said.

Ray also told me that subsequently Raoul contacted him and told him to meet him in New Orleans on March 20, 1968, less than three weeks before King was killed. When Ray arrived in New Orleans he said he was told that Raoul had gone to Birmingham and that he expected Ray to meet him there in two days. Ray arrived a day late in Birmingham since he became confused and took a highway to Montgomery by mistake.

Raoul and Ray traveled to Atlanta together. There, according to Ray, Raoul "told me that he wanted me to buy a large-bore deer rifle with a telescopic sight. He said that if the rifle was approved of by the buyers that I was to get about a dozen more and also about 200 cheap rifles. The good one had to be new, the others they didn't care about."

Ray said that since he had Alabama identification it might be better if he went back to Birmingham to buy the rifles. Raoul agreed. Ray said, "We met in Birmingham and Raoul and I got the address of a rifle place, Aeromarine Supply, out of a newspaper advertisement, which said they had a lot of rifles." According to Ray, Raoul gave him about $750 and told him to buy the large-bore deer rifle. Ray purchased a rifle and showed it to Raoul in a Birmingham motel. He said Raoul was displeased—"said it was the wrong kind." Raoul pointed out to Ray the rifle that he preferred from the catalogue and Ray called the store and said that he wanted to exchange it. Ray exchanged rifles. Raoul told him, he said, to meet him "in Memphis on April 3 in the evening at the Rebel Motel and to bring the rifle." Ray said that he did meet Raoul as planned and that he was told that he was to go back to Birmingham in a few days to purchase some more rifles and "a lot of cheap foreign rifles so that they could be shipped to New Orleans." Ray said that "before he left he said I should meet him the next day at four o'clock in the afternoon at a rooming house at 422½ South Main Street. He wrote down the address and said to meet him in the bar downstairs if he was not in the rooming house." Ray said that he met Raoul in Jim's Grill on the afternoon of April 4, 1968, and that subsequently they went together to a room in the rooming house. "When we got there Raoul said we would be there for a few days 'so bring the Mustang around and get your stuff out of it and bring it up here.' He also said to get a pair of infrared binoculars at York Arms, a store that was nearby." Ray did purchase binoculars but the sales clerk told him that the store did not carry the infrared variety.

Ray said that when he returned to the rooming house he brought his suitcase to the room. "I also brought the bed spread from the car since I was going to have to sleep in the room for a few days."

Quite obviously Ray's location at the time the shot was fired remains the single most important question in considering the case against him. It has been pointed out that he has vacillated when asked to establish that locale. Ray conceded the accuracy of that accusation when I inquired and now he explained it this way. As in the case with much of the evidence, this matter has neither been tested by cross-examination nor has it been offered in a courtroom under oath.

"I wanted to testify at the trial. Lawyers can say and the judges can agree that if you don't testify it can't be held against you. But jurors want to see you. They want to hear the defendant talk. I didn't kill King and I wanted to testify. Toward the end of our arrangement, when it was breaking down, old man Hanes came in to see me. He said, 'Huie wants to know where you were when King was shot.' I was surprised that Huie didn't ask me long before. I might have told him then. Now I said, 'Tell Huie it could have happened this way.' Then I told him a story about me waiting in the car, Raoul running down the steps and jumping in the back seat of the car. I said 'Tell Huie that Raoul pulled a sheet over him in the back seat.' I mentioned a sheet because Huie is so interested in the Klan I thought he would appreciate it. It never happened that way at all. The next morning young Hanes came in to see me. He said Huie is mad. 'He doesn't want to know how it could have happened, he wants to know how it did happen.' I just sort of smiled. I wasn't going to give away my testimony to the other side in advance."

I asked Ray if he would tell me where he was when Dr. King was murdered.

"Yes, I'll tell you. It looks now as if I may not get a trial at all so I'll tell you what happened."

Our conversation took place in the library of the Brushy Mountain Penitentiary. I was the first visitor to see him after the United States Supreme Court had denied his application for a trial.

He said, "I was sent out of the rooming house eight or ten times that day. I was almost never in there. As to the bathroom I'm not sure I was ever in there at all. It had no special meaning for me at the time. But I was in and out of the room I had rented all day—mostly out of it."

I asked why his fingerprints had not been found in the room. "Well," he said, "the doors did not have door knobs for one thing. They had a hole to stick a finger through and a leather strap to pull."

Ray returned to the narrative. "I was sent to the drugstore, to the gun shop, twice to the place that sold binoculars, to taverns. Late afternoon I was sent to a gas station to check out the car, to get air in the spare tire. I did that and drove back toward the rooming house on South Main. The place was filled with police, blocking off the street. Something had happened and I knew I had to get out of there. I was a fugitive and I could not afford to get stopped by the police. I turned down a street before the rooming house and started to drive away. I was later told that a police officer waved me on through but I don't remember that happening.''

I asked Ray where he went. He said, ''I began to drive toward New Orleans. I had the car radio on and the announcement came that King had been shot. It was dark by then. Maybe about seven o'clock when I heard that news. But even then I wasn't sure about what had happened. I didn't even know that the Lorraine Motel was behind the rooming house. I didn't know that King was staying there. I didn't even know that King was in town.''

I asked Ray when he determined for the first time that he had some involvement with the events that led to Dr. King's death. ''Well, I kept on driving and then the news report came over the radio about King being shot and the suspect, a white man, had escaped from the area in a white Mustang. I was driving a white Mustang. I had just left the area. It wasn't hard at that time for me to put two and two together and decide that I was it.'' Ray said, ''Then I just wanted to get far away from Memphis. I had good reasons to leave. I wanted to get away from the police. A convict, a fugitive wanted for killing King. I didn't think I had a chance. Anyway, even if I did I still owed time to Missouri and there would be the additional time for escaping. I had to get away before I was caught by the police or anyone else.''

According to Arthur Hanes, Jr., Ray was fleeing for his life. ''He knew all of a sudden that he was in deep trouble. I think it was not just the authorities Ray feared. He was afraid that Raoul or Raoul's friends might kill him. He knew by then, of course, that he'd been set up and he feared that as an important link to the killers he imposed a real threat. He was afraid that they would kill him.''

Certain elements of Ray's explanation of the events are subject to independent verification. I have been able to establish that Ray had been at the motels and restaurants that he spoke of and that he was there during the time frame that he gave. Yet those facts do not establish the validity of his essential claim that another was involved and directed him. Ray could have woven the fabric of his conspiracy story around the framework of a real set of facts. There are, I suggest, three areas of inquiry which might tend to confirm or challenge the essence of his story.

If Raoul was not a source of substantial funding for Ray during his months as a fugitive, what was the source?

Was the package containing evidence that would inexorably lead to him left on the sidewalk rather than placed in the Mustang?

Did he exchange rifles at the Aeromarine Supply Company after conferring with another as he claimed?

There has been speculation about how Ray's trips around the country and his trips to Europe were financed. Novelists have offered theories. The FBI conducted a relatively thorough investigation and was unable to establish any proof that Ray had been financed from the time of his escape from the prison at Jefferson City, Missouri, until the time of his arrest in London in any fashion other than Raoul, as Ray claimed. If Ray did receive substantial funds from other sources, those sources have escaped detection.

The troubling presence of the package containing evidence tending to link Ray to the crime creates a serious logical problem. If Ray acted alone, used the weapon that he purchased in Birmingham, and then was motivated to flee quickly from the scene, why did he take the time to pack the weapon in a cardboard box and then place his bulky belongings in a bedspread? Indeed, why had he not left the articles not required to kill Dr. King in the trunk of the Mustang before he fired the shot? If he was going to carry the rifle, binoculars, radio, clothing, and other articles from the bathroom, taking precious time to wrap them up, why did he leave them on the sidewalk? Why did he not just throw them in the Mustang parked a few feet away? The gratuitous placement by Ray of evidence that would, without doubt, lead to him is inexplicable. Ray's narrative of the events has the virtue of offering a rational explanation.

If Ray had discussed the characteristics of the rifle that he had purchased from the Aeromarine Supply Company with another who considered it to be unsuitable for the intended use, and then Ray exchanged the rifle for a more accurate or more powerful weapon, his narrative takes on an added authority. It is sometimes necessary for a juror to enter the mind of a defendant to determine if his testimony meets the crucial test of reasonableness. Since you, the reader, may be the only jury that James Earl Ray will ever have, an examination by you of his mental process at the time of purchase of the presumed murder weapon is important. Does it not seem likely that had Ray purchased the rifle with the intent of using it to murder Dr. King that he would have decided upon the weapon in advance of entering the store in order to spend as little time as possible with the store personnel? According to the state's hypothesis, the first overt act that Ray committed in his solitary plan to kill Dr. King was the purchase of a suitable weapon. Would Ray have not sought to complete that task expeditiously so that the salesperson might be less likely to identify him subsequently? Yet Ray, for some reason, did return to the Aeromarine Supply Company to exchange the weapon for a much more powerful and accurate one. Ray has told us of his view of the transaction with the Aeromarine Supply Company in Birmingham. Robert Wood and Donald Wood were the proprietors of the company on

March 29, 1968. According to Donald Wood, on that day Ray told him he was going deer hunting with his brother and that he needed a rifle for that purpose. Ray later recalled that he had said he was to hunt deer with "my brother-in-law." With the exception of that discrepancy, Wood fully corroborates Ray's narrative and provides, as well, details which tend to confirm essential elements in the narrative. Wood said that Ray looked over a number of rifles, seemed confused by the array of rifles available, and appeared to know even less about deer hunting. Ray selected a Remington Gamemaster. Wood affixed a telescopic sight to the .243 caliber weapon while Ray waited.

During the afternoon, Wood received a telephone call from Ray. Ray said that he required a "heavier gun" and that he wanted to exchange the weapon he had just purchased for a more powerful one. Wood agreed. He was, however, puzzled since the weapon he'd sold earlier in the day was more than adequate for deer hunting. Wood pointed out that he would prefer to make the exchange the next day when he would have time to mount the telescopic sight on the weapon he purchased. Ray agreed.

Wood said that Ray returned the following morning and chose a more powerful weapon, a Remington 30.06 rifle which fired a bullet that weighed approximately as much as the bullet for the .243 Remington.

Ray's account of the transaction at Aeromarine was confirmed both by Donald Wood and his father Robert Wood. Only the mysterious Raoul can corroborate or challenge Ray's account of why he exchanged weapons and risked a second visit to the location of his first overt act in the murder of Dr. King. We are left to ponder this question—Why did Ray exchange rifles unless someone advised him to do so after he had made the initial purchase?

Ray's explanation, whether truthful or not, claims the virtue of being reasonable. It also enjoys another distinction. During the twenty-five years that have passed since that day it remains the only explaination of the prolonged transaction.

In-depth interviews with potential witnesses, an examination of all of the voluminous working papers prepared by the original defense lawyers and their investigation, and days spent with Hanes senior and junior provided me with some insight into what might have been the affirmative case for the defense even had Ray not testified.

Arthur Hanes, Jr., a Princeton graduate and a sophisticated and urbane young Birmingham trial lawyer in 1968, told me what all trial lawyers know. "Hell, it wasn't our job to find out who killed King. We were there to defend Ray." This is the credo of the trial lawyer and it is, I suggest, an entirely proper approach when the role of the defense lawyer is examined in context. Students of history may be appalled by what may appear to be, and by what in fact may be, a cavalier attitude toward the facts. Yet, since historical truth is arrived at in one fashion and justice in the courtroom in another, the obligation of those who participate in a search for the truth is quite different from the responsibility of participants in the search for justice. The judicial experience as we practice it relies theoretically upon an impartial and wise judge, an impartial and open-minded jury, a state devoted to the discovery of evidence demonstrating the guilt of the defendant, and a defense dedicated to refuting that case. Should the defense lawyer abandon his traditional role and strike out on his own to learn and reveal the "truth," the delicate balance devised to create a fair and equal contest fails. It is for others to explore the facts to discover the truth. The suitable defense lawyer is an advocate for his client's case. It is in this light that the case, as seen and presented by the defense lawyers, should be understood.

Had Ray been tried, very likely the defense would have offered a serious challenge to several elements of the state's case. The jurors would have been required to determine if the shot was fired from the bathroom window; when and by whom the package that seemed to incriminate Ray was placed on the sidewalk; whether there was a deliberate police effort to allow Ray to escape from the scene; if the FBI deliberately allowed Ray to escape from the country before advertising their interest with him; why Ray's prints were not found in the bathroom; whether the bullet that killed Dr. King came from the rifle Ray had purchased; could the state prove that Ray had pulled the trigger that resulted in the fatal wound.

Among the most intriguing questions presented by the case against Ray as the lone killer are those that flow from the presumption that Ray rented a room at 422½ South Main in order to have a clear shot at Dr. King. Dr. King had not stayed at the Lorraine during his most recent visits to Memphis prior to April 1968. While the FBI had, since March 29, 1968, sought to drive King into that motel, Ray, presumably, would not have been aware of those efforts.

The prosecution alleges that once Ray learned that King was to be at the Lorraine it was obvious that a room at 422½ South Main would provide the perfect sniper's nest. In retrospect the casual observer might agree. However, an examination of the area either from the balcony at the Lorraine or from South Main Street reveals the true complexity created by the geography and topography of the site. From the Lorraine Motel balcony, it is not possible to see the building at 422½ Main Street. The rear of the building facing the Lorraine is entirely hidden by trees and bushes. From the Lorraine, one cannot even know that 422½ exists. The perspective afforded by an examination from South Main Street of the buildings located there does not reveal that by entering the 422½ address one will be able to see the Lorraine. A person familiar with the inner structure of the buildings might know that by entering 422½ and passing through a jerry-built impermanent corridor constructed of tin sheets and wood which connects 422½ with a separate building to its south a view of the Lorraine could be arranged. It is, of course, not impossible to enter the rooming house on South Main and arrive at a window which provides a view of the Lorraine balcony. It is, however, difficult to know that such a feat can be accomplished without advance knowledge of the connection between the two buildings and without knowing that the building south of 422½ is also a rooming house managed by the proprietors of the 422½ South Main establishment. The jurors might have been troubled by the failure of the prosecution to contemplate the curious complexity of the problem. They might have been stunned by the possibility that Ray had either inadvertently stumbled into a solution without even understanding the problem or that he had, as he had stated, been guided to the scene by someone with knowledge who had solved the problem for him.

If the jurors believed that Ray had managed to get to the bathroom window without help, as the prosecution had alleged, they would then have been confronted with the question of the origin of the shot. If the state had proof that the shot was fired from that window, it has not yet proffered it. It may very well be that a serious study of the autopsy documents, including contemporaneous notes, photographs, and X-rays, taken together with eyewitness testimony which may reconstruct the exact posture of Dr. King when he received the fatal bullet, will establish the angle of entry and thus the origin of the shot. In the absence of scholarly work by experts armed with the authority of the power of subpoena, who can say that he is content that the origin of the bullet is known? It is in this gray area of conjecture that the defense might have made significant gains. There were those in the Lorraine Motel courtyard and those on the balcony with Dr. King who believed that the shot may have been fired from a clump of bushes and scrub trees on the embankment between the rooming house and Dr. King and beneath the rooming house windows. As I have observed in the case of similar statements made by witnesses in the murder of President Kennedy, earwitness testimony is generally less reliable than eyewitness testimony. It is often difficult to identify the origin of a sound with precision. By contrast, it is relatively simple to state where one saw an event occur. There is some additional evidence which supports the defense theory that the shot was fired not from the bathroom window but rather from the bushes and trees on the embankment. This evidence, developed by the defense, should be examined as cautiously and evaluated as carefully as the evidence and statements proffered by the prosecution. This evidence, as in the case of the prosecution's allegations, has not been subjected to the crucible of cross-examination.

Solomon Jones was the driver of the car which transported Dr. King in the Memphis area. The vehicle had been made available by a local funeral parlor. In a statement Jones gave to the Memphis police authorities who questioned him on February 3, 1969, ten months after the murder, Jones said, "On the day of the shooting, I was on the ground beside the car, which was parked on the west side of the motel; I was on the north side of the car." While Jones was quoted by the police in an unsigned statement as having said, "Everybody was running and the yard was full of police, I was unable to tell who, if anyone, ran from the bushes." He had made earlier statements, some of them almost contemporaneous with the event, with a different emphasis. Jones told Renfro Hays, the defense investigator, and prior to that, news reporters at the scene, that he saw someone run from the bushes on the embankment immediately after the shot was fired. Jones said that the man had "something white" across his face. At one point Jones said that the man carried something in his hand.

On April 5, 1968, the morning following the murder, the Memphis *Commercial Appeal* quoted Jones as saying that just after the shot was fired he saw a man "with something white on his face" leave "a thicket across the street." Yet the police did not interview Jones until ten months had passed. Corroboration for the original observations made by Jones was furnished by Harold Carter. Carter lived at 422½ South Main. On April 4, 1968, he sat on a cardboard box on the embankment just in front of the clump of bushes and trees. If a shot was fired from that area he should have heard it. If a man fled from the area he might have observed him.

Carter was interviewed by Hays on August 25, 1968. He said,

That afternoon I was sitting out on the vacant lot behind the rooming house with Dude Wheeler and another man who works on the river. We were sitting there on some cardboard next to some bushes watching the people over at the Lorraine Motel as there was a lot going on over there. Just before six o'clock Dude and the other fellows left but Dude was supposed to come back. Then two men standing on the ground by the Lorraine Motel started calling up asking for someone to get Dr. King to the door. A man, I guess he was King, came out the door and came to the

182

**rail and started talking to these men on the ground. At the same
time I heard some one walking behind me from the other side of
the bushes. I thought it was Dude Wheeler coming back and I
didn't even look around. Then there was a loud shot from the
bushes right beside me. I looked around and saw the man
running away, north—I did not see his face. He was about my
size and he must have been young because he moved fast. He had
on dark clothes with a high necked white sweater. He had a rifle
or shotgun in his hand. When he got to the northwest corner of
the lot he took the stock off his gun and threw it in some bushes
and put the barrel under his jacket and stepped down on a barrel
and down to the sidewalk. Everyone was running to the motel
then. And he just walked on away from them.**

Carter told Hays that he was not anxious to become involved in the case.
For that reason he made no voluntary statement to the police. However,
during the evening of April 4th police officers interrogated all of the
residents of 422½ South Main. Carter said that when the police asked him
what he had been doing at the time of the murder and what he observed, he
answered them truthfully. The officers then took him to police headquarters where he was interviewed by detectives. Carter said he told the
detectives about the origin of the shot and of the man who fled from the
bushes. Carter said, "They called me a damn liar!" After the detectives
had made it plain to Carter that his allegations were not acceptable, he was
left alone for awhile.

**When they talked to me again I told them I didn't know anything,
I never got around to telling them where the gunstock was. I have
nothing to hide about this, I never saw that man before or since
that I know of. If the police had treated me like a human being I
would have told them everything I knew.**

Carter later signed a statement which was witnessed by Hays in which he
said that he was reluctant to sign a statement about his observations
"because I don't want to be thrown in jail like Charlie Stephens was."

On June 19, 1968, *The New York Times* published a review of some
of the evidence by Martin Waldron, a veteran investigative reporter. The
story ran under the headline "Evidence Hints a Conspiracy in Slaying of
Dr. King."

Waldron began:

**From the moment of the assassination of the Rev. Dr. Martin
Luther King, Jr., on April 4 evidence has accumulated to suggest
that he was the victim of a conspiracy. Several bits of evidence**

indicate more than one person may have been involved in Dr. King's slaying. Others point to the possibility that the murder may have been a hired killing.

Waldron considered the official response to the evidence tending to establish conspiracy.

The Federal Bureau of Investigation has refused to comment. Attorney General Ramsey Clark has said several times that the FBI has not uncovered any evidence of a conspiracy.

Mr. Clark said, however, that the investigation did not end with the arrest of James Earl Ray in London on June 8. If others are involved, he said, the FBI will find them.

During the halcyon days of 1968, before the United States Senate had informed us that the FBI destroyed evidence, suborned perjury and committed perjury to prevent the Warren Commission from learning who killed President Kennedy, and operated as well a squad determined to destroy Dr. King, it was easier to believe that the FBI might be interested in finding the assassins. Mr. Clark's assurances were no doubt comforting to many. But to a few, including Ray, his two lawyers and his one investigator, the evidence that raised doubts for Waldron had raised serious questions for further exploration.

The first matter that Waldron addressed himself to as one which indicated "that there may have been a conspiracy" was "a vivid description broadcast over the Memphis police radio network on the night of April 4 of an automobile chase that never took place."

The broadcast, made at the time Ray was fleeing from the city southward, attempted to establish the flight of the alleged assassin to the northeast.

Arthur Hanes, Sr., told me that he had listened to the official recording of the Memphis police radio broadcasts for the evening of April 4. He had taken handwritten verbatim notes of the broadcast which he gave to me. At 6:10 P.M. the radio broadcast the message "6:10—Information subject [or suspect] may be in late model Mustang going north on Main." Hanes said, "Now where did they get that information from. There is not a single witness who they can produce who claims that they saw anyone get into a white Mustang and leave the scene."

At 6:36 the police radio broadcast this message. "6:36—60 at Jackson and Hollywood. Mobile unit. East on Summers—from Highland exceeding speed limit. Blue 66 Pontiac going over 75 mph. Three white males in blue Pontiac. North on Jackson." And at 6:48 the radio broadcast this message. "White Mustang is shooting at Pontiac. Austin Peay. Approaching the road going into Naval Base." While the police concentrated upon an apocryphal gun battle in one part of town, according to Ray, he drove out of town in the opposite direction.

To this date, no adequate official explanation of the police radio broadcast has been offered. When I asked Frank Holloman, who had been the director of the police department on April 4, 1968, for an explanation he said, "Oh, it is nothing serious. It was just a teen-ager involved in a prank." That appears to be the official explanation. I asked Holloman if the teen-ager was arrested and prosecuted for obstruction of justice since quite possibly he had aided a murderer escape from the area. While Holloman paused for a moment, I asked if the teen-ager's radio license had been revoked. Holloman appeared troubled by the questions and then answered, "I don't recall if we ever found out who it was. If we didn't, then we couldn't arrest him." I agreed with Holloman's logic and asked how the police could learn the age of the suspect from the radio broadcast without learning his identity. Holloman pondered the question for a long moment and then said, "Well maybe we did locate him and that's how we got his age. I just don't know."

Had the case been tried while Hanes and Hanes represented Ray, the defense would have been prepared to explore this area of evidence that indicated the possibility of conspiracy. An examination of the broadcasts by the police over the two frequencies they employed revealed false or inexplicable references to the fleeing white Mustang at 6:10 P.M., 6:12 P.M., 6:35 P.M., 6:48 P.M., and 6:53 P.M., as well as a reference to an abandoned Mustang at 5:42 P.M. Approximately twenty minutes before the shot was fired a broadcast stated that "Tac 11 [Tactical Squad] has witness who saw white Olds pull away from Lorraine before police arrived."

The broadcast at 7:37 P.M. said "complete curfew in effect." Exactly ten minutes later the police reported "Tac units to start cruising from Lorraine. Homicide has completed investigation." There is very little evidence to dispute the police assertion that less than two hours after Dr. King had been murdered the police had finished their work. The unexamined clues, the unfollowed leads, the unexplored circumstances that led toward a conspiracy to kill Dr. King remain today unexamined, unfollowed, and unexplored by those in Memphis or in the Department of Justice.

Martin Waldron was concerned by evidence showing that Ray, using the alias Eric S. Galt, left "a trail of free spending" indicating that he had been financed by others. The Hanes law firm also focused upon that matter. Ray explained that he was paid by Raoul and he quite specifically supplied the amounts paid, the dates and places of payment, the denominations of the bills and the services that he performed. The FBI, through news leaks attributed by *The New York Times* to "quoted FBI 'sources,' " responded that Ray had probably robbed a bank in Alton, Illinois, on July 13, 1967, and taken $20,000. Waldron wrote that "other evidence indicates that Ray may have been living in Toronto at this time." In any event, Ray was never charged with the crime and the only evidence of his possible involvement in that crime was the statement of one woman in the bank who allegedly said that one of the two robbers resembled photographs of Ray. There exists no reasonable explanation of Ray's funding for the period of time preceding the murder of Dr. King, other than Ray's own explanation. While his explanations may not be accurate, they remain unchallenged by a viable prosecution alternative.

Waldron was also concerned that Ray used four aliases in Canada and in his trips about the United States and ultimately to Europe. The names Ray operated under were Ramon George Sneyd, Eric S. Galt, Paul Bridgeman and John Willard. All four men existed. All four men lived in Toronto. All four men were approximately the same height and weight as James Earl Ray, and like Ray, all four had dark hair. All four men gave the appearance of being the same age as Ray. The evidence indicates that Ray used the name Galt in Birmingham, Atlanta and Los Angeles; the name Willard in Memphis; the name Sneyd in Toronto and London; the name Bridgeman in Toronto.

The question that troubled Waldron and the defense attorneys is how did Ray, unknown in Canada, assemble documents from four men who resembled him physically and who did not even know each other. Did Ray have assistance in choosing the aliases? The prosecution failed to investigate this intriguing question and failed to comment upon it when presenting the case against Ray. Indeed neither the jurors nor the trial judge were informed of any of the distressing details which might have discommoded the case against Ray as the lone assassin. The unexplained false radio broadcasts, Ray's unexplained well-financed trips, the unexplored four remarkable aliases, the unrefuted evidence that indicated that the shot may have originated from a place other than the bathroom window, and the difficulty in knowing that by entering 422½ South Main one could arrange for a view of the motel balcony were neither commented upon by Ray's prosecutors when they presented the case against Ray to the court and jury nor alluded to by Ray's lawyer, the renowned Percy Foreman of Houston, Texas.

Indeed, why did Ray plead guilty when the state would have had a most difficult and perhaps an impossible task of establishing a *prima facie* case against him, and when such a strong affirmative defense was available to him? And why did Foreman, Ray's trial counsel, offer no resistance to an arrangement which sent his client to jail for ninety-nine years in a state where the death penalty had not been carried out for many years?

Chapter Twenty-Five

THE PLEA
by Mark Lane

Those who assert that Ray alone killed King offer as proof Ray's plea of guilty. That plea, however, can not be dispositive of the many and serious questions raised by the evidence. When closely examined, the plea itself, in fact, tends to support the other evidence of a prearranged plan to murder Dr. King and to cover up the evidence of that conspiracy.

When Ray entered his plea before Judge Battle, he stated that there had been a conspiracy to murder Dr. King. He has consistently held to that position. Over the years he has told all of his attorneys that there had been a conspiracy. He made that statement to the Hanes defense team, to their successor, Percy Foreman, and to the lawyers who have since represented him. He explained the details of the conspiracy to his lawyers and to Huie before he entered the plea and he elaborated upon those details when he spoke with me later.

The curious circumstances surrounding the arrangement for the guilty plea hardly do credit to our oft-repeated claims of due process in difficult cases and raise yet additional questions. Was a deliberate effort made to induce Ray to plead guilty so that the full facts might be successfully concealed? An examination of the development of the various episodes that led to the courtroom ritual in which the guilty plea was offered and accepted may provide the answer.

Ray was imprisoned in the Shelby County Jail in Memphis in maximum security until he pleaded guilty. During the months that he was jailed, bright lights were kept on him twenty-four hours each day. Closed circuit cameras monitored his every move. Guards were present in the cell with him while other guards watched him from the other side of the bars. Microphones in the cell picked up and magnified every sound that he made. Even his breathing was heard. Months later when Ray described the conditions in the cell during a civil suit against Foreman and Huie he testified, "As I stated, maximum security jail, lights on twenty-four hours a day, steel plates over the windows, two television sets watching me all the time . . . no fresh air.'' Ray testified that his conversations with his attorneys were overheard by the guards. He said that the listening devices were so sophisticated that the guards ''could hear a roach walk across the floor.'' Ray said that Foreman ''often spoke very loudly when talking with him.'' I was always warning Mr. Foreman about talking so loud. A lot of times he would talk loud on purpose so they [the guards] could hear him. A lot of times he had them sign documents as witnesses.'' Ray said that he did not wish to speculate about which conversations the guards had overheard. ''I think you would have to talk to the guards to find out what they heard and what they didn't hear.'' He did say that on one occasion ''one of them told me he heard some of Mr. Foreman's conversations one time.''

Two months after Ray had been confined under the extraordinary conditions imposed by the Memphis authorities, Arthur Hanes, Sr., filed a motion requesting an order directing the Shelby County Sheriff to ''cease and desist from the use of television lights, cameras and microphones to constantly surveille the Defendant.'' The attorney said that ''the presence of said illumination and surveillance has deprived Defendant of the opportunity to rest or sleep and has a tendency to cause Defendant to be nervous and disturbed and constitutes an electronic form of cruel and unusual punishment.''

The Attorney General, Phil Canale, filed an answer stating that the television cameras were required ''as a security measure to protect the defendant Ray as well as to keep the defendant Ray from effecting an escape.''

During 1976, Leona Zanetti and Pamela Spack, two investigators with the Citizens Commission of Inquiry, interviewed Phil Canale. They asked him about the presence of microphones in Ray's cell. He replied:

Well, we had a big hearing on that down there when, ah, one of his lawyers filed something, some motion about the fact that he was, ah, his health was going bad, and surveillance and everything, and we had a hearing, and, ah, the doctor testified, the jailers testified, and, ah, we had a full blown hearing on it. As I recall it there was always some light in the cell there . . . I think Hanes also said that he had to lie on the floor to talk to Ray because the place was bugged. Well, there was never any indication of bugs, I never heard of any, anything that came out of the cell. I'm sure that I would have heard it if anything came out of there, you know. But yes, I think there was some illumination in there at all times.

However, that same year the United States Court of Appeals for the Sixth Circuit concluded that Ray's prison conversations had been monitored and that such electronic surveillance was "improper."

Eight years before, on November 22, 1968, Judge Battle had ruled that "the security complained of is for the benefit of the defendant" and that "the measures taken for the security and protection of the defendant are reasonable."

Two months after Hanes had applied to Judge Battle for some relief from the oppressive jail conditions, Michael Eugene, an English solicitor who had been appointed to represent Ray's rights in London, saw Ray. He was astonished by the deterioration in Ray's condition. He said that Ray looked sick, weak, and nervous.

When James Earl Ray pleaded guilty, a reporter from the Chicago *Daily News* interviewed his brother, John Ray. John said that he had doubted that his brother would plead guilty but that the strain of being under constant observation in his cell by guards and closed circuit television must have affected him. "All the time he has spent up there in his cell may have affected his mind. He can't even go to the bathroom in private."

When I interviewed Jerry Ray, another brother, in December 1976, he said that Foreman's efforts to convince James to plead guilty were substantially aided by the defendant's condition.

He couldn't sleep. Those bright lights on all the time. Always being looked at. No air conditioning. No fresh air. Never any daylight. Never any night. I guess it was kind of like a concentration camp. You ended up doing things you ordinarily wouldn't do. James was sort of out of his mind at the time. He hadn't seen outside, even through a window, for four months. Never knew whether it was night or day. It was the kind of conditions that big shots in this country are always complaining about in other countries."

In *Spandau*, a remarkable prison book, Albert Speer, the convicted Nazi war criminal, discussed the conditions to which he was subjected as a military prisoner. Speer had been sentenced at Nuremberg to serve a twenty-year term. He explained that "the prison regulations are strict" because another convicted war criminal had just hanged himself. To prevent another death, his cell was not entirely darkened. He wrote that at first "the cell is poorly illuminated at night by a light placed outside." Speer added "at night we live in twilight." Later in his imprisonment at Spandau all of the lights were extinguished before ten o'clock. Indeed the rules required, he wrote, "that all cells had to be dark at ten o'clock."

190

The experience at Spandau, the ultimate maximum security military prison, was not pleasant. Yet Speer, in describing the conditions there, wrote of his regular visits with other prisoners which occurred many hours each day, his work in the garden with the other prisoners, the walks in the courtyard, the window in his cell which permitted a view of the stars at night, and fresh air both night and day.

In my view all prisons that I have seen offer artificial and brutalizing experiences. Yet Speer, a major war criminal, was not subjected to the dehumanizing denial of sensory perception that the elaborately contrived circumstances imposed upon James Earl Ray. If the torture that Ray was subjected to was not designed to weaken his resistance and to drain his resolve it nevertheless should have been quite clear to counsel, the prosecutors and the court that such a result was predictable, indeed, very likely inevitable.

It appears that the most important decision that Ray made after his arrest was to discharge the Hanes defense team and retain Percy Foreman. I believe that the father and son team was adequately prepared to represent Ray at trial and that the evidence against him was minimal and insufficient to convict him. Once Foreman entered the case the inexorable march toward a deal—the guilty plea and a ninety-nine year sentence—was underway.

Arthur Hanes, Sr., remembered quite clearly his last day as attorney for Ray. "We learned of it on Sunday, November 10. We, Art Junior and I, went to the jail to see Ray at about 8:30 at night. The guard said the sheriff wanted to see me. I went to the Sheriff's office and they showed me a Xerox copy of a handwritten note from Ray. It said 'Dear Mr. Hanes, I thank you for all you've done for me, however I've decided to change lawyers and obtain other counsel. Sincerely, Jim.' I said, 'Well, Percy Foreman was in his cell four or five hours today while you were driving here from Birmingham.'"

Hanes added, "Foreman had the original of my letter from Ray. How he was allowed to get in there and see my client about our case I never did find out for sure."

A substantial question also remains as to why Foreman visited Ray in his Memphis jail cell. On a January 2, 1976, CBS-TV broadcast an interview of Foreman conducted by a CBS reporter, Dan Rather. Rather asked Foreman how he got into the case. The following colloquy ensued:

Foreman: His brother, Jerry, had written me almost from the beginning, asking me to get in the case, and I refused—until I had a letter from James Earl Ray himself. And when he asked me to

come, I did go from Texas to Memphis, and talked with him, and I was employed.

Rather: You're aware that he now says that—James Earl Ray, that is—that he never asked you to get into the case?

Foreman: No, I wasn't aware of that. That's the first I ever heard of it. I have his letter.

Rather: If Mr. Foreman had his letter, he does not have it now. We asked to see it. We were told it had been lost.

When I asked Ray why Foreman had made that initial visit to him in November 1968, he said, "I really don't know. I was surprised to see him. Of course, I knew he was a famous lawyer. He told me that several times. He said he had tried a thousand murder cases, that almost no one ever went to jail and that just one was executed. He said that my case was the easiest one that he had seen."

Ray prepared a statement of his case in affidavit form from his cell in the Memphis Criminal Court on August 31, 1970. In that document, he explained his relationship with Foreman.

On or about November 10th, 1968, Mr. Percy Foreman, a Texas licensed attorney came to Shelby County Jail and asked to see me.

I agreed to see Mr. Foreman although I never contacted him directly or indirectly requesting any type of legal assistance.

After the amenities I saw that Mr. Foreman had the contracts I had signed with Mr. Hanes and Mr. Huie.

I asked his opinion of them. Mr. Foreman came right to the point, he said he had read the contracts and had concluded that the only thing Hanes and Huie were interested in was money. He said they were personal friends and if I stuck with them I would be barbecued.

I told Mr. Foreman I was concerned with certain aspects of the contracts, such as the inference of a trial date deadline, but that since I had signed the document there wasn't much I could do.

Mr. Foreman replied there was something I could do, that he could break the contracts if I hired him. Since I had been taken advantage of due to a lack of education in such matters.

I asked him what his position would be if I did engage him in relation to contracts with book writers and retaining a Tennessee licensed attorney.

He said there would be no stories written until after the trial was over and that it was necessary that Tennessee licensed counsel be retained to advise and assist with Tennessee laws.

I also asked Mr. Foreman how he would finance the trial. He said let him worry about that. That when the trial was over he would make a deal with some book writer but that he wouldn't compromise the defense with pretrial deals.

He said that his fee would be $150,000 for the trial and appeals, if necessary, and that as a retainer he would take the 1966 Mustang I had, which I signed over to him. Mr. Foreman also asked me to sign over to him a rifle the prosecution was holding as evidence. Although there was a question of ownership, I also signed this item over to him. I then wrote out a statement for Mr. Foreman dismissing Mr. Hanes and stating I would engage Tennessee counsel.

During November 1969, when Ray testified against Foreman in a civil suit, he said much the same thing.

Ray: Mr. Foreman came to jail. I will explain the surroundings. When Foreman came to the jail, evidently, my brother, someway, had contacted him when they found out they were going to make an effort to keep me off the stand. So Mr. Foreman come to jail and it was a complete surprise to me. He asked if I would let him in to see me and I said to let him in. When Mr. Foreman came to talk with me he had these contracts in his hand. He had them all, all my previous contracts, so after just some general conversation Mr. Foreman mentioned these contracts and I asked him what he thought of the contracts and he told me that the only thing Mr. Hanes and Mr. Huie was interested in was money. He said he studied those contracts and if I stuck with them I would be barbecued. That's Mr. Foreman's lingo for the electric chair.

Q: What else did Mr. Foreman say about those contracts?

Ray: Well, he didn't . . . we didn't discuss them deeply. We didn't go into any legal reasons, anything legal. The only thing he said, he said Mr. Hanes and Mr. Huie had been friends a long time and that's why they got involved in these contracts. That's what he said.

Q: What did Mr. Foreman propose at that time?

Ray: Well, he told me if he had been on the case to start with or if he was on it now he would never . . . would never become involved with no contracts on books until after the trial was over and he told me if he took the case we could forget about the books until the trial was over.

Q: Did you employ Mr. Foreman as your attorney?

Ray: Yes, I employed him . . . I got him.

Q: When?

Ray: At that time, going in that conversation, after he made those charges and I was just . . . it was just enough substance in what he said to make me believe it and, of course, what give me the impression he had plenty of money to finance the cause without compromising the case to book writers and I thought maybe it was a possibility Mr. Hanes didn't have that much money. I agreed to discharge Mr. Hanes.

Q: Just sort of get down to telling us what you said and what Mr. Foreman said in that conversation about the contracts, the contracts of employment as well as the book contracts. Did you employ Mr. Foreman?

Ray: Yeah. As far as Mr. Foreman, he said I would pay him $150,000 straight fee and he would handle all the appeals until the trial was over, carry it all the way to the United States Surpeme Court. I agreed to that and we made two or three other arrangements. One, that it would be necessary to hire a Tennessee counselor. I even stipulated this in the paper I wrote up relieving Mr. Hanes.

Q: What was the stipulation about hiring Tennessee counsel?

Ray: The paper is on record down there in Shelby County Court about the necessity of hiring Tennessee counselors.

Q: Was any Tennessee counsel hired?

Ray: No, there never was any counsel hired.

While Ray has been consistent regarding his dealings with Foreman, the latter has vacillated. Foreman had originally stated that Ray's brothers, John and Jerry, asked him to enter the case. Later he said that Jerry alone had invited him. On November 11, 1968, he told Martin Waldron of the *New York Times* that Jerry and John had forwarded a request, evidently an oral one, from James. Later he told Dan Rather that he had received a letter from Ray. Ray's denial that he had sent a letter, together with Foreman's inability to produce it, tends to support Ray's version of the events.

The brothers, Jerry and John Ray, said that they met Foreman for the first time on the day that Foreman also met James in his Memphis jail cell. Jerry told me that "the only time my dad ever saw Foreman was when Foreman was in St. Louis, he saw us all together. My mother is dead. My dad and John and me saw Foreman in St. Louis once. But John and me saw Foreman in Memphis. We would go over to Memphis to see James and we'd see Foreman. This is after he was the lawyer for James. I never did see him until the day he became James' lawyer."

I asked Jerry if Foreman talked about the defense for James.

Not much. He used to have us come over to his hotel room and he'd send down for a bottle of Scotch, he liked Scotch, and he'd drink and tell me about all these other cases he won. Then he'd say this would be the easiest case he ever had. He said my brother's case would be. He said they had no real evidence against James. He said, "They have no actual evidence." He said, "I've got guys out before where they had evidence against them but they don't have evidence against James."

On November 11, 1969, Foreman testified in an action brought against him by James Earl Ray. He said of John and Jerry Ray, "I had not met them officially or personally except over the telephone, in telephone conversations prior to the Sunday morning that I came." The morning he referred to, he explained, was the day that he met James Earl Ray in prison. Foreman then testified that he did not talk to Huie until "approximately a week later." Unexplained by that testimony is how Foreman was able to secure the contracts among Hanes, Huie, and Ray before meeting any of them.

Foreman has said that within an hour of reading about Ray's arrest in London he ordered his secretary to begin a file on the case so that he would be prepared in the event that someone asked him to enter the case. Foreman has often boasted that he has represented more than 1,000 persons accused of murder and that he has only lost one man to the executioner. Major newspapers and national magazines have repeated that allegation as fact.

Not as thoroughly publicized was Foreman's indictment by a federal grand jury in Dallas in July 1975, for conspiring to obstruct justice and for obstructing juctice. Indicted with him were Nelson Bunker Hunt and W. Herbert Hunt, both sons of the millionaire H. L. Hunt. In essence the grand jury charged that the Hunts employed two men to conduct alleged wiretapping and that Foreman was given "a secret payment of $100,000" in order "to guarantee the silence of prospective witnesses." The indictment charged that the Hunt brothers paid the $100,000, which constituted Foreman's fee, to prevent his two clients (the men employed by the Hunts) from telling the truth to the grand jury. The charge against Foreman was that, in 1970, he conspired to pay witnesses to go to jail rather than permit them to tell the full truth about the principals involved with them in the criminal conspiracy. Foreman allegedly participated in the crime to secure a large sum of money for himself and in order to protect the other members of the conspiracy. He never informed his clients that he was really serving another master. According to a story written by Martin Waldron in *The New York Times*, Senator Eastland took an interest in the case:

> **There have been widespread allegations that political pressure was brought in Washington to keep the Hunts from being prosecuted. Senator James O. Eastland of Mississippi, the chairman of the Senate Judiciary Committee, made several inquiries about the case to the Justice Department. Senator Eastland has vigorously denied reports that he was paid $50,000 to do this.**

As the case against the defendants began, Foreman stated that he was too ill to participate. After Senator Eastland had expressed a concern, those defendants on trial, including Nelson Bunker Hunt, were permitted to plead no contest to reduced charges and fined.

In 1969, James Earl Ray had charged that Foreman, perhaps acting on behalf of an unknown principal, had maneuvered him into a position in which he was forced to remain silent about the principals involved in a criminal conspiracy. Ray went to jail, remained silent, and the principals were not revealed.

The next year, according to a federal grand jury, Foreman entered into a conspiracy on behalf of principals unknown to his clients. The plea entered by his codefendants, does not weaken the viability of the grand jury's indictment nor does it threaten the viability of Ray's account of his relationship with Foreman.

After Foreman became Ray's attorney by dazzling him with his almost unblemished record of victories, and by assuring him that no book or magazine contracts would be entered into and all previous ones revoked, according to Ray, Foreman embarked upon a campaign for more book contracts. In his August 31, 1970, affidavit, Ray wrote:

> **During this early period of Mr. Foreman's tenure he once suggested I confirm, in writing, some theories being propounded**

by another novelist, one George McMillan who, in collaboration with a phrenologist, was writing another novel concerning the case.

Mr. Foreman said the pair would give us $5000.00 to use for defense purposes. I rejected this suggestion.

Then later Mr. Foreman transported a check to the jail for $5000.00 for me to endorse. He had received the check from the novelist William Bradford Huie and that would I let him have the money to give to Nashville attorney, John J. Hooker, Sr. as a retainer fee. I agreed to this.

Also during this period I suggested to Mr. Foreman that rather than printing more pre-trial stories we instigate some type legal action to prevent the publishing of stories, especially the more rancid type articles such as was appearing in *Life* magazine.

Mr. Foreman rejected this suggestion saying: "Why stir up a barrel of rattlesnakes." Still, later, on or about Jan. 29th, 1969, Mr. Foreman transported a contract to the jail and advised me to sign it. "See contract Ct. records."

Mr. Foreman saying it would take considerable funds to finance the suit and pay John J. Hooker, Sr.'s fee.

On or about February 3rd, 1969, Mr. Foreman transported still another contract to the jail and advised me to sign it. He told me the law suit was progressing well, that he could prove I was innocent, and the trial would start in the near future.

I also signed this document being reassured because the document stipulated that Mr. Foreman would represent me at "trial or trials" pending in Shelby County, Tennessee: in exchange for me signing the document. "see contract Ct. records."

There was no mention of "cop-outs" in the contract and it seems "cop-outs" are not legally classified as trials in Tennessee.

Foreman testified on November 11, 1969, that he did not "do business" regarding the publication of books until "about the 25th of January 1969," and that he did so then only because "Ray ordered me to do so." The testimony continues:

Foreman: I mentioned selling some pictures to *Life* Magazine and I made the contact with *Life* and *Life* sent a man to see me, the Senior Editor of *Life* that I am acquainted with and I relayed my conversation to Mr. Ray and Mr. Ray said, "Well, we have started with Mr. Huie and with *Look*. I don't see any reason to be contacting or communicating with anyone else. Why don't you get in touch with Mr. Huie?''

Q: And that was the last week in January?

Foreman: It was about the 25th of January, my best judgment. I only say that because it was three or four days before the 29th of January and from the time around the 25th to the 27th of November until the 29th of January, I had no communication, conversation, written or otherwise, with Mr. Huie and didn't intend to have any.

Q: After your discussion with Mr. Ray when did you contact Mr. Huie?

Foreman: I would just have to estimate this but it was sometime between the 25th of January and the 29th of January, I would guess possibly the same day.

Q: And when did you agree upon a contract—there is one written out and dated, but did you agree on a contract at that time that was later put in written form?

Foreman: I never discussed any terms or contracts except the assignment from James Earl Ray to me dated January 29, of which I just presented you a copy and I would not have taken all of the rights of Ray as they had been reconveyed to him save at his request.

Foreman testified that although Huie was writing stories stating that Ray was guilty it was "absolutely not" damaging to the defense since Ray had agreed before January 29, 1969, to plead guilty. Ray has consistently denied that he agreed to plead guilty during January 1969. A contract signed by Foreman and Ray on February 3, 1969, tends to support Ray's contention. That contract obligates Foreman to represent Ray at a trial or at trials presently pending. In exchange for that agreement, Ray gave all of his rights to the Huie book, including possible motion picture rights, to Foreman. It seems unlikely that Foreman could have extracted those rights from Ray in consideration of Foreman's silent appearance at Ray's side while he entered the plea of guilty.

Foreman's sworn statement that he had not talked to Huie about his interest in the book prior to January 25, 1969, was challenged by Huie. In the book, *He Slew the Dreamer,* Huie wrote:

Early on Wednesday morning, November 27, 1968, I met Mr. Foreman at the statue of the Texas Ranger at the Dallas airport. We drove to Fort Worth, where he made a brief courtroom

appearance. Then we had lunch, and altogether, we talked for several hours.

According to Huie, Foreman wanted Hanes out of the contract so that he "could have what Hanes had had." Huie said that Foreman told him, "So you get Hanes out and let me in, then, goddamn it, get to work and write us a good book and make us a good movie and make us some money."

Considerations as to how and why Foreman entered the case are important and interesting, but the attention of a serious inquiry must focus upon what he did after he became the attorney of record. I believe that the record reveals that Foreman was not prepared to go to trial. The implications of that statement are awesome, especially since during the period when he should have but failed to make a thorough examination of the facts, he was assuring Ray and his family that he was going to try the case and win it. Foreman's conduct constrains one to consider the nature of his commitment.

Young defense lawyers are often appalled when they learn that their client has a rather protracted yellow-sheet indicating a substantial criminal record. Experienced trial lawyers understand that such a record may be useful if it portrays a defendant very different from the one likely to have committed the crime in question. Ray had a not insubstantial record of petty thefts and robberies. Yet his *modus operandi* did not indicate that he would kill. A thorough examination of his record by the FBI revealed one fist-fight. He never fired a weapon at a human being. Percy Foreman might have made much of Ray's nonviolent background. Instead of probing that record, Foreman dismissed the subject stating that "all of a man's cells change every five years." Therefore, Foreman reasoned, past character attributes and previous experience and actions are irrelevant since each five years "a new man" with all new cells emerges like a moth from a chrysalis. Foreman's pseudoscientific analysis, offered quite seriously, might have been amusing had the circumstances been different.

This cavalier attitude characterized Foreman's approach to the evidence. When Judge Battle accepted Foreman as Ray's lawyer he made it plain that the case was to be tried in the near future. He ordered Foreman to prepare for trial quickly and indicated that he would be loathe to grant any additional delay.

Foreman knew that in order to be ready he would be required to secure and study the voluminous Hanes files, debrief Hanes, Sr., and Jr., quickly, interview Hays, their investigator, and send his own investigators into the field at once. Foreman evidently took none of those essential and basic steps.

Arthur Hanes, Sr., told me that on the Sunday that Foreman became counsel he spoke with Foreman about the files.

Hanes, Sr., also told me that upon being discharged by Ray he did want to be paid for the services that he had rendered. Subsequently, however, he said that he had offered all of his files and full cooperation to Foreman without charge.

Foreman called us on a Monday morning and said he was coming to Birmingham that afternoon. That was about three or four weeks after we were relieved of the case, about the end of November 1968. We said "fine." He told us his flight number and Art, Jr., met him at the airport and brought him to the office. We showed him what we had, advised him he was welcome to everything he could see. We said, "You can have it all; you're the trial lawyer now." We tried to outline the case for him, to tell him what we knew. He didn't seem to be too interested. We offered him everything we had. He took nothing with him.

Arthur, Jr., interjected at that point, "He wasn't interested in the case. He wanted to drink some Scotch, eat some dinner, and talk about his famous cases. He also told us about how he made speeches all over the country."

I asked both lawyers how much time Foreman spent looking at the thousands of pages of documents, reports, photograph interviews, and trial briefs that comprised the Ray file in the Hanes office. Arthur, Sr., said "about ten minutes." He added, "then we took him to dinner. We called and made reservations for him because he said he wanted to go to Miami. We took him to the airport and put him on a plane to Miami. We offered him our files. He could have taken the originals. The whole thing. He was welcome to. If he had wanted photocopies we would have made them. He didn't want anything."

I asked Hanes, Sr., what he thought of Foreman's actions. He said, "My judgment is that the man never even considered trying the case. Far as I can ascertain he never prepared and he never investigated. He never considered giving James Earl Ray a trial. For what reason, I don't know."

Renfro Hays said that he was never asked by Foreman to share the results of his investigation. Foreman, nevertheless, said that the Hays investigation was worthless.

Foreman's description of his investigation was made under oath. He testified, "I investigated the case and had the case investigated. As a matter of fact I spent, I don't know how much money." He said that he questioned James Earl Ray about the crime "anywhere from thirty to seventy-five hours." The difference between thirty and seventy-five is considerable. If Foreman had questioned Ray two hours a day from the time he was retained until he pleaded Ray guilty he would not have had sufficient time to have amassed seventy-five hours of interrogation. Foreman was ill for a good portion of that time and in Memphis, where Ray was imprisoned, only rarely.

Ray told me that Foreman never asked him if he had fired the shot on April 4th, or if he had been in a conspiracy with others to kill Dr. King. Foreman confirmed Ray's assertion. Manuel Chait, a staff correspondent for the St. Louis *Post-Dispatch,* reported on March 11, 1969, following the guilty plea, that "after the sentencing Foreman, answering questions from reporters, said he never had asked Ray specifically whether he had been involved in a conspiracy." And Jerry Lipson, a staff writer for the Chicago *Daily News,* reported on that same day that "throughout his tenure as Ray's lawyer, the bear-sized Texan said, he never discussed the slaying directly. 'I never asked Ray that question,' he said, when asked if Ray had told him he had pulled the trigger." It is apparent to me that the most significant aspects of the case are: Was there a conspiracy to murder Dr. King? And did Ray pull the trigger? Yet the only two men who participated in the conferences, Foreman and Ray, both state that Foreman never inquired about either.

Ray told me that he recalled vividly one occasion when Foreman did touch upon the case in a conversation with him.

> Foreman came to see me and he brought a batch of pictures with him. He had about ten or fifteen pictures. Most of them were pictures of Cubans or that's what they looked like to me. They were all white except one. Foreman said to me, "These are people that the FBI wants to get out of circulation." He said that the FBI said they were pro-communist or anti-communist and that the FBI wanted me to identify one or more of them. I told Foreman that I did not want to get involved in making a false ID. He said the FBI wanted an ID of one or more of them, that they wanted to get them out of circulation. I said I would not identify any of them. He looked at me and said that if I picked one out and said he shot Martin Luther King the FBI would arrest him and transport him to Memphis. I said, "No, I don't want to get involved in that type thing for various reasons." When it was clear that I was not going to make a false identification Foreman

**said to me, "Is that your last word on the subject?" and I
answered, "Yes." Then he left.**

I asked Ray if any of the men looked familiar to him. He thought for a
moment and I remembered again his style. He had said he would give me
leads to follow and refute false charges that had been made against him
but that he was not an informer and would not finger anyone. Then he
said, "I recognized one picture. It was a man who may have been a Klan
member. I never met him but I think I did see his picture in a newspaper.
There was another picture that was familiar. It is hard to recognize a
person and make a certain identification from a snapshot. But Foreman
showed me a picture from the FBI of three men in Dallas. Just after
Kennedy was killed. The three looked like they were under arrest. One of
them looked like, and might have been, Raoul."

I have seen the photograph Ray referred to. In the photograph three
men in Dealy Plaza, Dallas, appear to be under arrest, shortly after the
assassination of President Kennedy. No available Dallas police department record makes reference to such an arrest and the names of the three
men, apparently in police custody, have not been revealed by the local or
federal police authorities. One of the men in that photograph, the smallest
and the slightest of the three, bears a striking resemblance to the artist's
sketch of the presumed murderer of Dr. King. The sketch was utilized by
the local and federal police in a search for the murderer. It was created by
an artist employed by a Memphis newspaper in conjunction with witnesses who said they saw the man flee through the rooming house corridor
and from the rooming house just after the shot was fired.

As we talked in the small library of the Brushy Mountain Penitentiary
Ray recalled another occasion when Foreman had discussed a peripheral
aspect of the case with him. The atmosphere was relaxed for the warden,
Stonney Ray Lane (not related to either Ray or me), had been most
hospitable in arranging for a comfortable room where Ray and I could talk
without interruption or surveillance. Warden Lane had met me at the gate
and had driven me to the maximum security section of the prison where
Ray was confined. Will Rogers once said that he never met a man he
didn't like. I never understood how that could be. In any event I never saw
a prison that I did like. But Warden Lane proved a kind and considerate
host and Ray and I talked on in relative calm and isolation.

Ray said, "One time Foreman came into the cell with a long list of
places that had been robbed: banks, supermarkets, insurance companies.
It was quite a long list with maybe fifty or sixty places on it. He said the
list came from the FBI. I don't know if the FBI gave it to him or Huie got it
from the FBI to give to him. He told me once, 'Huie's got real good

connections with the FBI. Even better than mine. Huie can get things from the FBI in three or four hours that would take me three or four days to get.' ''

Ray said that Foreman asked him to look over the list. "He wanted me to check off the places that I had robbed from the FBI list of unsolved crimes. Foreman said 'the FBI wants to be able to explain your source of money.' It was the craziest thing I ever seen. I told him 'I got the money from Raoul. He paid me for various jobs that I did.' Foreman said that the FBI wanted me to check off some of the places from the list. I just looked at him and said 'If I cop out to robbing a place I didn't rob someone is going to put me under oath and I won't be able to supply the details when they ask about them.' He said 'Yeah, that's right' and he finally put that long list away."

Ray recalled other subjects that the two men discussed as well.

Then at a later date when attorney Foreman visited me he had several duplicated typewritten sheets of paper with him; one clause in the sheets cleared the novelist William Bradford Huie and *Look* magazine of damaging my prospects for a fair trial because of their pretrial publishing ventures; another clause, that if I stood trial I would receive the electric chair.

I told Mr. Foreman that Mr. Huie and *Look* magazine were able, legally and financially, to look out for their own interest.

Mr. Foreman's monologue was very strident that day in insisting that I sign the papers as I had to ask him several times to lower his voice to keep the guards, and open mike, from overhearing our conversation.

On November 11, 1969, when Foreman testified in a civil action brought against him in the United States District Court in Tennessee he was asked, "Who did your investigating work for you?" He answered, "Oh, different people. I had a number of students from the university at Memphis and I had—." Since he never finished answering, the attorney inquired, "Could you give us some names please?" Foreman, however, had no names to offer. He said, "I don't know the names. My god-amighty, man, they were students. There were at least seven or eight of them." Foreman was then asked if he had "any investigators that were not students." He testified, "I don't use investigators except students. Wherever there is a college my investigators are always students and preferably senior students. I would not believe a private investigator, under oath, anywhere in America." Later Foreman was asked if he could remember the name of at least one of his investigators in the James Earl

Ray murder case. He replied, "I never knew the names of the student investigators." Foreman was asked how he could have known that his investigators were reliable since he knew nothing about them, not even their names. How did he know, he was asked, that they might not give any information they uncovered to the prosecution. Foreman said, "Yes, sir, that's why I hired them, because a man has to have character to stay four years in law school or medical school." He continued, "They have spent four years in college and it takes character to make that."

Before a few minutes had passed Foreman said that "there were about six or eight" from the school. He secured them through the services of a teacher, he thought, but he added, "I don't remember the names of a single teacher there. I am in a trial all the time. I don't try to remember anything like that." It soon became apparent that Foreman could not even remember the name of the school from which the "at least seven or eight" or "about six or eight" students whose names he did not know had been referred by a teacher or teachers he could not remember.

Foreman's cavalier attitude toward the investigation of a capital case is startling. A trained and skillful investigator can make the difference between a conviction and an acquittal. Neither senior students nor trained investigators can function on their own. The investigators must, of course, conduct their inquiries into the areas considered to be relevant and potentially rewarding by the trial counsel. Their work becomes valuable only at the point of production—in the court room. Had Foreman worked closely with the investigators, he would have been able to evaluate their work, know what discoveries they made, and certainly he would have remembered some of their names. It is not necessary to speculate about the anonymous investigators who apparently developed not a single lead. Foreman later said that he did all of his own investigating and never relied upon others. Hugh Stanton of the public defender's office in Memphis served as cocounsel with Foreman. During November 1976 investigators for the Citizens Commission of Inquiry asked if his colleague, Percy Foreman, used any investigators in the Ray case. He answered, "No, he did not to my knowledge." When Stanton was asked what Foreman did do for the investigation, he was unable to think of a single contribution. Eventually he answered, "Why don't you ask him that. I'm not going to sit here, honey, and tell you what somebody else did."

Several months after Foreman's investigation had been completed and his client imprisoned at a Tennessee penitentiary to serve a ninety-nine year sentence, Foreman, while testifying, was asked if he had ever talked to Charles Q. Stephens and his wife, Grace. Charles Stephens was the only eyewitness against Ray, and his wife might have been the most important witness for Ray. Foreman did not know who they were; he asked if they were the owners of the rooming house. Foreman eventually admitted that he had not talked to either Mr. or Mrs. Stephens.

One of the lawyers who represented Ray after Foreman was discharged told me that Renfro Hays had been very anxious to assist Ray even while Foreman represented him. He said that Hays sent McCraw, the taxi driver, to see Foreman so that the new trial counsel might be informed that Stephens was drunk shortly before Dr. King was shot. During his testimony, Foreman acknowledged that he spoke with McCraw, whose name he could not remember. He said, "I talked to the cab driver that hauled him [Stephens] away from there." Actually McCraw told Foreman that he did not "haul him [Stephens] away" because Stephens was too drunk. Foreman had finally remembered a witness, although not by name, but he had forgotten the point of the witness' assertion. According to Foreman's successor, McCraw said that after he told Foreman that the state's only witness was too drunk at the crucial moment to be reliable Foreman said only, "Don't tell this to Stanton." Foreman had finally come across an important allegation for the defense and he was apparently determined not to share that evidence with his co-counsel.

The evidence reveals a sad and shameful story. Foreman, for reasons not known, had not adequately prepared to try the murder case although he constantly assured his ill-educated client and his brothers that he was more than ready for the easiest of all conflicts.

According to Ray, Foreman began a campaign to convince him to plead guilty soon after Ray had entered into a binding contract with him. Ray said he recalled the arguments Foreman advanced quite clearly.

Mr. Foreman gave me the following reasons why a guilty plea was necessary:

(One) He said the media had already convicted me and cited the pretrial articles written in *Life* magazine and the *Reader's Digest,* with the help of government investigative agencies as examples.

He also cited various articles printed in the local press, particularly the story in the *Commercial Appeal* dated November 10th, 1968, just two days before trial date.

Further, Foreman cited the record of the Amicus Curiae Committee saying neither the committee or trial judge would attempt to halt publicity unless it reflected on the prosecution case.

(Two) Foreman suggested, speciously, that it would be in my financial interest to plead guilty.

(Three) That the prosecution had promised a witness considerable reward money for testifying against me, that this witness had already been given a raise in a welfare check he was receiving from the government, that the prosecution was also paying his food and wine bills.

Further, that two Memphis attorneys had signed a contract with his alleged witness for 50 percent of all revenue he received for his testimony. They in turn would look out for his interest.

Mr. Foreman also gave me the following reasons why the prosecution wanted, and would therefore let me plead guilty:

(One) That the Chamber of Commerce was pressuring the trial judge and the Attorney General's office to get a guilty plea as a long trial would have an adverse effect on business, boycotts and such.

Further, that the chamber wasn't unhappy about Dr. King being removed from the scene—hence the acceptance of a guilty plea.

(Two) That trial judge Battle was concerned about the effects a trial would have on the city's [Memphis] image, and that the judge had even dispatched his Amicus Curiae Committee Chairman, Mr. Lucian Burch, to persuade some SCLC members to accept a guilty plea.

Ray told me that he had listened very carefully to Foreman's arguments and that he replied that he had wanted to stand trial. "I also remembered that he told me that it was an easy case to win. I thought we would win but even if we might lose I wanted to stand trial. Hanes knew that and they were ready. Now I know that I had made a terrible mistake firing them." Ray said:

Later, after considering all that Mr. Foreman had told me I said I still wanted to stand trial.

I told Foreman I agreed that the media had had an adverse effect on the prospects of my receiving a fair trial but I didn't think the public any longer believed every fabrication they read or saw on TV— therefore a possible fair jury verdict.

Mr. Foreman's reply was that if I plead guilty he could get me a pardon, after two or three years, through the office or Nashville attorney, John J. Hooker, Sr., as a relative of Mr. Hooker would then be Governor.

John J. Hooker, Sr., was a well-respected member of the Tennessee bar. His son was at the time a candidate for the office of Governor of

Tennessee. The political prognosticators predicted that Hooker could not lose. Foreman's association with Hooker, who later represented both Huie and Foreman when Ray brought a civil action against them, was related to Ray as the clincher in Ray's subsequent pardon application if he would but cooperate and plead guilty. Hooker, Jr., never did become governor; he was defeated. Yet his candidacy played an important part in ultimately convincing Ray to plead guilty.

On February 13, 1969, Foreman wrote a letter to Ray. In that letter Foreman said that there was a "little more than a 99 per cent chance" of a death penalty and a "100 percent chance of a guilty verdict." Ray began to wonder what had happened to "the easiest case" Foreman had ever encountered. Ray said that when he told Foreman he expected to be acquitted, Foreman replied that the prosecution could rig the jury. According to Ray, Foreman said, "the court clerk had been on the job for eighteen or twenty years." Ray said, "I was considering trying to relieve Mr. Foreman and get another attorney who would let me have a jury trial, but Judge Battle said that I was going to trial with Mr. Foreman and that was it. In other words, I was caught between Judge Battle and Mr. Foreman."

Even under those circumstances Ray decided to risk a jury trial. Ray said that he continued to give leads to Foreman and that Foreman refused to explore them.

> One time I told him that the police had made a statement that I was not within four miles of Dr. King when he was shot. So I told Mr. Foreman about that. Later he told me he called Mr. Holloman, the director of the police department but that Mr. Holloman would not let him have the statement. I said, "Why don't we get a discovery proceeding so we can force him to give us the statement," and Mr. Foreman said, "If we do that he might destroy the statement." I knew it wasn't logical but what could I do.

Ray said he felt trapped, caught between the judge who would not permit him to get another lawyer and his own attorney who insisted that he plead guilty. During this most difficult time, Ray was unable to sleep due to the constant bright illumination of his cell and unable to speak frankly to his attorney except in whispers due to the microphones in the cell which the trial judge had solemnly asserted were placed there for his own security.

Ray said that Foreman explained to him that if the state could prove that he had been involved in any criminal conduct, and that Dr. King died as a result of that conduct, that Ray could be convicted and executed as if he had fired the fatal shot. According to Ray, Foreman said that even if Ray had not known that there was a conspiracy to kill Dr. King he could be convicted because he had been part of it. "He told me that if they could prove I was just an accomplice I would be just as guilty as the other party."

Foreman was apparently discussing the legal concept of felony murder. If several men agree to participate in the robbery of a store, and all agree that none of them is to be armed and that none will harm any other person, and in the midst of the robbery one of the robbers pulls out a gun and kills anyone, either the proprietor, a bystander, or a fellow robber, all of the survivors may be tried for first-degree murder under the concept of felony murder. The theory is based upon the agreement to commit a felony and the death of anyone during the commission of the felony. Foreman extended the concept, Ray said, to cover his case. Ray had purchased a rifle illegally, and transported it across state lines in order to participate in the illegal sale of arms abroad. If anyone died as a result of that effort, Ray was led to believe, he was legally guilty of the murder.

At last Ray began to believe that he might be legally guilty even if he had not known of the conspiracy to kill Dr. King and even if he had not fired the fatal shot, as long as there actually was a conspiracy. Ray knew that he had participated in a criminal conspiracy to smuggle guns out of the country. He believed that one of those guns may have killed Dr. King.

Finally, Ray said, Foreman said, "If you force me to go to trial I will get that Negro judge Ben Hooks as co-counsel."

In an affidavit he filed with the Memphis Criminal Court, Ray said:

> **I knew from newspaper accounts that Mr. Hooks had resigned a judgeship to accept a position with SCLC.**
>
> **Therefore I told Foreman that having Mr. Hooks as a co-counsel would be a clear conflict of interest, more so than the grounds attorney F. Lee Bailey refused the case on. Foreman's reply was that as chief counsel he had the right to pick co-counsel.**
>
> **By this time Mr. Foreman had finally got the message over to me that if I forced him to trial he would destroy—deliberately —the case in the courtroom.**
>
> **I didn't know how he would fake the trial until I read the article he wrote for *Look* magazine, published April 1969.**
>
> **It was also my belief that I would only receive one trial—that appellant cts. probably wouldn't be looking too close for technical error in case of conviction—therefore I didn't want the one trial faked.**

On March 9, 1969, Foreman sent a letter to Ray which had the effect of assuring him that he would be given a potentially large sum of money if he did not alter his agreement to plead guilty to murder the following day and "if the plea is entered and the sentence [of 99 years] accepted and no embarrassing circumstances take place in the court room."

On March 10, 1969, James Earl Ray, accompanied by his lawyer, Percy Foreman, appeared before Judge Battle and pleaded guilty. Battle asked Ray if he was pleading guilty to murder in the first degree because he was "legally guilty of murder in the first degree as explained to you by your lawyers." Ray answered, "Yes, *legally* guilty, uh-huh." Foreman then addressed the court and jury.

Gentlemen of the Jury, I am Percy Foreman, permitted by his honor to appear, and it is an honor to appear, in this court for this case.

"I never expected, hoped or had any idea when I entered this case that I would be able to accomplish anything except perhaps save this man's life.

"All of us, all of you were as well-informed as I was about the facts of this case due to the fact that we have such an effective news media, both electronic and press and magazines. Took me a month to convince myself of that fact which the Attorney General of the United States and J. Edgar Hoover of the Federal Bureau of Investigation announced last July; that is, just what [Attorney] General Canale told you, that there was not a conspiracy.

At the first opportunity to speak Ray said:

Ray: Your honor, I would like to say something too, if I may.

The Court: All right.

Ray: I don't want to change anything that I have said. I don't want to add anything onto it, either. The only thing I have to say is, I don't exactly accept the theories of Mr. Clark. In other words, I am not bound to accept the theories of Mr. Clark.

Foreman: Who is Mr. Clark?

Ray: Ramsey Clark.

Foreman: Oh.

Ray: And Mr. Hoover.

Foreman: Mr. who?

Ray: Mr. J. Edgar Hoover. The only thing, I say I am not—I

agree to all these stipulations. I am not trying to change anything. I just want to add something onto it.

The Court: You don't agree with those theories?

Ray: I meant Mr. Canale, Mr. Foreman, Mr. Ramsey Clark. I mean on the conspiracy thing. I don't want to add something onto it which I haven't agreed to in the past.

Foreman: I think that what he is saying is that he doesn't think Ramsey Clark's right or J. Edgar Hoover is right.

I didn't argue them as evidence in this case. I simply stated that underwriting and backing up the opinions of [Attorney] General Canale, that they had made the same statement. You are not required to agree or withdraw or anything else.

The Court: You still—your answers to those questions that I asked you would be the same?

Ray: Yes, sir. The only thing is I didn't want to add anything onto them. That was all.

The Court: There is nothing in these answers to those questions I asked you, in other words, you change none of those?

Ray: No, sir. No sir.

The Court: In other words, you are pleading guilty and taking 99 years, and I think the main question here that I want to ask you is this:

Are you pleading guilty to murder in the first degree in this case because you killed Dr. Martin Luther King under such circumstances that would make you legally guilty of murder in the first degree under the law as explained to you by your lawyers?

Ray: Yes, sir, make me guilty on that.

The Court: Your answers are still yes?

Ray: Yes, sir.

The Court: All right, sir, that is all.

Ray had remained loyal to the only concept which he said might legally establish his guilt. There was a conspiracy, and because there was, he was *legally* guilty. The incurious attitude of the judge while the defendant stated in open court that others were involved in the murder remains inexplicable twenty-five years later. After the plea was entered, Judge Battle sentenced Ray to 99 years in a state penitentiary. The judge then addressed the jury and the press. He said:

The question might arise in many minds, "Why accept any plea at all? Why not try him, try to give him the electric chair?"

Well, I have been a judge since 1959, and I myself have sentenced at least seven men to the electric chair, maybe a few more. My fellow judges in this County have sentenced several others to execution. There has been no execution of any prisoners from Shelby County in this state since I took the Bench in 1959. All the trends in this country are in the direction of doing away with capital punishment altogether.

Well, that certainly explained why the state was eager for the plea, but left in doubt those who wondered why Ray's attorneys had arranged a deal which secured the maximum sentence for Ray.

The Judge, who had refused to inquire about the conspiracy to kill Dr. King when Ray invited him to do so, then discussed the absence of conspiracy.

It has been established by the prosecution that at this time they are not in possession of any evidence to indict anyone as a coconspirator in this case. Of course, this is not conclusive evidence that there was no conspiracy. It merely means as of this time there is not sufficient evidence available to make out a case of probable cause against anybody. However, if this defendant was a member of a conspiracy to kill the decedent, no member of such conspiracy can ever live in peace or lie down to pleasant dreams, because in this state there is no statute of limitations in capital cases such as this. And while it is not always the case, my 35 years in these criminal courts have convinced me that in the great majority of cases, Hamlet was right when he said, "Murder, though it hath no tongue, will speak with most miraculous organ."

Judge Battle had kind words to offer about Percy Foreman for he had played a decisive role in arranging for the guilty plea.

The defendant is represented by able and eminent counsel. All his rights and all the safeguards surrounding him have been zealously and conscientiously observed and adhered to.

The Judge felt called upon to praise the system of justice that had brought about such an irrefutably fair result.

I cannot let this occasion pass without paying tribute to Tennessee, Southern, American and Western Free World Justice and security which was truly a team effort involving scores and even hundreds of persons.

Having defended Foreman, Tennessee, the South, and the Western Free World, Judge Battle closed with a modest eulogy for Memphis.

> This court, nor no one else, knows what the future will bring, but I submit that up to now we have not done too badly here for a "decadent river town."
>
> If I may be permitted to add a light touch to a solemn occasion, I would like to paraphrase the great and eloquent Winston Churchill, who, in defiant reply to an Axis threat that they were going to wring England's neck like a chicken, said, "Some chicken, some neck."
>
> I would like to reply to our Memphis critic, "Some river, some town."
>
> Is there anything else?

What else could there be?

Ray was transferred to a state penitentiary to begin serving his long sentence. As soon as he was removed from the oppressive and blinding atmosphere of the Memphis jail he wrote a letter to Judge Battle.

> Dear Sir,
>
> I wish to inform the honorable court that the famous Houston Attorney Percy Fourflusher is no longer representing me in any capacity. My reason for writing this letter is that I intend to file for a post-conviction hearing in the very near future and don't want him making any legal moves unless they're in Mr. Canale's behalf.
>
> Sincerely,
> James Earl Ray

He later submitted a sworn statement to the Memphis Criminal Court explaining what happened to him after he wrote the letter.

> After I wrote the March 13th letter to Judge Battle indicating I would ask for a trial, corrections Commissioner Harry Avery strongly advised me not to seek a trial.
>
> He said if I didn't I would be treated like any other prisoner and would be released from isolation at the end of the prescribed six weeks. But if I persisted in asking for a trial he couldn't promise anything—he said he was speaking for the highest authority.

Just one week after Judge Battle had sentenced Ray, he granted an interview to Bernard Gavzer of the *Washington Post*. In that interview, Battle said that he accepted the plea because "had there been a trial, there could have been the possibility, in such an emotionally charged case, of a hung jury.'' He added that Ray ''could have perhaps been acquitted by a jury.'' So much for justice in this part of the Western Free World.

On April 15, 1969, *Look* magazine, in an article by Percy Foreman, credentialed as ''attorney for James Earl Ray,'' purported to prove that Ray acted alone in the murder of Dr. King. Foreman offered his theories, claiming that he had spoken with Ray for ''40 hours'' and concluding that Ray ''didn't tell me any of this: it is what I believe he thinks.'' On October 10, 1976, Foreman was interviewed by Roger Aldi, an intelligent and informed newsman. For the first time Foreman was pressed to provide some details. A transcription of that part of the program follows.

> **Aldi: Mr. Foreman, from a defense perspective, from what I could gather, there is no way to trace the bullet that killed Dr. King to the rifle that James Earl Ray admittedly did purchase in Birmingham.**
>
> **Foreman: It is true that the, uh, . . . there were no ballistics, that was an FBI report on that bullet. But that is not the only way to get convicted of murder.**
>
> **Aldi: The state's only real witness to place James Earl Ray at the scene at the time of the murder apparently was dead drunk at the time.**
>
> **Foreman: Well, you've been reading a bunch of things that have been collected by somebody with a Jewish name—I forget his name, uh, and all of this—what you're probably doing is rewriting the book.**

When the program was broadcast, Aldi interjected the following comment at this point:

> **I don't know what book Mr. Foreman was referring to but his answers to other questions about evidence that might have proved James Earl Ray innocent were dismissed in a similar manner. And the situation did not get better when I asked him about what he reportedly told James Earl Ray before the decision to plead guilty.**

Their dialogue continued:

> **Aldi: Did you ever tell James Earl Ray that the state would get some kind of blue ribbon jury, and it was a sure conviction?**
>
> **Foreman: Now listen, Mr. Aldi—I'm tired of listening to this horse shit. I told your James Earl Ray exactly what it was my**

duty to tell him. And I pointed it out to him—sometime while I was on this case in Memphis there were at least five or six major cases tried with serious verdicts. And each one of them—I didn't tell him anything. I discussed with him whatever was in the papers about the other cases.

On January 14, 1970, James Earl Ray, in his lonely cell in a Tennessee penitentiary learned that Arthur Hanes, Sr., his first trial attorney in the case, had been quite ill. He wrote to him:

Dear Arthur,

I have read in the paper where you have been a little under the weather.

I trust those young nurses will have you back in condition before you receive this letter.

Sincerely,

James Earl Ray

P.S. At least you don't have Percy Foreman for a doctor.

PART SEVEN

KALEIDOSCOPE

Chapter Twenty-Six

"THEY/HE SLEW THE DREAMER"

by Mark Lane

During the years that followed Ray's initial effort to secure a trial, after entering a plea of guilty before Judge Battle, a few books have been written purporting to tell the truth about the events of April 4, 1968. Perhaps the two most important books on the subject are *He Slew the Dreamer*, by William Bradford Huie, and *The Making of an Assassin*, by George McMillan. One can, on occasion, tell a book by its cover. The titles of both books about James Earl Ray make it quite clear that the authors were convinced of his guilt. Huie said that after Ray was arrested, "I decided to try to persuade him to sell me information." He wrote to Ray that "if you want to deal with me, I will have a contract drawn for us to sign, and I will pay you a substantial sum of money." He told Ray in that introductory letter that "Americans yearn to know the whole truth about why and how" the murder of Dr. King was accomplished. In many letters to Huie, Ray described in exquisite detail his view of the conspiracy to murder Dr. King. Yet, although Huie's book was published in 1970, on December 25, 1976, *The New York Times*, in a front-page story headlined "Conspirator Hunted in Dr. King Slaying," published an article which said, "In March 1969, when Mr. Ray pleaded guilty to killing Dr. King, he told the court that he did not agree with statements by the prosecution and by his own defense attorney that there was not conspiracy involved. However, Mr. Ray had never explained what he meant." Evidently, a problem had arisen somewhere between Ray's telling of the tale to Huie and its publication by Huie.

There is no doubt that Ray understood that his prospective biographer, Huie, had prejudged the case against him even before he had begun his inquiry. In the first letter sent by Huie to Ray, through his attorney Arthur Hanes, Sr., he wrote, "Obviously you were involved in

Dr. King's murder." Later, when Percy Foreman tried to insinuate George McMillan into the scene by arranging yet another publishing deal, this one between McMillan and Ray, the defendant, this time exercising sound discretion, declined. Foreman had brought McMillan to the jail cell, but Ray refused to see him.

Why did Ray enter into a business arrangement with Huie when he suspected, not without reason, from the outset that Huie's prejudice might overcome the facts? Ray explained in testimony offered by him in the Federal District Court in an action that he subsequently brought against Huie and others.

> **Well, the only reason I signed this contract there, well, I was under obligation to Mr. Hanes. He made three trips to London and I didn't have no money to pay him. I think I had $150, something like that, so I, originally, suggested that Mr. Hanes try to raise the defense money or something, but he thought the book would be best and so I more or less had to go along with the recommendations of the attorneys and I signed the contract in order to raise money for the defense. Mr. Hanes didn't want to get involved in—in the pauper's—in other words, more or less Court appointed people to work on the defense. That's one reason I signed the contract.**

Later Ray testified about the new book contract that involved both Huie and Foreman.

> **This here was a little different, the way I got involved with Mr. Foreman and the way I got involved with Mr. Hanes. After Mr. Hanes had been dismissed at the recommendation of Mr. Foreman, I—I—Mr. Foreman told me there couldn't be any contracts until after the trial was over. He also made the statement in open Court, I think, that he wasn't going to—Mr. Foreman made the statement he wasn't going to pan his profession to the press, or something of that nature, so I was under—I was under the impression there wouldn't be no contract when Mr. Foreman took the case until after the trial was over.**

> **Q. After you were under that impression there would be no contracts with Mr. Foreman—are you talking about book contract or some other kind of contract?**

> **A. No, book contract with Mr. Huie, he—we discussed this when he took over the case. That was one of the stipulations, that contract bookwriting wouldn't interfere with the trial. Mr. Foreman said he had enough—in other words, enough money**

that he wouldn't get obligated with book rights to finance the case, in other words, Mr. Foreman financed the case on his own until the trial was over and then he could get his money.

Q. Then subsequent to that, about how long was it until you did sign the contracts with Mr. Foreman and Mr. Huie, or did you?

A. Yes, I did, but this—Mr. Foreman, he—these contracts came up in a more or less—another money matter—do you want—I would have to explain that to start with.

Q. Go ahead and explain it.

A. Like I said, Mr. Foreman made the public statement that he could finance the case himself until the trial was over and he would have me sign a contract for the book to pay him off and his fee was supposed to be $150,000 and he would take care of all expenses and finance the jury trial and everything but after he had been on the case, I am not positive now, I will say two or three weeks, and he came to see me and he told me he was going to hire one of the best attorneys in Tennessee. He talked to several of them and he mentioned Mr. Hooker here, Senior, personally, and so he told me it was going to take quite a bit of money, so I thought maybe he was hinting around wanting more money for the contract. Of course, I know attorneys like money. I said, I told him to just take all that contract when this trial was over and go ahead and hire Mr. Hooker or whoever you want to as long as we can get the right kind of trial.

So, sure enough, a few days later he came up with a contract with Mr. Huie, and Mr. Foreman said he was—the contract would give, I think, Mr. Foreman sixty percent and Mr. Huie forty percent, so I signed it under those—believing that we were going to have all these high powered attorneys and everything. What we got was the Public Defender.

The contract among Huie, Ray, and Hanes stated that it was "for the purpose of establishing the truth" regarding "the assassination of Martin Luther King, Jr.," and "the alleged participation of Ray therein." It was entered into during July 1968. Three months later Huie told the press that "Ray delivered to me a first installment of 10,000 words written in longhand, a month ago. Since then he has delivered 10,000 words more." Quite clearly Ray cannot be held accountable for the failure of communication upon which *The New York Times* commented.

When Huie testified on his own behalf in the federal action filed against him by Ray he made a most intriguing disclosure. He testified that he originally planned to call the book "They Killed the Dreamer" and that later the title was changed to "He Killed the Dreamer." Huie was incorrect. He had originally entitled the book "They Slew the Dreamer" and then changed the title to "He Slew the Dreamer." Quite obviously there had been a change in concept from a book seeking to prove a conspiracy to one asserting that Ray acted alone.

When he testified as a defendant in November 1969, Huie sought to explain how and why the change had occurred. He was asked who had made the decision to change the title.

> I did. You see, all publishing plans and interests in the King case, many people sitting in New York assumed from the beginning that Ray didn't make the decision to kill Dr. King, meaning conspiracy. Gallup Poll showed eighty-four percent of the people in the United States wanted to believe in conspiracy as regards murders of Jack Kennedy or Bobby Kennedy or Dr. King. All publishers and editors want is books about conspiracy. They want you to prove conspiracy and show conspiracy.

Actually the Gallup Poll did not measure what the American people "wanted to believe" regarding a conspiracy; it was intended to reflect what the people did believe.

Huie then volunteered a bit of testimony which was quite surprising, perhaps astonishing, to me.

> As an aside, if I may, I was offered $250,000, not returnable, by a group of publishers soon after the murder of Jack Kennedy to write the first of the books questioning the Warren Commission Report, what was to be the Warren Commission Report, the authoritative statement. I went to Texas with private detectives who worked with me before and we worked for two weeks and came back and talked to the Attorney General, Bobby Kennedy, and I convinced myself that Jack Kennedy was killed by Lee Harvey Oswald and that Oswald never met Jack Ruby, his own assassin, before in his life. Therefore, I couldn't write a book that would have been economically profitable, and, therefore, had to decline the money because I simply believed Oswald acted alone and Bobby Kennedy, the Attorney General, whose office had all the facts that had been released, believed it and therefore, I don't know why I should disbelieve it.
>
> I went along on this business of a Ray conspiracy reluctantly,

so all of the projections as to what the Ray story might be worth was based on the assumption that they did kill the dreamer. That there was a "they" in the story, and early in the story, I, myself, reluctantly, went along on a conspiracy.

On occasion one comes across a joint venture in the publishing industry where a hardcover firm and a paperback company do a contract together for a book. However, in the highly competitive book publishing industry groups of publishers do not usually join together to publish a work. I remember the period prior to the publication of the Warren Report quite well. During that period almost every major publisher in the United States declined to publish my book based on the subject and it was not until after a conservative English firm in London agreed to publish *Rush to Judgment* that an American publisher did publish the book. It is safe to say that major publishers in the USA were not anxious to publish books questioning the Warren Commission Report during 1964. The advance offered to me by an American publisher was $5,000 for world rights to my book, not $250,000. It is true that after 1966 when *Rush to Judgment* was published and became the number one best-selling book in America that year, and the next year in paperback form, other manuscripts on the subject were more easily able to find publication. Yet, Huie's testimony was in relationship to a much earlier time, a period prior to the publication of the Warren Report itself. More troubling is the assertion that his two-week inquiry into the assassination of President Kennedy disposed of all the troubling questions. Thirty years later most Americans, including a majority of the members of the Congress, are still not satisfied.

Huie continued with his testimony.

I went along with the theory. There were several bits of evidence. The first thing I found that seemed to indicate to me that someone other than Ray made the decision to kill Dr. King—I never had any doubt from the beginning that Ray was the murderer himself, but the question was in my mind whether Ray himself made the decision to kill. So I believed, for several weeks in August and September, oh, until early in November, until Ray took the step to postpone the trial. For instance, I believed that someone other than Ray had made the decision. That was a mistake. I made a horrible mistake because I went along with the conspiracy theory for a while. I could not find any evidence that other people were involved and Ray, who had failed to provide me or anyone any

believable evidence that anyone else was involved, so I had to change my plans and inform everybody, magazine publishers, book publishers and everybody, which I did, I think, possibly, around December 1st, that I couldn't travel on a conspiracy; that I could not identify any person; I couldn't sustain a proposition that someone other than James Earl Ray made the decision to kill Dr. Martin Luther King. I had to back off and I would never have written anything else about Ray except that I had already committed myself and already made a mistake and I had to try to correct it and it is something that is a very grave disappointment to me.

Huie's statement that "I never had any doubt from the beginning that Ray was the murderer" places in rigid context his approach to the evidence in the case. In this respect he shared with George McMillan (whose work we will explore fully in the next chapter) a prejudice that precluded the consideration of the delicate shading of testimony. Huie and McMillan operated from a commitment to preconceptions. The prosecuting authorities in Memphis, Huie, and McMillan continually observed that major portions of the evidence had to be rejected because they did not fit in with what had been presumed—the lone guilt of Ray. Thus, the official version of the events could hardly be distinguished from the epistle published by those claiming to possess independent judgment. Huie then explained why he decided that there had been no conspiracy.

The postponement—Ray's desire to postpone the trial was one of the things that caused me to decide, because I thought the decision to postpone the trial was very ill-advised from Ray's point of view.

Although Huie said that the desire to postpone the case was "one of the things" that brought about his decision that there had been no conspiracy, he, at that time, offered no other consideration that led him to that conclusion. The determination to seek a continuance in this case, as in most pending matters, was made by trial counsel, not by the defendant. While such a decision may have been ill-advised, it is difficult to understand how such an application could logically have any bearing on the question of whether or not there had been a conspiracy to murder Dr. King. In the absence of some more substantial argument proffered by Huie his dramatic change is, in my opinion, unconvincing.

According to Huie's testimony, before he contracted to write *They* or *He Slew the Dreamer*, he entered into an agreement with *Look* magazine through its Vice President and general counsel, John F. Hardy. "At that time we foresaw two articles," he testified. He added, "They paid me $10,000 on what I was anticipating writing at that time."

Huie did write two articles for *Look* which were published in November 1968, three months after Ray's first installment of 10,000 words reached him and more than two months after the second installment was in his hands. Since Huie had solved the John F. Kennedy assassination in two weeks, even though ten months and 25,000 interviews by the FBI were required to assist the Warren Commission to its conclusion, two or three months to look into Ray's allegations would seem to be more than adequate for him. He evidently thought so. His first article was entitled, "The Story of James Earl Ray and the Conspiracy to Kill Martin Luther King." The second, "I Got Involved Gradually and I Didn't Know Anybody Was to be Murdered." In the November *Look* articles Huie makes it quite apparent that he believes that a conspiracy took the life of Dr. King and Ray was utilized, perhaps unwittingly, by that conspiracy.

In April 1969, *Look* published a third article by Huie. This story, "Why James Earl Ray Murdered Dr. King" reflected Huie's new position. In his appearance in the Federal Court in Memphis Huie, when asked how much *Look* paid him for all the articles responded, *"Look* paid me $62,871.85." A conclusion can be drawn from Huie's testimony that *Look* paid him $5,000 for each of the first two articles in which Huie stated that there was a conspiracy and more than $50,000 for the third and shortest article which he entitled "Why James Earl Ray Murdered Dr. King." It would appear, therefore, that Huie successfully rebutted his earlier testimony in which he claimed that publishers only desire and, therefore, pay handsomely for conspiracy stories.

It is, I suggest, truly instructive to make at least a cursory examination of Huie's three magazine articles before looking at the book which he later published.

In the first article, published on November 12, 1968, Huie described Ray's escape from the Missouri State Penitentiary at Jefferson City, his trip to Canada, and his fateful meeting with a blond Latin, approximately thirty-five years of age, to whom Ray referred only as Raoul.

Ray wrote to Huie that after arriving in Canada he did not plan to return to the United States. Huie asserted that Ray wrote that his decision to remain out of the country was "certain." Ray's efforts, according to Huie, were directed toward securing a passport and sufficient funds to leave Canada for Europe.

McMillan, and other supporters of the theory that Ray broke out of jail solely for the purpose of assassinating Dr. King, could not be expected to believe Ray's assertion. Huie, however, wrote, "I believe it's true that he never intended to return to the United States."

According to Huie, Ray frequented the Neptune Tavern in Montreal where he "sort of let the word get around that he had had a little trouble down in the States, that he was looking for I.D. and capital, and just might be available for activities that didn't involve too much risk." This, said Huie, "resulted in a contract." The contract was with Raoul. According to Ray, he and Raoul met at least eight times during the next three weeks to explore Raoul's suggestion that identification papers and cash might be provided to Ray if he assisted in various efforts. Ray said that he had just about run out of funds at that point. He held up the manager of a house of prostitution and stole approximately $800. Of that effort Ray said, "I hated to take a risk like that, but I figured that if I held up a whorehouse they probably wouldn't report it, and I guess they didn't."

While developing a relationship with Raoul, Ray met and cultivated a relationship with a Canadian woman who he had hoped would assist him in securing a passport.

Between August 8 and August 21, 1967, Ray met with Raoul at least five more times.

Huie wrote that Raoul had offered a six point deal to Ray:

One—They were to meet in Windsor on August 21, 1967, at the railroad station.

Two—Ray was to furtively transport packages for Raoul in a series of border crossings between the United States and Canada in his used car.

Three—Ray was then to travel to Alabama by surface transportation (train or bus) after selling the car.

Four—Ray would receive from Raoul living expenses and a sum to purchase an appropriate automobile.

Five—After Ray had undertaken and accomplished several more tasks Raoul would provide $12,000 and a passport and other means of identification.

Six—Raoul required that Ray remain incurious about the projects and seek to secure no information that Raoul did not provide voluntarily.

According to Huie, Ray later explained the dilemma that had confronted him and informed Huie that he was in a quandary. He was more than reluctant to return to the United States and face the possibility of being returned to the penitentiary in Missouri. However, he had almost no money left and he had been unable to secure adequate identification. He said that he had agreed to meet Raoul in Windsor but was planning to ask the Canadian woman who lived in Ottawa if she would help him get a passport.

Later Ray told me the same thing. He said, "I had sworn to myself never to come back to the U.S., to this snake pit. If the Canadian woman was willing to arrange for me to get a passport I never would have come back. If she said she would help me then I never would have met Raoul in Windsor, I never would have bought the rifle in Birmingham and I never would have been in Memphis on April 4th."

Huie sought to check out each of the allegations made by Ray. In almost every instance Huie went to the address indicated by Ray, found the relevant witnesses, and was satisfied that Ray had been truthful.

Huie met and interviewed the Canadian woman. He was evidently overcome with her beauty for he made repeated references to her appearance. He wrote that he was surprised that such a very attractive woman could have been interested in James Earl Ray. Later when I told Ray that I wanted to interview his Canadian friend he smiled and asked, "Is that because she's an important witness or because you believe Huie's description of her?" He added, "She isn't beautiful at all. She is a real nice person and just an average-looking middle-class woman." I said Huie had gone on at some length about her beauty and Ray answered "Well, she is beautiful compared to him."

Huie wrote that he met and interviewed the Canadian woman. Huie's published account of that interview is in all major respects identical with what Ray told me had transpired. Ray had driven to Ottawa to see her. As they drove around the capital city she pointed out where she worked and various other government buildings in the vicinity, including the nearby headquarters of the Royal Canadian Mounted Police. Thus did Ray discover that his Canadian friend was a government employee. He had almost decided to risk telling her the truth, or part of it, in an effort to enlist her in his plan to receive a passport. He was about to ask her if she would swear on an official government form that she had known him for two years. The proximity of the government buildings, the Mountie headquarters and his discovery that she worked for the government caused him a moment's panic. He decided not to ask for her help. The alternate plan, to meet Raoul, had suddenly become the only viable route.

The Canadian woman said that when Ray left her "He said he had to meet a man in Windsor." He wrote to her, planned to meet her when she took her vacation, but a brief stop in Memphis intervened and they never met again. The romantic-tragic parting between Ray and his Canadian friend was but a precursor to the monumental tragedy that was to follow.

It is apparent that Huie accepted as fact the major portions of Ray's lengthy statement, and that in addition he was satisfied that Ray's allegations, which were readily subject to verification, had been verified by his own inquiries. In most instances Huie gave the impression that he believed Ray and in some instances he stated that he did. The title of the article gave further credence to the belief that Huie believed that there had been a conspiracy to murder Dr. King. Yet it was not until the second *Look* article, which appeared two weeks later, that Huie publicly offered his conclusions.

Huie said that he had communicated with Ray for two months and had traveled throughout the United States and into Canada in an effort to verify Ray's allegations. He decided, he said, that the conspiracy to murder Dr. King began approximately eight months before King was shot. He concluded that "Ray was drawn unknowingly into this plot" during August 1967 in Montreal. He added that two weeks before the assassination Ray "did not know" that there was a plot to kill King or that the conspiracy was in any way aimed at King. Huie assured his readers that he knew more about the conspiracy to murder Dr. King than he was able to publish at that time. Some other evidence proving the conspiracy could, he stated, be released at the trial.

Huie wrote that the outline of the conspiracy to assassinate King began to become "visible" to him. He explained that if it was not clear to the readers it was only that he "could not reveal all that I have found to be true" about the conspiracy to murder Dr. King. What he discovered, said Huie, about "this plot" to murder Dr. King, he could reveal only after the trial.

There was no trial. Huie was, therefore, at liberty to share with America the additional, and no doubt sensational, details of the evidence that he had uncovered regarding the conspiracy against the United States of America.

However, in his third article published in *Look* in April 1969, Huie instead assured us that Ray acted alone or was involved in a "little conspiracy." Huie added that if there had been a little conspiracy, "I now believe that James Earl Ray was probably its leader not its tool or dupe." Huie never did enlighten us regarding the evidence he had previously uncovered, and the draconic conspiracy against our entire nation had been transformed into a small one if one existed at all. Huie certainly had the right, indeed the obligation, to inform us of his new insights and of the evidence that had led him to shun his previous conclusions. Yet he offered with his new conclusions no new evidence upon which they could be based. It appeared that Huie had simply changed his mind and was not prepared to share with his readers the reason for that dramatic metamorphosis.

Huie asserted that Ray killed Dr. King because he wanted "status among criminals and their guards," since he knew he would spend many years in prison. Huie also claimed that Ray killed Dr. King because he expected Alabama Governor George C. Wallace to be elected President on November 5, 1968, "and that President Wallace would promptly pardon the murderer of Dr. King." These two motives offered so firmly by Huie appear to be mutually exclusive. And these two important sentiments attributed to Ray by Huie appear in a form that sharply contrasts with the manner that Huie had adopted, and was so faithful to, in the first two articles. Huie did not quote Ray directly in the April article regarding his motivation, nor did he state that Ray had been his source. Yet Huie offered no other source for his startling conclusion. From a relatively careful author who quoted accurately and in context and who had conducted his own not inconsiderable research, most of which he was anxious to permit his readers to participate in, Huie had been transformed into an author who offered his own conjectures.

Huie concluded his curious article by stating that Ray "deliberately" placed his possessions, including a rifle with his fingerprints on it, and other items, including a transistor radio which he knew carried his prison identification number, on the sidewalk. He did this, said Huie, because he wanted to leave "his calling card" so that the FBI and all of America would know that he had killed Dr. King.

If Ray did want the FBI to know, why is it that thirteen days after the FBI laboratory in Washington, D.C., had received Ray's rifle and binoculars with his fingerprints on them and Ray's radio which "clearly bore his prison I.D. No. 00416" that the FBI was not looking for Ray? Why had the FBI not picked up Ray's calling card? Almost one hundred American cities were in flames as black communities throughout the country indicated an interest in the case. If ever there was a need for immediate and effective public action, the need was present and apparent on the days beginning with the evening of April 4. Yet on April 17 the FBI issued wanted posters charging Eric Galt with the crime. The fingerprints and the radio belonged to Ray not a man named Galt. One wonders if Huie ever contemplated the possibility that Ray had been given two weeks to leave the country by the FBI in the grand conspiracy which he had found to be directed against the United States of America.

If Ray had wanted the glory, even at the cost of spending the rest of his life in jail, he seems to have abandoned that aspiration. By insisting that he is innocent he lays no claim to the glory of having murdered Dr. King and suffers nevertheless the prospects of a lifetime spent in a rural Tennessee penitentiary.

As the reviewer assesses the two November 1968 articles, the April 1969 article, and *He Slew the Dreamer,* he is confronted by a great debate waged between Huie and Huie over the responsibility for the death of Dr. King. The earlier Huie offered facts, relevant interviews, and conclusions based upon the evidence he had presented. The subsequent Huie offered conclusions. In the first *Look* article, Ray was presented as a man who "was proud" that in all of his crimes he "had never hurt anybody." In *He Slew the Dreamer*, Ray was "an antisocial man capable of murder." The book was little more than an extension of Huie's April *Look* article, with a brief analysis of the sanitation workers' strike, and comment upon Huie's own commercial encounters with Ray and Percy Foreman.

Regarding the historic strike, Huie said that the city had been orderly: "Then agitators brought disorder." He added, "The mayor was winning this battle and the cheap laborers were losing when Dr. King came to help them."

Huie reported that on November 27, 1968, he had told Percy Foreman that he had made a mistake by getting involved in the Ray case. He said he told Foreman, "Now I wish that I had never gone into the case at all," and added:

> **And speaking of mistakes, I believe you've made one. This is not your sort of case. You let them get you to Memphis where the old fire horse couldn't resist another race to the fire. But a week after you begin trying to work with Ray you'll know that there is no defense, and you'll be as sick of the case as Hanes was. You did Art a favor by replacing him; you just haven't realized it yet.**

Yet Hanes was neither anxious to leave the case nor sick of it; he was, in fact, anxious and eager to try the case and confident that he would win it. According to Huie:

> **Mr. Foreman liked my three-way contract with Ray. All he wanted was for Mr. Hanes to get out so he could have what Mr. Hanes had had. "I like the idea of owning 60 percent of one of your books," he said, "while you own only 40 percent. So you get Hanes out and let me in, then, goddamn it, get to work and write us a good book and make us a good movie and make us some money."**
>
> **"I don't mind you having the money," I said. "But your client hasn't met his obligations. I want to know how, why and when he decided to kill Dr. King."**
>
> **"He may be incapable of telling anybody that," Mr. Foreman said. "You know why he did it. I've seen him only briefly, and I already know why he did it."**

With Ray's biographer and lawyer convincing each other before trial that Ray was the assassin even in the absence of proof that he was, Ray's chances for a fair trial were severely diminished.

After Huie had seen the light he sought to convince both the defense lawyer and the trial judge of Ray's lone guilt. In his book Huie spoke of a conversation he had with Judge Battle which took place when it was presumed that the case was to be tried.

Huie said that he showed the judge the contract that he had entered into with Ray and then said:

I don't want any secrecy about this contract, Judge. I'm showing it to you, and I'll show it to any reporter who wants to see it. This contract is an effort to do what your court can't do: to find the truth about why Dr. King was murdered. When you try Ray your trial will be necessary but disappointing because you can establish only what is already known: that Ray came to Memphis and killed Dr. King. At great financial cost you will spend weeks hearing witnesses from five countries give testimonies which already has been published. And after your trial every thoughtful American, white and Negro, will feel cheated because you will not have answered the question that matters most: why?

Huie reported that "the judge broke in to agree with me," Judge Battle, according to Huie, said, "All we can get are a few facts and perhaps a conviction. But we can't get much truth."

According to Huie, Ray's biographer, defense lawyer, and trial judge had all reached a conclusion regarding the defendant's guilt before the trial began. And, according to Huie's account, he had played a part in the process which culminated in that result. Yet in three articles and in a book he was unable to offer any substantial basis for that conclusion.

Perhaps the most telling critique of Huie's work is to be found in his own book. There he stated that he decided that Ray had lied to him about an escape from prison. Huie said that he had deliberately published "false" material in the *Look* article to show Ray that he would publish "false" material in lesser crimes if "he would help me establish the truth about the murder." Huie never did explain why he thought Ray would be more inclined to tell the truth to a man who had not insisted upon it but who had, in fact, demonstrated his contempt for the truth by knowingly publishing a false statement. As we depart from Huie's odd work, are we not constrained in our analysis of his important role to ponder his peculiar approach to the truth and subject all of his writings on this matter to close scrutiny?

An examination of Huie's statements on the subject, oral and written, reveals that he now supports the position that Ray acted alone. During February 1977, Huie also stated that he had heard from an informant that Ray's rifle had not been used to kill King and that a man, whom he named, had purchased the real murder weapon. According to Huie, that man, the informant said, was connected with organized crime.

Huie followed his new revelation with the publication of an article in the March/April 1977 issue of *Skeptic*, appropriately subtitled "The Magazine of Opposing Views" in which he insisted that Ray alone had murdered King. Huie libeled those who wished that the matter be investigated, saying that those who called for such an inquiry were "publicity-seeking congressmen, bureaucrats and conspiracy racketeers." He attacked Dr. King as well stating that "his sexual track record" revealed that he had "exercised often with assorted maids, wives, and widows." He added that J. Edgar Hoover "may have been a homosexual." He concluded his article by asserting that those who doubted the FBI version of the murder were panderers and that "forced to choose between a murderer and a panderer, I'll support the murderer every time."

Huie's vacillation regarding the central question of conspiracy was perhaps never more apparent than in his attempt to inform the members of the grand jury in Memphis of his thoughts. Attorney General Phil Canale and his two assistants questioned Huie, who was then under oath. In that brief appearance on February 7, 1969, Huie swore that "I started with the assumption that a Negro might have been involved in it [the plot to kill Dr. King]." He also said that "I have never had the slightest doubt that Ray and Ray alone killed Dr. King." Then he insisted that "I still think Ray was assisted [in the murder of Dr. King]." After assuring the grand jury that Ray acted alone in the murder, Huie concluded by stating that "It is my belief that this [the conspiracy to kill Dr. King] is a simple story involving maybe no more. than two men and no more than four."

Chapter Twenty-Seven

THE MAKING OF
AN ASSASSIN
by Mark Lane

As the members of Congress contemplated the future and the proposed
budget of the Select Committee on Assassinations, which promised to
conduct the first thorough investigation into the murders of Dr. King and
President Kennedy, they were able to read a review of *The Making of an
Assassin* by George McMillan which was featured in the *Washington Star*
on December 12, 1976. McMillan has been foremost among journalist-
writers defending the official findings of the investigations of both the
Kennedy and King assassinations; he give evidence of having access to
sensitive information sources far beyond the reach of most senior reports,
and has access to prestigious forums of American journalism, including
the Op-Ed page of *The New York Times*. The task of reviewing McMillan's
book was not assigned to an ordinary book reviewer but rather to Jeremiah
O'Leary, an "investigative" and intelligence report for the *Washington
Star* and later the *Washington Times*, who, as it turns out, is not an
ordinary reporter either. He wrote:

> **Reflecting on the tidal wave of assassination books that erupted
> after the murders of President John F. Kennedy, Dr. Martin
> Luther King and Sen. Robert F. Kennedy, it is a professional
> pleasure to encounter a volume that reflects a solid six years of
> original research instead of ivory tower thumbsucking.**
>
> **It is especially timely that George McMillan is now in the
> book stores since a House Select Committee on Assassinations is
> about to embark on a full-scale investigation of the murders that
> shook the world in the 1960s. McMillan, unlike most of the
> assassination authors, did not rely almost wholly on the work of
> such entities as the Warren Commission, the FBI and various
> police departments.**

O'Leary added that McMillan did not bother to analyze "the official reports." O'Leary was quite correct there. There appears to be little indication in McMillan's work that he explored the documents, read witness' reports, examined the transcripts of the various hearings, listened to the illuminating Memphis police radio broadcasts, examined the crucial FBI ballistics reports, or glanced at the FBI and Memphis police fingerprint records. Why this approach should be considered a virtue becomes clear only when we learn more about O'Leary. But first to McMillan and his book. The review concludes

The House Select Committee, among others, should take the reporting of George McMillan into account when it begins probing the murder of King. McMillan has done a good deal of the committee's work already when it comes to deciding whether the world knows all there is to know about Ray and why he set out to kill Dr. King and did so with nearly as much skill as the fictional "Jackal" of screen and novel. This is a most important book, and extremely timely, since the King assassination will soon be probed by a committee which does not have six years in which to reach a conclusion.

The reader who has come this far knows far more about the murder of Dr. King than does McMillan after his "solid six years of research," that is, if McMillan shared with his readers all he learned. A cursory examination of the index of *The Making of an Assassin* reveals that McMillan did not even mention Ed Redditt, the black detective who had been in charge of security for Dr. King in Memphis. The other police officer assigned to Dr. King, W. B. Richmond, is not mentioned either. The two black firemen so strangely detailed to another assignment on April 4, Floyd Newsum and N. E. Wallace, are not mentioned either. Lest the reader be given the impression that McMillan ignored the black witnesses only, we hasten to point out that he is indeed an equal opportunity omitter of relevant data. Neither Arthur Hanes, Sr., nor Arthur Hanes, Jr., the only two of Ray's lawyers who were familiar enough with the case and ready to try it, are mentioned in the book. Nor is Renfro Hays, who was the only responsible investigator for the defense. Nor is Percy Foreman, who entered Ray's pleas to the charge and who brought McMillan to Ray in an effort to make a deal for the remaining rights of his story. Ray refused to see him. Ray testified on November 22, 1969, in a civil action he had instituted against Huie and his former lawyers. At that time he explained why he would not see McMillan: "Well, the first time I saw Mr. Foreman in court after our court appearance dismissing Mr. Hanes, he brought in another writer. He wanted me to exchange information with George McMillan. I had heard his name and, of course, I had heard of this fellow's writing. I didn't want to get involved with any other writers and I thought we would just stick with Mr. Huie."

McMillan did not mention Ralph Abernathy or Andrew Young or Jesse Jackson, or many of the other eyewitnesses. J. Edgar Hoover, who had wanted to destroy Dr. King, who had waged an unequal and secret war against him, was not mentioned. There is no reference to Frank Holloman, the director of the Memphis Police and Fire Departments, either.

If McMillan's book, published in 1976, was the result of six years of effort, then the work began in 1970, after he spoke with Martin Waldron, a *New York Times* reporter. *The New York Times* reported this illuminating remark by McMillan on March 13, 1969: "I have always believed James Earl Ray did it alone," he said. "This guy is a loner. And I have never investigated any aspect of a conspiracy, which has left me free to work on his biography." Fair enough. McMillan did not wish the facts of the crime to interfere with his work. In any event, he knew that Ray did it alone before his research began, so why should he have concerned himself with the evidence? His book reveals him to be a man of his word. Nowhere in the work is there any indication that he betrayed his original prejudice. Under the circumstances, I think we are entitled to know why O'Leary admired this book so much and why he recommended that a serious study of the crime by a Select Committee should begin with a frivolous bit of fluff.

Approximately one year after Dr. King was murdered, Hoover told a friendly news source that it was Robert Kennedy who had requested that Dr. King's telephone be covered by FBI electronic devices, but that Kennedy "was persuaded by our people not to do it in view of the possible repercussions," and because Dr. King's constant traveling made a wiretap impractical. The friendly news source ran that false explanation of the episode, as Hoover requested. The Church committee examined the Hoover memorandum on the question and revealed the news source to be Jeremiah O'Leary.

On November 30, 1973, it was revealed that the CIA had forty full-time news reporters on the CIA payroll as undercover informants, some of them as full-time agents. Two months earlier William F. Colby, then the director of the CIA, ordered a review of the practice since legitimate reporters were concerned that agent-journalists seriously compromised the integrity of the American press in general and might cripple the ability of reporters to function overseas. It seems clear that an agent-journalist is really an agent, not a journalist. When a conflict arises between writing the truth or concealing it in what may be conceived of as the best interests of the intelligence agency, the latter concept must prevail if the reporter is to continue his relationship with the agency. Indeed his intelligence relationship is designed for the purpose of resolving such conflicts in that fashion. Another function of the agent-journalist is to publish false information which the agency writes to have released. The agent-journalist concept contravenes and endangers the fundamental principles of the First Amendment, for the right of the people to a free press includes not only the right to publish a newspaper but the right of the people to information that is not covertly manipulated by a secret police agency.

In 1973, the American press was able to secure just two of the forty names in the CIA file of journalists. The *Washington Star* and the *Washington Post* reported that one of the two was Jeremiah O'Leary.

The Making of an Assassin, to put it charitably, does not focus on the events of April 4th. Indeed, McMillan devotes just seven pages to those events. The allegations which comprise those pages are presented as if they were fact, but upon reflection it is clear that we are being treated instead to the imaginings of a biased mind. Let us, for example, examine McMillan's restatement of the final moments.

He [Ray] was going to make his shot from the bathroom. He raised the small window as far as he could, and knocked out the rusty screen. It fell two stories to the ground.

He rested the rifle on the windowsill and aimed it.

To do so meant that he had to stand in the bathtub, lean one arm against the wall. There was something inglorious in that, and something fatefully typical of Ray and his crimes. He was going to carry out the most important single act of his life and he had to do it with his feet in the old, stained, rooming house tub.

He watched through his binoculars until King came out on the balcony, until he was sure it was King. He aimed carefully and, at 6:01 P.M., he fired a single shot which hit Martin Luther King in his right jaw, shattering that side of his face, and which went on into his body to lodge in his vertebrae. King fell back on the balcony, mortally wounded.

Since McMillan claims that Ray was alone at that fateful moment and since Ray has consistently denied that he fired the shot, or was in the bathroom when it was fired, is it not fair to ask McMillan for his source? Quite obviously, there is no source—there can be no source.

Further in his recitation of events McMillan states, "Without telling King, Memphis police had put a security guard around the Lorraine." There are but two serious errors in that sentence. Dr. King's supporters had asked for police protection and knew that Redditt had been there. Redditt was then removed by the police officials and that removal was made without notification to Dr. King and his supporters.

As we turn from McMillan's brief but flawed recitation of the crucial events to his chosen thesis, the life and times of James Earl Ray, we are challenged again to decide whether his allegations in this area are real or imagined.

A major source of material for McMillan's book is Jerry Ray, James Earl Ray's brother. Indeed, Jerry Ray is quoted so often and in regard to such decisive matters that one wonders if the book could have been written without his remarks. Jerry has stated that he is convinced his brother is innocent and that he knows nothing that would indicate that his brother might be guilty. How then could McMillan make use of such a man in a book dedicated to the proposition of Ray's sole guilt? McMillan explains, "I would not place any value at all on any of the stories he told me about his brother's innocence." Yet, if McMillan was convinced that Jerry Ray lied regularly—"Of course he lied to me," he wrote—how could he rely upon him at all? Sociologists define as moral density the condition of those who can walk down a crowded street and, due to their rigid preconceptions, see only persons of their own class. Critics might observe that even authors may suffer from a strain of this tendency to select so capriciously.

According to McMillan's book, Jerry Ray had told him that he "agreed with Jimmy's ideas about King;" that "Jimmy was going to Birmingham to take out citizenship papers in Alabama;" that "he believed that if he killed King in Alabama, or killed him anywhere in the South, it would help if he showed he was a resident of Alabama;" that "Jimmy was getting caught up in the Wallace campaign;" that "he was talking as much that night in Chicago about getting Wallace in as he was about rubbing King out;" that "he had it in his head that it would help Wallace if King wasn't around." According to McMillan, Jerry and Jimmy spoke by telephone on the morning of April 4th. Without doubt, the most impressive words attributed to Jerry Ray by McMillan are those which reported Jimmy's last words to Jerry that morning. McMillan assures us that at that historic moment Jimmy had said, "Jerry, tomorrow it will be all over. I might not see you and Jack for a while. But don't worry about me. I'll be all right. Big Nigger has had it."

A serious evaluation of *The Making of an Assassin* requires, I believe, an interview with Jerry Ray. I spoke with him at some length. He denied making every serious quotation attributed to him by McMillan. His denials were not merely general but contained specific information to support his assertion that McMillan had invented the "quotations" which were attributed to him. He told me that it could not be said that he "agreed with Jimmy's ideas about King," since he had never discussed Dr. King with his brother. He said that not only did he not say that "Jimmy was going to Birmingham to take out citizenship papers in Alabama," but that he did not even understand that sentence when he read McMillan's book since his brother was already a citizen: "How could he talk about citizenship papers? I don't understand that." He said that he never said that James was in the Wallace campaign; that he did not know if he ever worked for Wallace, and that the only indication that he had been in the campaign was that "I read that he was in one of those books but I never asked him about it." He also allowed that he was growing somewhat suspicious about books as reliable sources after his experiences with McMillan. He said that his brother had never mentioned Dr. King's name to him or in his presence and that he could not understand how Wallace's campaign for election might be improved by Dr. King's death.

Regarding the historic telephone call on the morning of April 4th, Jerry could also say that he was not the best source regarding James' calls that day since he did not speak with him by telephone or in person on April 4th and that he had not spoken with James for approximately three months before that day.

During several conversations with Jerry Ray I noticed that although his manner was informal in general, he referred to his brother almost invariably as James. Yet in McMillan's book, all of the reconstructed conversations attributed to Jerry find him referring to his brother as Jimmy.

If McMillan had merely exchanged Jimmy for James a few times in his text, no harm would have been done. I know that Jerry referred to his brother as James in talking to me because I tape recorded all of our conversations and subsequently listened to them and then reviewed the transcripts prepared from the tapes. I can not imagine any other responsible way to write a book based, at least in part, upon interviews. I wondered if McMillan had tape recorded his interviews with Jerry Ray as well. I began by asking Ray that question. He said that in his meetings with McMillan there never was a tape recorder visible. He said that McMillan may have had a hidden machine, but he doubted it. He said

McMillan might have tape recorded telephone calls. In fact, he said he suspected that McMillan did monitor telephone conversations. He added that he never discussed matters of substance with McMillan on the telephone.

Jerry Ray subsequently told me that he had just written to the House Select Committee on Assassinations and offered to testify before that body. He suggested that his sworn statement about what he contended were McMillan's fabrications be taken. He said that he agreed to take a lie detector test. He also told me that he had just been questioned by two men from the Department of Justice and asked about the statement attributed to him by McMillan. He said that he told them that McMillan had made up the quotations and that he was ready to accompany them to the FBI office and submit to a polygraph examination there.

It seemed inappropriate for me to publish Jerry Ray's allegations without securing and publishing in full the response of the author whose veracity and competence had been challenged. I called McMillan numerous times at the telephone listed for his address in Frogmore, South Carolina, which appeared on the last page of his book. No one answered. His publisher, Little, Brown, informed me that his "real address" could not be revealed. I then explained that a major source for the book Little, Brown had recently published had told me that McMillan had invented the statements attributed to him. I said that I was anxious to ask McMillan to comment upon Jerry Ray's charges and that I fully intended to publish his response. I was then given McMillan's telephone number in Cambridge, Massachusetts. On that day, December 20, 1976, I called him for the purpose of securing his denial that he had made up the Ray "quotations" and to discover whether he had any tape recordings or other proof to support his assertions. Our conversation was brief.

Lane: Hello. George McMillan?

McMillan: Yes.

Lane: This is Mark Lane. How are you today?

McMillan: Uh . . . (pause) . . . OK.

Lane: I'm doing a book about the murder of Dr. King. There will be a chapter in the book dealing with your book. I've talked with Jerry Ray who, obviously, is a very important source for you, and he denies telling you almost everything you quoted him as saying in the book. I wonder if you have any recordings of these interviews with him.

McMillan: Mr. Lane, I'd just rather not talk with you.

Lane: You'd rather not talk?

McMillan: Yep.

Lane: Well, will you tell me Mr. Ray is wrong when he denies that he made those statements to you?

McMillan: You must have not listened to me. I said I'd rather not talk.

Lane: You won't even deny that you made up what Mr. Ray says.

McMillan: You still must not have listened to me.

Lane: What did you say?

McMillan: I said, you must still have not listened to me.

Lane: Yes, I'm just asking if you will deny—

McMillan (interrupting): I said I'd rather not talk.

Lane: You'd rather not talk. And you won't even deny Ray's charge that you made up those quotations.

McMillan: Uh.

Lane: I mean, it couldn't take you very long to say you didn't make them up.

McMillan: You want me to hang up, or do you want to hang up?

Lane: Well, I don't want to hang up and I don't want you to hang up. I just want you to answer the question as to whether or not Mr. Ray's charge . . .

McMillan (interrupting): I've already told you I don't want to talk with you.

Lane: You won't even answer that question.

McMillan: I told you, I don't want to talk to you.

Lane: You have said that, yes.

McMillan: OK.

Lane: Very good. I'll send you a copy of the book.

McMillan: Thank you.

Lane: You're welcome.

McMillan did not deny Ray's charges. He did not claim to have any proof that his book was accurate. I was struck by the contrast between Jerry Ray's offer to make his statement under oath, before a possibly hostile body, while being monitored by a polygraph and to answer all questions put to him and McMillan's refusal to deny the Ray charges or to suggest that he had proof relating to the integrity of his book.

I spoke with Jerry Ray again and told him of my conversation with McMillan. I said that McMillan had seemed very tense. Ray was in an expansive mood and he said, "I wouldn't blame McMillan if he were mad at me." Ray then discussed his relationship with McMillan:

Ray: One time down in Atlanta, I was talking to him on the phone, and I had a couple people around me listening in. I told him that I really had something for him, that I had a couple of names that would make his book and would even help solve the case. I said that it was dangerous and I couldn't talk about it much around here. I'll give you a call. Later I called him, and he flew in from Cambridge and stayed at a hotel. I told him, "This is dangerous stuff I'm talking about. . . . I'm going to give you two names that will solve the case for you . . . One name is Rudolph Stroheim, you check him out. . . ."

Lane: Rudolph Stroheim? You made that up?

Ray: Yeh, I made that up. I said, check him up in Germany.

Lane: Did you tell him East or West?

Ray: I think I said Hamburg.

Lane: Oh.

Ray: So I said, "Check Emmett Daniels of Fort Leonard Wood, Missouri." But before I gave him the names, I made him give me a thousand dollars. I said that this was a dangerous business but that I would give him the names for a thousand dollars.

Lane: Is there an Emmett Daniels?

Ray: No such guy.

Lane: Well, then you made the whole thing up.

Ray: I made the whole damn thing up. So when he got back to Cambridge, he hired some guys, and he paid some guy over in Germany to check that out. So they checked all the old Nazi files, all the files they could check, and there wasn't any Rudolph Stroheim. So they checked with Fort Leonard Wood, and there was no Emmett Daniels. Then he called me up. "Jerry," he said, "I've spent so much money checking this stuff out—all these phone calls, and paying these guys—and there's no Stroheim over there that could be connected with him, and no Emmett Daniels within Fort Leonard Wood." I laughed, and said, "Well George, thanks for the thousand, and you come up again in another month, and I'll have another story for you."

Stroheim was a wrestler in Atlanta, that's how I thought of his name. And Emmett Daniels—I thought of Emmett Kelly, the

238

clown, and I said to McMillan "you're a clown, and I just put Daniels on the back of it."

Then I laughed. Every time I took him for some money, he said, "Jerry, you shit on me. You shit on me again."

But he was so damn desperate with the book—I'd wait maybe eight or nine months and I'd give him a call again and say, "This time I'm on the level. . .no more bullshit." It'd take him awhile, and then he'd be on the plane back up. Last time—he thought I was bankrolling James when he got out. So he said to me, "If you show me some bankbooks or something. . ." Why, I've only had one bank account in my whole life, and that was in Missouri. So I said, "You come up here, and I'll show you the damn bankbooks where it shows so many thousand dollars that I withdrew—I'll give you that bankbook." I said, "I'll go over and get it." So he's on the plane up—when he came up, I had asked him up on a Saturday afternoon, and the banks were closed—I told him that the president was out and I couldn't get my bankbook. But I got my money anyway. When he got back, he found out there was no such thing.

Lane: How much did he pay you for that?

Ray: I only got five hundred that time.

Lane: Five hundred? Not bad.

Ray: Then the last time I took him was in St. Louis a year ago this month. I went down to see James, and did a lot of traveling, and when I got back, I was a little short of money, so I called George up.

Lane: He's your banker?

Ray: Georgie-pie—I called him Georgie-pie. And he's always wanting some pictures of my family then. You know, mother, my dad, and James when he was a little kid. We got pictures like that, but we would never give them to him. I told him, "My sister left, and I'm holding all these damn pictures. If you want to buy some pictures, come on up." It took a while, but he finally flew up.

Lane: He flew from Cambridge again?

Ray: He flew up from Cambridge again . . .

Lane: To Chicago?

Ray: This was to St. Louis. I met him at the airport, and I had got these damn pictures from an antique shop. I didn't get them, my sister got them.

Lane: They weren't of your family?

Ray: Not one of them was.

Lane: —Old, yellow—

Ray: Yeh, these were old pictures, antique pictures. One was supposed to be my grandmother, and one was supposed to be Lucille when she was a baby—we had one picture that looked something like James. This was taken back in the Forties, and it was on a boat, but I had cut the picture half up where you couldn't see the boat. So I sold him all these pictures.

Lane: How much did you get for them?

Ray: I got two and a half for them. He keeps going down all the time, as he keeps getting taken for all that money.

He still thought they were genuine, and he went back, and I asked him if he was going to use them, and he said he didn't know. So I said, "Well, if you don't, send them back, because I paid a dollar for them at that damn antique shop." He was hotter than hell that time. He said, "No more money, because my book is finished anyway." I said, "Well, put in some good words about me in your book, because I'm your friend." Actually, what it was, he was so damn desperate.

Partial corroboration for Jerry Ray's assertions may be found in a letter sent to John Ray, another brother, by George McMillan on September 14, 1973. In that letter McMillan said that Jerry Ray had told him a lot of things. McMillan wrote that subsequently Jerry sent him a tape recording in which Jerry said he had conned McMillan. McMillan then, according to his signed letter, discarded the material from Jerry. However, as his deadline for the book approached, McMillan said that he reviewed it and then changed his mind and finally decided to use it.

McMillan admitted that he was going to publish material that he had received from Jerry after his source, Jerry, told him the material was false.

McMillan pleaded with John to give him some information for his book as his deadline was fast approaching. He agreed to pay John for a statement adding the provision that he wouldn't pay in advance. McMillan closed by asking for photographs of the Rays. Evidently any picture of any one might do.

McMillan's letter raised a new question. Were the Department of Justice and the FBI assisting cooperative authors, who seemed certain to support the official version of the events, while denying access to relevant material to others? McMillan wrote that he was going to go to Memphis and see the FBI file on the case which was available to him.

When it became known in 1976 that the Department of Justice was conducting an inquiry into the murder of Dr. King, Donald Freed, a professor, researcher, author, screenwriter, and investigator in Los Angeles, wrote to the Department. Freed offered to share information with the investigation. The Justice office wrote back that it was Department policy not to share information with any private citizen.

After NBC announced that Abby Mann was writing an original screenplay on the life of Dr. King and it became clear that he was going to devote part of the drama to Dr. King's death, a woman lawyer in Los Angeles contacted Mann. She said that she wanted to arrange a meeting between Mann and Assistant Attorney General Stanley Pottinger. She told Mann that Pottinger could talk to him about the murder of Dr. King and another matter. Pottinger subsequently met with Mann in Los Angeles. Pottinger talked about the possibility of a conspiracy to kill Dr. King and about the investigation that the Justice Department had conducted. Pottinger has disclosed that the Department of Justice had asked for an advance copy of George McMillan's book which they thought might be helpful in the investigation.

Now one may ask, did the Justice Department decline to seek information from Freed, a private citizen, who together with his associates had conducted a serious and important investigation into the murder of Dr. King, while it sought out McMillan, a private citizen? According to McMillan, the FBI agreed to make its file available to him. Why? These questions focus on who George McMillan is.

McMillan led off the acknowledgments by thanking "my wife, Priscilla Johnson McMillan, without whom this book would not exist." There is no reason to doubt the accuracy of that statement. Priscilla Johnson McMillan and George McMillan have played a part, as a team and separately, in shaping events during the last decade in America. One researcher, Jerry Policoff of New York City, has closely followed, and on occasion commented upon, the assignments and undertakings of the McMillans. For his troubles the Boston law firm of Hausserman, Davidson and Shattuck, attorneys for George and Priscilla McMillan, have threatened to sue him.

In 1959, Priscilla McMillan, as Priscilla Johnson, first came to our attention after she had conducted an extensive interview in Moscow with

Lee Harvey Oswald, very soon after his arrival in the Soviet Union. This interview appears to be the longest ever given to any American journalist by Oswald. Soon after both the President and Oswald had been murdered, Johnson wrote about the origin of her interview for *Harper's Magazine*. "I had sought him out a few hours earlier on the advice of an American colleague in Moscow. A boy named Oswald was staying at my hotel, the Metropol, the friend casually remarked. He was angry at everything American and impatient to become a Russian citizen. 'He won't talk to anyone,' my colleague added, suggesting that, as a woman, I might have better luck."

Johnson's discretion in referring to the contact who led her to Oswald is apparent. He was in her story "an American colleague," "the friend," and finally "my colleague." The man who sent her to Oswald is John McVickar, who at that time was one of two officers in the consular section of the American embassy in Moscow. The "us" he referred to in his conversations with Johnson was the American Embassy in Moscow.

In June 1964, Richard Edward Snyder testified before the Warren Commission. He said that during 1959 he was employed at the American Embassy in Moscow as the consul and as the second secretary. He testified, "up until the time I left Moscow, Oswald was my baby." He also testified, "I know Priscilla Johnson talked to him." Snyder admitted under the questioning of Gerald R. Ford, then a member of the Congress and the Warren Commission, that he had sent out a dispatch to Washington in 1959 about Oswald's presence in Moscow and his desire to renounce his American citizenship which carried the notation "Press informed." He testified that "Priscilla Johnson, I think, was one of the first to be aware of Oswald." Although McVickar, the only other officer in the consul section of the Embassy in Moscow, had sent Johnson to Oswald, Snyder testified "just how she became aware of him, and just where I became aware of her knowledge of him, I don't know. But this, I think, was quite early in the game." Snyder indicated that on December 1, 1959, he sent an airgram to the State Department with intelligence about Oswald. Regarding that information he testified "this was the statement of the correspondent." When asked to identify "the correspondent" he replied, "This was Priscilla Johnson."

When McVickar testified, he referred to his debriefing of Johnson about the Oswald interview, an event which took place just after she had completed debriefing Oswald. McVickar asked how the American Embassy had learned when Oswald was going to leave his hotel and that he might be given training in electronics. In both instances McVickar said that Priscilla Johnson was the source. McVickar then produced a memorandum that he had prepared after debriefing Johnson. In it he said, "I pointed out to Miss Johnson that there was a thin line somewhere between her duty as a correspondent and as an American." He later wrote, "She seemed to understand this point."

When Johnson testified before the Warren Commission, she identified the man who suggested she interview Oswald as "Mr. McVickar, the consul." She testified that she believed McVickar told her about Oswald on November 16, 1959, "and that on coming home from the Embassy, coming to the Metropol, I went straight to Oswald's room, and therefore that would have placed my original conversation with Oswald probably on the 16th, my writing the story and my second conversation with McVickar on the 17th, and my filing of the story on the 18th."

Not long after the assassination, Priscilla Johnson entered into an agreement with Harper and Row to coauthor with Marina Oswald, the widow of Lee Harvey Oswald, a book about Marina. It was reported that the advance was $100,000. During that time Marina was being held in quasi-captivity and her contacts with the outside world were being monitored by the federal police authorities. I made several efforts to interview Marina Oswald but her agent and her lawyer, both provided by the United States Secret Service, said that I could not meet with her because the government wanted no one with her who could influence her testimony (other than the FBI agents who met with her regularly); they were concerned that some outsider might "plant" some documentary evidence for her to come upon; and above all, Marina should not talk to anyone about the facts until her book was published.

Priscilla Johnson did, however, meet with Marina Oswald before Marina had completed her testimony, and oddly enough Marina came upon an important document that she had evidently not seen before she was with Priscilla Johnson.

On September 6, 1964, Marina Oswald, still in what the government referred to as "protective custody," testified before the Warren Commission at the U.S. Naval Air Station in Dallas, Texas. Very much a matter of concern was the allegation that Oswald had gone to Mexico City and visited both the Soviet and Cuban Embassies while there. Years later it was revealed that the CIA had misled the Warren Commission about events surrounding those visits and had destroyed certain relevant evidence that might have demonstrated that Oswald had not been there. In 1964, however, the ill-informed Warren Commission was examining evidence about Oswald's Mexican trip.

Senator Richard Russell, then a member of the Commission, reminded Marina that she had previously testified that Lee had told her in

New Orleans that he said he was going to Mexico City. At that time Marina had no documentary evidence to support the allegation that Lee had actually gone to Mexico City. In September, however, Marina presented a ticket stub. She testified, "I found the stub of this ticket approximately two weeks ago when working with Priscilla Johnson on the book. Three weeks ago I found the stub among old magazines, Spanish magazines, and there was a television program also in Spanish and there was the stub of this ticket. But this was, you know, a piece of paper and I didn't know this was a ticket." She discovered that it was a ticket, she testified, when she showed it to Priscilla Johnson. Russell obviously did not believe the story. He asked why Lee would keep magazines in Spanish if, as Marina had previously testified, he could not read Spanish. Marina replied, "It was not a Spanish magazine." Russell asked how this document could possibly have escaped the extensive search of the FBI agents who were looking for such evidence and who had examined every scrap of paper. There was no responsive reply.

Priscilla Johnson's relationship with Marina Oswald for the purpose of writing a book which would tell Marina's story has been offered as the prime reason why Marina would not talk about the facts, many of which she alone knows. However, thirteen years after the contract was entered into, the book had not yet been published. A Warren Commission document (C.D. 49 page 24) which was supplied to the Commission by the FBI states, "On November 23, 1963, Mr. Jack Lynch, United States Department of Defense (USDD), Security office, telephonically advised Special Agent in Charge (SAC) Allen Gillies, Oswald had been contacted in Moscow by three employees of the State Department, whom he identified as John McVickar, Priscilla Johnson, and Mrs. Stanley G. Brown. Lynch indicated each of the above persons had interviewed Oswald in Moscow."

The law firm engaged by George and Priscilla in October 1975 for the purpose of threatening Jerry Policoff (the retraction demanded by the lawyers was not published and no legal action was taken) wrote to the editor of *New Times*, the magazine that published Policoff's article, stating, "As to the allegations of her being an undercover government employee throughout this period, there exists not even the slightest reasonable foundation for such an allegation. Mrs. McMillan has never seen the purported 'unpublished Warren Commission document listing her as a State Department employee.' "

The statement that Mrs. McMillan had not seen C.D. 49 is untrue. On May 11, 1975, I was a panelist, along with Priscilla J. McMillan and others, at the A. J. Liebling Counterconvention in New York City.

Anthony Lukas was the moderator. The proceedings were preserved by a tape recorder and a transcript from that record reveals:

> **Lane: I wonder if I could just interject for a second, Tony. I think that Mrs. McMillan has played a really active part in this, being one of the few people to question Lee Harvey Oswald in Moscow, having access to Marina Oswald after some eleven years on a book which hasn't yet come out. And I know that you told me before I met you today for the first time that you were working for the North American Newspaper Alliance at the time you conducted that interview. I wonder if you've seen Commission Document 49, an FBI report which reads as follows: "on November 23rd, 1963, Mr. Jack Lynch, of the United States Department of State Security Office, telephonically advised Special Agent in Charge, Allen Gillies, Oswald had been contacted in Moscow by three employees of the State Department, whom he identified as John McVickar, Priscilla Johnson, and Mrs. Stanley G. Brown. Lynch indicated each of the above persons had interviewed Oswald in Moscow." I wonder if you were at any time, or at that time employed by the State Department, if you're familiar with this document, or if you've tried, if it's incorrect, if you've indicated to the Warren Commission that the United States Department of State's Security Officer had made a mistake when he gave that information to the FBI.**
>
> **McMillan: Well, no I'm not familiar with the uh doc . . . with the document. Uh, John McVickar was the vice-counsel who was present the first day Oswald went in to uh, put down his passport. And uh, he was, he did work for the State Department. Mrs. Brown was the wife of the Agricultural Attache, and she was sort of a receptionist in the consul's office, and I suppose she was authority in the State Department. But, uh, that was a mistake about me and I wouldn't bother to correct that mistake. I worked for the North American Newspaper Alliance and I didn't work for anyone else.**

As soon as I read the document to Priscilla McMillan I passed it along to her so she could read it. Her lawyer's statement, made almost four months later, was based upon incorrect evidence given to him by his client or an error on his part.

When the Warren Report was issued during September 1964, two of its strongest supporters in the news media were Harrison Salisbury and Anthony Lewis, both of *The New York Times*. They wrote introductions to commercial publications of the report. Two months later, when the Commission published the twenty-six volumes of evidence, Lewis, who had had the volumes in his possession for just a few hours, wrote in a front page story for *The New York Times* saying all of the evidence they contained proved that Oswald was the lone assassin. Since it took me almost an entire year to read the volumes, I wondered how Lewis had been able to move through the material so quickly and then assure the readers of the *Times* that the evidence was consistent with the Commission's verdict, when it was not. Later Salisbury urged David Belin, the Warren Commission lawyer most committed to the preconception of Oswald's lone guilt, to write a book attacking the critics of the Warren Report and defending its essential findings. *The New York Times* published that book and Salisbury wrote the introduction. The book was then reviewed in *The New York Times Book Review* on November 10, 1973, by the team of Priscilla Johnson and George McMillan. Although Belin was the most vocal of the apologists for the Warren Report, the McMillans said of his book, "It is as if Lee Harvey Oswald had lived and there had been a trial." It would have perhaps been more accurate to suggest that it was as if Lee Harvey Oswald had died and there had been a lynching.

During April, 1967, the CIA staged one of the major coups in its history. It arranged for the defection from the Soviet Union of Svetlana Alliluyeva, the daughter of Joseph Stalin. When Alliluyeva arrived in the United States, the Voice of America, the broadcasting service of the United States Information Agency, sent news of her arrival all over the world, including the Soviet Union, where it was broadcast in Russian. Radio Free Europe, a "private broadcast operation" funded by the CIA, dispatched the word throughout Eastern Europe from its studios in Munich. During the great international brouhaha following her defection, Svetlana Alliluyeva spent her days in seclusion, at a site approved by American intelligence and the State Department, with George and Priscilla Johnson McMillan. The site was the home of Priscilla McMillan's parents. *The New York Times,* upon the arrival of Stalin's daughter, said that it would publish her forthcoming memoirs. Priscilla McMillan was assigned by Evan Thomas—who had edited William Manchester's defense of the Warren Report for Harper and Row and who would also supervise the editing of the Alliluyeva book—to translate Svetlana Alliluyeva's work for Harper and Row, the same publishers that had been waiting so patiently for Priscilla to finish the Marina Oswald biography. Alliluyeva and Lee Harvey Oswald had perhaps shared but one moment in common, both had been interviewed in Moscow by Priscilla Johnson McMillan before leaving for the United States.

When George McMillan's *The Making of an Assassin* was published, *The New York Times Book Review* assigned Anthony Lewis to review it. Before examining the Lewis review it is important to understand what the McMillan book claims to be. McMillan never even examined the voluminous files on the case maintained by Arthur Hanes, Sr., and Arthur Hanes, Jr.—the only lawyers who conducted an investigation and were prepared to try the case. There is, in my view, no way to review the case against James Earl Ray and his possible defense without making a thorough search through those files. Hanes Jr., told me, "I was astonished that McMillan did not come to our office as you did and spend days, as you did, going over the more relevant witnesses' statements, public reports, etc."

McMillan can, I suggest, be excused from failing to examine the evidence (although I would not elevate that failure to a virtue as did Jeremiah O'Leary) since he devoted almost none of his book to an assessment of the crime. He presented, instead, a biased biography of James Earl Ray and relied very substantially for that portrayal upon a man who now says that he falsified the record. Yet, even if McMillan were accurate where has he led us? He portrayed Ray as a racist, a man who had committed crimes, a man with a burning hatred of Dr. King and an obsession to do him harm. From this profile McMillan makes a quantum leap to the conclusion that Ray killed Dr. King and that he acted alone while doing so. McMillan's profile may describe Ray, although somewhat inexactly, but it would describe Hoover as if it were custom made for him. Ray may or may not have hated King, but unlike Hoover he never sent a letter to him encouraging him to kill himself.

Yet, if we were to presume that Ray wanted to kill King and that as McMillan states, his obsession to do so was rather widely known, have we established as fact that he did so and that he acted alone? Viable alternatives to McMillan's theory may rest upon McMillan's allegations as if they were fact. If Ray wanted to kill King, is it not possible that he organized a group to assist him? Is it not possible that a group planning to kill King picked up Ray because of his known propensities in that area and involved him, knowingly, in their effort? And is it not possible that a group planning to kill King picked up Ray and utilized him as the decoy and fall guy as he has insisted? To establish that Ray hated King and wished to kill him, which I suggest is contrary to the known evidence, is not to establish that he did so or that he acted alone and that there was no conspiracy.

Yet Lewis, in his major piece in *The New York Times Book Review,* concluded that McMillan's book "is a powerful, a devastating book" and then asks, "Will this brilliant piece of hard reportorial work end the attempt to find a conspiracy in the murder of Martin Luther King, Jr.?" He laments, "of course not," and explains, "as long as there are people unwilling to accept the pain of such deaths [President Kennedy, Robert Kennedy, and Dr. King] without some more satisfying reason—a political reason—the search will go on. And, I have to add, as long as there are self appointed 'investigators' who make an industry of finding conspiracies. The day I sat down to write this review, a newspaper carried a story about the latest theory of a man who got into the business in 1963. (I omit his name because publicity is gratification in this ghoulish business). The headline said: WAS DR. KING SET UP TO DIE?" Yet it is Lewis who attempted to buttress government dogma regarding the assassinations for thirteen years. His early and continuing advocacy of the conclusions of the Warren Report in stories in *The New York Times,* his book reviews and book prefaces, together with his panegyrical remarks in place of a critical analysis of the McMillan book established, I believe, an unblemished record of support for conventional and official doctrines regarding these assassinations that have been widely rejected.

The day I sat down to write this chapter the Gallup poll, published in the *Washington Post* on December 26, 1976, revealed that only 18 percent of the American people believed that James Earl Ray was the lone assassin of Dr. King and only 11 percent believed that Lee Harvey Oswald was the lone assassin of President Kennedy. Those statistics, in the face of the coordinated efforts of leaders of government, intelligence organizations, and their friendly media sources, stand as a monument to the good common sense of the people.

Unlike Anthony Lewis and George McMillan, James Earl Ray finds himself, on the issue of his lone guilt, among the majority of the American people.

Ray told me that "there are many statements in the McMillan book that are not true." Ray said,

McMillan makes me into a political activist for George Wallace. It's hard to discover the origin of a false statement here because Huie, McMillan, Foreman and the FBI all seem to feed from the

same trough. I was a fugitive, hiding out. I wasn't crazy enough to become active in a political campaign. I never even registered although once I considered registering under an assumed name to get a voter registration card because it is good identification. When you cross into Canada they always ask for a voter registration card. But I never did register or work in any political campaign under my right name or under an assumed name.

I asked Ray if he had any idea how McMillan or Huie had come upon the notion that he had been a political activist for Wallace. He said,

In December 1967, I took a woman to register to vote. She said she had a boy friend who was doing five years for marijuana. She registered and I think she did register for Wallace. That was the only time I was ever around any registration place. Later on she said to me that she wanted to get her boy friend out of jail, that she needed influential friends. I told her if she wanted help she should get into some organization that had influence. So she changed her registration to Republican. That was the extent of my political work. With a few more workers like me to depend on Wallace wouldn't even have gotten on the ballot.

Ray also spoke with me about McMillan's assertion that James and Jerry Ray had rendezvoused in a Chicago hotel the day after James had escaped from jail and talked there about killing Dr. King.

First of all when Jerry and I met in Chicago there were only the two of us there. We both know that we never talked about King. We talked about my getting out of the country. I was a fugitive trying to escape. Since there were just the two of us there and we both have always denied this charge about talking about King, what basis does McMillan have for his story? Ask him for some evidence for that charge—he won't have any, he can't; there isn't any.

I then asked Ray if his meeting took place in Chicago the day after he had escaped.

No, that's wrong too. It took me a week to get to Chicago after I escaped from Jeff City, Missouri. I walked. It takes a long time to walk on railroad ties. It takes a long time to cover fifty miles because you'd be surprised at how many houses are sitting right near railroad tracks. If there was a light in the house or if there were dogs there I'd circle around into the woods maybe for two or three miles. I slept during the day and walked at night. One time

two railroad workmen came by on a handcar. I was under a trestle. It was April but it was cold so I had a little fire going. The fire attracted them, I imagine. They came over and talked to me. I imagine the FBI might have heard about that and checked it out and interviewed the men since I told Huie about it.

Ray expressed his dissent from *The New York Times* review in a letter he mailed to Anthony Lewis on December 29, 1976. There too Ray pointed to errors in the McMillan book.

Mr. Anthony Lewis; Co
Columnist
New York Times

re: Book review

Dear Goody Two-shoes:
Sometime ago I received a copy of the review you did on your New York Times fellow, George McMillian's, published novel titled "The making of an Assassin". And all of it's "brilliant revelations". It would appear that one of the most heretofore significant long suppressed (a Nixon conspiracy?) revelation's by McMillian was that yours truly, while in the Missouri big-house, used to rant and rave when Dr. King appeared on the tube shouting & sobbing, "somebody's gotta get him" "somebody's gotta get him". Now I didn't read ole Mac's novel (just the Time mag. article) but I guess he also has me devouring the proverbial carpet, ect. ect. Anthony, when Mac was spoon feeding you all these turkey droppings as revelations did he also tell you that TV'S were not permitted in the Missouri penitentiary during my entire sojourn therein?*

In *The Making of an Assassin,* McMillan had written:

In 1963 and 1964, Martin Luther King was on TV almost every day, talking defiantly about how black people were going to get their rights, insisting that they would accept with nonviolence all the terrible violence that white people were inflicting on them until the day of victory arrived, until they did overcome.

*Ray's letter to Lewis concluded:
"But having to assume legally that you do consider McMillan's novel the last word on the case I'll herein issue collectively to you and the above referred to literati an invitation to consider carrying your prissy asses before the select committee, and I shall do likewise with my midwest tobacco-road one, and we shall let under oath testimony determine the facts."

Ray watched it all avidly on the cellblock TV at Jeff City. He reacted as if King's remarks were directed at him personally. He boiled when King came on the tube. He began to call him Martin "Lucifer" King and Martin Luther "Coon." It got so that the very sight of King would *galvanize* Ray. "Somebody's gotta get him," Ray would say, his face drawn with tension, his fists clenched. "Somebody's gotta get him."
[Emphasis in original]

In this instance both McMillan's and Ray's allegations were susceptible to proof. In February 1977, I spoke with Bill Armontrout, the associate warden at the Missouri Penitentiary at Jefferson City. He told me that during 1963 and 1964 no television sets were available for any of the inmates. Television sets were placed in a TV room with limited access in 1966 and television sets were permitted in the cells and the cell-block for the first time in early 1970. Ray had escaped from that prison in 1967. Under those circumstances one wonders where McMillan, who had never spoken with James Earl Ray, but who did speak with Huie, who in turn had never spoken with Ray, secured his information. The allegation that Ray "boiled" when King was there on the tube in 1963 and 1964 was graphic enough, as was the charge that the sight of King would *"galvanize"* (emphasis present in the original) him but since these events never took place either McMillan or his informants must be credited with a lively imagination.

PART EIGHT

FOR A DAY IN COURT

Chapter Twenty-Eight

THE APPEAL
by Mark Lane

Although Ray was evidently threatened by the authorities and advised by his former lawyer not to proceed with an appeal, he did write to Judge Battle, as we have seen.

Battle neither responded to the letter nor treated it as an application to withdraw the plea previously entered, to set aside the conviction, to vacate the sentence or, in the alternative, to set a date for a hearing at which time such a formal application might be made. Ray was without counsel and his letter could have been considered by Battle as an attempt at a formal application. Instead Battle left for a vacation in Florida. When he returned on March 31, 1969, he found another letter from Ray waiting for him. In that letter dated March 26th, Ray asked Battle to consider it to be a formal application "for a reversal of the 99-year sentence." Ray also asked the judge to appoint "an attorney or the public defender to assist me in the proceeding." Ray wrote, "I understand on one avenue of appeal, I have only 30 days in which to file."

Battle showed the letter to James Beasley, the Assistant Attorney General who had presented the case against Ray. Three lawyers, J. B. Stoner, Richard J. Ryan, and Robert H. Hill, Jr., had all indicated that they were interested in representing Ray. Battle asked Beasley to find out who Ray wanted to represent him. It was improper, I believe, for Battle to involve the attorney who prosecuted Ray in an aspect of Ray's defense efforts. This act emphasized yet again the close working relationship between the court and the prosecuting authorities even as Ray's appeal was being initiated. The legal canons of ethics proscribe such conduct. Battle could not ethically call upon the prosecutor to play a role in the determination of counsel for Ray. Beasley should not have responded. Beasley said he determined that Ray wanted all three lawyers to represent him. He then called Battle to inform him of the fact. But Battle's telephone remained unanswered.

254

Just before Beasley called Battle, Richard J. Ryan had called upon the judge in his chambers. Ryan told me that he had asked the judge to set a hearing for Ray's application for a new trial. Battle responded, he said, by stating that he had the matter "under advisement."

At approximately five o'clock Beasley visited Battle's chambers. He entered the room to find Judge Battle dead. He died, the medical examiner later reported, of a coronary insufficiency. He had fallen across his desk, his head on the last letter from James Earl Ray.

Ryan told me that with Battle's death he and the other lawyers for Ray were quite certain that their client was assured a new trial. Ryan said,

Ray's letter was an adequate application for a new trial. Just to be sure I perfected it by filing a formal application. We had thirty days to get it in and we filed it in a timely fashion. The law of Tennessee is really clear on this question. If a judge should die or go insane after an application for a new trial is filed and before he rules upon it the application is automatically granted. There has never been an exception in Tennessee since that statute was adopted by the legislature.

Judge Arthur J. Faquin emerged as Battles' successor. Ryan said,

He was working with Battle through the whole case. He just said at the hearing held at the end of May 1969 that Ray had pleaded guilty voluntarily and that was it. The laws of Tennessee just did not apply anymore. The reason is that there was a conspiracy to kill Dr. King, probably the FBI or CIA were in on it and they did not want this case being re-opened.

On January 9, 1970, Ray's application to the Supreme Court of Tennessee for a writ of *certiorari* was denied. The court, in a memorandum decision, denied the application with a vehemence rarely matched in appellate court opinions. The court pointed out that "the defendant was represented by privately retained able counsel." The court added that "The defendant upon the advice of his well-qualified and nationally known counsel pleaded guilty to murder in the first degree, the offense with which he was charged, a cold-blooded murder without an explained motive."

The court continued:

In Tennessee, as in all other liberty loving civilized countries, ambush killers are not looked upon with much favor, to say the least. In a country where you do not shoot a sitting duck or a fowl unless in flight; where a rabbit or other game of the field is allowed its chance to run; and where one does not shoot down his

fellowman unless that man has committed an overt act that would justify the defendant in so doing, jurors are inclined to deal harshly with such defendants.

And the court concluded that Ray

. . . willingly, knowingly and intelligently and with the advice of competent counsel entered a plea of guilty to murder in the first degree by lying in wait, and this Court cannot sit idly by while deepening disorder, disrespect for constituted authority, and mounting violence and murder stalk the land and let waiting justice sleep.

Judge Faquin had ruled against Ray in contravention, I believe, of Section 17-117 of the Tennessee Code Annotated, the relevant statute. The Court of Criminal Appeals of Tennessee refused to grant the petition and finally the Supreme Court of Tennessee refused to hear the arguments. Ray then chose to make an appeal to the federal court system. During April 1970, the lawyers who had been representing Ray withdrew from the case.

Bernard Fensterwald, Jr., now deceased, was a Washington, D.C., lawyer and native of Tennessee who became counsel for Ray. He was associated in December 1972 as Ray's attorney with Robert Livingston, a Memphis lawyer, and James Lesar, then recently admitted to the bar in Washington, D.C.

There were at least two potential bases for Ray's application to the federal court system for a new trial: the allegation that Ray had been coerced into making his guilty plea and the allegation that important new evidence had subsequently been uncovered. In my opinion, the first was the weaker of the two, being inherently more difficult to establish and sustain. Much more compelling, and far easier to sustain, it seems to me, would have been an allegation that hitherto undeveloped evidence strongly suggested that there had been a conspiracy to murder Dr. King. The mysterious transfer of Detective Ed Redditt and the equally mysterious transfers of fireman Floyd Newsum and N. E. Wallace would, alone, have raised serious questions which the prosecution would have had difficulty answering.

Ray's attorneys brought their action for a writ of *habeas corpus* to the United States District Court for the middle district of Tennessee in the form of a petition and a supporting Memorandum of Facts. This Memorandum of Facts, hyperbolically headed "A Sham, A Farce, and a Mockery," was signed by Fensterwald, Lesar and Livingston. Where it adopted an aggressive and rhetorical tone (it concluded with the potentially offensive charge that Ray's treatment by the courts "was, in effect, a legal lynching"), it was doubtless designed to make the federal court sit up and take notice of the case. What other effects that may have had on the court's attitude can only be surmised.

At one point the memorandum referred to the narration of a lawyer as "perjury," although, since the lawyer had not made a statement under oath, the charge was incorrect. At another point, the memorandum charged that Judge Battle (then deceased) and others were "participants in these illicit meetings [which] have revealed, in part, this corruption of the judicial process."

But, as I have suggested, probably more important than what the memorandum did say was what it did not. By this time there existed a substantial number of leads that could, with further investigation, have developed new evidence that could have provided the basis for granting a new trial.

Harold Weisberg, the defense's investigator, had in 1971 written a book, *Frame-Up,* in which he referred only briefly to Detective Ed Redditt (whom Weisberg calls "Reddick"), dismissing him as a police spy and never inquiring into the matter of his removal from the scene shortly before Dr. King was shot. Similarly, he did not explore the importance of the observations of the other police officer on the scene, W. B. Richmond (whom Weisberg variously calls "Richardson" and "Richman"). He did not refer to either of the black firemen by name and summarized the twenty-five year high-level association of Memphis Fire and Police Departments Director, Frank Holloman, with the FBI merely by characterizing him as "a former FBI agent." At no point in *Frame Up* did Weisberg, who later claimed that he was the only one who had ever been Ray's investigator, claim to have interviewed any of these men.

On the strength of this, one may speculate that Ray's defense team was either unaware of the significance of these leads or simply did not choose to develop them. What is apparent is that they did not use them.

Ray's application to the District Court was denied. The matter was appealed to the United States Court of Appeals for the Sixth Circuit, which remanded the matter to the District Court for an evidentiary hearing. After the hearing it was again denied. On further appeal, the Court of Appeals affirmed the District Court's denial. It was finally submitted to the United States Supreme Court on a writ of *certiorari.* That application, too, was denied.

When I met with Ray, at his request, and interviewed him at the Brushy Mountain Penitentiary in Petros, Tennessee, Ray was receptive, cordial, and outgoing. I told him that I was writing this book and he said that he hoped, unlike the others, that I wanted to be accurate. He wrote to me several times, and requested me to visit him again. I subsequently spent the major part of a weekend in February 1977 in Petros in extended conference with him.

This book is, of course, not intended to present the case for James Earl Ray. It focuses upon the events which transpired in Memphis on April 4, 1968, and the events which led up to the fateful moment that day as well as the incidents that followed. In the course of telling that story it becomes clear that James Earl Ray has been poorly treated, that his basic rights have been denied and that should he be granted a trial more of the facts about the murder of Dr. King might be known.

James Earl Ray was charged with a heinous crime. He and the American people have been denied the opportunity to witness an open inquiry into that murder, in which the evidence is offered under oath and subjected to the cross-examination required by our adversary system. Some may contend that Ray waived his right to a trial. Under the circumstances which prevailed I do not believe that such a waiver may be valid. In any event, the American people have entered into no such waiver and our right to know has been obliterated by actions seemingly beyond our power.

Chapter Twenty-Nine

THE BEGINNING
by Mark Lane

In February 1975, I founded the Citizens Commission of Inquiry (CCI). The CCI was mandated, through citizens' lobbies, to urge the Congress to reopen the investigation of the assassination of John F. Kennedy; further research revealed the need to pursue also the investigation of the death of Dr. Martin Luther King, Jr.

Many prominent citizens joined the CCI as advisers and active participants on our Executive Committee: among them John Adams, of the United Methodist Church and the Southern Christian Leadership Conference, a veteran of Kent State and Wounded Knee; Richard Barnet and Marcus Raskin, Directors of the Institute for Policy Studies; Robert Borosage, Director of the Center for National Security Studies; Morton Halperin, a former Assistant Secretary of Defense; researchers and writers Mary Ferrell, Donald Freed, L. Fletcher Prouty, and George O'Toole, a former computer specialist with the Central Intelligence Agency, and an author of several articles and books, including *The Assassination Tapes*. We were also joined by scientists and scholars interested in truth in government such as Nobel prize-winner Linus Pauling, astronomer Steven Soter, and philosopher Josiah Thompson.

As Director of the CCI—and while teaching at the Columbus School of Law, of the Catholic University of America—I was able to recruit a work force of student interns to conduct research and to assist in the formation of chapters of the CCI. The intern program was expanded to other colleges and universities, including the University of Massachusetts, Antioch College, Boston University, and the University of Pennsylvania.

The CCI was funded entirely by lecture fees I earned while speaking at colleges and universities throughout the United States; because the CCI lobbied as part of its program it was unable to achieve tax-exempt status and therefore could not attract foundation or other large gifts.

One advantage of my speaking at scores of institutions since 1975 was that at many of the schools a community-wide CCI chapter was formed. Each chapter, with guidance from the national CCI, operated autonomously, educating the community and motivating citizens to influence their Congressional representative to support a new investigation. We already knew that a majority of the American people did not believe the Warren Report and that the new information about Dr. King's death, and James Earl Ray's apparently induced guilty plea, had raised many additional questions. Now the old objections no longer had any meaning, and could not deter the determined citizenry—"What good would it do? It won't bring them back. Why stir it up? You can still have doubts about Lincoln's assassination, too." The people now insisted that their representatives, in whom the power had been vested, go to the enormous, complex, expensive, but worthwhile and necessary effort of determining the truth. The natural bent of most may be toward simplicity; but the Vietnam War and Watergate had shown the simplicity, while consonant with goodness and innocence, was not a match to the arabesque designs of the lie merchants. No sooner was one lie revealed than another took its place, and layer upon layer, like the integuments of an onion, needed to be removed before the truth could be approached.

CCI's first Congressional contact was Representative Henry B. Gonzalez of San Antonio, Texas, who had been in the Dallas motorcade on November 22, 1963, when President Kennedy was assassinated. Congressman Gonzalez had harbored doubts about the adequacy of the findings of the Warren Commission. Later he stated that he was also not satisfied with the official explanations of the deaths of Dr. King and Senator Robert F. Kennedy, and the attempted assassination of Governor George Wallace. Congressman Gonzalez believed that these assassinations were the responsibility of Congress to investigate, and ultimately to stop:

> **After all, these assassinations changed the course of history, thwarted democratic process, eliminated options, baited domestic unrest, and caused great harm to the collective national psyche—the extent of which I strongly feel it is the Congress' responsibility to assess.**

Gonzalez introduced House Resolution 204 in the United States House of Representatives on February 19, 1975, which called for a select committee of seven members of the House to study the assassinations of President Kennedy, Senator Robert Kennedy, Dr. King, and the attempted killing of Governor Wallace. The process of ultimately passing a resolution calls for the collection of cosponsors (other Congress persons who indicate their support of the bill). When a resolution goes through the Rules Committee, the greater the number of cosponsors, the greater may be the change of the resolution being reported out of the Rules Committee to the floor of the House. The bill is then read, some debate may ensure, and a vote then takes place. Of course, before the vote, the work of vote gathering has already been done.

At first, Gonzalez's proposal was met with little enthusiasm. Representatives Stuart McKinney, Republican of Connecticut, and Henry Reuss, Democrat of Wisconsin, were among the 64 cosponsors who submitted letters to the Rules Committee in support of H.R. 204, but the majority of the Rules Committee was opposed to it.

Representative Thomas Downing, Democrat of Virginia, however, became interested enough to introduce H.R. 498 in May 1975 which proposed a select committee "That would study and investigate the circumstances surrounding the death of the President." In a "Dear Colleague" letter, a common form of correspondence between members of the House, Representative Downing asked that those "interested in knowing the truth" list themselves as cosponsors.

Downing also said, in the same letter, "It has surprised many of you, I know, that I have taken this interest. Let me assure you that this is not an emotional concern with me. I have seen sufficient evidence to indicate that the Warren Commission left unanswered a number of questions which I feel bear directly on the assassination."

Downing's interest was a surprise to many of his colleagues because, in his almost two decades on the Hill, he had generally expressed conservative viewpoints, and had stuck usually to the maintenance of his own Congressional First District in Virginia.

But this was to be Downing's last term on the Hill; he had announced his retirement and his desire to spend more time with his family. This foray into a subject of national interest was to be his swan song.

There were, then, two resolutions before Congress, and while some Congressmen supported both, there was a clear division between Gonzalez's and Downing's. Although Downing's resolution seemed to be gaining in the number of sponsors over Gonzalez, there were members of the House who felt that Downing's resolution would not pass without the support of the black members of the House, and the black members would also be in favor of investigating Dr. King's murder.

At the behest of Mr. Downing, I presented before members of the House and their aides many unanswered questions along with available evidence. The CCI conducted public seminars and conferences during the summers so that informed citizens could better persuade their Representatives on this subject.

Representative Bella Abzug, Democrat of New York, Chairperson of the Government Information and Individual Rights Subcommittee, in an Oversight Hearing of the National Archives and Records Service connected with Freedom of Information Requests and Declassification, contributed toward the hopes of passage of Resolutions 204 or 498. Her committee, in an open hearing on November 11, 1975, questioned Dr. James Rhoads, Archivist of the United States and Acting Chairman of the Interagency Classification Review Committee. The Committee was able to determine that the "Warren Commission was *never specifically given the power* by the President under the Executive Order to originally classify its transcripts and memos. In effect, then, hundreds of Warren Commission documents were withheld from the public for years when there was no sound, legal basis for it."

Representative Don Edwards, Democrat of California, Chairman of the Sub-Committee on the Civil and Constitutional Rights of the Judiciary, and a former FBI agent, conducted hearings on the FBI's involvement in the destruction of a note delivered by Lee Harvey Oswald to the Dallas FBI office shortly before the Kennedy assassination. The hearings established that an FBI official ordered Special Agent James Hosty, an FBI agent, to destroy the letter and that Hosty was then ordered by an assistant director of the FBI not to disclose that episode to the Warren Commission.

The CCI participated in the efforts of this committee, including the preparation of questions to witnesses. My association with Don Edwards dated back to the confirmation hearings, before the Senate and the House, for the designation of Gerald R. Ford to be Vice-President of the United States. During Ford's examination before the Senate Rules Committee he was asked whether he had used any classified material in the writing of his book, *Portrait of the Assassin*. Ford had responded, under oath, that all of his sources were those freely available to the public and unclassified. Before Ford went before the House Committee on the Judiciary for examination, Don Edwards called me in St. Paul, Minnesota, where I was trying the Wounded Knee case, and asked me if Ford's assertion was true. I replied that it was not, and at Edward's request flew to Washington, went to the National Archives and requested the material on which Ford had based his first chapter, "The Commission Gets Its First Shock." The Archivist, Marion Johnson, reported to me that the material, a transcript of a meeting of the Commission, was and always had been classified *Top Secret* and not available to the public. I gave this information to Don

Edwards, who then questioned Ford at the House confirmation hearing. Ford stated that he had made an "inadvertent error" in using the classified material for his book, for which he had received an advance of $10,000. Edwards then commented that Mr. Ford's unauthorized disclosure of the information was against the law and is covered by the "same statutes used to prosecute Dr. Ellsberg for allegedly releasing the Pentagon Papers." Edwards asked Ford to comment on his "apparent violation of the law or on the truthfulness of your testimony to the Senate?"

Senator Richard Schweiker, Republican of Pennsylvania, took a leading role in the discoveries of the Senate Committee on Intelligence Activities, chaired by Senator Frank Church, Democrat of Idaho, when it held hearings on illegal activities of the intelligence agencies in April 1976. The fifth and final report of the Select Committee particularly dealt with the performance of the intelligence agencies regarding the investigation of the assassination of President Kennedy.

Senator Schweiker became vitally interested in the subject and explored it fervently on his own; he gained access to the most restricted materials in the Archives, and became one of the most knowledgeable members of Congress on the assassination. CCI staff members conferred with the Senator while he gathered his information.

The Committee's final report stated that it had

developed evidence which impeaches the process by which the intelligence agencies arrived at their own conclusions about the assassination, and by which they provided information to the Warren Commission. This evidence indicates that the investigation of the assassination was deficient and that facts which might have substantially affected the course of the investigation were not provided the Warren Commission or those individuals within the FBI and the CIA, as well as other agencies of the Government, who were charged with investigating the assassination.

Once the Select Committee released its final report, however, its activities were concluded. Since that time the Senate has publicly indicated no desire to explore the matter any further.

In the months following the formation of the CCI, I briefed scores of members of Congress, hundreds of congressional aides, including legislative assistants and administrative assistants, and I lectured at almost 200 colleges, law schools, and universities. Almost 150 autonomous chapters of the CCI had helped to generate hundreds of thousands of letters, telegrams, and signatures on petitions to members of Congress. One hundred and thirty-seven members of Congress had sponsored either the Gonzalez resolution, the Downing resolution, or both. In March 1976, the resolutions were presented to the Rules Committee. The committee refused to refer the matter to the floor and the issue seemed inert for the 94th Congress.

We considered plans to begin again with the 95th Congress which would convene in January 1977.

Abby Mann had for sometime sought to write a screen play about the life of Dr. King. NBC television commissioned the work and Abby asked me to join him in Memphis to assist him in gathering some information about Dr. King's death.

Les Payne, a black newspaper reporter for *Newsday*, had written some unheralded stories about events in Memphis that had preceded the murder there. Donald Freed, the West Coast chairman of the CCI, had introduced me to Payne and I was impressed with his knowledge of the case and with his obviously determined and incisive reporting. Freed arranged for Payne and Mann to talk by telephone. Since Payne had written about Ed Redditt's removal from the scene his information was, I thought, of great importance. I agreed to meet Abby Mann in Memphis and to seek confirmation for Payne's observations.

I arrived at the Holiday Inn Rivermont two hours before Abby did. When he called my room from the lobby I told him to join us at once—for my long series of interviews with Ed Redditt had already begun. I introduced Abby to Ed Redditt and our investigation was underway. All that Payne had written was established again, confirmed in tape recorded interviews by the witnesses he had talked to, and corroborated by many additional witnesses he had not.

Together, in three days in Memphis, Abby and I interviewed Floyd Newsum and N. E. Wallace, the two firemen who had been so precipitously transferred from Fire Station Two; Frank Holloman, the former FBI official and former director of the Memphis Fire and Police Departments; Richard Ryan, a former lawyer for Ray; various officials of the fire and police departments; newspaper reporters; Reverend Samuel "Billy" Kyles, who was to have been Dr. King's host at a dinner at his home on April 4th; and others.

We left Memphis with a growing feeling that little of the truth about Dr. King's murder had ever been published. Together we called upon Coretta King following a Sunday service at the Ebenezer Baptist Church in Atlanta at which Daddy King, Martin's father and minister emeritus, delivered a moving sermon. In a small vestry room we shared the results of our incipient inquiry with Mrs. King. We talked about the need for an in-depth investigation by a Congressional committee armed with the power to subpoena witnesses and to examine all relevant documents and other physical evidence. Abby's commitment to a film about Dr. King's life and death took him to the cities and towns that Dr. King had visited and transformed—from Montgomery, Alabama, to Chicago, Illinois. My commitment to the facts about Dr. King's death took me within a few miles of the Canadian border to Constable, N.Y., where, with April Ferguson, the associate director of the CCI, we learned from Arthur Murtagh about the destroy-King squad maintained by the FBI in Atlanta.

In August 1976, I called upon three black members of Congress; Andrew Young of Georgia; Yvonne Burke of California, at that time the chairperson of the Black Congressional Caucus; and Walter Fauntroy, the delegate to Congress from Washington, D.C. I told them what we had learned in Memphis. I played a tape recording of the interview with Murtagh. I saw their growing anger transform itself into a desire for action. It was agreed that at the meeting of the Caucus that day a demand would be made for an investigation. The Caucus endorsed the demand unanimously and chose Fauntroy as its leader in the effort to create a Congressional inquiry.

As the presidential campaign was approaching its climax, a meeting was arranged with Coretta King, the leaders of the Caucus and the leaders of the Congress, Carl Albert, the Speaker, and Thomas P. (Tip) O'Neill, the heir apparent to that position in the 95th Congress. The leadership acceded to the requests, firmly put by the others present. At one point it had been suggested that "since we are in the closing days of the 94th Congress and there is so little time to act before the Congress expires why don't we wait for a few months until January?" Mrs. King, speaking, I am told, gently but without hesitation replied, "We have already waited more than eight years too long."

The leadership informed the Rules Committee that the resolution should be reported out. While CCI chapters helped to develop a mass campaign of support through meetings, radio and television programs, and a telephone network, Walter Fauntroy maneuvered the newly-drafted resolution through the intricacies of the Congressional procedure. The new resolution, sponsored by Fauntroy, Gonzalez, and Downing, called for the establishment of a Select Committee on Assassinations to examine all of the facts surrounding the murders of President Kennedy and Dr. King.

The resolution cleared the Rules Committee on September 15, 1976, and reached the floor of Congress two days later. The people, some in the

Congress, others at colleges, union halls, churches, and in the streets had done their work well. The resolution passed by a vote of 280-65. A Select Committee had been formed, and within days, funded. Richard A. Sprague was chosen to be its general counsel and staff director. The investigation was underway.

Sprague brought with him the credentials of a long-time successful prosecutor, a real-life Philadelphia lawyer whose relentless investigative techniques and determination led to the classic investigation and presentation to a jury of a conspiracy to murder the Yablonski family in Pennsylvania. His work up to that time had won him the almost unanimous accolades of the news media. Sprague had served as an assistant to Arlen Specter, the Philadelphia District Attorney. Specter had played an important role as a Warren Commission lawyer; he had helped to design the implausible single bullet theory which provided the basis for the Commission's implausible conclusion.

Before the Committee's mandate had expired with the closing days of the 94th Congress the attacks upon the Committee and upon Sprague began.

Ben Franklin of the Washington bureau of *The New York Times*, who had written admiringly of Sprague, was taken off the assignment to cover the Committee. David Burnham, who had dealt with corruption or alleged corruption in Philadelphia politics, was given the assignment instead.

With Burnham leading the attack, and George Lardner, Jr., of the *Washington Post* and Jeremiah O'Leary of the *Washington Star* aiding and abetting his stories, what appeared to be a campaign against the Committee and its counsel was well underway. This trio ignored the work of the Committee to publish and then comment upon stories about Richard Sprague, some of them ten and fifteen years old, that Burnham had resurrected from the ancient clippings in the morgues of Philadelphia newspapers.

Among the stories that they did not cover as the events transpired was the action of the Memphis authorities after the announcement that a committee of Congress would investigate the assassination. The mayor ordered the police to burn all of the files—180 boxes of them—that comprised the entire history of the domestic intelligence division of the Memphis police. Why was Redditt pulled off his assignment? On September 10, 1976, the answer to that and a hundred other questions may have gone up in smoke. Why had the police protection been reduced? Were FBI agents surveilling Dr. King on the evening of April 4th? Why had the black firemen been transferred? Despite the best efforts of the

American Civil Liberties Union to prevent the official destruction of the files, the court order that they secured was served one hour too late; the records were gone. The facts could very likely be established only through a painful and careful reconstruction of the events.

Yet in January of 1977 the re-establishment of the Congressional committee with the authority to undertake such a project suddenly was in doubt with the new Congress. A *New York Times* editorial denouncing Sprague and questioning the wisdom of re-establishing the Committee was another blow to the hopes of the American people that at long last the facts might be uncovered and revealed. The stories of three newsmen had been effective. Why have *The New York Times*, the *Washington Post*, the *Washington Star*, and other major newspapers failed to meet and interview the relevant witnesses referred to earlier in these pages? Why have these publications instead focused upon the presumed errors of the Congressional investigators and published recurrent attacks, some of them containing dubious charges, against the committee's staff?

One of the black members of the Select Committee—Congressman Harold E. Ford of Memphis—charged that the FBI had hired former agents to lobby against the continuation of the investigation.

The stories, and the actions of the intelligence agencies, seriously eroded support for the investigation. In February 1977, the Rules Committee reported a compromise resolution to the floor. It placed the Select Committee on probation for two months; required that the committee adopt a modest budget; and stated that during the first week of April 1977, the Congress might decide to reestablish the Committee or perhaps forever end any hope of such an inquiry.

During the evening of February 1, 1977, on the eve of the vote, I spoke at Morse Auditorium at Boston University. Hours before I had telephoned Dick Gregory whom I had located in a dentist's chair in Boston where he was about to undergo dental surgery. I told him that I thought we should engage in an all night vigil in support of the resolution that night. He suggested the house in Brookline, Massachusetts, where John F. Kennedy was born. At the conclusion of my remarks at Boston University, I announced that Greg and I were going to walk to the house where John Kennedy was born and stand there in a silent vigil until the dawn brought in a new day with the hope that we might soon learn about his death. Two hundred people, students, professors, and others walked with us for the better part of an hour through that frigid winter night. When we arrived, it was nineteen degrees below freezing. Various reporters dropped in through the night. One person delivered a message that Steve Krause of the Boston office of the UPI wanted me to call him. I did so. I told him we were maintaining a silent prayerful vigil. He seemed receptive and almost supportive.

The next afternoon I arrived in Washington just in time to witness the debate on the resolution on the floor. The closing remarks were made by Representative Robert E. Bauman of Maryland.

He said that the *Washington Post* called the Select Committee "perhaps the worst example of Congressional unquiry run amok." Bauman then made a charge that caused considerable concern on the floor. He said:

> **I am well aware that this matter arouses certain passions. Last night the Speaker was subject to a public demonstration in Massachusetts warning that "They are watching Tip O'Neill, what you do in this matter," a statement from Mark Lane who has been a champion of such an investigation.**

When I inquired later that day, I discovered that Bauman based his allegation against me upon a UPI story. During the vigil I had not mentioned Tip O'Neill; I had not led a demonstration against him, or stated, or implied that we were watching him.

I secured a copy of the UPI story that had misled Bauman. It carried a Nicholas Daniloff by-line and read:

> **The night before the House debate, comedian and activist Dick Gregory and author Mark Lane led a group of about 200 people in an all-night vigil outside John F. Kennedy's birthplace in Brookline, Mass.**
>
> **"This vigil is to let Tip O'Neill know we're watching him," said Richard Feldman, a spokesman for the group.**

On February 4th. I wrote to Congressman Bauman and acquainted him with the facts. On February 7th he asked for and received unanimous consent from the House to correct the permanent record. On that occasion he admitted his error and apologized for any inconvenience to me that he may have caused. I wondered who Richard Feldman was. Clearly he was not a "spokesman" for the "group" since there was no formal group. I called Daniloff and asked him who Feldman was. He answered, "Feldman, you got me; who is he?" I referred him to the UPI story that carried his by-line. He read it and said, "I'll be damned. I did write the story but I never quoted Feldman, whoever he is, and I never put those words in there." I asked him who did quote Feldman and he said, "The only person who could have changed my story, and I can't imagine why she should, would be the overnight editor, Elizabeth Wharton." I called her and apprised her of the facts. She said, "That Feldman quote was not in there in Daniloff's story. He's right, he did not put it in there. And neither did I. This is the first I've heard of that quote and I saw the story when Daniloff wrote it. I did not change it and so far as I know it went out without any quote from Feldman. This is strange. This is very strange. All I can say, Mr. Lane, is that it could not have happened, but it did." It did. A phantom quote from a mystery person emerged in a UPI story from the Washington bureau in a fashion that remains an enigma to the Washington bureau of UPI and found its way onto the floor of Congress as a weapon against the investigation. The compromise resolution passed by the narrow margin of 237 to 165. The Committee was given a two month reprieve.

Twenty-five years have passed since the death of Dr. King. The American people have not been given details about the pathological hatred that Hoover's FBI betrayed toward Dr. King. Neither have we been told why the black witnesses were officially stripped from the scene the night before the murder nor why the police officer in charge was removed on an implausible pretext just before the fatal shot was fired. The witness and security stripping was directed by a former high-ranking FBI official. Mystery surrounds the failure of the FBI to seek James Earl Ray until April 19th, fifteen days after the murder in spite of the presence of the fingerprints on the presumed murder rifle.

The bullet taken from Dr. King's body was examined by an FBI agent whose conclusions raise more questions than they answer. The bullet has not yet been adequately tested. It may not have been fired from Ray's rifle.

Ray's claim that he was induced into entering a guilty plea is supported by much of the known evidence. His claim that a man named Raoul moved him about has never been tested by a comprehensive investigation and remains a viable theory.

The cover-up of facts surrounding the murder, including the publication of news stories, false information leads to authors of books and magazine articles, and direct lobbying against a Congressional investigation by intelligence and spy organizations requires that we ask what it is that is so feared by so few. And ask as well how powerful the few must be to influence and control so much.

The present available and known evidence leads inexorably to the conclusion, I believe, that persons employed by the Federal Bureau of Investigation in 1968 must be considered to be prime suspects in the murder of Dr. Martin Luther King, Jr. Even should the facts ultimately acquit those persons, to permit the FBI, under these circumstances, to conduct the only authorized investigation into the murder is, I believe, to profane our concept of justice and to betray our pretensions of decency. Indeed, an investigation conducted by the Department of Justice which relied upon the original FBI investigation would enjoy limited credibility.

Let the Congress act.

Let the truth be known.

POSTSCRIPT

POSTSCRIPT - 1977

by Mark Lane

"Just this morning, Mr. Speaker, one of the major wire services reported that the Justice Department after months of investigation had concluded that James Earl Ray acted alone in assassinating Martin Luther King, Jr." So spoke Representative James Quillen in leading off the debate in opposition to the resolution to establish a Select Committee to investigate the assassinations of President Kennedy and Dr. King.

Quillen was quickly challenged by Yvonne Burke, a member of Congress from California and formerly the Chairwoman of the Congressional Black Caucus.

> I have been trying to see that report. I have been advised that the material in that report is too sensitive. As a member of the Committee on Appropriations and a member of the Subcommittee on State, Justice, Commerce and the Judiciary, the committee that has jurisdiction over the Attorney General's office and the Justice Department, I find it very irregular that I have not been able to see that report.
>
> I also find it irregular that the Justice Department had 12 to 15 deputies originally assigned to this investigation, that those deputies came back with a report to Assistant Attorney General Pottinger concluding that there should be an independent investigation, but that as a result there was another person appointed, Michael Shaheen, and that person has now come up with a report that was on the former Attorney General's desk at least 2 weeks ago, although the Attorney General has been gone for some weeks. This morning, the report was leaked.
>
> The Justice Department told me this morning that they know nothing about the leak.

The alleged conclusion of the report prepared under the direction of a former Attorney General, Edward Levi, had been leaked to a news service, after a new Attorney General had taken office and on the very day that the Congress was to consider the matter. Members of Congress were unable to secure the report. The shadow of a previous administration had been conjured up to blur the distinctions between the present and past and between the executive and legislative branches of government.

The report, entitled *Report of the Department of Justice Task Force to Review the FBI Martin Luther King, Jr., Security and Assassination Investigation*, dated January 11, 1977, and leaked on February 2, 1977 (it was thereafter officially released on February 19, 1977, by then new Attorney General, Griffin Bell), was intended to be the final solution to the doubts that had been raised regarding the murder of Dr. King. Instead, it raised more questions than it could answer.

The mission of the task force, said the Department of Justice in its report, was to respond to the "widespread speculation on the possibility that the Bureau [FBI] may have had some responsibility in Dr. King's death and may not have done an impartial and thorough investigation of the assassination."

On November 24, 1975, Attorney General Levi directed Stanley Pottinger, the Assistant Attorney General in charge of the Civil Rights Division at Justice, to undertake a review of the files of the Department of Justice and the FBI to determine whether the investigation into the assassination of Dr. King should be reopened.

On April 9, 1976, Pottinger submitted a memorandum to Levi which embodied the results of his three-person study.

During May 1976, after Pottinger's work was completed, I became aware of the strange circumstances regarding the removal of Redditt two hours before Dr. King was killed and the transfer of Newsum and Wallace the night before. Don Freed, Les Payne, and I discussed the matter in New York City. Later Freed and I explored the matter with Abby Mann in Los Angeles. On June 13, 1976, Pottinger met with Mann in Los Angeles. The meeting had been arranged through a Los Angeles woman lawyer. At that meeting Mann expressed doubts about the official reconciliation of the facts by the FBI and the Department of Justice, citing as troubling examples of unexplained occurrences the transfer of the black firemen and the removal of the black police officer.

However, the report by the Department of Justice reveals that the question of Redditt's untimely removal and the Newsum and Wallace transfers was not even considered by the Department of Justice until July 1976, after Mann had raised the matters with Pottinger. More than eight years had passed since the assassination of Dr. King and the Department of Justice had not even contemplated the substantial questions raised by the witness and security stripping. Levi, then aware that the mysterious removal of the officer and firemen might be illuminated in Mann's NBC-TV screenplay and in this book, evidently began to prepare a defense against the facts.

The Department of Justice panel was established to continue the investigation, and Pottinger's assistant, Michael Shaheen, served as its investigator. Shaheen's work was incorporated into the final report issued by the Department of Justice.

The serious questions contemplated by the Justice Department inquiry were:

1. Why were only two police officers assigned to Dr. King on the evening of April 4, 1968?

2. Why was one of those officers, Redditt, removed so precipitously two hours before the murder?

3. Why were the only two black firemen removed from the scene of the murder the night before it occurred?

4. If Raoul did not provide Ray with funds as Ray claimed, where did Ray secure the many thousands of dollars that he expended from the time he escaped from the Missouri Penitentiary until his arrest in London?

Before the inquiry began it was necessary to determine who was to conduct it. A memorandum from Levi was published in the Justice Department's report on the King assassination. It referred to the earlier efforts made by Pottinger and reads, in part, as follows:

The review is not complete. Mr. Pottinger and all those who have commented upon his memorandum recommend that the review be completed. Mr. Pottinger also has made other recommendations upon which there is some difference of opinion. In my view, it is essential that the review be completed as soon as possible and in as thorough a manner as is required to answer the basic questions. In view of what has already been done, and the tentative conclusions reached, special emphasis should be given to the fourth question. In conducting this review you should call upon the Department to furnish to you the staff you need.

Levi had decided that the "thorough" investigation was to be conducted by his Department of Justice. Levi's delicate language regarding Pottinger's "recommendations" and the "difference of opinion" that existed tended to obfuscate the central question that Pottinger had raised.

On March 25, 1976, as Pottinger's survey of the records was nearing completion, he said that he would recommend that Levi appoint a committee made up of people outside the FBI, outside the Department of Justice, and *outside the government* to investigate the assassination of Dr. King. Pottinger said that new doubts and suspicions about possible FBI involvement in the murder required an independent inquiry. He said that for "reasons of credibility" the investigation should be conducted by persons independent of the Justice Department which has control over the FBI. Pottinger urged that the new committee look into such questions as whether there was any FBI complicity in the murder and whether the FBI violated any law in its harassment of Dr. King.

These were the "recommendations" that Pottinger had made. The "difference of opinion" that Levi referred to was his own categorical rejection of the Pottinger suggestion that anyone outside his department be entrusted to examine the evidence.

The Department of Justice embarked upon its secret investigation by establishing two categories of evidence for the Department of Justice report. Appendix A contained irrelevant or easily obtainable and previously published data for the most part, including the titles of several books about the assassination, maps of Memphis, a floor plan of the second floor of the rooming house, and various FBI memoranda. It purportedly consisted of eighteen exhibits. However exhibits 12, 17, and 18 were designated as "classified" and were not published.

The documents referred to in the Department of Justice report which seemed to bear some relationship to the case were all placed in Appendix B. All of the documents in Appendix B were classified and none can be examined by the public. Appendix B became a *Catch-22* kind of depository for all governmental doubtful propositions, for the evidentiary basis for all FBI speculations, and for all Justice Department theories.

Its *modus operandi* determined, the Levi task force began its work.

Why were only two police officers, Redditt and Richmond, assigned to Dr. King on the afternoon of April 4, 1968? In fact, did FBI agents witness the murder? The shameful record of FBI harassment of Dr. King established that he was subjected to electronic surveillance through telephone wiretaps and planted microphones in cities that he visited all over America, including Los Angeles, Washington D.C., and New York. He was followed and spied upon in cities throughout the country by an army of FBI agents. Does it seem likely that Dr. King was not subjected to any FBI surveillance at the time of his death and during the hours preceding his death? The report said only that the FBI "unequivocally assured the task force that there was no electronic surveillance of Dr. King in Memphis. It was explained [by the FBI] that Memphis was not in the mainstream of Dr. King's SCLC activities." The Justice Department task force relied entirely upon the suspect agency to resolve this important question. FBI records were apparently not examined. The FBI interview relied upon by the report was placed in Appendix B and is not available for examination. The explanation offered by the Bureau appears to be of little value since Dr. King's activities were subjected to continual electronic surveillance in many cities which were not in the mainstream of SCLC activities. In addition Dr. King's continuing commitment to the struggle of the sanitation workers, along with the efforts of his aides, Reverend Abernathy, Andy Young, Bernard Lee, and others, demonstrated yet again that Memphis was very much in the mainstream of SCLC activities. The report stated that "FBI agents did observe the sanitation workers' strike activities for intelligence purposes." Yet, nowhere in the report does the Department of Justice disclose if any of those agents observed Dr. King during the hours before his death or at the time of his death. The interviews relied upon by the report to establish the FBI position on this question were placed in Appendix B and cannot be seen.

Inspector G. P. Tines of the Memphis Police Department (MPD) told the task force that six or seven officers were assigned to place Dr. King under surveillance and to provide security for him on April 3rd. The report of Tines was made part of Appendix B and is unavailable. According to the report, the security detail of four or five men operated in the area of the Lorraine Motel "until they were ordered to headquarters by Chief J. C. Macdonald at approximately 5:05 P.M." on April 3, 1968. According to the report, Tine said "he was not conferred with and has no idea why the security detail was removed from Dr. King after 5:05 P.M." While the report asserted that Macdonald had ordered the security detail to leave the area of the Lorraine Motel, also according to the report, "Former Chief Macdonald has no present recollection of the security detail." The interview with Macdonald was made part of Appendix B and cannot be seen. The report stated that "the security detail was not resumed on April 4, 1968." It relied for that conclusion upon the secret reports of two MPD Inspectors which were incorporated in a document in appendix B.

On April 4, 1968, according to the report, Detective Ed Redditt and Patrolman W. B. Richmond were the only MPD officers in the vicinity of the Lorraine Motel. The Justice Department's investigation failed to determine if FBI agents were present at the time. It failed to investigate the possibility of FBI electronic surveillance at the time. The Justice Department was unable to discover why Redditt and Richmond were the only two police officers assigned to Dr. King on the evening of April 4, 1968. All of the evidence that the task force of the Justice Department examined regarding this aspect of the investigation was placed in Appendix B. None of it can be seen.

The second question considered by the Justice Department concerned the removal of Redditt from the scene two hours before the murder. The report stated:

> **At approximately 4:00 P.M., Redditt was ordered by telephone to leave the fire station and report to headquarters where he was advised that threats had been made on his life. He was, therefore, ordered to move his family into a motel under an assumed name by Frank Holloman, former Director of Police and Fire, Memphis, Tenn.**

Redditt stated that he was not called to headquarters as the result of a telephone call but that Lt. Arkin arrived on the scene and drove with him to headquarters. The source for the version published in the report is an interview with Frank Holloman. That interview remains secret and assigned to Appendix B. According to the report:

> **Redditt was taken home in a squad car, but refused to move his family because of a sick relative. At about the time the squad car arrived in front of Redditt's residence, it was announced on the radio that Dr. King had been shot. After a couple of days, Redditt did not hear any more about the threat on his life.**

An interview with Redditt was given as the source for that data. That interview also remains secret as part of Appendix B.

The matter was properly posed. The question before the task force was evident. Why was Redditt removed? The task force could not discover the answer. A secret report by Inspector Tines, filed in Appendix B, was given as the source for the story that a man named Philip R. Manuel, an investigator with Senator McClellan's investigating committee, had told the MPD that an informant in Mississippi said that the Mississippi Freedom Democratic Party (a liberal, nonviolent, interracial political movement within the Democratic Party) had made plans to kill a "Negro lieutenant" in Memphis and then later called to say that the "Negro lieutenant" was in Knoxville, not Memphis. This slender reed provided the only information the Justice Department could secure to form the basis for its conclusion regarding Redditt's removal. However, according to the report, "Philip R. Manuel neither has a present recollection of providing the information regarding the threat to the MPD, nor does he have a memorandum of the event."

The Manuel interview is, of course, secret and is, of course, in Appendix B. The reader may recall that Redditt told me, and very likely told the Justice Department as well, that he was introduced to the Secret Service agent by Holloman at MPD headquarters and that other law enforcement officials were present as well. Redditt's recollections appear to preclude the possibility that Manuel was the source of the information. Together with Manuel's own lack of independent support for the story, it appears to fall. The story attributed to Manuel regarding an unnamed "Negro lieutenant" in Memphis should not have led the Memphis police to Redditt in any event. Redditt was not a lieutenant. He was a detective with a rank of warrant officer. Following the publication of the Department of Justice's report I called Manuel and asked him if he had ever met Redditt. Manuel refused to discuss the matter with me, stating only, "I have made complete statements to the Department of Justice and the House Select Committee on Assassinations." Since the Department of Justice's statements are unavailable, stored in Appendix B, I visited Richard Sprague, the General Counsel and staff director to the House Select Committee on Assassinations. He said, "Manuel's statement was that he refused to talk to us unless we served him with a subpoena. We don't have that power now, so we have no statement from him." On March 1, 1977, I called Ed Redditt. He described for me the Secret Service agent he had seen on April 4, 1968, at Police Headquarters. Redditt said, "He was approximately 5 feet 11 inches tall; weighed about 200 pounds; light complexion; hair that was not dark, probably light brown." Later that evening I secured the description of Philip Manuel from an associate of his. He was described as being "approximately 5 feet 6 inches tall; 160 pounds in weight; an olive complexion and black hair." The Department of Justice's speculation that Manuel was the source for the story that led to Redditt's removal had apparently been refuted by the evidence. I wondered if the Department of Justice's investigators had confronted Redditt with Manuel or if they had even secured Redditt's description of the Secret Service agent from him. On March 3, 1977, I called Redditt and asked him about the Department of Justice's interview with him. He said, "They never asked me to describe the Secret Service agent who supposedly brought the death threat from Washington. They never showed me a picture of Manuel. They never told me that they had located a man who they thought had conveyed the threat." The Department of Justice had failed to conduct the most elementary investigation to determine if Manuel could have been the person who conveyed the threat to the Memphis authorities. The Department of Justice had failed to ask Redditt if he could identify Manuel. The Department of Justice had failed to send Redditt a copy of its report; I read relevant portions to him. When Redditt learned that Manuel had called the Memphis Police Department on April 5, 1958, "and advised them that a threat was on the life of a 'Negro lieutenant' in Knoxville, rather than Memphis" he was amused. He observed, "Yet headquarters did not release me from my 'house arrest' at that time—on April 5. They kept me there after that, still saying that I was the subject of a death threat. Manuel's story is a hoax, they evidently just won't tell the truth about why I was removed just before Dr. King was murdered." The report does not allege that Manuel called the Knoxville Police Department to inform them of the newly located threat or that the Memphis Police released Redditt from his protective custody status just after or as a result of the telephone call by Manuel to the Memphis Police Department in which he allegedly corrected his previous error.

Why were the only two black firemen assigned to Fire Station Two, which was located near the Lorraine Motel, removed from the scene of the murder the night before it occurred? Here again the investigation by the Department of Justice confirmed all of the findings of our investigation. The report reads:

As of April 3, 1968, Norvell E. Wallace and Floyd E. Newsum were the only black firemen assigned to Fire Station No. 2 of the Memphis Fire Department (MFD). Wallace was working the night shift on April 3rd and Newsum was scheduled to report for the day shift on April 4th. Both of these individuals actively supported the sanitation workers' strike, attending their rallies and making financial contributions.

In our interview of Wallace (Interview July 8, 1976, App. B.) he stated that at about 10:00 or 10:30 on the night of April 3rd his captain told him that a call had come in requesting that a man be detailed to Fire Station No. 33. He was immediately detailed to No. 33 although it was raining and he was preparing to go to bed. Wallace further stated that while Fire Station No. 33 was understaffed as a whole, there was no shortage of personnel for the pump truck on which he worked. Otherwise, he does not know why he was detailed.

Also, on the night of April 3rd Fireman Newsum, in a wholly personal capacity, attended a rally at the Mason Temple where

Dr. King made his last speech. When he returned home (about 10:30 P.M.) there was a message for him to call Lt. J. Smith at the fire department. When he called, Lt. J. Smith ordered him to report to Fire Station No. 31 on the morning of April 4th rather than Fire Station No. 2. Newsum claims that Fire Station No. 31 was overstrength at the time and his detail made his company short. Moreover, he says he never has received a satisfactory explanation why he was detailed. However, he did say that Lt. Barnett at one time told him he was detailed at the request of the police. (Interview of Floyd E. Newsum, July 8, 1976, App. B.)

Again the facts had posed the question. The Department of Justice could only report:

Interviews of past and present members of the MFD have failed to disclose the individual who initiated the order or the reason for detailing Wallace and Newsum.

The interviews of the past and present officers of the fire department are all secret. All have been made part of Appendix B. The investigation was able to establish that Wallace's Company at Fire Station Two "was operating at minimum strength after he was detailed; whereas Company No. 33 to which he was detailed operated at one over the minimum strength after the detail." Similarly, the records revealed that "Newsum's Company No. 55 at Fire Station 2 was operating at minimum strength after the detail but Company 31 to which he was detailed operated at one over minimum strength after the detail." The Department of Justice, failing to discover who initiated the order to remove Newsum and Wallace and failing to discover the reason for the order, was nevertheless willing to speculate:

Our investigation has not disclosed any evidence that the detail of Wallace and Newsum was in any way connected with the assassination of Dr. King.

The conclusion may be accurate since the investigation apparently uncovered no evidence regarding the cause for the transfer.

The report of the Department of Justice rejected out of hand Ray's claim that he had been financed by Raoul. The report concludeded;

Indeed, the overwhelming evidence indicates that Ray was almost totally alone during the year after his escape from the Missouri State Prison.

The evidence which impressed the Justice Department lawyers as being "overwhelming" was not shared with the readers of the Report. It too was placed in Appendix B.

If Raoul did not provide Ray with funds, who did?

The facts disclosed that Ray had traveled extensively after he escaped from the Missouri Penitentiary. The Department of Justice conceded that "in addition to normal living expenses, Ray made several substantial purchases, e.g., cars, photo equipment, dance lessons."

The report stated that

These expenditures suggested that he had financial assistance and hence possible co-conspirators. Therefore, the Bureau was particularly interested in determining his sources of income.

Hoover went to extreme lengths in an effort to determine if Ray had been involved in any robberies or burglaries anywhere within the United States.

The report disclosed that

On April 23, 1968, the Director advised all field divisions to consider Ray as a suspect in any unsolved bank robberies, burglaries or armed robberies occurring after April 23, 1967. The results were negative.

Six days later Hoover enlisted the entire law enforcement apparatus in the United States, federal, state and local, in another such effort.

On April 29, 1968, the Director in a teletype to all SAC's ordered that all law enforcement agencies which maintained unidentified latent fingerprints be contacted and requested that fingerprints of Ray be compared in order to determine his past whereabouts and possibly establish his source of funds. Again, negative results were obtained. The Director, on May 14, 1968, reminded all field divisions that Ray had spent a considerable amount of money from April 23, 1967, until April 4, 1968, and advised that a source for these monies had not been determined. The Director ordered that photographs of Ray be displayed to appropriate witnesses in unsolved bank robberies and bank burglaries. These efforts and all others to date, with one exception, have proved fruitless. The Bureau investigated the possibility that Ray participated in a bank robbery at Alton, Illinois, in 1967, but it was established that he was not a participant.

Hoover then involved the Canadian and Mexican police in an effort to explain Ray's income.

Reports from the Royal Canadian Mounted Police indicated no known robberies or burglaries which could be connected with Ray.

Unable to secure any evidence that Ray robbed or burglarized a single establishment in spite of its unprecedented efforts to do so the FBI fell back upon a guess:

It is the Bureau's opinion that Ray most likely committed on a periodic basis several robberies or burglaries during this period in order to support himself.

The Department of Justice concluded its report regarding Ray's "Sources of Funds" more enigmatically.

It held, "The sources for Ray's funds still remain a mystery today."

Indeed, to the Department of Justice every relevant area regarding the murder of Dr. King still remains a mystery today. The report confirmed the accuracy of our investigation. It posed to the American people the questions that our investigation had posed to the Department of Justice. Yet it provided not a single relevant answer.

A substantial portion of the report was devoted to a section designated IIC and titled "The Story of James Earl Ray." The Department of Justice relied upon Huie's book, *He Slew the Dreamer*, for many of his findings about Ray. In just the opening eight pages of Section IIC, it cited that book more than twenty times as the source of information about Ray. The report relied upon Huie's description of Ray's relationship with a Canadian woman who Ray considered asking for assistance in securing a passport. When Ray discovered that she was a government employee, he decided not to ask for her help. Huie had written in *He Slew the Dreamer* that when he interviewed the Canadian woman she told him that Ray was a racist. According to Huie, Ray had said to her that those people who "know niggers hate them." I asked Ray about that remark when I saw him in prison. He said that he had never made such a remark and that he doubted the Canadian woman told Huie that he had. The Canadian woman was reluctant to discuss this matter. I spoke with her attorney. He said, "We were going to sue Huie for attributing remarks to her that she did not make, but since Huie never mentioned her name in the book or articles I didn't think we had a legal case. If he had mentioned her name we would have sued because he made statements that were not true." The Department of Justice should have examined Huie's record in this matter thoroughly before relying upon him as the source. Huie's confusion of fact and fiction appears to have predated his work in the Ray case. In 1960, Huie brought an action in the United States District Court for a preliminary injunction against the National Broadcasting Company, Inc. (NBC), on his copyright on a story entitled "The Hero of Iwo-Jima." NBC had commissioned a television program entitled "The American" which Huie claimed was based upon his work. The court denied Huie's motion since in his book he claimed that the story was true, but before the court he demonstrated that episodes previously offered as fact were actually "the product of his imagination." Historical facts are not subject to copyright laws; works of fiction are. The court said that Huie was estopped to say that his book was fiction after having claimed in that book that it was true.

When the then new Attorney General, Griffin Bell, released a report on February 18, 1977, he expressed reservations about its conclusions that Ray acted alone. His doubts encouraged members of the Congress to move on with their investigation into Dr. King's death. On Sunday, February 27, 1977, the *Washington Star* published a lengthy and strong defense of the report and in conclusion contained an attack upon the new Attorney General as well. The story that appeared on the front page of the editorial section of the newspaper was written by George McMillan. We had come full circle. The Department of Justice and Huie had provided information for McMillan's book. McMillan's book and Huie's book had been used by the Department of Justice's report. George McMillan then praised the report saying he liked it even better than the Warren Commission Report. On a personal note, McMillan added to his endorsement of the report that the critics of the official version had ignored him. He wrote, "The task force report takes on what has been a key point in the argument that the King assassination was a conspiracy: it is the myth that Ray was only a two-bit punk who had no motive and therefore must have been paid to kill King.

"I confess to having tried to lay this myth to rest myself. I spent six years on a biography of Ray—*The Making of an Assassin*—only to have my book treated among assassination buffs as if it did not exist." I trust that this book will help to remedy the situation of which McMillan complained. While McMillan was quite certain that the report concluded that Ray was not paid to kill Dr. King, the report itself was not so unequivocal on that point. In discussing motive, the report said, "Yet, Ray's apparent hatred for the civil rights movement, his possible yearning for recognition, 'and a desire for a potential quick profit' may have, as a whole, provided sufficient impetus for him to act, and to act alone."

On the afternoon of March 3, 1977, I met at the Department of Justice in Washington, D.C. with four of the five members of the Task Force and Michael Shaheen, who had directed their work. I informed them of Redditt's description of the Secret Service agent whom he had seen in

Memphis on April 4, 1968, and asked if that matched Manuel's description. The Task Force member who had interviewed Manuel said that he had never seen Manuel. He explained that, instead, he had talked briefly with Manuel by telephone. Manuel's physical attributes were relevant as was Redditt's description of the Secret Service agent, yet the Task Force members said that they had not inquired about the Secret Service agent when talking to Redditt and neither seen Manuel nor inquired about his physical description.

The report reveals that Redditt was interviewed on July 8, 1976; Tines, who related the Manuel story, was interviewed the following week. However, the telephone call to Manuel was not made until the end of September 1976. The Task Force member who had called Manuel asked me, "Why should I have conducted a long interview with Manuel? What could I have asked him after he said to me that he didn't remember the incident, had no memorandum about it, but was willing to accept the Memphis Police Department's account of it?" I said, "You might have asked him if he remembered calling the Knoxville Police Department to alert them to the threat. You might have asked him if he ever recalled telling any police department during his life that there was a contract out on one of its officers and if he thought it likely that he could forget such a dramatic moment. You might have asked him if he met Redditt on April 4th in the police station. You might have asked him for his height, weight, and hair color so that you could check that information out against Redditt's description of the Secret Service agent."

At that point, the Task Force member interrupted to say, "We do not interrogate witnesses." Another Task Force member said, "You don't have to tell us what questions to ask."

One of the younger Task Force members asked me what more could be done to investigate the Manuel story. I suggested that the Knoxville Police Department should be called to see if a threat had been relayed to that office on April 5, 1968; that a thorough investigation of the incredible story that the threat originated with the Mississippi Freedom Democratic Party should be made; that the Memphis police officials, including Holloman, should be asked why Redditt was confined to his house for days after the Memphis Police Department had been informed, on April 5, that he was not the presumed target and why Redditt had never been told, until I called him in March 1977, that he had in fact not been the target for the alleged contract killing. I noticed that no one associated with the Task Force made any notes.

I asked the government lawyers if they had determined in their search of the FBI's secret files whether Redditt, Newsum, Wallace, or Richmond had ever been questioned by the FBI in the investigation. Shaheen said that the FBI had not questioned any of the four men and that the first time any of the four had been questioned by federal employees was in July 1976.

Carl T. Rowan, perhaps America's most influential black journalist, wrote, in the *New York Post* on February 19, 1977, ''Very clearly the FBI is suspect.'' He added, ''We may never know the truth—but we must search for it.'' Rowan underscored the necessity for an investigation independent of the FBI and those associated with it in the Department of Justice by disclosing a startling fact. He wrote, ''While James Earl Ray was fleeing some FBI operatives were trying to sell me the spurious line that Russians had killed King because of some hitch in his relations with 'Soviet spies.' '' Within four hours after Dr. King was murdered the FBI had taken possession of Ray's rifle and binoculars which bore his fingerprints. Yet subsequently FBI personnel were alleging that Russians had killed King.

The Department of Justice did not examine, in its report, the failure of the FBI to seek Ray from the outset, in spite of the fingerprints which led inexorably to him. The report did not explore or disclose the fact that the original circulars advertising his escape from the Missouri Penitentiary inexplicably bore not Ray's, but another man's, fingerprints. The report did not disclose or explore the false stories circulated by the FBI regarding the suggested culprits, from Hoover's talk of ''a jealous husband,'' to his employees' allegations about Russian spies.

Attorney General Bell reacted to the report, which was prepared during a previous Administration, by stating that it did not adequately answer the apparent questions. He felt, he said, that the question of a conspiracy to murder Dr. King survived the report and remained a viable one.

Indeed the report raised more questions than it answered. Only a serious, sober, and thorough investigation conducted by persons not afraid of what the evidence might reveal will suffice. And that investigation, to be effective, must not husband away its evidence beyond the perception of the people in a bin marked Appendix B.

APPENDIX

Appendix One

THE FUNERAL
by Dick Gregory

Martin Luther King had said time and time again that he would probably die fighting for civil rights. He felt that he was a likely target for the same type of violence that struck John F. Kennedy and others who tried to pave the way for freedom for all people. He had talked to his close friends about dying. He had mentioned to his wife, Coretta, that he, just like President Kennedy, was despised by many who were against integration, and that in a sick nation, violence was common. Martin Luther King died just the way he said he might; by an assassin's bullet; the way millions of Americans had hoped he wouldn't. He died in a town where he might not have been except for the garbage collectors' strike which was affecting blacks in Memphis in a way that was soon to be recognized as one of the single most important accomplishments of the civil rights movement. Martin Luther King died alone. He was not a victim of a bombing or a fire affecting a group of people, but rather he was the center of attraction. Reverend Andrew Young had always predicted that if violence ever struck the inner circle of civil rights leaders, it would probably hit them all at once. He felt that the entire movement and its leadership would be wiped out at the same time. It surprised him that Dr. King died alone with his close friends standing watch.

For more than ten years now, King had been under the constant pressure that had built up during his entire career in the civil rights movement. It had not been easy for this man who had lived with threats for such a long time. Many of the threats had become a regular part of his life along with the hatred and the lies that he and his family had to contend with.

King was labeled a national security threat and J. Edgar Hoover called him "The most notorious liar in the world." The FBI subjected King to massive and complete surveillance, smear campaigns, and blackmail. They tapped his phones. The way the FBI used to operate in the South was like a black guy would call them and tell them that the Ku Klux Klan was threatening his family. Two agents would come out to his house, warm their hands on the cross burning on the front lawn, take the black guy's fingerprints, and then leave. The FBI is hung up on fingerprints. If they can't get any fingerprints they can't solve anything. If a cat could figure out a way to rob banks just by using his feet, the FBI would never

288

catch him! Black folks in America rate the FBI like they do the swine flu shots . . . "Use it at your own risk."

A secret FBI document dated March 4, 1968, issued this revealing directive:

Prevent the rise of a messiah who could unify, and electrify, the militant black nationalist movement. [Malcolm X] might have been such a messiah; he is a martyr of the movement today. [King could] be a real contender for this position should he abandon his supposed obedience to white liberal doctrines.

Maybe this accounts for what many have called his premonition of death. It was on the night of the Kennedy assassination that Mrs. Edith Scott Bagley in Atlanta recalls a statement made by King. She says he returned to his home all shook up, upset, and going to pieces. "This is the way I'm going," he said. He seemed to have even prepared his loved ones for the fate that would eventually come his way. They, too, lived in constant fear, and the pressure was building in all of them. Dr. King's younger brother, Reverend A. D. King, had taken the pulpit on the day of the funeral and cried out, "America, your day of death is coming."

It was hot and muggy the day of the funeral. Women were dressed in black with hats and gloves. Their bodies would soon feel the overwhelming heat and humidity of the warmer-than-usual spring day in Atlanta. Men, dressed in their best suits, knew that they would soon feel the urge to loosen their ties in order to find a bit of comfort from the heat. But the atmosphere on this day soon made everyone unaware of the heat, and very much aware of the large crowd that poured into the church and onto the streets. Martin Luther King was dead, and for the first time since before the announcement of his death, the public was looking at him as his body lay at rest in the church where he had preached so many times.

More than a hundred thousand mourners crowded outside the Ebenezer Baptist Church and onto the streets. They also lined the sidewalks on the route leading to the campus of Morehouse State College where another memorial service would be held. There were hundreds of familiar faces. Celebrities were the first to begin pouring in. They hoped to get a good seat inside the church so they could see and hear the services. But there were just more people than the church could accommodate. There was seating space for 750 persons. Loudspeakers were set up so that those in the basement and those outside could hear. Among the celebrities I was able to see were Sammy Davis, Jr., Diana Ross, Eartha Kitt, James Brown, Lena Horne, Aretha Franklin, Nancy Wilson, Wilt Chamberlain, Mr. and Mrs. Harry Belafonte, Berry Gordy, Thurgood Marshall, Richard Nixon, Hubert Humphrey, Whitney Young, Roy Wilkins, Floyd McKissick, James Farmer, James Foreman, John Lewis, Julian Bond, Floyd Patterson, and Jackie Kennedy. Johnson Publishing Company President John H. Johnson and *Jet* Editor Bob Johnson were there. They had been a big force behind King's being built as a leader. For years *Jet* and *Ebony* had followed his cause, and now they would do tribute to the man who so often made their covers and filled their pages with news of the ongoing struggle for civil rights. As I watched the expressions of the SCLC members I knew that they were going through a special type of pain. They had walked with King, marched with him, and watched a whole movement turn a nation around; and now he was gone. I wondered how these ministers would be affected by it. Many of them I knew personally, people like Hosea Williams, James Bevel, Ralph Abernathy, Bernard Lee, C. T. Vivian, Fred Shuttlesworth, T. Y. Walker, Jesse Jackson, Walter Fauntroy, and Andrew Young.

During the first week of February Dr. King told his congregation at the Ebenezer Baptist Church what kind of eulogy he wanted at his funeral. One could say that King preached his own funeral before his death when he delivered the following sermon:

> Every now and then I guess we all think realistically about that day when we will be victimized with what is life's final common denominator, that something we call death. We all think about it. And every now and then I think about my own death, and I think about my own funeral. And I don't think of it in a morbid sense. Every now and then I ask myself, "What is it that I would want said?" And I leave the word to you this morning.
>
> If any of you are around when I have to meet my day, I don't want a long funeral. And if you get somebody to deliver the eulogy, tell them not to talk too long. . . . Tell them not to mention that I have a Nobel Peace Prize, that isn't important. Tell them not to mention that I have three or four hundred other awards, that's not important. Tell him not to mention where I went to school.
>
> I'd like somebody to mention that day, that Martin Luther King, Jr., tried to . . . love somebody. I want you to say that day, that I tried to be right on the war question. I want you to be able to say that day that I did try to feed the hungry. I want you to be able to say that day that I did try in my life . . . to visit those who were in prison. I want you to say that I tried to love and serve humanity.
>
> Yes, if you want to say that I was a drum major, say that I was a drum major for . . . righteousness. And all of the other shallow things will not matter. I won't have . . . the fine and luxurious things of life to leave behind. But I just want to leave a committed life behind.

AS HE DIED TO MAKE MEN HOLY, LET US DIE TO MAKE MEN FREE

A free man is a man with no fears. Martin Luther King, in life, was about setting men free. Martin Luther King was killed in the process of setting men free. President Emeritus of Morehouse College, Dr. Benjamin Mays gave the eulogy at Martin Luther King's funeral.

Eulogy of Dr. Martin Luther King, Jr.
Atlanta, Georgia — April 9, 1968
By Benjamin E. Mays

To be honored by being requested to give the Eulogy at the funeral of Doctor Martin Luther King, Jr., is like asking one to eulogize his deceased son—so close and so dear was he to me. Our friendship goes back to his student days at Morehouse College. It is not an easy task; nevertheless, I accept it, with a heavy heart and with full knowledge of my inadequacy to do justice to this man. It was my desire that if I pre-deceased Doctor King, he would pay tribute to me on my final day. It was his wish that if he pre-deceased me, I deliver the homily at his funeral. Fate has decreed that I eulogize him. I wish it might have been otherwise, for after all, I am three score and ten and Martin Luther is dead at thirty-nine.

Although there are some who rejoice in his death, there are millions across the length and breadth of this world who are smitten with grief that this friend of mankind—all mankind—has been cut down in the flower of his youth. So, multitudes here and in foreign lands, queens, kings, heads of governments, the clergy of the world, and the common man everywhere, are praying that God will be with the family, the American people, and the President of the United States in this tragic hour. We hope that this universal concern will bring comfort to the family—for grief is like a heavy load; when shared it is easier to bear. We come today to help you carry the load.

We have assembled here from every section of this great nation and from other parts of the world to give thanks to God that He gave to America, at this moment in history, Martin Luther King, Jr. Truly God is no respecter of persons. How strange! God called the grandson of a slave on his father's side, and said to him: Martin Luther, speak to America about war and peace; about social justice and racial discrimination; about its obligation to the poor; and about nonviolence as a way of perfecting social change in a world of brutality and war.

Here was a man who believed, with all of his might, that the pursuit of violence, at any time, is ethically and morally wrong; that God and the moral weight of the universe are against it; that violence is self-defeating; and that only love and forgiveness can break the vicious circle of revenge. He believed that nonviolence would prove effective in the abolition of injustice in politics, economics, in education, and in race relations. He was convinced, also, that people could not be moved to abolish voluntarily the inhumanity of man to man by mere persuasion and pleading, but that they could be moved to do so by dramatizing the evil through massive nonviolent resistance. He believed that nonviolent direct action was necessary to supplement the nonviolent victories won in the federal courts. He believed that the nonviolent approach to solving social problems would ultimately prove to be redemptive.

Out of this conviction, history records the marches in Montgomery, Birmingham, Selma, Chicago, and other cities. He gave people an ethical and moral way to engage in activities designed to perfect social change without bloodshed and·violence; and when violence did erupt it was that which is potential in any protest which aims to uproot deeply entrenched wrongs. No reasonable person would deny that the activities and the personality of Martin Luther King, Jr., contributed largely to the success of the student sit-in movements; in abolishing segregation in downtown establishments; and that his activities contributed mightily to the passage of the civil-rights legislation of 1964 and 1965.

Martin Luther King, Jr., believed in a united America; that the walls of separation brought on by legal and de facto segregation, and discrimination based on race and color, could be eradicated. As he said in his Washington Monument address: "I have a dream!"

He had faith in his country. He died striving to desegregate and integrate America to the end that this great nation of ours, born in revolution and blood, conceived in liberty and dedicated to the proposition that all men are created free and equal, will truly become the lighthouse of freedom where none will be denied because his skin is black and none favored because his eyes are blue; where our nation will be militarily strong but perpetually at peace; economically secure but just; learned but wise; where the poorest—the garbage collectors—will have bread enough and to spare; where no one will be poorly housed, each educated up to his capacity; and where the richest will understand the meaning of empathy. This was his dream, and the end toward which he strove. As he and his followers so often sang: "We shall overcome someday; black and white together."

Let it be thoroughly understood that our deceased brother did not embrace nonviolence out of fear or cowardice. Moral courage was one of his noblest virtues. As Mahatma Gandhi challenged the British Empire without a sword and won, Martin Luther King, Jr., challenged the interracial wrongs of his country without a gun. And he had the faith to believe that he would win the battle for social justice. I make bold to assert that it took more courage for King to practice nonviolence than it took his assassin to fire that fatal shot. The assassin is a coward; he committed his foul act and fled. When Martin Luther disobeyed an unjust law, he accepted the consequences of his actions. He never ran away and he never begged for mercy. He returned to the Birmingham jail to serve his time.

Perhaps he was more courageous than soldiers who fight and die on the battlefield. There is an element of compulsion in their dying. But when Martin Luther faced death again and again, and finally embraced it, there was no external pressure. He was acting on an inner compulsion that drove him on. More courageous than those who advocate violence as a way out, for they carry weapons of destruction for defense. But Martin Luther faced the dogs, the police, jail, heavy criticism, and finally death; and he never carried a gun, not even a knife to defend himself. He had only his faith in a just God to rely on; and the belief that "thrice is he armed who has his quarrels just." The faith that Browning writes about when he says: "One who never turned his back, but marched breast forward: never doubted that clouds would break; never dreamed that right through worsted wrong would triumph; held we fall to rise, are baffled to fight better, sleep to wake."

Coupled with moral courage was Martin Luther King, Jr.'s capacity to love people. Though deeply committed to a program of freedom for Negroes, he had love and concern for all kinds of peoples. He drew no distinction between the high and the low; none between the rich and the poor. He believed especially that he was sent to champion the cause of the man farthest down. He would probably say that, if death had to come, I am sure there was no greater cause to die for than fighting to get a just wage for garbage collectors. He was supra race, supra nation, supra denomination, supra class, and supra culture. He belonged to the world and to mankind. Now he belongs to posterity!

But there is a dichotomy in all this. This man was loved by some and hated by others. If any man knew the meaning of suffering, King knew. House bombed; living day by day for thirteen years under constant threats of death; maliciously accused of being a Communist; falsely accused of being insincere and seeking the limelight for his own glory; stabbed by a member of his own race; slugged in a hotel lobby; jailed over twenty times; occasionally deeply hurt because friends betrayed him—and yet this man had no bitterness in his heart, no rancor in his soul, no revenge in his mind; and he went up and down the length and breadth of this world preaching nonviolence and the redemptive power of love. He believed with all his heart, mind, and soul that the way to peace and brotherhood is through nonviolence, love, and suffering. He was severely criticized for his opposition to the war in Vietnam. It must be said, however, that one could hardly expect a prophet of Doctor King's commitments to advocate nonviolence at home and violence in Vietnam. Nonviolence to King was total commitment not only in solving the problems of race in the United States, but in solving the problems of the world.

Surely this man was called of God to do this work. If Amos and Micah were prophets in the eighth century, B.C., Martin Luther King, Jr., was a prophet of the twentieth century. If Isaiah was called of God to prophesy in his day, Martin Luther was called of God to prophesy in his time. If Hosea was sent to preach love and forgiveness centuries ago, Martin Luther was sent to expound the doctrine of nonviolence and forgiveness in the third quarter of the twentieth century. If Jesus was called to preach the Gospel to the poor, Martin Luther was called to give dignity to the common man. If a prophet is one who interprets in clear and intelligible language the will of God, Martin Luther King, Jr., fits that designation. If a prophet is one who does not seek popular causes to espouse, but rather the causes which he thinks are right, Martin Luther qualified on that score.

No! he was not ahead of his time. No man is ahead of his time. Every man is within his star, each in his time. Each man must respond to the call of God in his lifetime and not in somebody else's time. Jesus had to respond to the call of God in the first century, A.D., and not in the twentieth century. He had but one life to live. He couldn't wait, even though he died young. How long do you think Jesus would have had to wait for the constituted authorities to accept him? Twenty-five years? A hundred years? A thousand? He died at thirty-three. He couldn't wait. Paul, Galileo, Copernicus, Martin Luther, the Protestant reformer, Gandhi and Nehru, couldn't wait for another time. They had to act in their lifetime. No man is ahead of his time. Abraham, leaving his country in obedience to God's call; Jesus dying on a cross; Galileo on his knees recanting; Lincoln dying of an assassin's bullet; Woodrow Wilson crusading for a League of Nations; Martin Luther King, Jr., dying fighting for justice for garbage collectors—none of these men were ahead of their time. With them the time was always ripe to do that which was right and that which needs to be done.

Too bad Martin Luther King, Jr., died so young. I feel that way, too. But, as I have said many times before, it isn't how long one lives, but how well. It's what one accomplishes for mankind that matters. Jesus died at thirty-three; Keats and Marlow at twenty-nine; Shelley at thirty; Dunbar before thirty-five; John Fitzgerald Kennedy at forty-six; William Rainey Harper at forty-nine; and Martin Luther King, Jr., at thirty-nine.

We all pray that the assassin will be apprehended and brought to justice. But, make no mistake, the American people are in part responsible for Martin Luther King, Jr.'s, death. The Memphis officials must bear some of the guilt for Martin Luther's assassination. The strike should have been settled several weeks ago. The lowest paid in our society should not have to strike for a more just wage. A century after Emancipation, and after the enactment of the 13th, 14th and 15th Amendments, it should not have been necessary for Martin Luther King, Jr., to stage marches in Montgomery, Birmingham and Selma, and go to jail over twenty times trying to achieve for his people those rights which people of lighter hue get by virtue of their being born white. We, too, are guilty of murder. It is time for the American people to repent and make democracy equally applicable to all Americans.

If we love Martin Luther King, Jr., and respect him, as this crowd testifies, let us see to it that he did not die in vain; let us see to it that we do not dishonor his name by trying to solve our problems through rioting in the streets. Violence was foreign to his nature. He warned that continued riots could produce a Fascist state. But let us see to it also that the conditions that cause riots are promptly removed, as the President of the United States is trying to get us to do. Let black and white alike search their hearts; and if there be any prejudice in our hearts against any racial or ethnic group, let us exterminate it and let us pray, as Martin Luther King, Jr. would pray if he could: "Father, forgive them for they know not what they do." If we do this, Martin Luther King, Jr., will have died a redemptive death from which all mankind will benefit. Morehouse College will never be the same because Martin Luther came by here, and the nation and the world will be indebted to him for centuries to come. It is natural that we here at Morehouse would want to memorialize him to serve as an inspiration to all students who study in this center.

I close by saying to you what Martin Luther King, Jr., believed, that if physical death was the price he had to pay to rid America of prejudice and injustice, nothing could be more redemptive. To paraphrase the words of the immortal John Fitzgerald Kennedy, permit me to say that Martin Luther King, Jr.'s, unfinished work on earth must truly be our own.

SPEECH OF SENATOR ROBERT C. BYRD

SENATE—Friday, March 29, 1968

The Senate met at 9 o'clock a.m., on the expiration of the recess, and was called to order by the President pro tempore.

Rev. Edward B. Lewis, D.D., minister, Capitol Hill Methodist Church, Washington, D.C., offered the following prayer:

We come to Thee, Heavenly Father, with a very present need. We acknowledge that the bonds which hold the human family together have been broken. Our wisdom has been lacking, our hearts have become increasingly hard, our divisions between man and man, race and race, nation and nation are more apparent from day to day. None of us are free from fault. We have a deep hurt as we look at the world today.

Yet we must look up and see Thee longing to help us. This spring morning gives us new hope in Thy creation. From the dull earth of winter, we see nature reborn in splendor. We remember the words of Jesus, ''Marvel not that I said unto you, 'You must be born again.' '' Man's nature, O God, needs the touch of a new birth in Thee.

With a new birth in our hearts, our eyes are not dimmed by deep-seated prejudices that feed fear, our attitudes are not stirred by resentment. Our hope is in new opportunities of peace.

We pray for our worthy leaders. Give wisdom, patience, steadfastness, courage, and the gift of love. Here are our minds, our hearts, our lives. Make us anew. We pray in the name of our Lord and Master. Amen.

THE JOURNAL

Mr. LONG of Louisiana. Mr. President, I ask unanimous consent that the Journal of the proceedings of Thursday, March 28, 1968, be approved.

The PRESIDENT pro tempore. Without objection, it is so ordered.

MEMPHIS RIOTS AND THE COMING
MARCH ON WASHINGTON

Mr. BYRD of West Virginia. Mr. President, we have been hearing for months now that Dr. Martin Luther King, Jr., has been planning a march on Washington and a "civil disobedience campaign" in the Nation's Capital in April.

Yesterday, Mr. President, the Nation was given a preview of what may be in store for this city by the outrageous and despicable riot that Martin Luther King helped to bring about in Memphis, Tenn.

If this self-seeking rabble-rouser is allowed to go through with his plans here, Washington may well be treated to the same kind of violence, destruction, looting, and bloodshed.

In Memphis, people were injured, stores were looted, property was destroyed, terror reigned in the streets, people were beaten by hoodlums, at least one Negro youth is known to have been killed, and massive rioting erupted during a march which was led by this man. It was a shameful and totally uncalled for outburst of lawlessness, undoubtedly encouraged to some considerable degree, at least, by his words and actions, and his presence. There is no reason for us to believe that the same destructive rioting and violence cannot, or that it will not, happen here if King attempts his so-called poor people's march, for what he plans in Washington appears to be something on a far greater scale than what he had indicated he planned to do in Memphis.

When the predictable rioting erupted in Tennessee, Martin Luther King fled the scene. He took to his heels and disappeared, leaving it to others to cope with the destructive forces he had helped to unleash.

He was due in Washington today, to conduct discussions in furtherance of the demonstration planned for this city. However, as a result of the tragic happening of yesterday, he canceled the conferences in Washington for today. Nonetheless, I do not believe that the implications of the ugly events of yesterday will be lost on local residents—despite the widespread sanction and support that has been offered to King by churches, the YMCA, and many other organizations in the Nation's Capital. I hope that well-meaning Negro leaders and individuals in the Negro community here will now take a new look at this man who gets other people into trouble and then takes off like a scared rabbit. If anybody is to be hurt or killed in the disorder which follows in the wake of his highly publicized marches and demonstrations, he apparently is going to be sure that it will be someone other than Martin Luther.

Mr. President, what occurred yesterday in Memphis was totally uncalled for—just as Martin Luther King's proposed march on Washington is totally uncalled for and totally unnecessary. He himself has been publicly quoted as saying that he thinks nothing constructive, so far as congressional action is concerned, can come out of his campaign here. Yet he says he is coming anyway. Why? To bring about another riot?

Mr. President, the main difference that I see now between what Martin Luther King plans here and what happened in Memphis yesterday is that the Memphis riot he precipitated might best be described as a hit-and-run riot, in view of his flight, while he was promised that his demonstration in the Federal City may last all summer.

Ostensibly, Martin Luther King went to Memphis to do the same sort of thing he has promised to do here—to "help poor people." He has billed his Washington march as a "poor people's crusade." In Memphis he went to lead striking garbage workers in a march to "help" them, but today, in the aftermath of Thursday's stupid and tragic occurrence, the Negroes he purportedly wanted to help are far worse off than they would have been if he had never gone there, for many are in jail and many are injured—and most certainly race relations have been dealt a severe setback across the Nation, as they have been in Memphis.

Is Washington now to be subjected to the same destruction and bloodshed?

Martin Luther King had no business in Memphis, he should never have gone there for the purpose of leading the protest march—just as he never should come here for the purpose of conducting a poor people's demonstration. There can be no doubt that he must be held directly responsible for much of what took place in Tennessee, and he will have to bear the onus for whatever takes place in Washington if he carries through on his threatened demonstration here.

King, himself, has talked of a crisis-packed situation in connection with his projected Washington demonstration and the erection of his proposed "shanty town," wherever it is to be located, whether among the Tidal Basin's cherry trees, on the Mall, in the District of Columbia Stadium, or elsewhere.

This man, who suffers from the delusion that only his eyes have the divine insight to detect what is wrong in our country, claims he wants to dramatize the plight of the poor. He has declared:

Bitter experience has shown that our Government does not act until it is confronted directly and militanty.

With this as his deceitful theme, King intends to demand greater and more unrealistic governmental subsidies in a year when the Federal Government is already spending over $25 billion annually to help the poor.

His plan for creating a crisis-packed situation, which he so often foments, is to bring 100 initial demonstrators to the Nation's Capital on April 22 to pressure Congress and Federal executives for more adequate health care and education, increases in jobs and incomes, and numerous other actions. Larger masses of people will begin moving in on April 26, according to a news story written by Willard Clopton, which was published in the *Washington Post*, of March 28, 1968.

Never before in history has an administration, a Congress, or a Nation's citizenry as a whole devoted as much effort and action toward alleviating the problems of poverty and discrimination. Yet, in the midst of this, the pious Dr. King ominously declares:

We have a national emergency. The prospects of cities aflame is very real indeed, but I would also remind America of the continuing violence perpetrated daily by racism in our society.

If King goes through with his plans now, he will indeed create a crisis-packed situation in Washington, just as his presence created an explosive situation in Memphis.

There are very real dangers, Mr. President—as yesterday's rioting clearly showed —in the sort of irresponsible actions King indulged in in Memphis, and in what he is planning here. The warning signals should be raised, if, indeed, they have not already been. There are dangers from the leader himself, as he so thoroughly demonstrated by not being able to keep down violence in Memphis despite his vaunted policy of nonviolence. And there is certainly danger in the type of gathering he envisions here.

Mr. President, I call attention to one paragraph in an article written again by Willard Clopton, entitled "Riot Spurs Review of March Here," which was published in the *Washington Post* of this morning. The paragraph reads as follows:

One of the Campaign's organizers said of the Memphis eruption, "It looks like we were 'had' by the extremists . . . We weren't prepared."

He indicated that the SCLC's usual precautions against violence such as the posting of numerous marshals and monitors, were overlooked yesterday.

King intends to create a black hole of despair with people packed together with pigs and chickens in a "shanty town" lacking sanitation. Surely he must know that to change hearts it is not necessary to turn stomachs. It can be assumed that, however, if yesterday's flight by King from the disorder he had helped to generate was any indication of what he might do here, the "Messiah" himself will not share the squalor he plans and that instead he will be conducting a lay-in at a posh Washington hotel to dramatize some imaginary discrimination there.

In his typical fashion, King intends to build a powder keg village and then plead that no one play with matches nearby lest destruction occur. He lays down the fuses around such a situation, however, with his semantic storehouse of volatile phrases such as "bloodless war," "direct action program," "crisis-packed situation," "dramatic confrontation," "attention-getting activities," "pressure," and "civil disobedience."

King's semantic gyrations have not fooled the American public, because violence has followed him like his shadow. Just as Shakespeare's Iago goaded Othello, the Moor, into committing outrage, King, the ever-correct phrasemaker, manages with saccharin words to produce sanguinary results.

He preaches nonviolence as a characteristic of disobedience. But the new civil disobedience is "civil disturbance." Riots, bombing, and violent protest typify the civil disobedience of today.

The marches in Milwaukee and Chicago last year were chaotic, and the Memphis march Thursday was disastrous. King has called for nonviolence here, but there are people allied with the poor people's campaign who call for the overthrow of the American Government by violence. Martin Luther King may have been a powerful man in the civil rights movement up to now, but it seems almost impossible to expect that he can control such large groups of militant activists as those he expects to join him in the demonstration here. Or, Mr. President, does he really expect to control them?

Both Stokely Carmichael and H. Rap Brown, if he can get out of jail, have agreed to march with Dr. King on the latter's terms—nonviolence—but how can we, or King, be sure of this? How can we be sure that another Memphis will not erupt? How can we be sure that King's lieutenants will not again have to say, "It looks like we were 'had' by the extremists. We were not prepared."

It is a well-known fact that riots begin when there is some uniting spark to excite a mob. All it would take in a situation like a Washington camp-in would be for some incident to turn the modern Coxey's Army King is raising into an angry, and ugly mob.

If Dr. King's plans to obstruct passage into the departments of the Government and buildings on Capitol Hill are carried out, it is certain that these actions will be met with a counterforce. There would be violence, and there is a great possibility that someone could be injured or killed.

Washington citizens and businessmen are concerned about their city. They do not want Washington to be torn apart by riots or discord.

Washington businessmen have been meeting with District officials and among themselves to draw up plans for the possible coming of the campaign. Hotel Association President Hudson Moses was quoted in the Washington Post on March 1 on what the city might lose as a result of the demonstration. He said:

Several of our members told me they have had group cancellations specifically because of the march. . . . It will cost this city millions of dollars in indirect loss of business and taxes.

Martin Luther King's main target, in Washington, Mr. President, is the Congress, because it has not passed all of the broad legislation that he seeks.

From the beginning, this Washington march and demonstration—if it really seeks the goals that King claims for it—has been poorly conceived and poorly planned. It must be obvious to anyone that people who have to be recruited and trained will not be coming to Washington of their own volition. This will be no spontaneous demonstration, Mr. President, no grassroots movement. This task force he wants to bring here, by King's own admission, must be recruited and "trained."

Some of the recruits, it is said, will come from cities that went up in flames last summer. One can only assume that they will be riot-hardened veterans. One can properly ask, I think: What sort of "training" are they now being given?

Why, Mr. President, do citizens, if their cause and their grievances are just, have to be trained? It seems to me that there is something very sinister here. I am aware, as I have indicated before in these remarks, that Dr. King has said that his tactics will be nonviolent. But when he sets the stage for violence, how long can his "trained" army and the malcontents, disrupters, militants, and hoodlums already here be expected to remain nonviolent in Washington's long, hot summer?

Mr. President, they may have learned their lessons well from King, who once said:

I do feel that there are two types of laws. One is a just law and one is an unjust law. I think we all have moral obligations to disobey unjust laws. I think that the distinction here is that when one breaks a law that conscience tells him is unjust, he must do it openly, he must do it cheerfully, he must do it lovingly, he must do it civilly, not uncivilly, and he must do it with a willingness to accept the penalty.

King lovingly breaks the law like a boa constrictor. He crushes the very life from it. His willingness to accept the penalty, which is supposed to set him apart from the common lawbreaker, can be judged by his irritation at a court decision which upheld a 5-day jail sentence for King recently. Faced with the prospect of accepting the penalty, King intoned that the decision would "encourage riots and violence in the sense that it all but said that Negroes cannot redress their grievances through peaceful means without facing the kind of decision that we face." Analyze this comment, if you will. Although King states the court decision did not declare that Negroes could not redress their grievances, he seems to say just the opposite and warns that the dire consequences are riots and violence. The English language is like putty in King's hands, but his incantations are loaded with hidden land mines.

Apparently the hoodlums in Memphis yesterday followed King's advice to break laws with which they did not agree. This has been a cardinal principle of his philosophy—a philosophy that leads naturally to the escalation of nonviolence into civil disobedience—which is only a euphemism for lawbreaking and criminality and which escalates next into civil unrest, civil disorder, and insurrection.

Mr. President, I have previously urged, in discussing this matter with the Justice Department, that the Federal Government seek a court order to enjoin Martin Luther King and his pulpitless parsons from carrying out their planned poor people's campaign in the Nation's Capital. In the light of yesterday's bloody chapter of violence which erupted with the visit of Martin Luther King to Memphis, I again urge that the Federal Government take steps to prevent King from carrying out his planned harassment of Washington, D.C. An ounce of prevention is worth a pound of cure. It is time for our Federal Government —which in recent years has shown itself to be virtually spineless when it comes to standing up against the lawbreakers, the hoodlums, and the Marxist demonstrators—at least to let the Nation know, in no uncertain terms, that it will not allow this Nobel Peace Prize winner to create another Memphis in the city which serves as the seat of the Government of the United States.

Law-abiding citizens, both Negro and white, in Washington and elsewhere, deserve no less from a government, the first duty of which is to preserve law and order.

PERCY FOREMAN LETTER
to James Earl Ray

Dear James Earl:

You have heretofore assigned to me all of your royalties from magazine articles, book, motion picture or other revenue to be derived from the writings of Wm. Bradford Huie. These are my own property unconditionally.

However, you have heretofore authorized and requested me to negotiate a plea of guilty if the State of Tennessee through its District Attorney General and with the approval of the trial judge would waive the death penalty. You agreed to accept a sentence of 99 years.

It is contemplated that your case will be disposed of tomorrow, March 10, by the above plea and sentence. This will shorten the trial considerably. In consideration of the time it will save me, I am willing to make the following adjustment of my fee arrangement with you:

If the plea is entered and the sentence accepted and no embarrassing circumstances take place in the courtroom, I am willing to assign to any bank, trust company or individual selected by you all my receipts under the above assignment in excess of $165,000.00. These funds over and above the first $165,000.00 will be held by such bank, trust company or individual subject to your order.

I have either spent or obligated myself to spend in excess of $14,000.00, and I think these expenses should be paid in addition to a $150,000.00 fee. I am sure the expenses will exceed the $15,000.00, but I am willing to rest on that figure.

Yours truly,

/s/ Percy Foreman

Appendix Four

THE RIGHT TO KNOW
by Mark Lane

Early in the morning on Saturday, February 5, 1977, I began a drive from my home in Washington, D.C., to Brushy Mountain penitentiary in Petros, Tennessee to visit with James Earl Ray. I picked up a copy of the *Washington Post* at a gasoline station and read a story published under the headline "Critics of Warren Report Objects of CIA Campaign." Sometime earlier I had brought an action against the CIA under the Freedom of Information Act for all of the documents about the Warren Report. On Friday, February 5th, a CIA officer informed me that some 900 pages of material were available. A student volunteer at the CCI drove to CIA headquarters at Langley, Virginia, and picked up the package Friday afternoon. I had planned to read the material upon my return from Petros. The CIA had evidently released the same material to the media and the *Washington Post* had published an Associated Press story. The Post version of the AP story said:

> **The documents show that the CIA examined copies of almost all books about the November, 1963, assassination, including one by then-Congressman Gerald R. Ford. A CIA officer called Ford's book "a re-hash of the Oswald case" and criticized its "loose" writing.**

On my next stop through Virginia I picked up a small local daily newspaper. There I read for the first time the complete version of the AP story, for the *Washington Post* story had excised all references to me (there were several in the AP Disptach) and most of the most dramatic and startling admissions about illegal CIA conduct contained in the documents. The CIA was not concerned that Ford's book was a "re-hash of the Oswald case" but in the March 1, 1965, memorandum prepared for Richard Helms, then the Director of the CIA, the anonymous CIA source (his name was deleted before the documents were released) made that observation about the book and then expressed concern that Ford had disclosed material about Oswald's relationships to the FBI. He concluded, "I felt, therefore, that the chapter, as written, could be used by the Lefties, Mark Lane, *et al*, to continue the campaign of which you are already aware." An examination of the then newly-released CIA documents, the original AP story and the abbreviated and sanitized version of that story published by the

301

Washington Post, provided an indication that even as the CIA's illegal and improper conduct was at long last being bared, the *Washington Post* continued editing and deleting disclosures related to the assassination.

CIA document number 1035-960 proposed a plan of action against the Warren Commission critics. It reads,

Action. We do *not* recommend that discussion of the assassination question be initiated where it is not already taking place. Where discussion is active however addressees are requested:

To discuss the publicity problem with liaison and friendly elite contacts (especially politicians and editors), pointing out that the Warren Commission made as thorough an investigation as humanly possible, that the charges of the critics are without serious foundation, and that further speculative discussion only plays into the hands of the opposition. Point out also that parts of the conspiracy talk appear to be deliberately generated by Communist propagandists. Urge them to use their influence to discourage unfounded and irresponsible speculation.

To employ propaganda assets to answer and refute the attacks of the critics. Book reviews and feature articles are particularly appropriate for this purpose. The unclassified attachments to this guidance should provide useful background material for passage to assets. Our play should point out, as applicable, that the critics are (i) wedded to theories adopted before the evidence was in, (ii) politically interested, (iii) financially interested.

The irrelevant and insulting questions that had followed me for a decade had been formulated and promulgated at CIA headquarters.

The document suggests that "a useful strategy may be to single out Epstein's theory for attack." Edward J. Epstein had written a book that tentatively raised some questions about the Warren Report. The CIA document explained that "Mark Lane's book" is "more difficult to answer as a whole." The three-page document urged that "reviewers" of books critical of the Warren Commission "might be encouraged to add to their account the idea that, checking back with the Report itself, they found it far superior to the work of its critics." Absurd arguments that have been put forth in the last decade in support of the Warren Report can be traced to the CIA document.

The CIA suggested that "in private or media discussion" various arguments "should be useful." Among those the CIA offered as most effective to destroy the impact of *Rush to Judgment* and other books critical of the Warren Report are these:

a. "No significant new evidence has emerged which the commission did not consider."

b. "Critics usually overvalue particular items and ignore others."

c. "Conspiracy on the large scale often suggested would be impossible to conceal in the United States."

302

d. "Oswald would not have been any sensible person's choice for a co-conspirator. He was a 'loner,' mixed-up, of questionable reliability and an unknown quantity to any professional intelligence service."

Reviewers and apologists for the Warren Commission offering themselves as freethinking iconoclasts have slavishly adopted the CIA's proposals and developed newspaper columns, major reviews and, on occasion, entire magazine articles around them. This has been so even though a wealth of newly-discovered significant evidence reveals that the Warren Commission did not secure the facts. The Select Committee on Intelligence of the United States Senate discovered that the CIA itself had withheld significant evidence from the Warren Commission. Conspiracies on a large scale, have of course, occurred within the United States. The Watergate episode and its cover-up involved a President, an Attorney General and many others. The evidence now available discloses that Oswald worked for the FBI and with the CIA; perhaps that does call into question the professionalism of those services as the CIA document might suggest.

For those reviewers and publications not perceptive enough to understand the CIA line, the agency was kind enough to furnish more assistance. Regarding one long magazine article defending the Warren Commission and attacking the critics the CIA boasted: "This was pulled together by [name deleted] in close conjunction with [name deleted]. We furnished most of the source material, proposed many of the themes and provided general 'Expertise' on the case."

In addition the CIA prepared a book review of *Rush to Judgment* on August 2, 1966, *before* the book was published. It began, "I reviewed the attached proof copy of the above book per your request." The name of the CIA official who requested the review was deleted. Another memorandum dated August 25, 1966, addressed to the "Director of Central Intelligence" carried this heading, "Subject: New Book: *Rush to Judgment* by Mark Lane." That seven page review was dispatched by the CIA to eleven different CIA departments including its Plans Department, known as the "Department of Dirty Tricks" within the agency.

Another CIA report dated January 4, 1967, stressed the income that I had reportedly earned from the book. Although William Manchester had earned more than ten times the amount I did for his defense of the Warren Report, the CIA, taking note of his income, indicated that he should be exempt from criticism and said that he should not "be classed with critics of the Commission." A CIA letter dated October 1, 1964, was sent to J. Lee Rankin, then the General Counsel of the Warren Commission. It too dealt with a critic, Joachim Joesten. A copy of the letter was sent by the CIA to the FBI, Department of State, and the Immigration and Naturalization Service. Attached to the letter was a document dated, "Berlin, 8 November, 1937." The letterhead read "Secret State Police (Gestapo), Gestapo Headquarters." It was addressed to "The Chief of the SS and of the German Police in the Ministry of Interior." The document said that Joesten "has seriously transgressed against his duty to remain faithful to his [the German] people and State by his anti-German conduct in foreign countries." It seems that Joesten had fled from Hitler's Germany to warn the people of Denmark to arm against the Nazis. The Gestapo ordered that Joesten's "German citizenship be revoked and that his possessions be confiscated and declared as forfeited to the State."

The Gestapo also claimed that Joesten was a leftist, a charge not infrequently made by that police organization against democrats during that period. In its letter, the CIA parroted the Gestapo charge. Why the CIA felt compelled to share it and the Gestapo's joint conclusions about Joesten with the FBI, State Department, and Immigration and Naturalization Service is not clear. One can surmise, however, that it was not intended to substitute for a welcome wagon greeting. Why the CIA letter, signed by Richard Helms, then Deputy Director for Plans (Dirty Tricks Department) was sent to the Warren Commission remains a matter of conjecture. Joesten, no doubt, thought that he had left all of that behind when he fled from Nazi Germany. He never did envision that three decades later, three leading liberals, J. Lee Rankin, a pillar of the New York Bar, Norman Redlich, formerly general counsel for the Emergency Civil Liberties Committee and Earl Warren, then Chief Justice of the United States, might one day pore over Gestapo documents to evaluate his political reliability. After all, Joesten did nothing more than question the conclusions of the Warren Commission Report.

I do not know how the CIA may react to this book or what demonic plans it may devise to interfere with the right of the American people to hear another view. I do not know who it may enlist knowingly or unwittingly in its crusade for darkness and its commitment to silence. It seems a pity that we may be required to wait yet another decade before that information becomes available to us. I think, in the circumstances, we are obligated to act against illegal and improper conduct rather than wait to read of it in anger and in sadness.

You have, I believe, the right to read this, and other serious and challenging books without the intervention of the CIA, the FBI, or other secretive government agencies. Perhaps we will soon view this time as a period from our troubled past. Perhaps the federal police will be forever restrained from poisoning the common well of knowledge that nourishes us only when our access to it is free.

INDEX

Abernathy, Ralph, 10, 15, 30, 58, 87, 117–118, 119–121, 233, 276, 290
Abzug, Bella, 262
Adams, James, 83, 84–85, 259
Aeromarine Supply Company, 152, 163, 175, 177, 178, 179
Albert, Carl, 265
Aldi, Roger, 213–214
Allgood, Clarence, 37, 39, 40
Alliluyeva, Svetlana, 247
American Civil Liberties Union, 267
Amicus Curiae Committee, 205, 206
Arkin, Lt., 131, 279
Armontrout, Bill, 251
Assassination Tapes, The (O'Toole), 259
Avery, Harry, 213
Avidson, Rodney, 154

Bagley, Mrs. Edith Scott, 289
Bailey, F. Lee, 159, 208
Bailey, Mel, 33
Baker, Howard, 77, 110
Barnet, Richard, 259
Barnett, Gerald, 126, 127, 280
Battle, W. Preston, 148, 166, 171, 188, 189, 199, 206, 207, 209, 211, 212–213, 216, 228, 254, 255, 257
Bauman, Robert E., 268
Beasley, James, 148, 152, 153, 154, 156, 157, 162–163, 164, 166, 167, 168, 171, 254, 255
Belafonte, Mr. and Mrs. Harry, 289
Belin, David, 246–247
Bell, Griffin, 273, 281, 285
Bevel, Jim, 30, 98, 108, 290
Billingsley, Orzell, 37, 39, 40
Birmingham News, 33, 38–39
Birmingham protest march, 26–31
Black, Kay Pittman, 107, 145, 146
Black Congressional Caucus, 265
Bond, Julian, 291
Bonebrake, George J., 156
Borosage, Robert, 259
Branch, Ben, 9–10, 121
Brewer, Bessie, 153, 164, 165
Brich, Phillip E., 156
Bridgman, Paul (James Earl Ray pseudonym), 186

Brooke, Edward W., 110
Brooks, Tyrone, 98
Brown, H. "Rap," 91
Brown, James, 291
Brown, Mrs. Stanley G., 245, 246
Brushy Mountain Penitentiary, 2, 176, 202, 257, 301
Burch, Lucian, 206
Burke, Yvonne, 265, 272
Burnham, David, 266
Byrd, Robert C., 108–110
    attack on Martin Luther King, Jr., in *Congressional Record*, 295–299

Canale, Phil, 148, 165, 166, 168, 189, 207, 208, 227
Canipe Amusement Company, 151, 153, 156
Canipe, Guy Warren, 153–154
Carmichael, Stokely, 53, 91
Carpenter, Ralph, 153
Carter, Harold, 182–183
Central Intelligence Agency (CIA), 232–233, 247, 301, 302, 303, 304
Chait, Manuel, 201
Chamberlain, Wilt, 289
Chastain, Wayne, 145
Chicago *Daily News*, 190, 201
Chicago Theological Seminary, 13
Church Committee, *see* Select Committee to Study Governmental Operations with Respect to Intelligence Activities
Church, Frank, 77, 263
Citizens Commission of Inquiry (CCI), 3, 134, 165, 189, 204, 259, 260, 261, 262, 263, 265, 301
Claridge (hotel), 107
Clark, Ramsey, 184, 210
Clayborn Temple, 124
Cohen, Jeff, 100–101
COINTELPRO (Counter Intelligence Program), 99, 102
Colby, William F., 232
Collins, Addie Mae, 39
"Colonel Klink," 61–62, 95–96
"COMINFIL" (Communist infiltration), 79, 81
Congress of Racial Equality (CORE), 13
Connor, Bull, 22, 35

305

"Conspirator Hunted in Dr. King Slaying"
    (*New York Times* article), 216
Copeland, Elizabeth, 153
Crozer Theological Seminary, 13
Curry, Izola Ware, 15

Daniloff, Nicholas, 268
Davis, Angela, 30
Davis, Sammy, Jr., 291
De Loach, Cartha, 77–78, 80, 108
Downing, Thomas, 261–262, 265
Dwyer, Robert, 148–152

Eastland, James O., 196
Ebenezer Baptist Church, 289, 290
Ebony magazine, 289
Edwards, Don, 262–263
Epstein, Edward J., 302
Eskridge, Chauncey, 150
Eugene, Michael, 190
"Evidence Hints a Conspiracy in Slaying of
    Dr. King" (*New York Times* article),
    183–184

Faquin, Arthur J., 255, 256
Farmer, James, 289
Fauntroy, Walter, 265, 290
Federal Bureau of Investigation (FBI), 60–71,
    152, 178, 184, 202–203, 226, 229, 244,
    249, 262, 269, 275, 285, 288–289, 301,
    303, 304
  accuses King of Communist domination, 80,
    92–93
  collects information about King, 83–84
  criteria for selection of agents, 62
  destroy-King squad, 265
  "dirty tricks" operation, 66
  Domestic Intelligence Division, 103–104,
    105
  hostility toward King, 6, 90–96, 136–137
  investigates bombing of 16th Street Baptist
    Church, 39–40
  investigates Southern Christian Leadership
    Conference, 80–81
  relationship to civil-rights movement, 5,
    60–62, 80, 88–96
  suggests "messiah" to replace King, 109
  "Two Squad," 65
"FBI Tied to King's Return to Memphis"
    (*Newsday* article), 99–100
Feldman, Richard, 268
Fensterwald, Bernard, Jr., 256
Ferguson, April, 265
Ferrell, Mary, 259
Fire Station Two, 124, 125, 128, 142, 264, 279
Ford, Gerald R., 24, 243, 262–263, 301
Ford, Harold E., 267
Foreman, James, 289

Foreman, Percy, 148, 163–164, 173, 186–187,
    188, 189, 191–192, 193, 194–195,
    196–214, 217–218, 227, 231, 249, 300
Frame-Up (Weisberg), 257
Francisco, Jerry Thomas, 150–151
Franklin, Aretha, 289
Franklin, Ben, 266
Frazier, Robert A., 157, 162
Freed, Donald, 241, 242, 259, 264, 273

Gallup Poll, 3, 219, 249
Galt, Eric (James Earl Ray pseudonym), 152,
    153, 154, 155, 185, 186, 226
Gandhi, Mahatma, 8, 17
Garner, Jimmy, 155, 156
Gaston Motel, 30, 33, 34
Gavzer, Bernard, 213
Gillies, Allen, 245
Goldwater, Barry, 77
Gonzalez, Henry B., 260, 261, 265
Gordy, Berry, 289
Gregory, Dick, 3, 5–8, 20, 22–24, 27–29,
    267–268
Gregory, Lil, 23–24

Halperin, Morton, 259
Hamilton (Chief, Memphis Fire Department),
    126
Hanes, Arthur, Jr., 160, 161, 177, 179, 185,
    188, 191, 199, 200, 231, 247
Hanes, Arthur, Sr., 22, 32, 159, 160, 161, 173,
    175, 184, 185, 188, 189, 190, 191, 192,
    193, 194, 195, 199, 200, 214, 216–217,
    218, 227, 231, 232, 247
Harper and Row, 243, 247
Harper's Magazine, 242
Hartnell College, 7
Hausserman, Davidson and Shattuck, 242
Hays, Renfro, 160, 182–183, 199, 200, 231
Hazlitt, William (quoted), 4
He Slew the Dreamer (Huie), 163, 198–199,
    216, 226, 227, 282
Helms, Richard, 301, 304
Hill, Lister, 33
Hill, Robert H., Jr., 254
Holiday Inn Rivermont Hotel, 9, 105–106,
    107, 109, 132, 264
Holloman, Frank, 9, 101, 102, 107, 127, 128,
    130, 131–133, 139–144, 185, 207, 232,
    257, 264, 277, 278, 284
Home Service Laundry Company, 154
Hooker, John J., Jr., 207
Hooker, John J., Sr., 197, 206–207, 208, 218
Hooks, Ben, 208
Hoover, J. Edgar, 83–84, 107, 144, 209, 210,
    229, 232, 248, 269, 281, 285, 288
  attempts to discredit King, 77–78, 79,
    82–83, 86–87
  attitude toward blacks, 80

Hoover, J. Edgar (*continued*)
    attitude toward civil-rights movement,
        88–90
    attitude toward Presidents, 65–66
    methods of controlling FBI, 60–61, 62,
        63–64
Horne, Lena, 289
Hosty, James, 262
House Resolution 498, 261, 264
House Resolution 204, 260–261, 264
House Select Committee on Intelligence (Pike
    Committee), 61, 72, 76
Hughes, Emmet John, 53
Huie, William Bradford, 160, 163, 164, 173,
    175, 188, 192, 193, 195, 197, 198, 199,
    202–203, 207, 216–218, 219–227,
    228–229, 231, 232, 249, 251–252, 283
Humphrey, Hubert, 289
Hunt, H. L., 195
Hunt, Nelson Bunker, 195–196
Hunt, W. Herbert, 195–196

"I Got Involved Gradually and I Didn't Know
    Anybody Was to Be Murdered" (*Look*
    article), 222
"I Have a Dream" (speech), 45–49
"I've Been to the Mountaintop" (speech),
    114–117, 119
Ingram, William B., 145, 146
International School of Bartending, 155
Invaders, 98, 99–101, 102, 118–119, 124, 130

Jackson, Jesse, 9–10, 99, 108, 119, 121, 290
James, Roy, 15
Javits, Jacob, 52
Jensen, Robert, 151–152
Jet magazine, 291
Jewish War Veterans (JWV), 51
Jim's Grill, 167, 175
Joesten, Joachim, 303–304
Johnson, Bob, 289
Johnson, John H., 289
Johnson, Lyndon B., 9, 51, 52, 66, 81, 82, 84
Johnson, Marion, 262
Johnson, R. T., 129
Jones, Solomon, 182
Jowers, Lloyd, 167

Katzenbach, Nicholas, 81
Kelley, Clarence, 32
Kelly, Asa, 88
Kennedy, Jacqueline, 291
Kennedy, John F., 20, 23–24, 29–30, 35, 66,
    81, 82, 249, 259, 260, 265, 272, 288
Kennedy, Robert F., 81, 83, 90, 232, 260
King, A. D., 30, 33–34, 38, 41, 112, 119, 120,
    289
King, Mrs. Alberta, 112, 120
King, Coretta Scott, 17–19, 77, 78, 87, 241,
    264–265, 286, 288

King, Martin Luther, Jr., 2, 22–23, 40,
    103–104, 109, 111, 149, 156, 160, 161,
    162, 165, 167, 168, 171, 172, 175, 177,
    178, 180, 181, 183–184, 185, 188, 206,
    210, 225, 227, 231, 232, 233, 248, 249,
    250, 251, 259, 260, 264, 265, 269,
    272–276, 283, 285, 288
    attacked for opposing Vietnam War, 51–53
    biographical background, 12–16
    criticizes FBI, 79–80, 90
    eulogy by Benjamin Mays, 290–294
    expresses distrust of FBI, 87
    final speech, 112–117
    funeral of, 8–9, 16–17, 288–294
    impact on thinking of black Americans,
        12–13
    leads demonstration in Memphis, 124
    leads protest march in Birmingham, 13
    leads protest march in Washington, 13
    opposes Vietnam War, 6–7, 50–51
    physical attacks on, 15–16
    relationship with Ralph Abernathy, 117–118
    security for at Memphis, 130–131
    speaking ability of, 16
    supports striking sanitation workers in
        Memphis, 13, 98
    worldwide leader, 21
King, Martin Luther, Sr. (Daddy), 112, 264
King, William B., 134–135
Kitt, Eartha, 291
Krause, Steve, 267–268
Ku Klux Klan (KKK), 20
Kyles, Samuel Billy, 10, 119, 120–121, 124,
    148–149, 150

Lane, Mark, 236–237, 245–246, 257, 302
Lane, Stonney Ray, 202
Lardner, George, Jr., 266
Lau, Thomas Reeves, 154, 155
Lawson, James, 98, 100–101
Lay, James Edward, 37–38
Lee, Bernard, 53–54, 276, 290
Lesar, James, 256
"Letter From Birmingham Jail," 42–44
Levi, Edward, 272, 273, 274–275
Lewis, Anthony, 246, 247, 248, 250–251
Lewis, John, 289
Liebling, A. J., Counterconvention, 245
Life magazine, 197–198, 205
Lipson, Jerry, 201
Liuzzo, Viola, 159
Livingston, Robert, 256
Look magazine, 163–164, 197, 203, 213,
    221–222, 225, 227, 228
Lorraine Motel, 9, 100, 105–106, 107, 108,
    109, 111, 120, 124, 125, 128, 130, 132,
    133, 134, 141–142, 145, 149, 151, 161,
    177, 180–181, 182, 185, 234, 276, 279
Louis, Joe (homemade brew), 34

Lowmeyer, Harvey (James Earl Ray
    pseudonym), 154
Lukas, Anthony, 245
Lynch, Jack, 245

McClellan, John, 277
McCraw, James M., 166–167, 205
MacDonald, J. C., 276
McGill, Ralph, 95, 103
McKinney, Stuart, 261
McKissik, Floyd, 289
McMillan, George, 197, 216, 217, 221, 222,
    230, 231, 232, 233, 234, 235–238,
    240–241, 242, 245, 246, 247, 248, 249,
    250, 251, 252, 283
McMillan, Priscilla Johnson, 242, 243, 244,
    245–246, 247
McNair, Denise, 39
McNamara, Robert, 35
McVickar, John, 242, 243, 245, 246
Maddox, Lester, 16
Making of an Assassin, The (McMillan), 216,
    230, 231, 235, 247, 251, 283
Manchester, William, 247, 303
Mann, Abby, 126–127, 139–144, 241, 264,
    273, 274
Manuel, Philip, 277, 278–279, 284
March on Washington, 5, 45–46
Marshall, Burke, 34, 39, 81, 82
Marshall, Thurgood, 291
Mason Temple (Memphis), 112, 113, 119,
    125, 281
Mays, Benjamin, 290–294
Memorandum of Facts (Fensterwald, Lesar and
    Livingston), 256–257
Memphis *Commercial Appeal*, 104, 107, 182,
    205
Memphis *Commercial Clarion*, 103, 104
Memphis garbage workers' strike, 55
Memphis *Press-Scimitar*, 99, 107, 145
Memphis Strike Strategy Committee, 98
Miller, Herbert J., Jr., 37
"Mini-Riot in Memphis . . ." (*New York
    Times* editorial), 104
Mississippi Freedom Democratic Party, 277,
    284
Mondale, Walter F., 77, 78–79
Moore, Daniel, 37
Moore, John, 63
Morehouse College, 13, 291, 292
Motley, Constance, 88
Murphy, C. M., 169
Murtagh, Arthur, 61–62, 63, 72–75, 76,
    90–96, 136–138, 265

National Association for the Advancement of
    Colored People (NAACP), 13
Neptune Tavern, 173, 223
New Times, 245

New York Post, 287
New York Times, The, 103, 183–184, 196,
    216, 218, 230, 232, 246–247, 248, 250,
    266, 267
Newsday, 99–100, 102, 264
Newsum, Floyd, 125–126, 127, 128, 129, 135,
    142, 231, 256, 264, 275, 279, 280, 284
Newsweek magazine, 53
Newton, Huey, 91
Nichols, Bob, 91
Nixon, Richard M., 66, 291
Nonviolence
    concept of, 5, 8
    opposition to, 14–15
Norville, Peyton, 37

O'Hearn, William W., 166
O'Leary, Jeremiah, 230–231, 232, 233, 248,
    266
O'Neill, Thomas P. (Tip), 265, 288
Orange, James, 98
Oswald, Lee Harvey, 242, 243, 244, 246–247,
    249, 301, 303
Oswald, Marina, 243–245, 247
O'Toole, George, 259

Panella, Mary Lucy, 154
Papia, Jim, 164
Patterson, Floyd, 289
Pauling, Linus, 259
Payne, Larry, 124
Payne, Les, 99, 102, 264, 273
Peay, Austin, 184
Peters, Annie, 155
Piedmont Laundry, 155
Pike Committee, *see* House Select Committee
    on Intelligence
Policoff, Jerry, 242, 245
Poor People's Campaign and March on
    Washington, 56–58, 98, 118
Portrait of an Assassin (Ford), 262–263
Pottinger, Stanley, 241, 242, 273, 274–275
Prouty, L. Fletcher, 259

Quillen, James, 272

Ramparts magazine, 54
Raoul, 173, 174–176, 177, 179, 185, 186, 202,
    222, 223, 224, 274, 280, 281
Raskin, Marcus, 259
Rather, Dan, 191–192, 194
Ray, Dewell, 164
Ray, James Earl, 23, 148–157, 158, 160, 162,
    164, 167–168, 171, 172, 173–179, 180,
    184, 185, 188, 191–192, 196, 198, 199,
    201–202, 203, 206, 207–208, 211, 212,
    217–218, 220–221, 232, 233, 234, 237,
    247, 248, 249, 250–252, 254, 255, 256,

Ray, James Earl (*continued*)
  257–258, 260, 272, 274, 280, 281, 283,
  285, 300
  conditions of imprisonment, 188–189, 191
  pleads guilty to murder of King, 148
  relationship with Percy Foreman, 192–194
Ray, Jerry, 190, 194, 195, 234–236, 237–240,
  250
Ray, John, 190, 194, 195, 240
Reader's Digest magazine, 51, 57–58, 205
Reagan, Ronald, 9
Rebel Motel, 152, 171, 175
Redditt, Ed, 100, 124, 125, 129–130,
  131–133, 134, 135, 141, 142, 143, 231,
  234, 256, 257, 264, 266, 273, 274, 275,
  276–277, 278–279, 283–285
Report of the Department of Justice Task Force
  to Review the FBI Martin Luther King,
  Jr., Security and Assassination
  Investigation, 273, 280, 282, 285
Reuther, Walter, 65
Rhoads, James, 262
Richmond, W. B., 129, 130, 131, 133–134,
  231, 257, 275, 276–277, 284–285
Robertson, Carol, 39
Robinson, James George, 15
Rooming house (422½ South Main Street,
  Memphis), 160, 161, 163, 164, 166, 167,
  168, 172, 175, 176, 177, 180–181,
  182–183, 186
Ross, Diana, 291
Rowan, Carl T., 287
Rush to Judgment (Lane), 84, 220, 303
Russell, Richard, 244
Rustin, Bayard, 98
Ryan, Richard J., 254, 255, 264

St. Louis *Post-Dispatch,* 201
Salisbury, Harrison, 246
Sanders, Jim, 25, 27, 28, 29
Santinella, Al, 91
Schwarz, Frederick A. O., Jr., 78–79
Schweiker, Richard, 84–86, 263
"Seat of Government" (SOG), 65
Select Committee on Assassinations of the
  House of Representatives, 3, 160, 230,
  232, 241, 265, 267, 272
Select Committee to Study Governmental
  Operations with Respect to Intelligence
  Activities (Church Committee), 77, 78,
  79, 81–83, 84, 103, 106, 108, 232, 263
Selma-to-Montgomery March, 5
Shaheen, Michael, 274, 283, 285
Shelby County Jail (Memphis), 188, 192
Shores, Arthur, 38–39
Shuttlesworth, Fred, 30, 35, 290
16th Street Baptist Church, 25, 30, 39–40
Skeptic magazine, 229
Smith, Coby, 102

Smith, John B., 101, 102
Smith, Lt. J., 125, 280
Sneyd, Ramon George (James Earl Ray
  pseudonym), 159, 186
Snyder, Richard Edward, 243
Soter, Steven, 259
Southern Christian Leadership Conference
  (SCLC), 13, 18, 26–27, 52, 61, 87, 93,
  107, 118–119, 276
Southern Regional Council, 79
Spack, Pamela, 165, 189
Spandau (Speer), 190–191
Specter, Arlen, 266
Speer, Albert, 190
Sprague, Richard A., 266, 267, 278
Stanton, Hugh, 204, 205
Stennis, John, 110–111
Stephens, Charles Q., 153, 165, 166, 167, 168,
  169, 172, 183, 204–205
Stephens, Grace, 165, 166, 168–170, 204–205
Stone, Charles E., 134
Stoner, J. B., 254
"Story of James Earl Ray and the Conspiracy to
  Kill Martin Luther King, The" (*Look*
  article), 222
Stride Toward Freedom (King), 15
Student Non-Violent Coordinating Committee
  (SNCC), 13
Sullivan, William C., 80, 83, 86, 94

Tatum, Roosevelt, 33–34, 36, 37, 38, 39,
  40–41
Teasley, Morris, 36–37
Thomas, Evan, 247
Thompson, Josiah, 259
Thurmond, Strom, 110
Tines, G. P., 276, 277
Tolson, Clyde, 65, 86, 108
Tower, John G., 77
Tri-State Defender, 102

United Press International (UPI), 270

Vietnam War, opposed by Martin Luther King,
  50–51
Vivian, C. T., 30, 290

Waldron, Martin, 183–184, 185, 186, 194,
  196, 232
Walker, Robert, 127–128
Walker, Wyatt Tee, 33, 290
Wallace, George C., 226, 249, 260
Wallace, Norvell E., 127, 128, 129, 135, 231,
  256, 264, 273, 279, 280, 284
Warren Commission, 243, 244, 245, 246, 260,
  262, 302, 303, 304
  Report of, 220, 246, 248–249, 260, 283, 303

Washington Post, 233, 249, 266, 267, 301, 302
Washington Star, 230, 233, 266, 267, 283
Watergate break in, 76
Weaver, Macon, 37, 38
Weisberg, Harold, 257
Wesley, Cynthia, 39
Wharton, Elizabeth, 268
Wheeler, Dude, 182–183
White, Byron R., 81
"Why James Earl Ray Murdered Dr. King" (*Look* article), 222
Wilkins, Roy, 91, 98, 99, 289
Willard, John (James Earl Ray pseudonym), 153, 164, 165, 172, 186
Williams (Chief, Memphis Fire Department), 127

Williams, Hosea, 30, 98, 290
Wilson, Nancy, 289
Wiretaps, 92, 96
Women Strike for Peace, 18
Wood, Donald, 178–179
Wood, Robert, 178–179

York Arms Company, 153, 175
Young, Andrew, 61, 62, 81, 87, 98, 99, 103, 107, 118, 121, 232, 241, 265, 276, 288, 290
Young, Whitney, 91, 279

Zachary, N. E., 151, 152, 153, 164, 168
Zanetti, Leona, 165, 189
Zorro (code name for Martin Luther King), 94